MW01630111

Yale Publications in the History of Art   Walter Cahn, editor

Yale University Press/New Haven & London

Esther da Costa Meyer

The Work of Antonio Sant'Elia Retreat into the Future

Designed by Nancy Ovedovitz and set in Minion type by Highwood Typographic Services, Hamden, Connecticut. Printed in the United States of America by Thomson-Shore, Inc., Dexter, Michigan and Cromwell Printing Company, Inc., Cromwell, Connecticut.

Library of Congress Cataloging-in-Publication Data
da Costa Meyer, Esther 1947–
The work of Antonio Sant'Elia: retreat into the future / Esther da Costa Meyer.
p. cm.—(Yale publications in the history of art)
Includes bibliographical references and index.
ISBN 0-300-04309-0 (alk. paper)
1. Sant'Elia, Antonio. 1888–1916—Criticism and interpretation.
2. Futurism (Architecture)   I. Title.   II. Series.
NA2707.S28M48   1995   94-39125
720'.92—dc20   CIP

A catalogue record for this book is available from the British Library.

The paper in this book meets the guidelines for permanence and durability of the Committee on Production Guidelines for Book Longevity of the Council on Library Resources.

10   9   8   7   6   5   4   3   2   1

Yale Publications in the History of Art are works of critical and historical scholarship by authors formerly or now associated with the Department of the History of Art of Yale University. Begun in 1939, the series embraces the field of art-historical studies in its widest and most inclusive definition.

Series logo designed by Josef Albers and reproduced with permission of the Josef Albers Foundation.

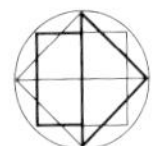

Frontispiece: Antonio Sant'Elia in his early twenties. (Photo: Collection of the author)

To my parents

Contents

Acknowledgments

A book, especially one's first book, is to a certain extent a collaborative project, the fruit of one's endless ruminations on a given topic, shored up by the scholarly advice and support of friends and colleagues. I deeply appreciate the generosity of Wendy White, Stefano and Benedetta Majnoni, Francesco and Margherita Majnoni, Gabriella Buonomo, Enrico Vitiello, Helen Chillman, Barbara Adams, Suha Gursey, Myriam and Sam MacDowell, and Daniel Recasens. The following scholars were kind enough to share their knowledge of Sant'Elia's work with me: Rossana Bossaglia, Manfredi Nicoletti, Alberto Longatti, Donatella Poli, and Jörn-Peter Schmidt-Thomsen. I gratefully acknowledge the help of Ellen Shapiro, who read early drafts of the manuscript and offered excellent advice. I also wish to thank my colleagues in the Department of the History of Art at Yale, many of whom were my professors, for their encouragement. I owe a special debt to Jonathan Weinberg, whose assistance at various stages of this project ranged from the sublimities of art history to the unfathomable depths of computer software.

In Como, the Museo Civico, the Biblioteca Comunale, and the Terragni Foundation spared no effort in facilitating my research. I also wish to thank the Ballarate family and Studio Logos for helping me with photographs. At Yale, the professional staffs of the Art and Architecture Library, the Beinecke Rare Book and Manuscript Library, the Audio Visual Center, and the Yale Slides and Photographs Collection were extremely helpful. Aldo and Andrea Zana provided me with last-minute photographs, which were swiftly and providentially flown from across the ocean. Mr. Paride Accetti kindly allowed me to publish his beautiful collection of drawings by Sant'Elia. My thanks as well to Mr. and Mrs. Charles Larson for their generosity.

I am grateful to Judy Metro, my editor at Yale University Press, for her patience as I prepared the final manuscript and to Karen Gangel, whose kindness and thoughtful editorial assistance approached the miraculous. The book benefited greatly from the careful reading of Susan Laity and Laura Dooley and from the excellent design of Nancy Ovedovitz. A grant from the Frederick W. Hilles Publication Fund helped cover editorial costs.

Maurice Besset, my undergraduate advisor in Geneva, Switzerland, first pointed me in the direction of architectural history: I thank him here for his faith in my work. I am much indebted to Thomas Beeby, dean of the Yale School of Architecture when I was finishing the manuscript, for allowing me to take a semester off and for awarding me the Symmonds grant. To Vincent Scully, my mentor at Yale, I owe a greater debt than I can ever hope to repay: he read every word of this manuscript in its previous incarnation as a Ph.D. dissertation. It was his advice, enthusiasm, and abiding love of architecture that encouraged me to pursue this book to the end.

Finally, I wish to thank my parents for a lifetime of unwavering support.

One **Birth of a Nation**

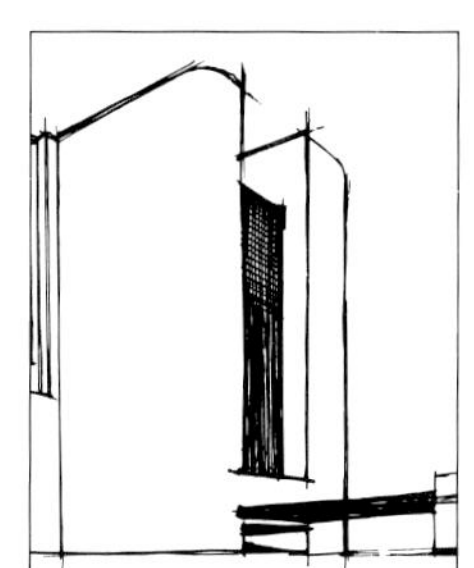

When Antonio Sant'Elia was born, in 1888, the Regno d'Italia was only twenty-seven years old.[1] The birth of a new state is rarely easy, and the case of Italy was no exception. Centuries of foreign domination to the north and unenlightened despotism under the Bourbons and the papacy to the south, as well as the political and economic stagnation that ensued, had prevented the very concept of a unified Italy from emerging earlier.

Unlike Germany, where cultural identity preceded political unification, Italy was first unified by force. Only after the fact could the state face the pressing need of devising a common cultural heritage that would give a semblance of historical inevitability to the recently and somewhat reluctantly assembled commonwealth. The situation was brilliantly summed up at the time in Massimo D'Azeglio's celebrated bon mot: "We have created Italy, we must now create Italians."[2]

The search for a national identity was a complex process that involved every field of human endeavor. In music, literature, art, and architecture there was the same earnest quest for a common denominator that would consolidate and legitimize unification and give expression to national, not regional, values. The brunt of this task devolved mainly upon the intellectuals who still felt a deep-seated skepticism concerning the legitimacy of the new nation. There was an underlying fear that its creation was the result of arbitrary decisions rather than the fulfillment of historical necessity. Out of this doubt arose the desire to forge a unitary culture, a desire that produced a long drawn-out crisis among the intelligentsia. Its effects were felt well into the twentieth century.

Nowhere is the complexity of the situation so clearly revealed as in the notorious language problem. The question whether nationality and language coincided was not new in history, but in the age of Romanticism it reemerged with an urgency hitherto unknown. The German Romantics were among the first, in modern times, to equate the two, thereby providing the cultural underpinnings for what was later to become the German state.[3] This lesson was not lost on the Italians of the Risorgimento, who saw in the choice of a national idiom an indispensable premise to the formation of a national consciousness.

But the gap between the Romantic aspirations of the Risorgimento and the everyday realities of postunitarian Italy was abysmal. At the time of unification only eight out of every thousand Italians spoke what was more or less arbitrarily chosen as the national language, that is, Tuscan.[4] The situation was compounded by an illiteracy rate of almost 50 percent at the beginning of the century.[5] At the time of Sant'Elia's birth Italy was still a mosaic of different ethnic and cultural groups in varying stages of development, held together by a weak and controversial government.

The repercussions of the language question in all aspects of Italian culture can hardly be overestimated. Given the urgency of the situation, aesthetic issues had become political liabilities. The arts—and architecture in particular—were pressed into service to advance the creation ex post facto of a national character. In architecture this problem assumed the form of an obsession with a national style that was to dominate professional circles on and off until World War II. Style was considered the visible expression of a common identity and was felt to confer, at least in retrospect, a sense of national identity. Influenced by positivism, Italian architects and critics believed that the distinctive characteristics of a nation could find expression in one style—and one only. The problem was to decide on the prerequisites of an architecture that adequately represented the new political reality of unified Italy. On the whole there was widespread agreement over the main tenets of this hypothetical style.

Foreign influences were to be shunned at all costs. Ugo Monneret de Villard, one of Italy's most enlightened critics of modern architecture in Sant'Elia's day, complained bitterly of the internationalist tendencies that Italian architecture had inherited from the nineteenth century: "One could almost say that in the great bustle brought about by the Napoleonic wars, the limits of the nations disappeared, and with the arrival of Romanticism, a time of cosmopolitan culture came into being: the most diverse tendencies of the most diverse countries in Europe fraternized among themselves and mingled."[6] Architecture was no longer based on the intrinsic needs and characteristics of each nation, on its way of life. "Those were troubled times for architecture," he continued, "architecture without personality, construction rather than art."[7] The absence of an identifiable style such as, say, the Gothic or the Baroque, haunted Italian architecture overtly and covertly for several decades and in times of political upheaval was manifested as chauvinism, and sometimes as xenophobia.

A national style in architecture not only precluded foreign influence, it ruled out individuality altogether. Only the ethos of a people, as revealed throughout the ages, could give birth to a truly national architecture. Personal originality was to be curbed: "It was the timeless perseverance in pursuing the same ideal, with the total sacrifice of one's personality to it, that produced those well-determined styles."[8] Whereas art is clearly capable of expressing an artist's personal ideas, "architecture . . . virtually requires that the spirit of an entire nation collaborate with the architect," since it must adapt itself to the peculiarities of a national ethos.[9] In other words, the new Italian architecture was to be evolutionary, not revolutionary.

If a national style was the expression of the genius of a nation, embodied by generations through the centuries, then only the past could sanction and inspire it. In a celebrated passage Camillo Boito, one of Italy's leading figures in the world of architecture, wrote that "for architecture to become the monument of an age and of a nation, it must be intimately connected with the past: the national characteristics come as much from the historical characteristics as they do from the natural ones."[10] In short, the new architecture of unified Italy had above all to be national; it had to express the corporate will; it could not be too personal; and it had to derive its inspiration and vocabulary from the past. Opinions diverged only when it came to deciding whether the new architecture should come from the wholesale adoption of a single historical style or from a judicious selection of characteristics from various periods. In either case, style had become virtually synonymous with history, or rather with historicism: the confusion between the two terms underlies the entire period of Italian architecture from unification up to World War II.

Many of Italy's leading architects, like their colleagues abroad, chose the Middle Ages as the most representative period in Italian history. They were interested in the representation and dramatization of the structural forces at play, such as one finds in Gothic architecture. Their choice was not, of course, dictated by aesthetic preferences alone: "One must note the coming together of the Romantic ferment, with the renewed predilection for history, the evocation of communal liberties, [and] the emergence of the national spirit, which consequently led the arts to an appreciation of the Middle Ages."[11] Indeed, in Italy medievalism had a strong connotation of nationalism not only in architecture but also in painting, sculpture, literature, and even music (opera in particular), fields in which it had become an ideal vehicle for the Romantic aspirations of the Risorgimento.

The medievalists could lay claim to one of Italy's most famous and influential architects of the turn of the century, Camillo Boito (1836–1914), the older brother of Verdi's librettist Arrigo Boito and himself a noted writer, essayist, and critic.[12] As a writer he was known mainly for his short stories, now largely forgotten except for the novella *Senso* (1883), which was adapted to the screen in Lucchino Visconti's famous eponymous film. Boito was a minor Ruskin. His own architecture, which bears some resemblance to High Victorian Gothic, is somewhat dry and deceptive, with its archaeological fidelity to historical detail.[13] But he was extremely influential as a professor of the history of architecture, a task for which he was eminently prepared thanks to his immense erudition and extensive traveling. And if he lacked the exalted fervor of a Ruskin or the universality of a Viollet-le-Duc, he had a bit of both and was a man of their caliber.

Boito had studied in Venice with Pietro Selvatico Estense (1803–1880), a learned architect, writer, and intellectual.[14] It was from Selvatico that he took one of the mainstays of his theoretical framework: the fundamental importance of descriptive geometry for the study of architecture, which Selvatico in turn took from Friedrich Froebel.[15] This stood Boito in good stead later, when he became professor of architecture at the Academy of Brera in Milan—where Sant'Elia was to study—a post he held for almost half a century until his retirement in 1909. He taught his students to study buildings in terms of their geometric components and to take as their starting point simple solids—cubes, cylinders, spheres—before tackling plans or sections. He fell short, however, of the ardent militancy of Selvatico, who introduced Froebel's ideas to Italy.[16]

Boito was a man of the Risorgimento, and he aspired to do for Italian architecture what Alessandro Manzoni had done for the Italian language: to create more or less single-handedly the architectural idiom of unified Italy.[17] This is made unmistakably clear in his use of linguistic metaphors when discussing architecture:

> The architect needs to feel that he is in possession of a style that is docile, adaptable to every need; . . . that does not dismiss preconceived forms; . . . that may have columns that are long, short, slender or squat; windows that are high, low, broad or narrow . . . with broad and protruding cornices or barely salient ones; a style, in short, like a language abounding in words and phrases, free in its syntax, imaginative and exact, poetic and scientific, and one that lends itself neatly to the expression of the most arduous and diverse concepts.[18]

The possibility of a modern architecture, stripped of any historical reference and born exclusively of contemporary needs and means, was something that Boito could not accept. On the other hand, despite the philological precision shown in his work as an architectural historian, the kind of architecture he called for should not be thought of as a slavish imitation of the past. What he advocated, like Viollet-le-Duc or his teacher, Selvatico, was a sort of neo-Gothic structuralism, that is, Gothic principles reinterpreted in the light of modern engineering. In his famous and influential essay "Sullo stile futuro dell'architettura italiana," he draws up a charter for the new architecture of unified Italy:

- it cannot spring from the mind of an architect;
- it cannot be new in plan;
- it cannot be made up of several old styles mixed together;
- it must not imitate any [style];
- it must be national;
- it must link itself freely to a single Italian style of the past;
- it must lose the archaeological character of that style in order to become fully modern.[19]

This "single Italian style of the past" was none other than Lombard architecture of the trecento, which he saw as possessing flexibility, structural honesty, and all the representational qualities indispensable, in his eyes, to a truly national architecture. And, he adds, this "rough but seminal Italian architecture which, for want of a better name, is usually called Lombard, shall become over the years, however developed, refined and remodernized, the architecture of the new Italy."[20]

Broadly speaking, the revival of Gothic architecture was to be found mainly, but not exclusively, in the north—Lombardy, Veneto, Liguria, Piedmont—areas in which such architecture had flourished in the past. Rome and the south, however, had always remained closer to the classicizing models of the Roman Empire and the Renaissance and had never made a secret of their age-old distaste for the Gothic. Rome's having been chosen the definitive capital of the new Italy strengthened that trend considerably. There a diffuse eclecticism was institutionalized by means of competitions for the most important governmental buildings in an attempt to disseminate a national style throughout the country.[21] Something vaguely approximating an architecture of unification, culled from the great monuments of the past, thus came into being and was used in the grandiloquent commissions of state, such as Giuseppe Sacconi's Monument to Victor Emmanuel (constructed between 1885 and 1911) and Guglielmo Calderini's Palace of Justice (1888–1910).[22]

Eclecticism was also reinforced by the extensive restoration program being carried out as part of the cultural agenda of unified Italy. The most significant buildings of the past were being repaired or completed as tangible proof of a teleological process that paved the way for modern Italy's historical destiny. Detailed plans, sections, and elevations of the buildings to be restored were given ample space in the periodicals of the day, much to the chagrin of younger architects, who hungered for the innovative trends they saw in other nations.

Architectural theory had played a crucial role in the Gothic Revival. The medievalists were perfervid moralists who liked or needed to proselytize, who wrote much and built relatively little. With the eclectics the reverse was true. The best textbook on their ideas remains the architecture itself, which is expressive to the point of loquacity.[23] Dozens of buildings—partly functional, partly commemorative—had to be erected to house the new ministries, and all were built on a grand scale with a wealth of detail and ornament that proclaimed the greatness of modern Italy and its link to the imperial Rome of the Caesars, via the papal Rome of the Renaissance and the Baroque. These buildings were as programmatic and as explicit as Boito's writings.

The opposition between medievalists and eclectics should not be stressed unduly, as both can be subsumed under the broader category of historicism. The two parties were not mutually exclusive, nor were they wholly determined by geography (a neomedieval north versus an eclectic south). Eclecticism carried the day, because most architects, including Boito himself, could be both neomedieval or eclectic, depending on the commission at hand.[24] For the purposes of modern architecture, the similarity of these two tendencies was far more important than their differences: the belief that the future of Italy's architecture lay in its past, but the past reinterpreted as myth. The Italian penchant for historicism thus had specific political connotations. Whether one chose Roman or Gothic, Renaissance or Baroque, as the quintessence of the Italian genius, the architecture of these periods was seen as the outward sign of a destiny made manifest only in 1870. Architecture was therefore made to serve a political purpose, that of helping legitimize unification.

In this quest, ironically, Italy was not unlike other European nations. The very search for a national style was related to the international scene. Germany, unified the same year (1870), likewise faced the need to forge a cultural identity for itself in the form of a national style that evoked or embodied its newly found unity. Using words similar to Boito's, the archaeologist Julius Lessing claimed that style, like language, could not be invented: it reflected the interaction of climate, environment, and human needs—ideas patently derived from Hippolyte Taine and the positivists. Following no less an authority than Gottfried Semper, Lessing advocated the use of the Renaissance as the style that best reflected the German ethos.[25] And in the *The Seven Lamps of Architecture* Ruskin had already called for a national English style in the form of the Gothic.[26]

By the beginning of the new century, however, the cultural problems brought about by unification, such as the search for a national style, had receded somewhat into the background, at least for the younger generation. Indeed, notwithstanding all the problems that attended its birth, Italy had begun to change rapidly and irreversibly. The most ostensible aspect of this transformation lay in its political geography. The industrial revolution had displaced the nation's center of gravity to the north. This move was dictated largely by the availability of cheap sources of energy owing to the abundant water network at the foot of the Alps. The advent of electricity in a nation so poor in coal and oil accelerated the process of industrialization, and soon the great Italian cities of the north began to produce motors and machines of every sort. To facilitate the circulation of manufactured goods, great tunnels were cut through the Alps: the Mont Cenis tunnel (1857–1881) connected Italy to France, and the San Gottardo (1872–1882) and the Sempione (1898–1906) linked Italy to Central Europe via Switzerland. Important engineering feats in themselves, these tunnels encouraged production and helped tie Italy's economy to that of the rest of Europe.

As a result Milan and Turin replaced the old historic cities of Rome, Florence, and Venice as the seats of economic power and, consequently, of cultural ferment. Thousands of *contadini* flocked to these great industrial centers in search of work in the new factories. Mass migration to the cities was followed by a building boom on an unprecedented scale in Italian history. Within a few years industrialization changed the face of the northern Italian cities beyond recognition; it also changed the tenor of life of a great part of the population accustomed to the sedentary social patterns of the agrarian economy still prevalent in the countryside. Industrialization quickly brought about social mobility and a new urban way of life that in turn fostered new cultural needs.

But culture and education, as institutionalized by the new state, were sadly out of step with those needs and with the whole changed physiognomy of unified Italy. The humanities lagged behind reality, lost in a vain and anachronistic search for a grandeur that was gone forever. This identification with the past conferred on the as-yet-modest status of the young state an aura of glory, an imperial pedigree as it were, that helped restore its self-confidence. It functioned as an antidote to the inferiority complex generated by confrontation with other European nations, the greatness of the past making up for the deficiencies of the present. The consequences of this state of affairs were disastrous, for nothing could have been further removed from the problems that beset the modern world, and Italy in particular, than those carefully contrived humanistic blinkers that excluded other equally valid responses to the situation. "Our path," grumbled one of Italy's leading intellectuals of the time, "is barred by seventeen million illiterates and five million Arcadians."[27]

The problem was not, of course, that historicism was wrong and modernism right. To compete in a market economy Italy had to revise its approach to design, as the more industrially advanced nations had already done. If its goods were to be competitive in world markets, it had to pose anew the question of ornament in an age of mass production, and this could not be done by looking exclusively to ancient Rome or to the Gothic for inspiration. The British Arts and Crafts movement had been among the first to formulate these questions, followed by the German Werkbund and related associations, as well as several Belgian and French Art Nouveau groups. Around the turn of the century these ideas made their first appearance in Italian architecture under the guise of a somewhat belated form of

Art Nouveau, when the question of a national style, though still a burning issue for the older generation, had ceased to attract the young. Indeed the Liberty, as the movement was called, appeared precisely as a protest against both the existence of a national style as such and the historicism in which it was couched.

ART NOUVEAU

Although Art Nouveau had great impact on architecture, it remained essentially an ornamental style and was used primarily in the decorative arts.[28] Art Nouveau flourished briefly during the last decade of the nineteenth century, culminating in the Paris exhibition of 1900. In the first years of the nineteenth century a sharp reaction against its often gratuitous excesses brought the Art Nouveau interlude to a close, the younger generation preferring the more restrained, geometrically oriented form language of the Secession.

The Italians thus turned to Art Nouveau just as it was losing ground everywhere else, when the curvilinear forms of French extraction were giving way to a new manner of expression: "A counter-movement had set in in Germany and Austria, with a parallel movement in Scotland. First came a tendency to abandon the original Art Nouveau ornamentation and to develop instead a geometrical play of similar elegance. . . . As early as 1902–1903 these trends had found adequate expression and Mackintosh, Hoffmann, Wagner, Olbrich and Behrens turned their backs on the style."[29] Only after the exhibition of decorative arts in Turin in 1902 did Art Nouveau gain wide acceptance within a certain sector of the public, but by that time it was hopelessly *retardataire,* and only within the context of the Italian situation can the movement be considered novel in any way. Its life span was short, and few architects practiced exclusively in that vein. After a few years the more enterprising practitioners had set their sights in a different direction, though the Liberty continued to flourish in debased and trivialized versions virtually until World War I.[30]

Originally, the term Liberty referred quite simply to the products manufactured by the famous firm that Arthur Lasenby Liberty founded in London in 1875, although the double entendre was obvious.[31] But by 1900 it had gained common currency as a synonym of Art Nouveau and of modernity in general. At the time, it was used interchangeably with "Floreale," which is now considered to be a distinctive aspect of Italian Art Nouveau—the unrestrained use of naturalistic, plantlike motifs, which covered objects and buildings alike.[32] Furthermore, the word referred at first to the applied and graphic arts: only much later did it come to designate an architectural style proper. Italian Art Nouveau, like its counterparts in Europe, was not limited to architecture but influenced all the decorative arts, literature and music included.[33]

More important, like the names of so many art movements at the turn of the century, this one too came into being with a marked intent of hostility. Art Nouveau was part of a conscious attempt to oust historicism from the artistic scene.[34] But in Italy historicism had merged with nationalism ever since the Risorgimento, and it was against this double-edged threat of nationalism and historicism that the Liberty architects tried to fight.

They came up against bitter opposition. The young architects who aspired to modernity were caught in a quandary born of a tragic misconception of the role of history in the definition of nationalism: how to be modern without ceasing to be Italian. Italy's leading architects had already given their implacable verdict, based on the spurious equation of style and historicism—which they took to be history. Modernity was the very negation of history and as such was not consonant with *italianità,* as Boito and his peers had categorically stated.

But the Liberty was also seen as a rejection of nationalism, and in this respect the old guard was quite right: "With Art Nouveau, Europe attempted a project of universal brotherhood. The most open-minded Italians adhered with enthusiasm to the invitation, which implied the emergence of a supra-national cultural community; but they found the way blocked by droves of zealots in search of a figurative [style] that expressed the concept of nationhood."[35]

For its contemporaries, the new art was fraught with political, and, more specifically, socialist, overtones that were more obvious then than they are now. The very internationalism of the Liberty was seen as a nod toward the Left. Conversely, nationalistic idioms in architecture were understood as an expression of political conservativism.[36] In England, too, the Arts and Crafts had openly flaunted its ties to socialism, particularly in the case of William Morris, Walter Crane, C. R. Ashbee, and Arthur Mackmurdo. The same happened in Belgium, where Victor Horta's Maison du Peuple was built for the Belgian Socialist Party. Recent scholarship has shown to what extent the Liberty was associated, in the minds of contemporaries, with militant socialism, particularly in Turin and Milan, the two strongholds of the Italian Socialist Party. The posters and even the membership card of the party were Liberty.[37]

It is hardly accidental that the Liberty took shape when and where it did. Giovanni Giolitti's term in office (1901–1914) undeniably ushered in an age of progress and prosperity hitherto unknown in Italy.[38] Not surprisingly, the new forms first appeared in the north, in Milan and Turin, where, as the result of the extraordinary impetus given to industrialization, a new social class was on the ascendant, the industrial bourgeoisie, a class without a tradition of its own with which to add luster to the new architectural typologies engendered by the fruit of its labors: railroad stations, department stores, factories, hotels. This upcoming managerial class—bankers, captains of industry, and the engineers who implemented their policies—was quick to patronize the new style. Influenced by positivism and its unshakable faith in progress, the new patrons of the arts were well connected with their European counterparts and as a result were up-to-date with regard to the avant-garde in art and architecture.[39]

The state and the ruling classes, on the other hand, flatly rejected the Liberty, because, having turned its back on history, the movement precluded representation and could not therefore be harnessed to their political purposes.[40] Florence and Rome thus offered far greater resistance to the new, largely because of the overwhelming presence of the past. For all its rhetoric, Art Nouveau was hardly free of history. In fact, the Liberty flourished precisely where the neo-Gothic had scored its greatest triumphs. Indeed, virtually all of Italy's Art Nouveau architects had been practicing medievalists and had inherited Ruskin's ardent love of nature.[41] It was they who took up the anticlassicist crusade from the neomedieval-ists, introducing nature, primarily foliage, into architecture as an antidote to history.[42] Because patronage in the new state was limited to a narrow segment of society, the industrial bourgeoisie, Liberty architects were often forced to be historicists in order to build.

THE TURIN EXPOSITION OF 1902

Without a doubt, the most important architectural manifestation of the Liberty in Italy was the international exposition held in Turin in 1902, an event that determined not only the course that modern architecture was to follow in Italy for the next few years but also the counteroffensive of the historicists. For the first time, the presence of a truly European avant-garde made itself felt on Italian soil, as perhaps had not happened for centuries.

The age was ripe for expositions: after the great Exposition Universelle of 1900 in Paris and the Darmstadt Künstlerkolonie show of 1901, the optimism inherent in the advent of a new century was materialized in the technological products of the Industrial Revolution.[43] Although the heyday of Art Nouveau was over—as the foreign entries made clear—the Turin show was one of the most comprehensive exhibitions of modern art of that period. Promoted by the Circolo degli Artisti di Torino and warmly supported by the magazine *L'Arte Decorativa Moderna*, this venture was an attempt to give a strong impetus to the decorative arts in Italy. The aim was frankly didactic: to show Italy what other nations were doing.

The program would have been bold enough had it been announced in France or Germany, but in Italy it stopped just short of the revolutionary. Social and economic considerations played a preponderant role from the very start, as the organizers stated in their manifesto:

> We would like this organic exhibition of design to aim not only at aristocratic characteristics of elegance and artistic beauty, but above all at those of a practical and industrial nature. In short, we would like artists and producers to lean not so much toward the creation of praiseworthy objects of luxury as toward the study of types of complete decoration, adapted to all homes and all purses, particularly the most humble ones, so as to promote a real, efficacious and total renewal of the environment.[44]

None of this was particularly original, but it was all very new to Italy. Artists were assigned a revolutionary role in society as creators of products that, at least in theory, were to become available to the lower classes. This involved a radical change in the notion of design, a shift in emphasis from the material to the formal aspect of the product: "Substituting the 'fetishism of the product or of the merchandise' by the fetishism of the project, of 'design,' that [notion of] 'beauty' shall in fact cease to be unique and unrepeatable precisely because of its infinite reproducibility, that is, because of its unlimited leveling expansion throughout the social sphere."[45]

Design for mass production thus implied a new concept of style, because the machine imposed certain stylistic norms and, of course, precluded others. Detailed historical trappings were not compatible with mass production. Modernity—if the absence of historical references can be so defined—was almost a mandatory prerequisite for mass production. The organizers also introduced the notion of total design: artists were encouraged to tackle every aspect of the domestic scene, from bookbinding to architecture, in order to create a truly modern environment.

Antihistoricism, as a fundamental basis for a modern style, was applied with even greater consistency to the architecture of the show. The guidelines for the exhibition buildings amounted virtually to a declaration of war on official doctrines concerning the notion of style, in that they categorically excluded any reference to the past: "Straightforward imitations of past styles will not be admitted . . . [but] only original products that give evidence of a decisive tendency toward renewal.[46] This was a radical departure from the official doctrines of the leading architectural circles, which had elevated the equation of style as history to an article of faith:

> In 1890 [date of the First Italian Exhibition of Architecture] style was seen as an abstract but potentially objective entity, rendered concrete by means of historical forms to which evolutionist science guaranteed a priori the faithful representation of the collective soul of the nation. In 1902, on the other hand, this certainty begins to waver. Historical reverberations no longer assured the adherence to reality. One began to tackle the problem of [architectural] language from the point of view of its social role, a role that is at once symbolic and practical.[47]

This was one of the most important contributions of the show: the shift of the notion of style from an openly national and historical idiom to an international and suprahistorical one. In this rejection of historicism, this tabula rasa of the past, one finds the confused but concrete beginnings of a modern architecture in Italy. A few years later, the futurists themselves would insist with greater virulence that antihistoricism was in fact a crucial component of modernity. They too were to shock their compatriots with their incendiary injunctions, the groundwork for which had already been laid in Turin.[48]

Needless to say, all these ideas had political implications and were themselves the fruit of deliberate political choice. In a sense the exposition of 1902 was the culmination of a long and dramatic fight for democracy that brought together intellectuals and certain sectors of the working class.[49] The show also coincided with the rise of the socialist movement, which registered some of its greatest triumphs during those same years. Indeed, there was a connection between socialism and the Liberty. Turin and Milan were the strongholds of the Italian socialist movement for the same reason they were the seedbed of modernity: as the two most industrialized cities of Italy, they contained the greatest concentration of blue-collar workers while also serving as centers for the radical reform of industrial design and the industrialization of the building trade. It is hardly surprising, therefore, that a number of socialist aspirations should find echoes in the guidelines of the show. Nothing did more to enforce a confusion between socialism and the Liberty than a slogan, innocuous enough, launched inadvertently by the artist and critic G. Beltrami in an enthusiastic article written in support of the initiative: "It will be the Socialism of beauty," exclaimed Beltrami referring to the express intention of the organizers to make the decorative arts accessible to all.[50] This slogan was typical of the atmosphere of euphoria and utopia that characterized the entire venture: many of the hostile reactions were directed not so much against the Liberty itself as against what was mistakenly taken for its political moorings.

In 1900 a competition took place to select the architects responsible for the exposition buildings. Most were awarded to Raimondo D'Aronco (1857–1932), at the time one of Italy's most original architects.[51] D'Aronco's career had been unconventional, to say the least. After a three-year apprenticeship in Austria as a skilled mason and a brief stint as a practicing architect in Italy, in 1893 he was summoned to Istanbul to work for the reigning sultan, Abdul-Hamid. D'Aronco's long stay in Turkey exposed him to Byzantine and Ottoman influences, as his use of exuberant detail, surface patterning, and unrestrained color clearly reveals.[52]

D'Aronco's pavilions were startlingly new—at least in Italy. Austrian influence in his work is overpowering, particularly Joseph Olbrich's designs for Darmstadt (1901). At times the extent of D'Aronco's debt reaches embarrassing proportions. The entrance gate to the exposition, for example, virtually plagiarizes the entrance at Darmstadt, as Olbrich noted bitterly: "This is typically Italian," he exclaimed sarcastically on his first visit to the Turin show.[53] And Charles Rennie Mackintosh, whose work was on display, claimed that the exhibition building was "the basest and meanest theft from what Olbrich did at Darmstadt."[54]

With regard to interior space, D'Aronco's work was very traditional. The form and sequence of the halls is entirely Beaux-Arts, in contradiction to the modernist exteriors or even the elevations. D'Aronco understood the Secession as a purely figurative phenomenon. He gave, as Giulia Veronesi said of Olbrich's work, a "pictorial solution to architecture."[55] Painting was his forte, as his Turin buildings show in the beautiful tessellated rhythm of the colors reminiscent of Klimt, with gold and pastel tones on a flat ground.

The two most interesting buildings were the central rotunda—taken, by D'Aronco's own admission, from Hagia Sophia—with an immense gilded dome hovering effortlessly over the central hall (plate 1), and the more original pavilion of automobiles (figs. 1,2). Al-

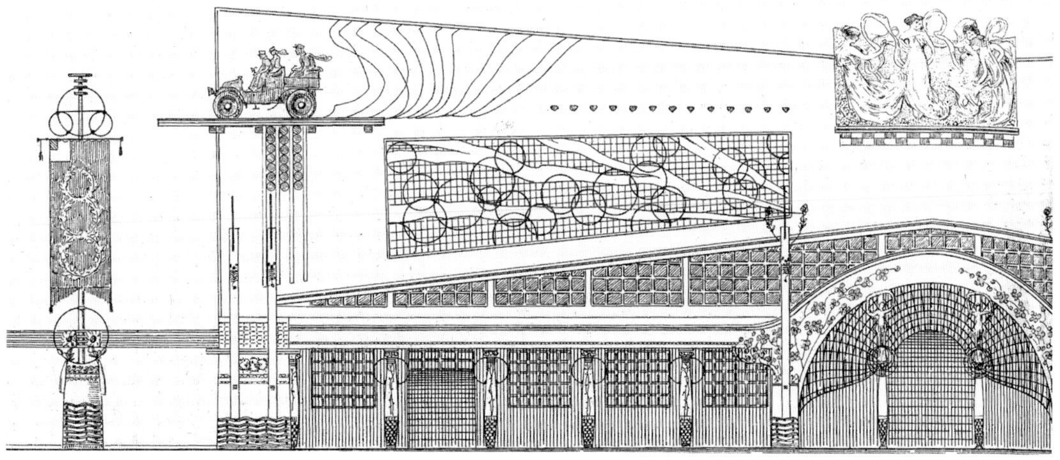

1. Raimondo D'Aronco. Automobile Pavilion, International Exposition, Turin, 1902 (detail). *L'Ingegneria Civile e le Arti Industriali,* 1902.

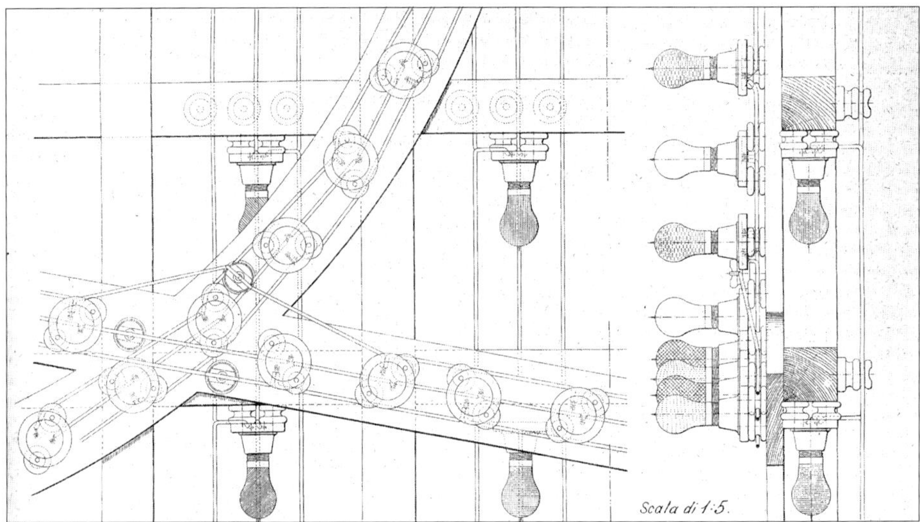

2. Raimondo D'Aronco. Electric lights of the kinetic facade of the Automobile Pavilion, Turin, 1902. *L'Ingegneria Civile e le Arti Industriali*, 1902.

though contemporary critics all but ignored the latter, it was a fascinating structure in which nine thousand electric light bulbs in the facade created the illusion of night and day and introduced the idea of kinesis into architecture.[56] How much Sant'Elia knew of this—he was an adolescent at the time of the show—is hard to gauge, but the Turin exposition laid the cornerstone for much of the architecture and architectural theory that was to follow: namely, antihistoricism, the search for an international architecture, the use of new methods and materials, and bold experimentation with color and movement.

This, then, was the architectural scene when Sant'Elia was born. On one hand there was a newly created nation still doubtful as to the wisdom of unification and avid for "proofs" of its ineluctability—proofs that historicists found in a national style reflecting the past. No such style—unmistakably Italian—emerged, but the hunger was there. At the opposite end of the spectrum stood the modernists, who looked to Europe for inspiration. They found in Art Nouveau an international style that had cut its ties with history and thus satisfied their craving for the new—new forms as well as new materials. Twentieth-century Italian architecture was to be racked by these two opposing tendencies that presided over its birth, with all the attendant political implications.

Antonio Sant'Elia was born on April 30, 1888, into a middle-class family of modest background in Como. His father, Luigi Sant'Elia, a hairdresser by profession, seems to have had a little money. Like his son many years later, he became a city councillor of Como. Little is known  of Sant'Elia's mother, Cristina Panzillo, except that she was born in Capua, near Naples, and that Sant'Elia was extremely fond of her. A younger brother, Guido (born in 1891), and an older sister, Giuseppina (born in 1884), both outlived their famous sibling. Tall and redheaded, Sant'Elia was an arresting figure, all the more since he excelled at several sports and made a name for himself at the local athletic club.[1]

We know little about his childhood. But he must have shown his aptitude for draftsmanship early, for in 1903, when he was fifteen, he enrolled at a local professional high school, the Istituto Gabriele Castellini.[2] This institute offered a rudimentary program in construction, metalwork, and industrial arts that enabled its students, most of whom were of humble origins, to earn a living after graduation. Sant'Elia chose construction. The curriculum was limited to building techniques, topography, and design. Students were taught how to supervise a construction site and follow a building through to completion. Accordingly, they left the school as master masons or building contractors, that is, as qualified cadres who knew how to apply design rather than to create it. There was no grounding in theoretical matters, and Sant'Elia's short career was severely handicapped by the lack of adequate schooling in this area, not to mention faulty orthography and syntax.

In 1906, after three years at the institute, Sant'Elia graduated as a *capomastro* (master builder). His final grades for the academic year 1905–1906 reflect his strengths and weaknesses: building techniques, 30/50 (written) and 40/50 (oral); topography, 43/50; design, 47/50.[3] One sees at this early stage a pattern that was to repeat itself throughout his career: he excelled at drafting but performed poorly in written exams. Sant'Elia had little inclination to write, and the paucity of documents in his own hand is one of the greatest obstacles to our knowledge of his work. Immediately after graduation, and like many promising and ambitious young Lombards, Sant'Elia left for Milan, "la capitale morale" of the country.[4]

Milan, then the cultural and financial hub of Italy, dominated the vast plains of the Po, halfway between the Mediterranean and the Adriatic, where international trade routes had converged for centuries. Under Napoleon, Milan had been the capital of the Cisalpine Republic and had benefited greatly from the enlightened administration of the French; decades later it had become to all intents and purposes the economic capital of Italy.

The opening of Italy's first power plants outside the city gave Milan an undisputed primacy in the production of electric power, a position that quickly transformed its economy. In the 1870s, the first great industrial plants became established in the periphery, and within a few years the entire city was surrounded by an industrial belt comprising vast modern factories. In 1903 Bianchi began to manufacture automobiles, followed by Alfa Romeo and Isotta-Fraschini. The Caproni plant, in Malpensa, began to manufacture airplanes in 1910. Each of these industries employed well over one thousand workers and constituted virtually a "city within a city."[5] More important, they boasted the most recent technological innovations of the period: vast sheds of iron and concrete, suspended iron passageways for pedestrians, private railroad systems, external elevators, steel bridges, all of which were widely publicized in the periodicals of the day. Many of the elements of Sant'Elia's famous Città Nuova projects of 1914 can be found in Milan's paleoindustrial hinterland (fig. 3).

Culture also received fresh impetus from industrialization. Foreign capital, attracted by industry, the promise of profit, and the proximity of foreign markets, helped intensify cultural exchanges, so that Milan was easily the most cosmopolitan city in Italy and the only one that could rightly claim to be both European and Italian. Here French art and literature were avidly welcomed and imitated.[6] Here, too, were Italy's greatest publishing houses: Hoepli, Treves, Sonzagno, and Bestetti e Tumminelli.

Upon arrival in Milan, Sant'Elia found lodgings in the heart of the city, in Via S. Vincenzo. Almost immediately he found work on the Villoresi Canal, an irrigation project then nearing completion that linked the Ticino to the Adda, north of Milan.[7] No information on his work there has come down to us, not even the length of his stay. But after a brief stint on the Villoresi, he found a job as draftsman in the city's Ufficio Tecnico (Department of Public Works).

Because many of the city's archives were destroyed during the bombings of World War II, attempts to determine the nature of his work have proved fruitless. Given his meager training, he was, in all probability, involved in straightforward detailing for the numerous projects sponsored by city hall. For the next few years almost nothing is known about his life, but he cannot have been impervious to the main architectural and urban developments taking place in Milan, particularly within the public works sector of the city administration.

At that time Milan was facing the worst housing crisis in its history. As a result of industrialization and the subsequent economic boom, the population of the city had almost doubled in the last quarter of the nineteenth century: in 1871, the city had 262,000 inhabi-

3. Luigi Repossi. Prestressed concrete sheds of the newspaper
Corriere della Sera, Milan, 1903–1904. *L'Edilizia Moderna*, 1905.

tants; by 1901 the population had reached 491,000, and by 1911, almost 600,000.[8] The situation took on alarming proportions as wave after wave of migrant workers from rural Lombardy flocked to the city in search of work.[9] Many had no alternative but to sleep in the large public dormitories, the *alberghi popolari*, built just outside the city walls.

As would be expected, a large part of public attention and official initiative was focused on housing. For years the reform-minded of society had been clamoring for a solution to this problem. Official reaction had been characteristically dilatory and timorous. Finally, in 1903, the city administration set up a vast program of low-income housing to be built over the next few years.[10] These projects were turned over to the building section of Milan's Ufficio Tecnico while Sant'Elia was employed there.

The city administration was also busy erecting the new infrastructure made necessary by demographic growth: hospitals, schools, day-care centers, new networks of water supply and sewage, transportation routes, stations, and bridges. Many of these projects introduced high standards of hygiene and technology previously unknown in Italy, such as elevators, modern heating, and ventilation systems.[11] Sant'Elia later incorporated in his Città Nuova a number of the innovations carried out by Milan's enlightened administrators.

The main concern of the Ufficio Tecnico, however, was Milan's new master plan. The year Sant'Elia arrived, the master plan created by Cesare Beruto was in force and was to remain so until a new plan was ratified in 1910. When approved in 1889, the former was already an anachronism. Based vaguely on Baron Georges-Eugène Haussmann's radial avenues for Paris and on Vienna's Ringstrasse, it consisted in a monocentric scheme that radiated out from the Piazza Duomo according to the old, threadbare, biological analogies dear to the positivists: "The plan of our city [seen] in small scale shows a great similarity with the cross-section of a tree; the ramifications and the concentric rings can be seen quite clearly. The plan is quite rational, and takes its inspiration from nature: we have, therefore, but given it a greater extension."[12] Beruto's arbitrary decision to create a monocentric plan influenced urban planning in Milan virtually up to World War II, suffocating the center of the city and clogging its main thoroughfares. In spite of these failings, it had the support of a group of Milanese industrialists with vested interest in the matter, particularly G. B. Pirelli, who has been partly credited with the main outlines of the scheme.[13] The plan served industry well, by providing quick and easy access from the center of the city to the periphery and vice-versa. It served speculators even better, by squeezing out of the available land the maximum number of lots for future dwellings.

Not only did the Beruto plan not solve any of Milan's most urgent urban issues, it actually added to them, aiming as it did at a purely technical solution to the problem. It was oriented toward opening up the dense, capillary system of the old Milan and imposing, with little regard for preexisting structures, an abstract system of star-shaped symmetries and geometric connections that echoed one another admirably on paper. No attempt was made to understand the city as a historical artifact with a past of its own.

The architectural climate of Milan at that time is significant because so little is known of Sant'Elia during these crucial, formative years. His reluctance and inability to express himself in writing and the fact that he lived his entire professional life in Milan, within twenty miles of his family and hometown, and had therefore no real need to do so, have left an unbridgeable gap in our knowledge of his work. It is only in January 1909 that he emerges from obscurity, with an appearance of one of his projects in *La Casa* (figs. 4,5), a magazine published in Rome and dedicated primarily to housing.[14] This project is of extraordinary importance not so much because of its inherent qualities as because it is the earliest known work by Sant'Elia and the first dated document of his professional career, a fact that should warrant it greater attention than it has received hitherto.[15]

The design represents a small villa, a two-story cube rising somewhat uncertainly from a small plot of land surrounded by trees. Just below the flat roof, a projecting cornice juts out to protect the house from the glare of the sun. The sharp angularity of the profile is echoed throughout—in the doors and windows, which seem to be carved out of the thick walls.

Sant'Elia's first project is a beginner's work with a beginner's weaknesses. Plan and elevation do not correspond exactly to each other: in elevation the house seems cubical, though the plan suggests otherwise. The scale hardly suggests human tenancy. As the editors of *La Casa* noted in 1909, there is a great discrepancy between outside and inside.[16] The lapidary simplicity of the exterior is not carried over into the conventional and some-

4. Antonio Sant'Elia. Study for a villa. *La Casa*, January 1909.

5. Antonio Sant'Elia. Interior of the villa. *La Casa*, January 1909.

what cramped interior—an Arts and Crafts living room with a most un-Italian inglenook. Perspective is also problematic: the fountain in the foreground is awkwardly designed and sited and reveals only a rudimentary grasp of the laws of projective geometry.

As in all Sant'Elia's works, the plan is an afterthought: the house was conceived of as a small object seen from the outside and then blown up. If placed side by side with the other (rare) plans designed by Sant'Elia, one finds no evolution whatsoever. The same static, hackneyed scheme prevails, a scheme he could have picked up—and no doubt did—from any construction manual.

This project represents something of an anomaly in Sant'Elia's oeuvre, in that it appeared long before any other known work of his and before he received any formal training in architecture. The few villas he designed later, and the one house he actually built, are all Art Nouveau (Liberty). From where did he derive the austere forms and the measured harmony of the massing in this early work? Its stripped classicism was unlike anything to be seen in Italy at the time.

Indeed the design, or at least the exterior, was cribbed entirely from a project by Joseph Olbrich (fig. 6) that had appeared in *Deutsche Kunst und Dekoration* in 1900, and two years later in the Milanese magazine *La Lettura*.[17] The scale, size, and point of view of the two designs are identical. So are all the main elements: the cubelike profile with the indented angle, the deep in-set windows with no moldings, the flat roof, and the cantilevered cornice above the windows. Thus, long before Sant'Elia had his first lesson in architecture, he had already come under the influence of the current that was to have the greatest impact on his work, the Viennese Secession. Nevertheless, it is significant that Sant'Elia borrowed only the perspective from Olbrich, not the plan, thus initiating a recurring pattern in his work. He was won over by the seductive charm of the Wagnerschule's characteristic mode of expression, which relied heavily on perspectives; interior space, for him, was clearly secondary.

6. Joseph Olbrich. Preliminary sketch for the Villa Habich, built in Darmstadt in 1901. *Deutsche Kunst und Dekoration,* May 1900.

Sant'Elia's earliest known project thus consists of architecture that is secondhand—and not very new at that, since Olbrich's sketch had been produced almost a decade earlier. And yet, borrowed or not, Sant'Elia managed to design a villa that, at the time, was undoubtedly the most modern building designed in Italy at the time. The absence of any reference to historicism on the facade, or to the Liberty, is proof of great originality within the context of contemporary Italian architecture.

The publication of his first project, and perhaps the strictures of the editors, encouraged Sant'Elia to pursue seriously a career in architecture. A few months after the project appeared, Sant'Elia resigned from his post at the Ufficio Tecnico in order to work for architectural studios, where he probably hoped to be given more specialized projects and to have the advantage of being under the constant supervision of architects.

THE ACCADEMIA DI BELLE ARTI DI BRERA

In November 1909, Sant'Elia enrolled in the *corso di architettura superiore* of the Accademia di Belle Arti di Brera. At the time, two educational options were open to a young Italian wishing to become an architect: the Politecnico or the Accademia di Belle Arti. The prestigious Politecnico of Milan was a product of the entrepreneurial spirit of the city's forward-looking industrialists. It was divided into two sections: civil engineering and civil architecture. The architectural courses were notoriously inadequate; they were never organically woven into the excellent engineering program and remained an ineffectual overlay. Nonetheless both the engineers and the architects who graduated from the Politecnico could legally practice architecture.

The equally famous Academy of Brera, however, lacked the sturdy faith in progress that was the foundation of the Politecnico: "At the other extreme, in the Institutes and Academies of Fine Arts, there persisted a form of education tied to the old patterns of the past, to the tradition of the Great Competitions of the French Ecoles des Beaux-Arts, and despite the reforms carried out in the different provinces, teaching was still based on copying and designing according to old styles."[18] The problem, of course, lay not in the copying of historical styles per se but in the fact that the academy permitted no other form of education.

The student body in the *corso di architettura superiore* consisted of a motley group of painters, sculptors, and artisans with limited education. Admission requirements were not rigorous: one had to have only an elementary education and be at least fourteen years old. Given the dearth of technical information imparted during this course, graduating students were not recognized as full-fledged architects. They left the academy with a degree in *disegno architettonico,* which did not legally entitle them to practice their profession, and had no choice but to take underpaid jobs in engineering firms, for whom they devised suitable facades to specification. Architecture, as taught by the Accademie di Belle Arti, was viewed as a strictly humanistic discipline. Indeed, however much architects deplored their inferior legal status with regard to their colleagues of the Politecnico, they were extremely proud of their Beaux-Arts training, which they believed placed them above the crass utilitarianism of engineers. The time-honored distinction between *artes mecanicas* and *artes liberales* died hard.

This dichotomy, which was institutionalized all over Italy, dragged on for years, until Camillo Boito succeeded in working out a joint program in architecture in which students of the Politecnico were invited to attend a two-year course on architecture at Brera. This exchange, it was believed, would enable engineers to acquire a more comprehensive background in architecture, while architectural students at Brera would benefit from close contact with the engineers. Unfortunately, despite joint curricula and docents, two wholly different types of professionals were produced by this system: "The students enrolled in the Politecnico graduated with a university degree in civil architecture. Those of the Academy, considered exclusively as artists, finished their studies with a diploma that conferred upon them a degree of 'Professor of architectural draftsmanship,' a title as pompous as it was useless, since it did not lead to the legal practice of the architectural profession. All this thanks to the absolute lack of any technical and scientific knowhow inherent in the profession itself."[19] This core curriculum was still in effect when Sant'Elia enrolled at Brera in November 1909.

Technology was not the only glaring lacuna of the Accademie di Belle Arti. Another serious flaw vitiated the educational system: the social dimension of design was ignored altogether. Centuries of economic and industrial stagnation, made worse by geographical isolation, had reduced Italian architecture to a position of hopeless insularity vis-à-vis the more open situation found in other European nations.[20] And over the years, the scant attention paid to social problems further deprived the profession of a vital blood transfusion that could have helped renew it from within, cut off as it was from all but the more conservative, immobile aspects of European architecture. Housing problems, which had become overwhelming in Milan by that time, were dismissed as a technical, not an architectural, question and thus fell within the province of engineers.[21]

Urbanism, so essential a part of architecture, was introduced into the curricula only in 1921. At the very moment that Italy was undergoing the greatest urban revolution of its history, architecture took refuge in monumentality and abdicated housing and urbanism to engineers and contractors. The debate concerning the problems that beset modern Italy and the solutions that architecture alone could give never took place: "The dialogue among architects had lost all tangibility: important topics were ignored because of incompetence, major social problems because of disinterest: not one reference [was made] to the movement of the garden cities . . . nor to the hygienic reform of the cities, nor yet to the movement on behalf of popular housing."[22]

Architecture emerged from the first fifty years of unification as a wholly anachronistic discipline, unable or unwilling to address the nation's major social problems, ignorant of modern technology, and fearful of any style not sanctioned by history. The teaching of architecture rested on an arbitrary division of buildings into two independent parts, structure and wrapping: the masonry box was the preserve of engineers, and the facades were the exclusive concern of architects. The latter became, as it were, the dressmakers of the building, incapable of relating the facades causally to what lay behind. "In general," as

Manfredi Nicoletti put it so masterfully, "architects were encouraged to be manipulators of skins."[23]

For all its shortcomings the Academy of Brera was then at the height of its fame as the first school of art and architecture in Italy.[24] Although the school was still dominated by Boito and the influential Luca Beltrami, the general orientation was eclectic: classicism and medievalism received equal emphasis. Beltrami's recent restoration of Milan's Castello Sforzesco, as well as the completion of the Duomo during those years, served to reinforce the historicist orientation. Records of the enrollment have survived. Sant'Elia presented himself on November 6, 1909, and signed up for the *primo corso comune,* offered to students from both schools.[25] It was to be followed by a three-year course of specialization devoted to architecture. Very little is known of his years at Brera. Records indicate that he took courses in perspective, ornament, and architecture and that his teachers were Giuseppe Mentessi, Angelo Cattaneo, and Gaetano Moretti, head of the academy.

Giuseppe Mentessi (1857–1931), head of the *scuola di prospettiva,* was a sort of secular saint in residence at Brera, revered by both colleagues and students.[26] Like his more famous friend Gaetano Previati, he came from a rural, poverty-stricken background in Ferrara, a fact that may have strengthened his belief in the social role of art. Commitment to the poor and the oppressed was not unusual in the Milan of the Scapigliatura and of Verismo—if anything, it was the rule. But the moral fervor that Mentessi put into his work and his attempt to elaborate a work ethic consonant with his goals as a painter were legendary: "His authority spurred us onward: his Franciscan love for art left us with our mouths agape. For him art was kindness, affection, faith; it was a quasi-philanthropic form of perfection: it was Goodness itself."[27]

Mentessi's work shows us a *vedutista* of great talent, with a penchant for the Baroque: violent light effects, dramatic atmosphere, and complex spatial arrangements on the diagonal (the famous Baroque *scena per angolo* of the Bibbienas). He also taught a separate course on scenography, assisted by the architect Angelo Cattaneo (1871–1936), with whom Sant'Elia also studied.[28]

But it was mainly Mentessi's teaching methods that were innovative. A born pedagogue, he tried to devise new ways of teaching geometry and perspective. In the first year, students were taught to draw geometric solids; during the second, they were directed to their elected field (sculpture, painting, or architecture); the third year was dedicated to the study of perspective *di sotto in su* (worm's-eye view). These classes represented everything Sant'Elia loved—pictorial architecture, with epic and dramatic overtones that only the two-dimensional medium of paint and paper could give. And yet he did not do well in Mentessi's seminar: his grasp on the matter remained intuitive rather than optical. His friends Gerolamo Fontana, a sculptor, and the architect Luigi Pellini both remember him as a poor student in this subject, as his grades clearly reveal.[29] But Mentessi's courses made an indelible impression on Sant'Elia, and he retained the worm's-eye view and the use of towering masses for years.[30] Mentessi himself remembered him fondly: "Sant'Elia is the last of the Comacine masters," he is reported to have said.[31]

But however praiseworthy Mentessi's work and pedagogy, the fact remains that his neo-Baroque scenography was wholly out of touch with contemporary experiments in theater design. More important, the worm's-eye-view perspective that Sant'Elia learned at Brera was in fact a form of romantic evasion, in that it was not controlled by a rigorous method of architectural notation. This approach was a means of distorting reality for scenographic purposes. The blunt fact that many, if not most, of Sant'Elia's surviving drawings were designed di sotto in su, with no indication of scale or measurements, bears this out. Sant'Elia thus learned the more pictorial elements of design at the expense of architectural ones.

Ironically, the professor in charge of the architectural section of the core curriculum at Brera was one of the most open-minded architects in Italy. In 1909 Gaetano Moretti (1860–1938) assumed the chair of *architettura superiore,* the most prestigious and influential position in the country. Camillo Boito, the formidable dean of Italy's architectural world, had just retired from this post, after forty-three years of teaching.

Moretti was a man of the younger generation and, though a former student of Boito, he was much more pragmatic in his approach to architecture.[32] He was not a fierce medievalist like his teacher, nor was he obsessed with finding an unequivocal "Italian" style for

7. Antonio Sant'Elia. Architectural study, ca. 1910–1911. Musei Civici, Como.

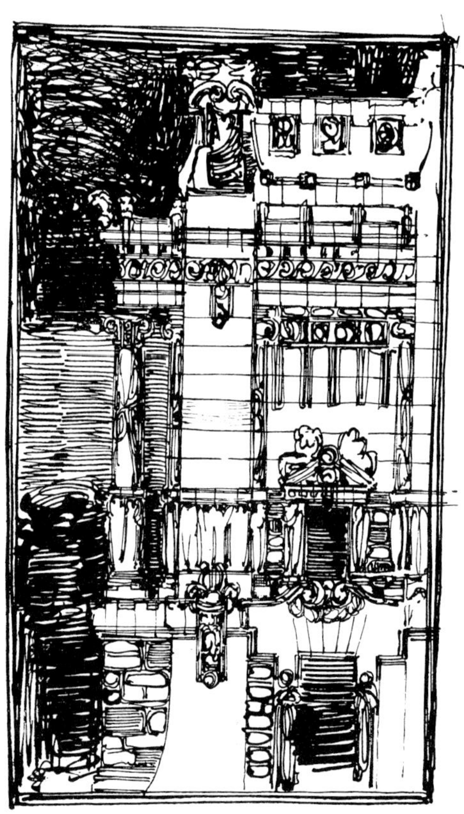

8. Antonio Sant'Elia. Architectural study, ca. 1910–1911. Musei Civici, Como.

9. Antonio Sant'Elia. Study of ornament and statuary, ca. 1910–1911. Banca Popolare di Lecco.

10. Antonio Sant'Elia. Study of a tomb inside a church, ca. 1910–1911. Banca Popolare di Lecco.

the architecture of unified Italy. Although Moretti was hardly a revolutionary, his tutelage came as something of a relief after the gravity of his predecessor. His unprejudiced eclecticism greatly influenced the students. Rather than use a preconceived style for commissions, Moretti adopted different styles for different projects. What made him attractive to the young was the wide range of his sources: he was among the first to introduce non-Western architecture into Italy.

Sant'Elia studied at Brera for two years. Records show that he passed his exams at the end of the first year and was promoted to the *secondo corso comune*.[33] After this he seems to have abandoned his studies or failed his exams. No works dating from Sant'Elia's term at Brera are known to survive, and the few extant drawings that may be linked to this period are difficult to date with precision. After the startling sobriety of his earliest known project, the villa published in 1909, these sketches show Sant'Elia at the most academic moment of his career.[34] Decoration overrides architecture. Swags, pediments, acroteria, architraves— the full panoply of Renaissance-oriented eclecticism, then current in official circles—is deployed (figs. 7,8). This style of draftsmanship also owes something to the architect

Giulio Arata, whose streamlined eclecticism found favor both with the young and with the academy.

Another group of early drawings, done around 1911, reveals that peculiar type of neomedievalism with Art Nouveau touches so much in vogue in Lombardy at the time (figs. 9,10). In fact, they have more to do with ornament than with architecture proper. The mourning knight with the long sword was borrowed from the monumental portal figures of the Hungarian pavilion designed by Emile Töry and Maurice Pogány for another international exposition, held in Turin in 1911 (figs. 11,12). These knights were to appear repeatedly in Sant'Elia's iconography, which, with few exceptions, was drawn largely from the Middle Ages. The quick, nervous line is characteristic of his earliest work, as is the use of *crayon gras* retouched in black ink.[35]

Sant'Elia's training at Brera did not palliate any of the weaknesses in his education. It seems to have encouraged his innate aptitude for draftsmanship and scenographic renderings without giving him a rigorous discipline to temper the romantic bent of his personality. Carlo Carrà, who studied at Brera from 1906 to 1908, has left a frank appraisal of the teachings of the academy in his autobiography: "I have often asked myself, without ever finding an answer, what relation the Academy of Brera had with art. Speaking in all frankness, I should say that I saw no relationship whatsoever." And he adds: "What I seek, rather,

11. Emile Töry and Maurice Pogány. Hungarian Pavilion, Turin, 1911. *The Studio*, September 1911.

12. Monumental entrance to the Hungarian Pavilion by Emile Töry and Maurice Pogány, Turin, 1911. Sculpture by Nicolas Ligeti. *The Studio*, September 1911.

is the complex contact that every institution must have with the living culture of its own age, and from that point of view the Academy of Brera contributed little or nothing at all to the artistic education of the young. On the contrary, it weighed heavily on the shoulders of the student rather than help him rise."[36]

Carrà's strictures are also applicable to architecture: for a brief period he attended Moretti's classes, one year before Sant'Elia enrolled in the same course.[37] For Sant'Elia, however, Brera functioned as a forum for discussion with the most promising artists and architects of Milan, many of whom were to play a prominent role in his life and work. It weaned him from his narrow provincialism and educated him to a national outlook.

The year 1909 marked a turning point in Sant'Elia's life: in January he published his first project, thereby achieving a modest notoriety of sorts, albeit in a restricted circle; in November he entered the august Accademia di Brera. By coincidence this was also the year in which F. T. Marinetti published the founding manifesto of futurism in Paris.[38] Whether Sant'Elia knew about it at the time is a matter of conjecture, but soon after its publication, the manifesto "Let's kill the moonlight" appeared in Marinetti's seminal magazine *Poesia*, published in Milan, and caused a great deal of excitement. It is hard to believe that Sant'Elia could have ignored the event.

Three **The Impact of Vienna**

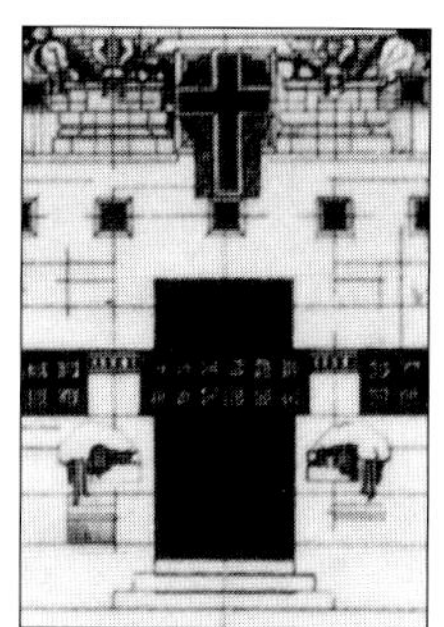

Late in 1910 Sant'Elia entered a competition called "Il Villino Moderno," organized by the Milanino Cooperative, a nonprofit association that had founded a garden city in Milan in 1908.[1] Eighty projects
were submitted and later exhibited, and Sant'Elia was awarded a *diploma d'onore* for his entry (figs. 13,14). The best designs, his own included, were
subsequently published by the magazine *Le Case Popolari e le Città-Giardino,* which
had helped sponsor the competition.[2]

Sant'Elia's *villino moderno* is a two-story house, with a short tower, resting on a
rusticated base. The massing is calculated to produce entirely different side elevations, so that symmetry is studiously avoided. Sant'Elia further tries to enliven his
design by contrasting the smooth plaster of the walls with the rough stone of the
base.

The plan is static and conventional, very similar, in fact, to that of his first published project of 1909. Here, however, it is repeated unimaginatively in both stories.
By 1910 this sort of picturesque villa was frankly old-fashioned. The difference between this house and his first published design is surprising. The earlier project,
borrowed from Olbrich, was far more original, with its crisp detailing and crys-
talline profile. Considering that Sant'Elia attended the Academy of Brera during the
two years that separate these designs, one begins to measure the extent to which
Italian schools of architecture were divorced from contemporary achievements in
the rest of Europe.

Sometime in 1911 Sant'Elia took the first of his rare documented trips outside
Milan, to Rome. He was accompanied by old friends from Brera, the architects
Luigi Pellini and Romeo Moretti and the painter Cantoni.[3] The year 1911 was emblematic in Italian history: the country was celebrating the fiftieth anniversary of
the proclamation of the Regno d'Italia of 1861, and a vast exposition, the largest
ever held on Italian soil, was planned as part of the festivities.[4] Italy wanted to show
the world that it was no longer the picturesque "Little Italy" of gondoliers and man-
dolins but a strong new contender on the European scene. The show was to be di-

13. Antonio Sant'Elia. Project for a villa. *Le Case Popolari e le Città-Giardino*, 1911.

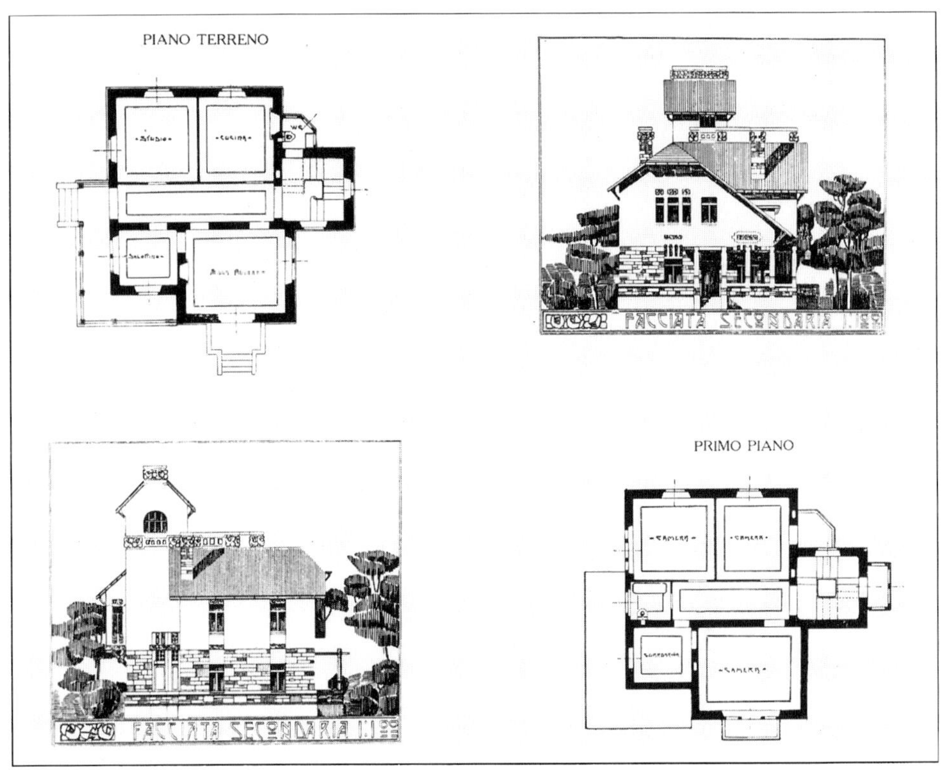

14. Antonio Sant'Elia. Plans and side elevations of the villa. *Le Case Popolari e le Città-Giardino*, 1911.

vided between Turin and Rome, the nation's first and third capitals, respectively. Rome was to house the exhibitions of art, archaeology, and ethnography, while Turin was to play host to industry and technology. Moreover, Rome was the site of the Ninth International Congress of Architecture as well as the Concorso Nazionale per le Case Popolari, both of which were planned to coincide with the international exposition.[5] There is no mention of dates, but Sant'Elia's trip must have taken place between the last days of March, when the show was inaugurated, and the end of the year.

The exposition gave rise to a major scheme of architectural and urbanistic renewal of the capital. New avenues, bridges, and piazzas had to be built to serve the numerous official buildings of the show. Rome's neo-imperial building boom had begun much earlier, when it became a capital, but the magnitude of the undertaking was such that many of the projects were only now being completed. Many had to be hastily completed for the inauguration. For the event Rome was finally unveiling to the world the two most famous architectural monuments erected after unification: Giuseppe Sacconi's memorial to Victor Emmanuel II, the Vittoriano (1885–1911), and Guglielmo Calderini's Palazzo di Giustizia, known as the "Palazzaccio" (1888–1910).

By 1911 these two monuments were something of an embarrassment to official circles: their colossal scale and sententious rhetoric were no longer in tune with the prevailing taste. But however much they may have been maligned at the time, there is no doubt that the sheer mass of these structures rising like man-made cliffs above the spectator and the

15. Josef Hoffmann. Interior of the Austrian Pavilion, International Exposition, Rome, 1911. *Der Architekt,* vol. 17, 1911.

orchestration of staircases and statuary on a grand scale greatly influenced Sant'Elia's projects of the following years.[6]

The temporary buildings erected to house the Italian exhibits had little to offer the visiting architect: their grandiloquent eclecticism was characteristic of international expositions all over the world. Nonetheless, the foreign pavilions included some remarkable works that were bound to be of interest: Edwin Lutyens's dignified neoclassical building, now the seat of the British Academy, the powerful Serbian structure by P. Bajalovich, and, above all, Josef Hoffmann's Austrian pavilion.

Hoffman's building was a revelation in both its architecture and its exhibits. It was a spare, U-shaped building with porticoes around a central courtyard, designed by Hoffmann as a showcase for the works of his two favorite artists, Gustav Klimt and the sculptor Anton Hanak.[7] Its dignified restraint pleased the modernists for its sobriety and the historicists for the elegance of its stripped classicism. The architects in charge of the architectural display in the interior were well known to Sant'Elia: Emil Hoppe, Marcel Kammerer, and Otto Schönthal. Their own work figured prominently in the exposition, together with sketches by Otto Wagner, Hoffmann, and other members of the Wagnerschule. A model of Wagner's Steinhof Kirche was exhibited, as well as reproductions of secessionist buildings in Vienna (fig. 15).[8] Klimt's art caused a sensation, especially since he visited the show in person. He was already quite well known in Italy, and in Rome in particular, having re-

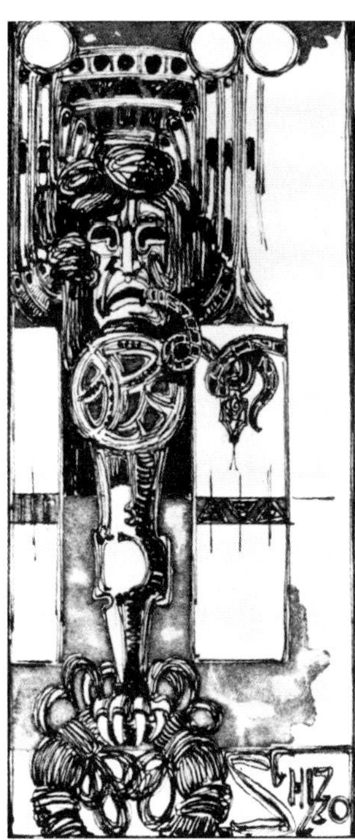

16. Antonio Sant'Elia. Ornamental sketch for an apartment building, 1911. Musei Civici, Como.

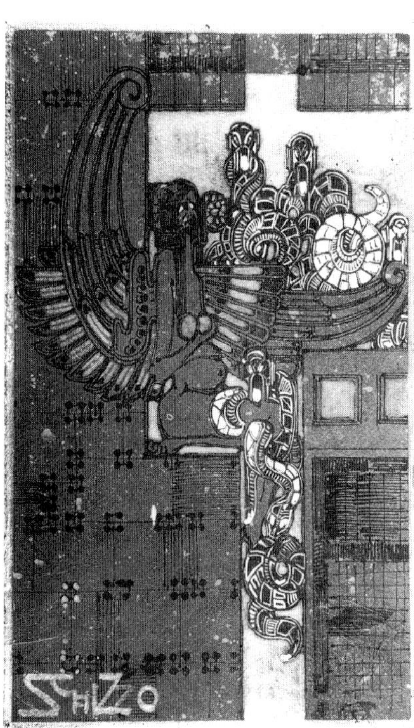

17. Antonio Sant'Elia. Ornamental study for an apartment building, 1911. Musei Civici, Como.

18. Antonio Sant'Elia. Ornamental study for an apartment building, 1911. Musei Civici, Como.

ceived a gold medal there in 1908. This time he was again awarded first prize for his entries.

Soon after his return from Rome, where the Austrian presence had been so overwhelming, Sant'Elia executed an extraordinary group of sketches, strongly influenced by the Secession (figs. 16–18). There are five such preparatory sketches, all done in pen and ink and retouched in gold. The final drawing, mounted on cardboard, is among the most exquisite ever designed by Sant'Elia (plate 2). It is a product of the refined fin-de-siècle sensibility, morbid and willfully decadent, so much in vogue among the symbolist painters of Milan.

Sant'Elia's project shows a relatively small, five-story apartment house liberally covered with grimacing masks, strange winged females, pythons, snakes, bats, and flowers. Each of the masks and figures is given an entirely different physiognomy and posture so that there is asymmetry within the overall symmetrical composition. Highly original wrought-iron gratings with a batlike appearance adorn the first two stories. Here Sant'Elia is far removed from the machine aesthetic of his later years: this sort of narrative could be executed only by means of craftsmanship.

This apartment building was his most secessionist work to date. It calls to mind Wagner's Majolikahaus (1898–1899), as well as the numerous projects for apartment buildings that his students were required to execute, all of which were famous for their graphic virtuosity. Sant'Elia's surface, like those of the Viennese, is treated as a large easel across which his macabre narrative can unfold. Sant'Elia, however, was looking at the Austrians partly through the eyes of their Milanese imitators. His teacher Gaetano Moretti, director of the Academy of Brera, did at least one project that influenced this design, an apartment house of 1911, which is patently derived from the Wagnerschule (fig. 19).[9] Sant'Elia's basic composition follows Moretti's: the building is divided horizontally by five stories and vertically by five rows of windows. Even the minute characters in Moretti's project, cursorily drawn, recurred in Sant'Elia's work until his death.

Giuseppe Sommaruga (1867–1917), the most original architect practicing in Milan in Sant'Elia's day, was also a seminal influence and one to whom Sant'Elia often turned for inspiration.[10] In a sense Sommaruga translated Wagner's lofty and elegant formulas into the earthier terms of Milanese dialect. His importance for the younger generation comes from the fact that he turned his back on historicist revivals while preserving the traditional *palazzo* typology as well as the Baroque masses filled with dramatic contrasts of light and shade. Yet the structural clarity of Wagner's work is buried under the rhetoric of the facade. Not surprisingly, Sommaruga's cautious modernism gained favor with Milan's industrial bourgeoisie, who sought the dignity of the palazzi and at the same time the frisson of being "moderne." His powerful Palazzo Castiglioni (1901–1903), one of the most notorious Liberty—if not libertine—buildings in Milan, came as a revelation to the young architects (fig. 20).[11]

From Sommaruga Sant'Elia learned to increase the complexity of the design as the eye moves upward. Not only do the decorative figures multiply but the windows also increase in size and number so that the hypertrophy of ornament is countered by the greater number of voids. Sant'Elia thus avoids any impression of top-heaviness that might otherwise

19. Gaetano Moretti. Apartment building, 1911. Archivio Storico Civico e Biblioteca Trivulziana, Milan.

20. Giuseppe Sommaruga. Palazzo Castiglioni, Milan, 1901–1903. (Photo: Courtesy of Archivio Fotografico Castello Sforzesco, Milan)

result. Also based on the Palazzo Castiglioni are the pairs of female nudes flanking the main entrance and the windows, the highly individualized figurative elements, and even the triads of minute windows in the basement. Another borrowing is the rustication of the first two floors so characteristic of Sommaruga, although Sant'Elia's interpretation is not heavy and lithic but planar and graphic.

The macabre asymmetrical gratings with stylized bats and serpents come from yet another local source. Wrought-iron work of this sort was a specialty of Milanese Art Nouveau architecture owing chiefly to the extraordinary craftsmanship of Alessandro Mazzucotelli (1865–1938), one of the greatest specialists of ironwork in Europe, whom Sant'Elia may have known personally.[12]

Sant'Elia has cloaked his borrowings in a highly personal idiom and has taken great liberties with the rules of architectural notation. The decoration overpowers the architecture: much more attention has been lavished on the minute details of the figures than on the architectural elements themselves.[13] One should bear in mind, however, that Sant'Elia's sources were often pictorial rather than architectural, in spite of the great influence of contemporary Italian buildings—an impact he was to deny in his manifesto. His graphic style during these years reminds one of the secessionists' architectural vignettes published in *Ver Sacrum* or *Der Architekt*. His design, like theirs, unfolds as an insubstantial image floating on white ground—a sort of architectural "black figure." Furthermore, Art Nouveau in all its manifestations (Secession, Jugend, Liberty) was never primarily an architectural style to begin with; it was, as so many scholars have pointed out, a type of design related to the decorative arts.[14]

The layout, with the frame cropping the image above and below—and thus withholding vital architectural information—stresses the identity, indeed the flattened oneness of figure and ground reminiscent of a poster. In this Sant'Elia clearly betrays his magazine sources. As Tschudi Madsen points out, "In architecture, too, we find a poster-like use of Art Nouveau motifs. The Viennese periodical *Der Architekt* contains a number of examples in the years just before and after 1900."[15] *Der Architekt* was one of Sant'Elia's favorite sources, as it was produced by the architects he most admired within the Wagnerschule.

Equally derivative of the Secession is his use of varied mediums on the facade. Although Sant'Elia did not leave any indication as to the materials, he was possibly thinking of a combination of metalwork for the bats and the serpents and ceramic tiles or terracotta for the female figures, while the floral decoration could be easily incised on a plaster surface. These are, significantly, the materials that Olbrich had used in the Secession building in Vienna (1898). There too masks intertwined with serpents occupy a prominent place on the facade.

The draftsmanship is superb, with webs of finely hatched lines enlivened with gold. There is a strong, almost abstract rhythm of forms, independent of the figures, that pulsates across the composition, producing a lively tesselated pattern. This play between abstraction and figuration is one of the most characteristic tenets of the Secession and of Klimt in particular, as is the overall conception of decoration as content.

These were the years of Klimt's greatest triumphs in Italy.[16] He was revered, flattered, and imitated, and it would be difficult to overestimate his influence on the architecture of the time: he was, after all, a painter of surfaces, and his flat, decorative style was embraced by architects trained in the academies of fine arts. For them, his stylized figures, so heavily dependent on abstraction, were an ideal means of articulating facades without lapsing into historicism. Sant'Elia, fresh from his Roman experience, was then at the height of his admiration for the Viennese master.[17] The decorative scrolls below the roof and the abundant use of gold are all traceable to Klimt. So too is the iconography that was unprecedented in architecture: bats, serpents, masks with contorted features, and strange female nudes of somewhat dubious occupation.

The reptilian imagery is striking. Writhing snakes festoon the facade, their menacing jaws open and their coils often intermingled with strange claws (fig. 16). It is true that a tradition of zoomorphic decoration existed in Milanese secessionist architecture, as seen in the many extant examples of snails, shrimps, and even elephant trunks. In Sant'Elia, however, the animal imagery takes on erotic overtones.[18]

The woman-serpent equation, a common topos in symbolist milieus, was part of the macabre eroticism that pervaded the representation of women in all the arts at the turn of the century.[19] This was an age that focused mainly on the satanic element of the *ewig Weibliche:* Flaubert's *Salammbô* (in which a woman embraces a python), the various Salomes of Oscar Wilde, Aubrey Beardsley, and Richard Strauss, the Lulus of Frank Wedekind, Alban Berg and, later, Georg Pabst.[20]

Sant'Elia's women, like Klimt's, are not only demonic but subject to decay and old age. With their sagging breasts and bellies and their eerie grimaces, they present an unusual type not found in the Italian tradition but common in that of northern Europe. In profile, Sant'Elia's standing women closely resemble the aged female in Klimt's *Three Ages of Woman* (1905), which Sant'Elia must have seen in Rome. Women and serpents are associated in the work of several fin-de-siècle artists: Klimt's *Jurisprudence,* also shown in Rome, and the numerous versions of Franz von Stuck's *Die Sünde* (Sin) of 1897, to name another northern artist whom Sant'Elia admired.[21] It is true, as Carlo Cresti remarks, that Sant'-Elia's angular figures are closer to the "asexual nudes of Toorop and of Minne."[22] But the manifest perversity of these grinning figures and the constant association with snakes are clearly a trope for the sort of sexuality in vogue among decadent artists. What Sant'Elia's figures lack is not eroticism per se but the overt lubricity of those of von Stuck, which were too sanguine to please the linear canon of Art Nouveau aesthetics.

The masks, too, are cryptic; their expressions of pain, anger, or spite may have been derived from literary sources. Cesare Lombroso's physiognomical studies on criminal anthropology were particularly important in Milan's artistic circles. Symbolist artists and writers were avid readers of his theories, which had great impact on their portrayal of women as evil, demonic beings.[23] Sant'Elia's friend Romolo Romani (1884–1916), who later joined the futurists briefly, was also interested in expressing psychic states through physiognomy and left a large oeuvre of fascinating portrait studies that Sant'Elia knew well.[24] Romani, interestingly enough, was one of the few artists in Milan who is known to have read Freud, as reflected in both the images and the titles of his art.[25] It was also Romani who introduced Sant'Elia to the lithographs of Charles Munch: the stylized contours of Sant'Elia's figures and their grimacing features attest to the impact of Munch's graphic work.[26]

Iconography such as this makes one wonder whether Gabriele D'Annunzio's crepuscular tales of stifling eroticism influenced Sant'Elia. Whatever the case, the moody, nocturnal colors, overcast skies, and vaguely mystical setting of these projects reveal the strong link between Sant'Elia and the Milanese symbolists, such as Gaetano Previati (1852–1920) and Vittore Grubicy de Dragon (1851–1920), whose works no doubt encouraged Sant'Elia's propensities toward the macabre.

Symbolism was the cultural matrix of the Milanese avant-garde. Marinetti's first poems, the early paintings of Umberto Boccioni, Luigi Russolo, and Sant'Elia himself, all owe a great deal to the circles of self-proclaimed decadent artists and writers. Romolo Romani had collaborated in Marinetti's magazine *Poesia* during its symbolist phase (1906 to 1908). Previati—a towering personality surrounded by that aura of misery and malediction that so became modern artists of the day—dominated the artistic scene during Sant'Elia's years in Milan. His luminous divisionism and the bold, sinuous lines of his symbolist paintings exercised a strong attraction on the young. Previati's two theoretical treatises, *La tecnica della pittura* (1905) and *I principi scientifici del divisionismo* (1906), were crucial precursors of futurist artistic theory.[27] Sant'Elia may have met him personally, since many of his friends, such as Boccioni, Romani, and Mentessi, frequented Previati's studio. In all probability, he saw Previati's one-man retrospective in Milan in 1910.

Symbolist literature was also of signal importance for Sant'Elia, especially the poetry of Baudelaire, the tales of Edgar Allan Poe, and the novels of Joris-Karl Huysmans and, of course, D'Annunzio. Poe struck a cord with Italian artists and writers, who were fascinated by the expressive potential of his sumptuous and gruesome settings.[28] Previati's illustrations of Poe were justly famous in their day. It has been suggested that Sant'Elia, who was no doubt familiar with them, may also have illustrated some tales of Poe,[29] as well as episodes from Dante's *Inferno,* but Jörn-Peter Schmidt-Thomsen has rightly questioned this assumption.[30] At any rate, the pervasive influence of symbolist art is manifest in his work, particularly between 1911 and 1912.

Funeral art and architecture were two of the most important outlets for the Liberty. Strangely enough, these areas afforded artists and architects great artistic freedom, as art and the age came together. The taste of the times, which ran to the macabre and the morbid, expressed itself not only in art but also in the work of writers like D'Annunzio, Huysmans, and Wilde, with their erotic variants of the death theme. Certainly Milan's large colony of symbolist writers and artists could find no more congenial atmosphere than that of the cities of the dead.[31] To this day the best anthology of fin-de-siècle art and architecture in Italy is Milan's Cimitero Monumentale, where hundreds of diminutive buildings attest to the creative vigor of their designers, while many of the full-scale city works of these same designers are perfectly anodyne: "In effect, instead of being a place of pain, the great Milanese cemetery is one vast museum of statues, an uninterrupted succession of marbles, bronzes, mosaics. None other, perhaps, is as rich in sculptural and architectural works."[32]

The same sinister women with their attendant snakes appear again in a superb project for a small funerary chapel or family tomb probably executed immediately after the apartment building (fig. 21). These angular women with sagging breasts and swollen bellies, one with a serpent around her torso, stand out all the more in this context, where they have no theological significance and they depart radically from established funerary iconography. Once more, the project is heavily influenced by Wagner, particularly with regard to the central plan (the circle-in-the-square). The drawing has the lapidary clarity of design and the massing of the Viennese master, although Sant'Elia is uncertain, as usual, as to how the dome really relates to the underlying structure. His technical weaknesses never really improve. Part of the problem stems, one suspects, from his difficulty in dealing with plans and sections and his dismissal of interior space.

This *tempietto* was the first of a series of centrally planned buildings designed at about this time, when the influence of the Secession on his work was at its highest point; such schemes seem to disappear from his work thereafter (figs. 22,23, plates 3,4). As mentioned

21. Antonio Sant'Elia. Funerary chapel, 1911. Collection of
Giovanni Pellini, Milan.

earlier, Sant'Elia had seen a model of Wagner's church of St. Leopold at Steinhof (1905–1907) in Rome, and he returns to that composition here.[33] Significantly, in the upper part of one of these designs (plate 4), Sant'Elia shows the cladding, presumably stone or marble slabs, held in place by bolts and clamps, as in Wagner's famous Postal Savings Bank as well as in the Steinhof church. This type of cladding, whether Sant'Elia knew it or not, actually harked back to Gottfried Semper's *Bekleidung* theory, which called for a clear separation between the load-bearing core and the wafer-thin wall. Unlike Wagner or his students, however, Sant'Elia constantly struggled with problems of scale, as these projects show. This sort of simplified cube capped by a dome almost precludes large dimensions unless articulated with great care so as to give the viewer a clear sense of scale.

WAGNER AND THE WAGNERSCHULE

These projects raise the question of the extent to which Sant'Elia was indebted to the Secession and to Wagner in particular. The extraordinary influence in Italy of Austrian and German art at the time was due, in part, to the close political ties established among members of the Triple Alliance.[34] Soon after the treaty was signed (1882), German and Austrian capital began to replace French capital, previously so crucial for industrialization, providing the economic foundation for the uneasy entente among the three powers. Two decades of economic domination, from 1896 to 1915, profoundly influenced the arts. Austrian art had pride of place in exhibitions of modern art in Italy, particularly in Venice, once a Hapsburg possession.[35]

With regard to architecture, the diffusion of Viennese influence in Italy came about primarily through secessionist periodicals and magazines, which were followed with great interest: *Ver Sacrum, Kunst und Kunsthandwerk*, and *Der Architekt*. So were popular German magazines, particularly those published in Darmstadt, *Deutsche Kunst und Dekoration* and *Innendekoration*, as well as *Dekorative Kunst*, from Munich. Italian periodicals such as *Emporium, Pagine d'Arte, L'Arte Decorative Moderna, L'Artista Moderno*, and *Arte Italiana Decorativa e Industriale* were also widely read. Although there were others, these, in particular, were the magazines that carried the spare, black-and-white graphics that Sant'Elia and other Liberty architects sought to imitate. Not surprisingly, the periodicals founded to propagate the style eventually ended up influencing that style itself.

Otto Wagner constituted a major source of inspiration for Milanese architects during those years.[36] Italians greatly admired his underlying classicism and stereometric volumes, which resembled in shape and size the palazzo of the Italian Renaissance, the time-honored habitat of the urban bourgeoisie. Wagner's rigorous symmetry in plan and elevation further stressed the bond between past and present architecture so that he appeared to be retrieving the classical heritage while turning his back on historicism. Equally important were his books: *Moderne Architektur* (1896), *Einige Skizzen, Projekte und ausgeführte Bauwerke* (three volumes: 1890, 1897, 1906), *Die Grossstadt* (1911), and *Die Baukunst unserer Zeit* (1914). But on the whole Wagner's written work had far less impact on Sant'Elia than did his projects. None of Wagner's books had been translated into Italian at the time, and

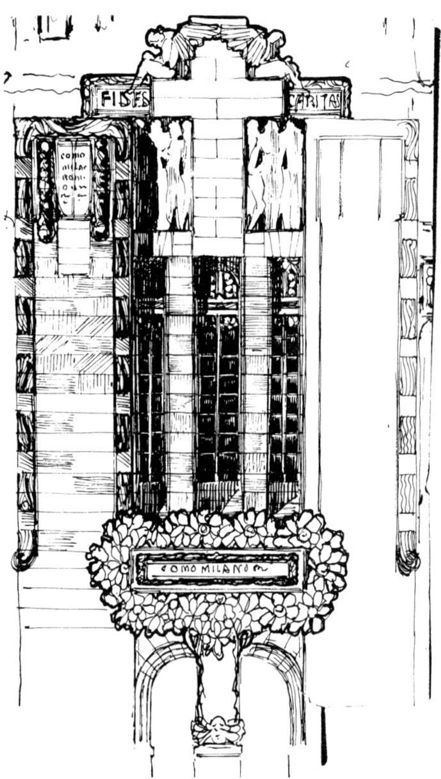

22. Antonio Sant'Elia. Funerary chapel, ca. 1910–1911. Musei Civici, Como.

23. Antonio Sant'Elia. Monumental building, ca. 1911–1912. Musei Civici, Como.

Sant'Elia was little inclined to read theory. Even so, he may have been exposed to Wagner's ideas on the future of the metropolis through colleagues or through books and articles popularizing Wagner's ideas.[37]

A distinction must also be made between Otto Wagner himself, with his emphasis on clarity of design and purpose, and the more lyrical works of his students, which had even greater appeal for Sant'Elia.[38] The architect and critic Giulio Arata, who was the first to mention Sant'Elia's debt to the Wagnerschule, saw this quite well: "In some drawings he imitates the rather cold forms of Margold or lets himself be influenced by the Austrian Wagnerian school."[39] Arata's penetrating observation was very much to the point: Margold came not from the Wagnerschule but from the Hoffmannschule, and his work lacked the spatial clarity that was characteristic of Wagner. E. J. Margold designed his projects by combining volumes in a tasteful manner, very much, in fact, like Sant'Elia.

The various albums of the Wagnerschule were a constant and treasured source of ideas. Sant'Elia's belongings at the time of his death were scattered, with the exception of the volume *Wagnerschule 1902*, which is the only book known to have belonged to him.[40] His friend Mario Chiattone owned at least two other albums, *Wagnerschule 1902–03* and *Wagnerschule 1903–04*.[41]

Most of the *Wagnerschülern* whom Sant'Elia admired had won the Rome prize and had spent part of their *Wanderjahre* in Italy, among them Josef Hoffmann, Josef Plečnik, Emil Hoppe, Otto Schönthal, Marcel Kammerer, Rudolf Perco, Wunibald Deininger and of course Olbrich, who had never been a student of Wagner's but had worked in his office. And yet, despite considerable experience sketching in the Roman countryside, these *petits maîtres* displayed an interest in landscapes that were thoroughly unclassical. Coming from Bohemia, Moravia, Slovenia, Croatia, or Hungary, they absorbed the more Romantic currents of the waning Austro-Hungarian empire, thus preserving the nostalgia inherent in Hapsburg culture.[42] Perhaps because of this they preferred landscape to cityscape, which was the setting that so interested Wagner. Many of their works show villas or buildings in isolation, surrounded by nature. But their work differed from Wagner's in another respect. While he made use of clear-cut elevations, these students, like Sant'Elia, preferred the worm's-eye view, which enhanced the Romantic nature of the project and conveyed a feeling that was lyrical and psychological rather than purely architectural. There is much truth to Otto Antonia Graf's remark that Sant'Elia should really be considered a belated member of the Wagnerschule.[43]

Meanwhile, war had broken out between Italy and Turkey: toward the end of September 1911, Italy invaded Libya on the slenderest of pretexts. A classic example of colonialist expansion, this war was waged chiefly to provide land for Italian settlers who were emigrating by the thousands. But there were other reasons. Italy's dreams of a heroic future after unification had come to nought. The great epic wars of the Risorgimento had ended in the tepid, bourgeois dynasty of the Savoy—a musical operetta rather than a heroic drama. The country continued to lag behind the Great Powers economically and culturally and was clearly relegated to a second rank among nations. Italy nonetheless thirsted for glory. In the first fifty years of unification, its literati had created not a unitary culture but a unitary myth: for half a century they had stressed the idea that modern Italy was in fact the old Roman Empire redivivus—hence the need for military exploits of resounding glory.

The Libyan campaign marked the first alliance between the futurists—or at least Marinetti—and the government, an alliance that was to repeat itself with sad monotony during World War I and again with the fascists' accession to power. From the Italian front in Libya, where he had gone as war correspondent for *L'Intransigeant*, Marinetti wrote the euphoric manifesto "War, Sole Hygiene of the World." And the conquest of Tripoli in the first days of October prompted the famous lines: "Today, we can admire nothing but the formidable symphonies of shrapnel, and the mad sculptures that our inspired artillery chisels with bursts of machine gun within the enemy ranks."[44]

Among the dissenting voices were those of the socialists, who tried desperately to mobilize the population against war. Ironically, their most inflammatory orator in Milan was a young firebrand named Benito Mussolini. In one of his most important socialist speeches of the time he declared: "Before conquering Trento and Trieste and Tripolitania, we must conquer Italy; must take water to Puglia, drainage to the Roman Ager, justice to the south, and the alphabet everywhere."[45]

It is unfortunate that we have no way of knowing what Sant'Elia thought about Italy's colonialist maneuvers in Libya, because such evidence might shed light on the vexing question of his participation in World War I a few years later. We do know, however, that by that time Sant'Elia was well acquainted with the futurists, Milan's enfants terribles. His friends Boccioni, Carrà, and Russolo were already militant members of the group. Together with Marinetti, they had even organized one of their notorious evenings in Como, Sant'Elia's hometown.[46]

During the last months of 1911, Sant'Elia fell under the spell of the Wagnerschule and worked hard to give his own projects a secessionist overlay. As the year drew to a close, Sant'Elia could look back and take stock of his situation: he had managed to publish one project—his second—in a respectable magazine. Encouraged by this modest success, he was eager to assert himself professionally at a higher level. The occasion presented itself in February 1912, when the nearby town of Monza announced a competition for the new cemetery.

THE MONZA COMPETITION

This was Sant'Elia's first important competition and one that attracted considerable attention nationwide. Sometime in 1911, he had dropped out of the Academy of Brera, a decision that was perfectly consistent with his ambition to achieve greater exposure. Given the state of affairs in Italian architecture at the time, competitions were far more useful than good grades or a degree from the academy. Older, more experienced architects might permit themselves the luxury of disdaining such events now and then, but the young desperately needed to make themselves known to public and patrons alike: "Even architects, in order to establish themselves in the public eye, no longer thought of schools or of academies: they took part in competitions announced by the new magazines, competitions that were not necessarily geared toward practical purposes but that served at least to make them known by means of impeccable draftsmanship."[47] This modus operandi was not unusual: Otto Wagner could not recommend competitions highly enough in *Moderne Architektur,* his primer for architectural students.[48]

Competitions also prompted a certain notion of style, understood in a very broad sense. Because most utilitarian structures were left to engineers, monuments were one of the main staples of the architectural curriculum. The simple fact that so many architects were vying with one another for monumentality only perpetuated designs of cyclopean size. The academies trained their students with this purpose in view, turning out urban scenographers, stage designers who aspired to orchestrate compositions of imposing dimensions while leaving the core of the buildings virtually untouched: "State pressure to revive the heavy heritage of one of the world's most prestigious historic traditions, and the contrast between that old glory and the frustrating present, mingled in a tragic inferiority complex. The result was a sort of irresistible love of gigantism and an eclectic celebration of the past; all public buildings had to demonstrate this, and later monumentality inspired Sant'Elia's architectural dreams as well as Mussolini's imperial realities."[49]

The Monza competition was no exception. The program called for a majestic structure, in keeping with the artistic traditions of Monza, once famous as the seat of the Austrian Regent in Lombardy. Sant'Elia had never before undertaken a project of this magnitude and wisely decided to team up with Italo Paternoster, a former colleague from Brera, who was himself from Monza and could therefore be of invaluable assistance. They completed the preliminary research together and presented their entry under the pseudonym "Crisantemo," with its overtones of Art Nouveau and the aesthetic movement.

It is impossible to assess the part played by Paternoster in their joint undertaking. All the surviving designs and reproductions seem to be by Sant'Elia alone. Only one of the final drawings for the project has come down to us. The others, which belonged to Paternoster, were lost and exist only as reproductions in a contemporary publication.[50] Also extant are a number of preparatory sketches, which give a step-by-step account of how Sant'Elia arrived at the final solution.

One of the earliest drawings for this competition, a central plan crowned by a dome (fig. 25), is clearly based on a project by Alois Bastl (fig. 24) published in Sant'Elia's treasured volume *Wagnerschule.*[51] But after this final attempt, the central plans of the Secession were abandoned, no doubt because colossal rotundas of this sort were not feasible.

In the remaining sketches Sant'Elia gave free rein to his imagination. The draftsmanship shows the quick, nervous line characteristic of his early years. Understandably for the project at hand, Sant'Elia looked chiefly to Milan's leading architects or more specifically to the typology that interested him—funerary architecture. Sommaruga's Ossario di Palestro (1893), with its unforgettable receding silhouette, is close to the design of Sant'Elia's pylons (fig. 26). Gaetano Moretti's colossal mausoleum at Crespi d'Adda (1896–1907) and Ernesto Pirovano's monumental entrance to the cemetery at Bergamo (1900–1913) were obvious points of reference. Gino Coppedè's Staglieno cemetery at Genoa (1904–1906) was another important precedent (fig. 27).[52] The apsidal termination of the sides, the stunted towers, and the cross-shaped windows all occur at Staglieno.

It was primarily from these sources that Sant'Elia derived the orientalizing features of

24. Alois Bastl. Project for a monumental building, ca. 1900.
(Photo: Collection of the author)

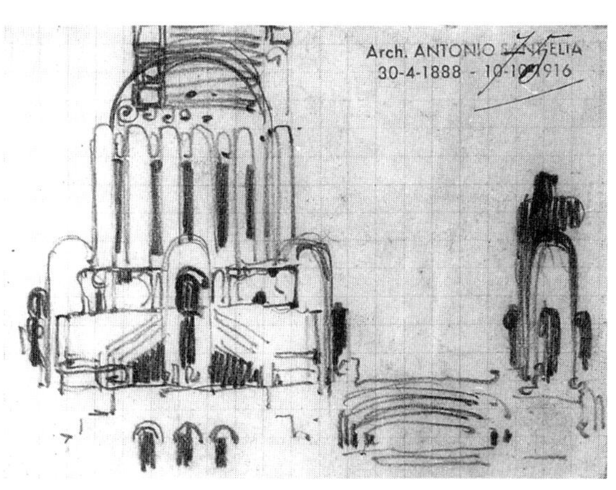

25. Antonio Sant'Elia. Preliminary sketch for the Monza cemetery(?), ca. 1912. Musei Civici, Como.

26. Giuseppe Sommaruga. Ossuary of Palestro, 1893. (Photo: Collection of the author)

27. Gino Coppedè. Entrance to the Staglieno cemetery, Genoa, 1904–1906. (Photo: Collection of the author)

his project, which were more pronounced in the preparatory sketches. Indeed, scale itself made prototypes from the Far East almost a necessity. In one of them, the central feature was a typical Indian stupa, later demoted to the corners (fig. 28). Interest in architecture of the Far East, more specifically the Khmer temples of Southeast Asia, was widespread at the time, particularly in the work of the Wagnerschule. This sudden "discovery" of the architectural marvels of the East was part of the broadening cultural horizon that followed in the wake of European colonialism.[53] Orientalism was introduced into Milan's architectural circles precisely by Moretti, Sommaruga, and Pirovano, who used it chiefly in their cemeterial buildings.[54] The characteristic Angkor Wat–like profiles of the great rounded masses were an apt metaphor for eternity now that the Greco-Roman canon, the Egyptian, or even the neo-Gothic were too timeworn to be of use.

The final project consists of some eleven drawings that include the statutory temple of fame (the *famedio*), the crematorium, the colombarium, a funerary chapel, and the site plan, as well as plans and sections. The only extant original, the perspective, is entirely in Sant'Elia's hand (fig. 29). It represents a temple of fame, the crowning glory of every Italian cemetery: a monumental core with exuberant decoration, set in a secessionist landscape of swirling clouds and stylized trees. A superb procession of mourners advances along the foreground, with languorous elegance and studied gestures of grief: "In the perspective, the group of priests and altar boys is transformed into a heraldic procession of an unknown sect, a fabled survivor of an arcane journey which undoubtedly called at Böcklin's Island of the Dead."[55]

The draftsmanship shows Sant'Elia at his Klimtian best: bold, sweeping lines and minute details are all rendered with ease and elegance. All the elements serve a twofold purpose of conveying architectural information as well as contributing to surface patterning. Colors are restricted to black, white, and gold and are handled with his customary brilliance. Yet despite the airy and graceful lines, the impression of weight and mass, virtually a prerequisite of Italian architecture at the time, is overwhelming. In designing the famedio, Sant'Elia no doubt tailored his style to suit the taste of his Lombard patrons, who frowned upon the calligraphic ornament of Art Nouveau, preferring dramatic sculptural masses in which every structural hint was swallowed up.[56]

28. Antonio Sant'Elia. Preliminary sketch for the Monza cemetery, 1912. Musei Civici, Como.

29. Antonio Sant'Elia and Italo Paternoster. Temple of fame for the Monza cemetery, perspective, 1912. Musei Civici, Como.

The elevation is harder to judge, because we have only reproductions to work from: it appears to lack the strong, incisive line and dramatic contrasts of the perspective (figs. 30,31). Color was its forte, and in its absence the whole seems flat and rather conventional. Surprisingly, the elevation does not agree with the perspective in detail, scale, or size, a fact that owes nothing to the quality of the photograph.

Sant'Elia's unprejudiced assemblage of volumes fails to give a consistent sense of scale; there is no yardstick by which to measure the whole. Too many decorative elements, of too many different sizes, only accentuate the ambiguity. So do the apertures that are either too large or too small. Depending on which detail one focuses on, the building seems either colossal or diminutive.

30. Antonio Sant'Elia and Italo Paternoster. Temple of fame for the Monza cemetery, elevation. *Concorsi di architettura in Italia,* Milan, n.d. (1912).

31. Antonio Sant'Elia and Italo Paternoster. Temple of fame, detail. *Concorsi di architettura in Italia,* Milan, n.d.

The plan looks very much like an afterthought carved out from the mass of the building once the design for the facade was completed (fig. 32). As a result, the relationship between plan and elevation seems almost fortuitous, as indeed the jury was quick to point out. Sant'Elia always had problems handling large-scale structures and complex spaces such as these. Given his penchant for monumental structures, difficulties inevitably ensued, because his plans were always contingent on the elevations rather than the reverse.

With regard to iconography, Sant'Elia's favorite characters make their appearance for the last time, having perhaps outlived their usefulness. Yet one almost feels his reluctance to part with them as his vocabulary begins to change. Serpents, now endowed with an abbreviated, sphinxlike torso and wings, glare threateningly from above, together with grimacing heads and skulls. When it came to representing death, Sant'Elia dwelled not so much on the peace of the resurrection, the *resquiescat*, but on the terror of the *dies irae*, though his iconography is rather secular. Large cross-shaped windows (of stained glass?) and highly stylized saints are the only nod toward traditional religious imagery.

The smaller buildings—the crematorium, funerary chapel, and colombarium—all differ in style from the monumental ones (figs. 33,34). They are more graphic and owe nothing to contemporary Milanese architecture. Vienna's Secession reasserts its hold: rectilinear lines take precedence over curves, planes over mass. The figurative elements are consigned to carefully delimited panels. These structures are no longer defined by dramatic masses and tenebrous chiaroscuro.

As these last drawings clearly show, Sant'Elia's style was beginning to evolve in a different direction: ornament is restrained, and there is an increasing tendency toward abstraction. Sant'Elia tries to make the architectural forms themselves more eventful. Elevations and massing gain in spatial complexity. Beauty is no longer a function of the figurative decoration but is to be found primarily in the abstract play of forms. What these smaller projects lose in drama, they gain in clarity of design. The influence of Otto Wagner's work, with its emphasis on structure, is slowly ousting the dramatic, massive forms of the Italian Liberty.

Contemporary sources allude to the great beauty of Sant'Elia's colors, which aroused the admiration of the public.[57] In his drawings for the competition they seem to have been even more vivid than his usual hues and were reminiscent of D'Aronco's glittering palette.[58] This heightened effect may, of course, have been due to Italo Paternoster. A pale reflection of the original colors is seen in a drawing of a cemetery ("Visione") by the architect Silvio

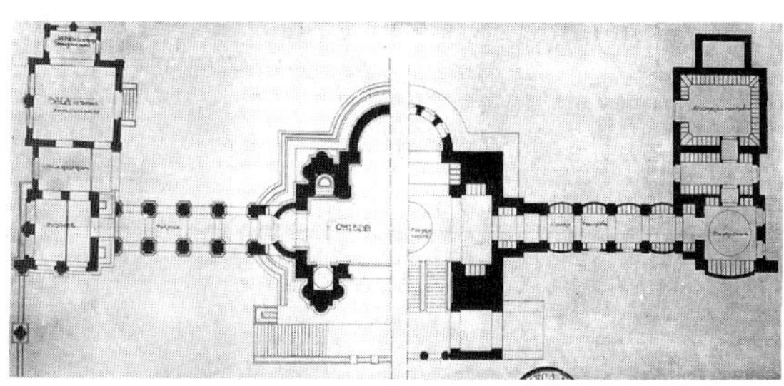

32. Antonio Sant'Elia and Italo Paternoster. Temple of fame for the Monza cemetery, plan. *Concorsi di architettura in Italia,* Milan, n.d.

33. Antonio Sant'Elia and Italo Paternoster. Crematorium for the Monza cemetery. *Concorsi di architettura in Italia,* Milan, n.d.

34. Antonio Sant'Elia and Italo Paternoster. Funerary chapel for the Monza cemetery, plan and elevation. *Concorsi di architettura in Italia,* Milan, n.d.

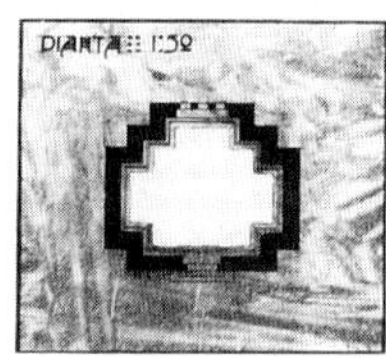

Gambini (1877–1948), dated December 31, 1913. Gambini came from the neighboring town of Busto Arsizio and must have had the actual drawings close at hand.[59]

The site plan is weak and unimaginative and fails to relate the separate buildings to the shape and size of the plot (fig. 35). The temple of fame faces the main road, blocking the view to the spacious grounds beyond, as was the case with most of the entries. The jury would have preferred a monumental building toward the back of the plot, thereby allowing a sweeping, grandiose view of the whole. Instead, landscape and buildings are not interrelated in a meaningful way: the pavilions are scattered about aimlessly and do not contribute any distinctive features to the landscape. Nor does the layout of the alleys and garden paths suggest purposeful itineraries for the visitor or satisfactory vistas for the eye.

"Crisantemo" was finally eliminated in the third and last round—an honorable outcome, considering that it was the first time Sant'Elia had faced a competition of this importance. The jury was no stranger to the two young architects, as it was headed by their former professor of architecture at Brera, Gaetano Moretti. Its verdict was published on October 19, 1912: the winner was the Florentine architect Ulisse Stacchini (1871–1947). Although the project by Sant'Elia and Paternoster was among the ten finalists, the jury did not spare its criticism:

> The jury recognizes that the project is marked by a felicitous originality however much it may have been inspired by Oriental forms. Nevertheless, the grandeur which is imparted by the composition in itself does not correspond to the dimensions given in plan. The Committee is forced to recognize this great drawback which destroys much of what is good in the project. The artistic composition, moreover, is not buttressed by a matching bravura in the indispensable technical part; on the contrary, the scant and, at times, nonexistent correspondence between elevations, sections, and plans constitutes a grave failure which the Committee cannot but deplore.[60]

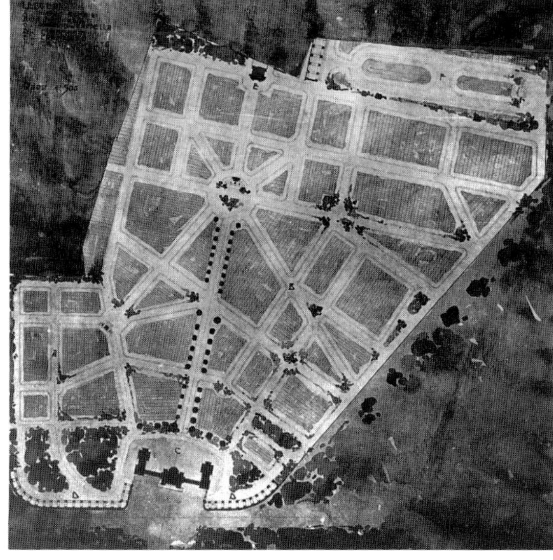

35. Antonio Sant'Elia and Italo Paternoster. Site plan of the Monza cemetery. *Concorsi di architettura in Italia,* Milan, n.d.

Their strictures were more than justified: there are too many concessions to the purely pictorial without the corresponding attention to architecture. In spite of these well-deserved criticisms, however, their work achieved a certain succès d'estime when all the entries were displayed at Monza. The public was captivated by the glowing colors and exquisite draftsmanship, by the exotic atmosphere and the procession of fabled characters. The project was also singled out for praise by various well-known critics and was published in

36. Antonio Sant'Elia. Funerary chapel, 1911–1912. Musei Civici, Como.

37. Antonio Sant'Elia. Study for the interior of a church.
Dated September 28, 1911. Banca Popolare di Lecco.

its entirety by the prestigious architectural publishing house Bestetti e Tumminelli in a book on Italy's best competition entries of the time.[61]

Among the other drawings of this period is a lovely undated sketch of a funeral chapel, which is one of Sant'Elia's most successful secessionist works (fig. 36). Although the project is not clearly identified, on the basis of style it would seem to be a preliminary sketch for one of the smaller buildings at Monza. The decoration is entirely abstract, except for two flat Byzantine-like saints. The design has all the charm and maturity of one by Mackintosh or Hoffmann. Everything is harmonious and beautifully proportioned. Ornament is not added on by increment but seems to grow out of the structural needs of the little building.

Another drawing that may be related to Monza shows one of the rare interiors left us by Sant'Elia, a church or a large funeral chapel (fig. 37). The Baroque sensibility and the theatricality of the point of view are undercut by a certain secessionist levity. Although the competition had not yet been announced—the drawing is dated September 28, 1911—its venue was common knowledge at Monza and would have been known to Paternoster.

A TRAIN STATION FOR MILAN

That same year, 1912, Sant'Elia also took part in a competition for Milan's new Stazione Centrale. The old railroad station, built in 1864, could no longer meet the needs of the expanding city. A competition for the new station was therefore announced in 1906, and it was won by the architect Arrigo Cantoni, with whom Sant'Elia was shortly to collaborate.[62]

Cantoni's project was a mixture of *Rundbogenstil,* a great favorite with designers of railroad stations, and Garnier's *style opéra,* which gave it a more genteel appearance.[63] The result—a design suited more to the nineteenth than to the twentieth century—did not quite satisfy the authorities. As a result, in 1912 the city administration announced a new competition for the facade of the station, leaving the shed to engineers.[64] The program called for two galleries in front of the station to shelter incoming vehicles from the weather. Because the approach streets and the railroad tracks were not on the same level, some sort of vertical transportation system was necessary to carry passengers and luggage from the street level below to the tracks above. Arrigo Cantoni and his partner, Paolo Vietti Violi, who were again competing for the commission, invited Sant'Elia to work in their prestigious studio, no doubt because of his great ability as a draftsman.

No preparatory sketches can be linked to this competition with certainty. His final project is thus known largely through old photographs (figs. 38–40). The facade consists of a long building crowned by a central dome, with two smaller ones accentuating the extremities of the vast structure. It is possible, of course, that the overall solution was Cantoni's and that Sant'Elia served exclusively as a draftsman.

As many critics have noted, Wagner's influence was paramount: "Sant'Elia, in effect, was not looking to the Wagner of monumental palaces but to [the Wagner] of bridges, and he transposed the vast scale of the latter to the great spaces of the station, throwing slender beams and metal arches across powerful vertical stone piles."[65] From the bridges and viaducts of Wagner's *Stadtbahn* scheme for Vienna, Sant'Elia took the massive masonry pylons, as well as the stylized eagles and wreaths adorning them.[66] Sant'Elia was also influenced by one of Wagner's projects for the ill-fated Franz-Josefstadtmuseum of 1902, particularly in the ornament.[67] The basic idea, however, came from a project by Rudolf Melichar, published in one of the famous albums of the Wagnerschule (fig. 41).[68] It was from Melichar that Sant'Elia derived the central dome and its connection to the shed below.

38. Antonio Sant'Elia. Stazione Centrale, Milan. Final project, elevation, 1912. (Photo: Courtesy of Musei Civici, Como)

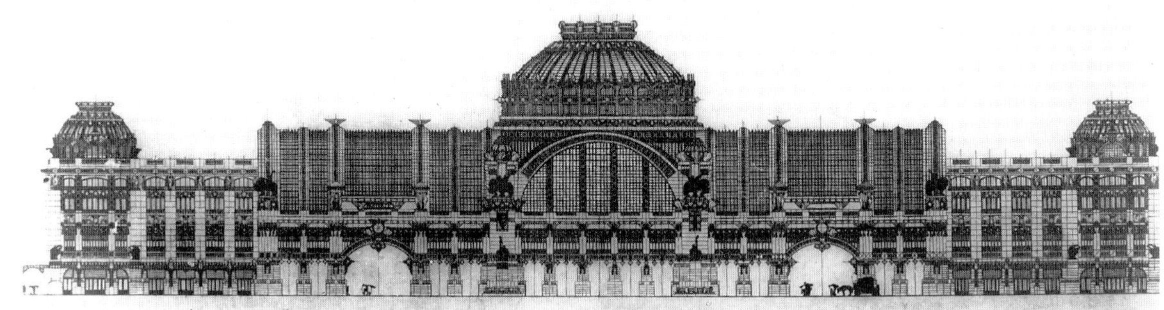

Plate 1. Raimondo D'Aronco. Central Pavilion, International
Exposition, Turin, 1902. Galleria d'Arte Moderna, Udine.

Plate 2. Antonio Sant'Elia. Apartment building, 1911. Musei
Civici, Como.

Plate 3. Antonio Sant'Elia. Monumental building, ca. 1911.
Banca Popolare di Lecco.

Plate 4. Antonio Sant'Elia. Monumental building, ca. 1911.
Musei Civici, Como.

Plate 5. Antonio Sant'Elia. Monumental building, ca. 1911. Musei Civici, Como.

Plate 6. Antonio Sant'Elia. Modern building, 1913. Musei Civici, Como.

Plate 7. (*opposite*) Antonio Sant'Elia. Modern building, 1913–1914. Collection of Paride Accetti, Milan.

Plate 8. Antonio Sant'Elia. Kiosk, 1914. Musei Civici, Como.

Plate 9. (*opposite*) Antonio Sant'Elia. Study for a church. Dated February 20, 1914, Milan, and initialed. Musei Civici, Como.

Plate 10. Antonio Sant'Elia. Study for a monument. Dated
February 21, 1914. Musei Civici, Como.

39. Antonio Sant'Elia. Stazione Centrale, Milan (detail), 1912. (Photo: Courtesy of Musei Civici, Como)

40. Antonio Sant'Elia. Stazione Centrale, Milan (detail), 1912. (Photo: Courtesy of Musei Civici, Como)

Iron technology is given great prominence in this project, while the use of masonry is restricted to thin strips between the bays. There was nothing revolutionary about these designs: Milan had long been accustomed to similar structures, beginning with Giuseppe Mengoni's famous *galleria* (1865–1877). But by relying almost exclusively on iron and glass, Sant'Elia negated the possibility of expressing unified Italy's epos in masonry and statuary, and Cantoni may have turned down Sant'Elia's fine drawings for this reason. Glass and iron were not considered noble materials and were felt to be appropriate only for industrial architecture or minor genres.[69] The taste of the times ran to cumbersome rugged monuments, not to the structural engineering of Mengoni or to the mature works of Wagner.

It is characteristic of Sant'Elia that however innovative his projects, the iconography was almost invariably drawn from the past. As a rule, historicism crept in with his statuary, in this case stylized versions of Michelangelo's *ignudi* from the Sistine ceiling, complete with the swags of oak leaves and the emblematic acorns of Julius II (fig. 40). Sant'Elia's hard-edged statues with grimacing features were also influenced by Romolo Romani, a great expert on contemporary art.[70] But the blocklike figures may also owe something to the Croatian secessionist Ivan Mestrovič, whom both Sant'Elia and Romani admired and

41. Rudolf Melichar. International exposition building, 1898.
Aus der Wagnerschule MDCCCIIC, Vienna, 1898.

whose work had been a revelation in the exhibition held in Rome the previous year.[71] Some of the surviving preparatory sketches for the statuary, until recently attributed to Sant'Elia, have now been convincingly ascribed to the sculptor Giovanni Possamai, an old friend from Brera who also worked in Cantoni's studio at the time of the competition.[72] They are very different in style from those of Sant'Elia and were in fact never used in the final project.

Cantoni's lack of foresight deprived the competition of one of its most interesting projects. His own design, which is far weaker than Sant'Elia's, was given seventh place in the final classification.[73] Once more the winner was Ulisse Stacchini. Although his project was executed many years later and with many modifications, its having been given first place was symptomatic of the change in the cultural climate. Few buildings have come in for so much opposition in Italy. Even Carroll Meeks, whose appraisal of official Italian architecture is usually fair and generous, is categorical in his criticism: "A bank of five sheds, among the most beautiful ever built, is entirely concealed from the piazza by a grotesque brontosaurus of a forebuilding."[74]

THE VILLA ELISI

Sometime during 1912, Sant'Elia designed his only surviving building, the Villa Elisi, in the resort of S. Maurizio, high above Lake Como (fig. 42). It was commissioned as a hunting lodge by the industrialist Romeo Longatti, of Como. Sant'Elia supervised the construction in person, and although the villa no longer reflects his original plans, it is one of the few works built entirely according to his ideas.

It is one of the many ironies of Sant'Elia's life that the man who would become so famous for his bold and visionary skyscrapers should have left behind nothing built but this parochial little house (apart from a small tomb in Monza). It is precisely because of its modesty that the Villa Elisi was deliberately overlooked for years. Only in 1962, at the time of the first serious retrospective of Sant'Elia's works, did Caramel and Longatti restore it to

42. Antonio Sant'Elia. Villa Elisi, San Maurizio (Como), 1912.
(Photo: Courtesy of Musei Civici, Como)

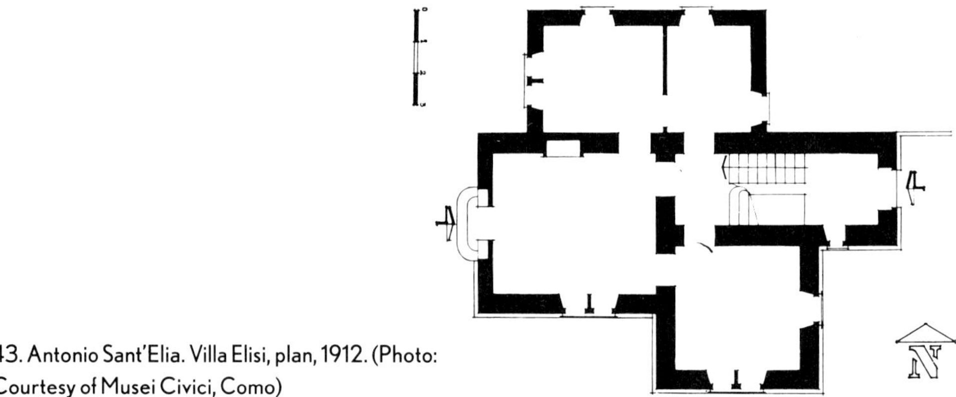

43. Antonio Sant'Elia. Villa Elisi, plan, 1912. (Photo: Courtesy of Musei Civici, Como)

the short canon of Sant'Elia's built works.[75] Although no sketches or documents survive, Sant'Elia's authorship is corroborated by members of his own family as well as by the family of his patron.

As has often been pointed out, the Villa Elisi is in fact a rustic version of Sant'Elia's *villino moderno* (fig. 13), though the massing is not as dynamic and the deep gables and pitched roof give it a faintly neo-Gothic appearance. But one can see the same tripartite windows opening onto a central balcony and the same attempt to enliven the facades with rustication and brick lintels. Decoration of the area beneath the gables was entrusted to the sculptor Gerolamo Fontana, a former colleague and fellow "Comasco." Fontana's frescoed trees, with their triangular and circular leaves, are liberal quotations from Olbrich's Ernst-Ludwig Haus, built a decade earlier in Darmstadt. In spite of its modesty, the plan is decidedly an improvement over that of the two published projects and shows a timid attempt to impart movement to the distribution of space (fig. 43).[76] Instead of the rigorous symmetry and axiality called for by Wagner, Sant'Elia preferred the more Romantic asymmetrical plan characteristic of the Floreale.[77]

The Villa Elisi is no different from hundreds of such villas erected in Italy at the time, by architects, speculators, or even amateurs. Nevertheless, as the only extant building by Sant'Elia, this villa has an importance wholly incommensurate with its all-too-modest qualities: it shows Sant'Elia's beginnings, as well as the plight of young Italian architects at the turn of the century, who oscillated uneasily between conservative projects for commissions and competitions and more original and personal work done in private.

ARCHITECTURAL MOUNTAINS

Toward the end of October Sant'Elia went to Bologna in the company of Italo Paternoster in order to take the qualifying exams for a degree in *disegno architettonico* from the Accademia di Belle Arti, which he had failed to receive from Brera. Candidates who passed the preliminary entrance exams were then admitted to the finals. On the whole, Sant'Elia did very well, even though these tests confirm the widening gap between his practical and theoretical capabilities. Once more he did brilliantly in drawing (receiving 67/70 in the entrance exams and 70/70 in the finals) but performed rather poorly on written and oral sections (49/70 in the essay question and 56/70 in the colloquium on the theory and history of architecture). His final grade, announced in December, was 242 out of 280.

Only three of his sketches can be linked to the exams at Bologna. Of them, one is a perspective of a monumental building, and another an elevation closely associated with it (figs. 44,45). A third drawing, hastily scribbled on a postcard to Mario Chiattone, is evidently related to these two.[78] These drawings probably represent a cemeterial hall of fame.[79] A few months earlier he had designed another such building for the cemetery at Monza, and it is natural that he should have chosen the same *parti* here: a towering central mass with a dark, squat entranceway linked to the smaller masses on either side by low horizontal structures (see fig. 30).

The design is also very close to the preparatory sketches for Milan's central train station. There seems to be some influence of Ulisse Stacchini on the stereometric volumes: the curves of the Monza cemetery have given way to crisp, rectilinear profiles.[80] Even the statuary seems more massive and cubelike. The crouching forms of the Stazione Centrale reappear. As usual, Sant'Elia's statuary figures look uncomfortable and load-bearing, even when they have no load to bear. His iconography, particularly from 1912 onward, was unorthodox and secular. It rarely strayed from the usual combination of knights armed with lances and rearing horses, one of the legacies of the Romantic medievalism in vogue at that time.

These drawings usher in a series of grandiose and enigmatic buildings that he designed soon after his return from Bologna, during the last weeks of 1912 (figs. 46–51). The new sketches occupy a transitional place in Sant'Elia's work, between the florid exoticism of the Monza period and the abstract *dinamismi* of the following year.[81] There is a notable shift away from the planar, graphic style of his earlier drawings to the heavy, unwieldy masses already seen in the Monza competition. All the decorative excesses of the Secession are pruned, even though the massing of the zigguratlike forms owes much to the Wagnerschule. Except for monumental statuary that appears on one or two sheets—and even here reduced almost to abstract monoliths—there is no decoration.

There are over one dozen drawings of this sort. Half a dozen or so are dated, and the remaining ones are so close to these that one can safely group two or three during the same week, if not the same day. All were executed in November and December of 1912.[82] The draftsmanship has changed dramatically: gone is the gold, the elegant arabesques, the graphic virtuosity. Color is restricted to one hue, if it is used at all. The outline is fuller, more spontaneous, as was always the case when Sant'Elia was casting about for new solutions.

Sant'Elia's *Stadtkrone* are colossal monolithic structures, punctuated by obelisklike towers or pylons and perched on high places. This impression of towering heights is enhanced by the staircase, which adds a psychological dimension to the architecture. All the

44. Antonio Sant'Elia. Study of a monumental building, perspective, 1912. Musei Civici, Como.

45. Antonio Sant'Elia. Study of a monumental building, elevation, 1912. Collection of Enrico Tarentini, Milan.

structures taper at the top, so that there is no separation between walls and ceiling, and vast, oblique surfaces stretch out between the towers (fig. 49).[83] Massive buttresses shore up the buildings, but their representational function far outweighs their structural one: whether they are meant to be of brick or of cement, these struts are overbuilt. Flying buttresses, which became a salient feature of Sant'Elia's late work, make their appearance for the first time, albeit in a wholly unorthodox position (figs. 47,48).

Elevations are rare in Sant'Elia's oeuvre: he preferred perspectives where the point of view is chosen for psychological effect. Although symmetrical, his drawings do not register as such. All the projects are rendered in worm's-eye view so that the rigorous symmetry and axiality of the building is thrown off balance. The adoption of such a low, off-center viewpoint dramatically enhances the foreshortening: the upper part of the building nearest to the spectator is often cut off by the frame, thus suggesting improbable heights, and a great part of the structure, seen diagonally, is heavily shaded (figs. 46–48). This bold telescoping of the building makes for dramatic contrasts of mass and void, light and shade, and is characteristic of theater design and scenography.

Sant'Elia's use of perspective distorts architectural reality. What is monumental in many of his projects is not the building in its conceptual purity but the pictorial rendering of the same. By choosing the worm's-eye view, Sant'Elia exalts the simplest architectural forms to the dimensions of a monument.[84] The objective elements are deliberately left aside, while the subjective ones—color, point of view, and landscape—are stressed. Here, too, the analogy with Hugh Ferriss is inescapable: "Ferriss," wrote Peter Blake, ". . . is so greatly interested in 'powerful' architecture that if he tried to sketch a birdhouse it would end up looking like Boulder Dam."[85] Were one actually to build the most theatrical of Sant'Elia's projects, the result would always fall short of the dramatic perpective used in the sketch. In that case it is Boulder Dam that would end up looking like a birdhouse. Witness the Monument to the War Dead built in Como by Giuseppe Terragni after one of Sant'Elia's designs (see plate 10). The impression of staid, solid mass that it exudes cannot

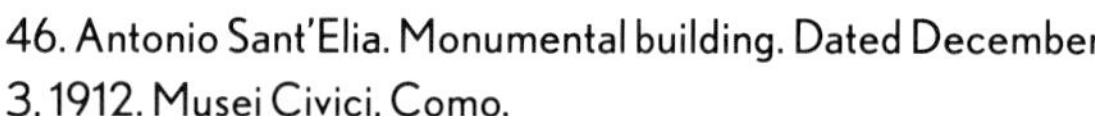

46. Antonio Sant'Elia. Monumental building. Dated December 3, 1912. Musei Civici, Como.

47. Antonio Sant'Elia. Monumental building. Dated November 21, 1912(?). Musei Civici, Como.

be put down entirely to Terragni or to the trials and tribulations of its history: it is due to the difficulty in translating Sant'Elia's essentially two-dimensional, scenographic projects into the medium of architecture proper.

Sant'Elia's cyclopean structures are virtually windowless. Many have no light source other than the small entranceways. The deliberate disparity between the towering heights and the diminutive openings at the foot of the vast, clifflike masses produces an impression of gloom and darkness, of physical oppression on the observer.[86] It is just this emphasis on mass and weight, unrelieved by any outlet, this attempt to convey a sense of mood to the spectator, that characterizes Sant'Elia as one of the forerunners of Expressionist architecture together with Hans Poelzig and Max Berg.

With their forbidding allure and endless flights of steps, these enigmatic monuments place the unseen and imaginary beholder in the position of a suppliant to some mysterious sect. A vaguely mystical aura surrounds them, as if these buildings expressed a deep, unappeasable yearning for the unknown such as one finds, for example, in the cosmic mountains of Wenzel Hablik, Bruno Taut, or those of the Wagnerschule.[87] Needless to say, neither plans nor sections were ever carried out. These impenetrable structures are more like mountains to be scaled than buildings to be entered. Sant'Elia conceived them exclusively as "pure scenographic exteriors."[88] They are, in other words, invertebrate, and one has difficulty imagining the gloomy interiors as other than unlit, shaftlike caves.

In fact, Sant'Elia introduces a new concept of nature and of architecture: instead of a building within a landscape he designs the building *as* landscape (plate 5).[89] His topography is almost entirely artificial. Gone are the secessionist landscapes of his earlier years. Even where the buildings must of necessity rest upon a hilltop, the surroundings are barely indicated, and the vast staircases lead up to the entrance as if from a void.[90] Gone also are human beings, dwarfed in absentia by these sinister masses.

But there is a code of sorts behind this topography. A hidden naturalism is at work here, seeking to elicit specific emotions in the observer. The overwhelming masses, accompanied by clifflike abutments, dramatic shadows, and long flights of steps, are like features of a landscape transliterated into architecture: the remote crag, the yawning abyss, and the Gothic ruin all find their counterparts in these buildings: "Instead of the predominance of voids, one sought to impress the spectator by means of mass. Massive walls, rugged and

48. Antonio Sant'Elia. Monumental building, 1912. Museo Civico, Cremona.

49. Antonio Sant'Elia. Monumental building, 1912. Museo Civico, Cremona.

50. Antonio Sant'Elia. Monumental building. Dated November 21, 1912. Musei Civici, Como.

51. Antonio Sant'Elia. Monumental building. Dated December 28, 1912. Musei Civici, Como.

powerful rustication, domes and colossal vaults, exaggerated arches. . . . And since what was important—and this was the fundamental tenet of romanticism—was above all the impression or emotion aroused in the spectator, one did not hesitate to falsify all things: the powerful masses of rustication were not cut in stone but modeled in artificial aggregate."[91] Much of this, of course, came from familiar sources such as Sacconi's monument to Victor Emmanuel, with its all-encompassing staircase, and Calderini's Palace of Justice. Or exhibition buildings such as the Hungarian pavilion by Emile Töry and Maurice Pogány, which Sant'Elia probably saw in Turin (see fig. 11).[92]

There was also a strong undercurrent of Expressionism in Milanese architecture, with its mass, pyramidal profiles, and dramatic chiaroscuro. Sant'Elia's remote, tapering structures are reminiscent of the temple-mountains of Southeast Asia that so enthralled contemporary architects. Sommaruga's mausoleums (fig. 52) and the orientalizing masses of Moretti and Pirovano were all crucial precedents in this respect. But Sant'Elia was primarily influenced by the most impressive of the Italian orientalists and the only one to have traveled to the Far East in person: Edoardo Baroncini.[93] A master at perspective, Baroncini was also an avid student of Indian architecture. Sketches of his travels throughout India caused a sensation in Milan's architectural circles and were later exhibited, together with drawings by Sant'Elia, at the show of the Association of Lombard Architects. Baroncini excelled in bold, theatrical foreshortenings with antlike human figures ascending endless

52. Giuseppe Sommaruga. Faccanoni Mausoleum, Sarnico,
1907. (Photo: Collection of the author)

flights of steps leading to vast, mysterious temples (fig. 53). He was more cinematic than Sant'Elia in his choice of perspective and point of view, both of which were closer to modern photography or even film than were the types of perspective taught at Brera.

Thus, less than two years before his ground-breaking manifesto, we find Sant'Elia looking to the most traditional aspects of contemporary Italian architecture for inspiration: the declamatory monuments of Humbertine Rome, Lombardy's ponderous funerary buildings and commemorative exhibition pavilions in general, as well as architecture from the Far East. But his main and inexhaustible source of inspiration was to be found in works of the Wagnerschulern, amply documented in the pages of *Der Architekt:* half-mythical, half-architectural images, rearing themselves at the edge of vast, clifflike embankments.[94]

Of all Wagner's students, none was more congenial to Sant'Elia than Emil Hoppe.[95] Many of the Hoppe sketches that Sant'Elia admired and emulated were drawn near Rome or Lucerne around the turn of the century and are really landscapes, heirs to a tradition stretching back to the nineteenth century (figs. 54,55). In these drawings, buildings play

53. Edoardo Baroncini. "Stairway at Benares," ca. 1913. *Vita d'Arte,* April 1914.

54. Emil Hoppe. Study for a monumental building, 1902. (Photo: Collection of the author)

55. Emil Hoppe. Study for a monumental building, 1902.
(Photo: Collection of the author)

the same role as ruins did in Romantic paintings. Mood landscapes, one might call them, as the artist has taken great pains to enhance the lyrical side of the works exactly as a landscape painter might, by devoting attention to the dramatic skies and clouds and even more dramatic siting. The individual, though still implied, is physically absent and overwhelmed by a none-too-friendly nature. The overcast skies and crepuscular atmosphere clearly connote gloom and foreboding. The ultimate source of all these works is the lingering Romanticism found in the paintings of Arnold Böcklin—his isolated or inaccessible buildings, deserted save for some lonely figure, funerary monument, or cypress.[96]

Sant'Elia succumbed easily to the somber charm of Hoppe's drawings. In their utopian and otherworldly isolation, his quasi-mystical projects suggest the same sense of expectation and of catharsis that one finds in the work of the Viennese master.[97] Rejecting the past, but not yet anticipating the future, the work of Hoppe had a timeless quality that served Sant'Elia well in the absence of a new, ahistorical architectural idiom.

THE "DINAMISMI"

In 1913 Sant'Elia produced a magnificent series of drawings known as dinamismi (figs. 56–59), a term that is apocryphal and partly misleading. Sant'Elia named few of his drawings. In this case, the futurist poet Escodamè (the pseudonym of Michele Leskovitch) chose the name because of the resemblance of these drawings to a series of drawings by Boccioni called dinamismi, also done in 1913. The futurists always exaggerated the influence of their movement on others, to the detriment of all other currents. The term was subsequently taken for granted and used uncritically, as if Sant'Elia were putting into practice Boccioni's programmatic ideas. In fact, these drawings owe as much to Emil Hoppe and to the Wagnerschule as they do to Boccioni.

The dinamismi are a series of tall, tapering forms with vast, smooth surfaces and bold arrises that cut deep into space. In hindsight it is difficult to see how revolutionary they were. Except for Adolf Loos's Steiner House (1910), this degree of abstraction in architecture was unprecedented. Like the mysterious monolithic structures of the preceding years, most of these buildings have no windows or even doors. Yet the impression of heavy, static masses has given way to that of bright planes stretched taut around a central core. All are shown in isolation, without a context. Color, previously used to convey mood, is conspicuously absent in almost all the sketches. Here we find a new monumentalism, lightweight rather than massive, but still scenographic: the dinamismi are an exercise in pure form with which Sant'Elia attempted to purge his language of the decorative hypertrophy of the Liberty without any attention to functional or technical considerations. He had finally found a way to deliver his architecture from the pictorialist impasse of the previous years.

There was, however, no corresponding spatial breakthrough. Although less massive than his previous work, these structures are hardly less pyramidal: in Sant'Elia's architecture, the envelope almost always suggests load-bearing masonry. Furthermore, none of these buildings has plans, nor do they fit any clear, unequivocal purpose or typology. The architectural data imparted by Sant'Elia are always given in terms of volume rather than

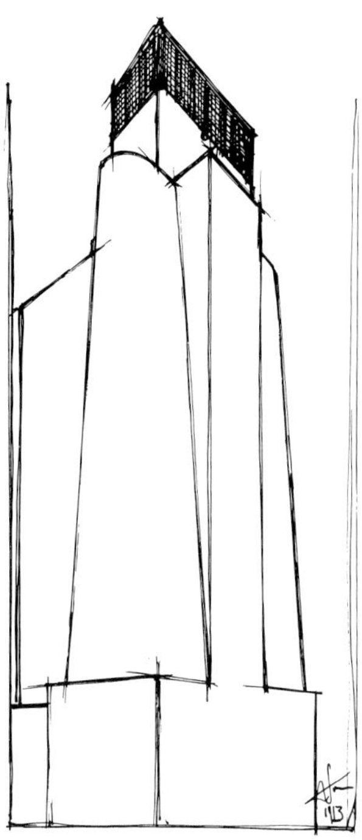

56. Antonio Sant'Elia. Study for a modern building. Signed and dated 1913. Musei Civici, Como.

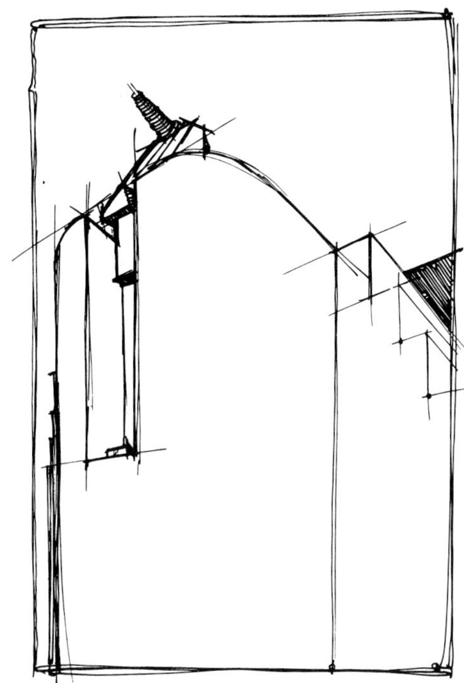

57. Antonio Sant'Elia. Study for a modern building with stylized monumental figure, 1913. Musei Civici, Como.

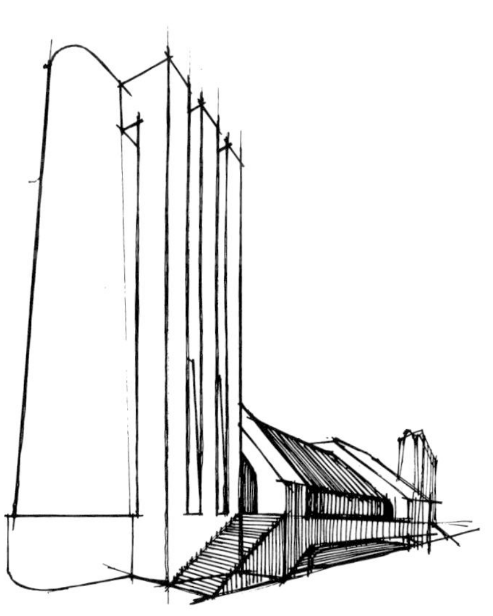

58. Antonio Sant'Elia. Modern building, 1913. Musei Civici, Como.

59. Antonio Sant'Elia. Modern building, dated 1913. Musei Civici, Como.

of space.[98] The low viewpoint, which exalts the building beyond that which the elevation alone would permit, produces a disparity between real and apparent form. Nevertheless, one should not impugn these drawings as mere scenography. The dinamismi are fleeting visions, caught on the wing by the nervous, impetuous gestures of Sant'Elia's pen (plate 6). His purpose was not to present prototypes for actual buildings but to seek out a new architectural idiom beyond historicism. In this respect, the dinamismi bear a striking resemblance to the works of Eric Mendelsohn, which were roughly contemporary.[99] Mendelsohn's sketches also give an impression of energy and motion which, significantly, he also called "dynamism," although in his case the term encompassed a more complex notion than Sant'Elia's.[100] More important, he was drawn to the same kinds of modern building types as Sant'Elia—factories, hangars, stations—and was equally fond of combining the same forms in buildings of different purpose.

With the dinamismi Sant'Elia attempts to free his architecture from the literary associations of symbolism. Ornament is abolished altogether. The sinuous, fluid line that so loved to lose itself in arabesques is now limited to marking the arrises. In this sense, the dinamismi are revolutionary: the shift from the heavy, twilit temple-mountains to these clean, clear volumes in black and white, unencumbered by any decoration, is equivalent to the transition from figuration to abstraction that Kandinsky and others were exploring at this time.[101] With these sketches Sant'Elia broke, at least temporarily, with one of the mainstays of Western tradition. As Karel Teige remarked, Sant'Elia was the first to attempt to work outside historical styles in Italy.[102]

Sant'Elia's new syntax is made up of a limited number of elements that he would use again and again in different permutations: the cylinder, the pyramid, the canted buttresses. But whereas in the former phase of granitic masses the forms merged into one another, in these the underlying solids retain their individuality (plate 7). The final composition is the result of an aggregative play of masses, undecorated, and with emphatic flat surfaces (figs. 60–64). It is possible too that Froebel's ideas, handed down from Selvatico to Boito and possibly to Mentessi, however diluted, left vestigial traces in these works, making Sant'Elia a Froebelian twice or thrice removed.

Initially Sant'Elia used only a few basic forms. Then, when the main components of his new grammar were worked out, he began to group them in more complex structures, particularly in the beautiful series of power plants which appears toward the end of 1913 (figs. 65–68). Sant'Elia's power plants are highly romanticized buildings, festooned with electric cables, and far removed from the utilitarian structures actually built in Lombardy. They are, in other words, poetry rather than prose and reveal an awe-struck admiration for the topic rather than a profound understanding of how these vast complexes work. Again, the worm's-eye view is used throughout, in conjunction with dramatic foreshortening. Considering the age and the context in which they were produced, the dinamismi are startlingly new, not only stylistically but thematically as well. What was the source of their inspired modernity?

Carlo Ragghianti was the first to suggest that the stage designs of Gordon Craig and Adolphe Appia may have had some influence on the spare, lean idiom of these drawings,

60. Antonio Sant'Elia. Modern buildings. Dated June 23, 1913,
Milan. Musei Civici, Como.

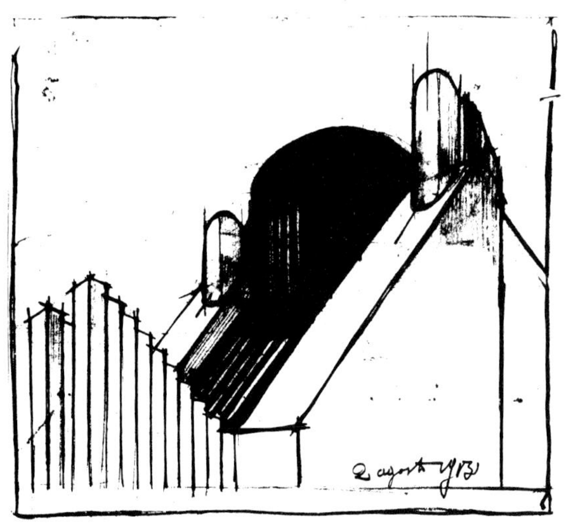

61. Antonio Sant'Elia. Modern building. Dated August 2, 1913. Musei Civici, Como.

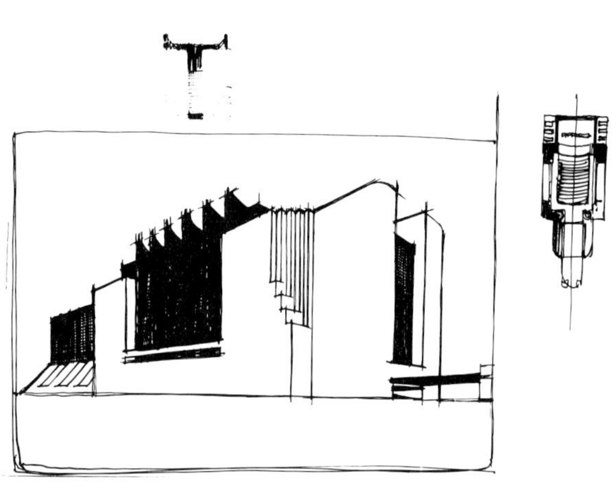

62. Antonio Sant'Elia. Monumental building (auditorium?), 1913. Musei Civici, Como.

63. Antonio Sant'Elia. Industrial building (hangar?). Signed and dated 1913. Musei Civici, Como.

64. Antonio Sant'Elia. Modern building, 1913. Musei Civici, Como.

particularly with regard to the "ambiguity of scale" evident in Sant'Elia's sketches.[103] Appia's *Espaces rythmiques* dates from 1909. Craig's *On the Art of the Theatre* appeared in 1905, and his *Towards a New Theatre,* dedicated to the Italians, in 1913. In the same year the Arena Goldoni was founded in Italy, and its productions helped popularize the works of the two stage designers. But by then their abstract stage sets were already widely known in Italy through foreign magazines. Although Appia's lapidary forms, particularly the stairways, were aimed at enriching interior space—never Sant'Elia's forte—they had a certain influence on the architecture of the exterior shell.[104] The question must remain open: one cannot rule out this possibility although the formal evidence itself is inconclusive.[105]

Adolf Loos likewise comes to mind with his ascetic and lapidary forms. Years ago Reyner Banham claimed that Sant'Elia may have heard of "Ornament and Crime" through Marinetti, though Boccioni is a more likely candidate.[106] Loos's manifesto was republished in *Der Sturm* in 1912, the year of the futurist exhibition in Berlin, when both Boccioni and Marinetti were in personal contact with Herwarth Walden. Boccioni, in fact, had the issue translated at his expense.[107] But the lack of formal analogies between the two seems to invalidate this claim. If Sant'Elia did hear of "Ornament and Crime," it was more likely to have influenced his ideas, although even that is doubtful. As for Loos's architecture, Sant'Elia was always too much of a Romantic to be swayed by such a rigorously *sachlich* design as that of the Steiner House.

Futurism undoubtedly exercised a powerful influence on these drawings. Boccioni's own *dinamismi*, that is, the studies in interpenetration of geometric shapes done in pen and ink, were obviously an important precedent for Sant'Elia, who must have been struck by the high degree of abstraction, the successful attempt to convey a sense of motion, the elimination of detail, and the tensile energy of Boccioni's lines. One should not, however, overestimate the impact of Boccioni's *dinamismi* on Sant'Elia, who was not attracted to theory nor to the sort of intellectual astringency that is evident in Boccioni's art. Sant'Elia preferred ready-mades, images he could adapt with minor changes rather than processes in which he had to work out all the intervening stages. Furthermore, Boccioni's iconography never focused on anything as radically innovative as Sant'Elia's power stations: on the contrary, Boccioni's imagery was truly urban, industrial, and modern only in his writings. In Sant'Elia's *dinamismi*, on the other hand, the change in imagery is as striking as the change in style.

One cannot overemphasize the fact that futurism influenced Sant'Elia as much by its literary imagery as by its art. With regard to electricity, no one had showed more enthusiasm than the futurists. Marinetti had sung its praises in various works, from his play *Elettricità* (1913) to the manifesto "Geometrical and Mechanical Splendor" (1914). For a while he even toyed with the idea of naming his movement *elettricismo*.[108] It is true that by this time both Russolo and Carrà, as well as Balla in Rome, had produced various paintings of electric lights, but these had no manifest influence, at least stylistically, on Sant'Elia.

Sant'Elia eagerly absorbed this many-sided apologia of modernity and made the new icons of futurist literature his own. Power stations had interested him ever since his work on the Villoresi Canal. The grand scale of the much-vaunted Lombard dams and their

65. *above left* Antonio Sant'Elia. Power station. Initialed and dated August 9, 1913, Como. Musei Civici, Como.

66. *left* Antonio Sant'Elia. Power station, 1913. Musei Civici, Como.

67. Antonio Sant'Elia. Power station, 1913. Musei Civici, Como.

68. Antonio Sant'Elia. Power station, 1913. Musei Civici, Como.

smooth, unadorned surfaces must have impressed him greatly. But at the time, the seventeen-year-old Sant'Elia was little more than an inexperienced master builder. It was only when he made contact with the futurists that Sant'Elia began to take a more active interest in industrial architecture, that is, typologies beyond the pale of the academic curriculum but extolled by Marinetti and his circle.[109]

Although these were the first drawings by Sant'Elia to be clearly influenced by futurism, that influence is primarily thematic.[110] The *dinamismi* are not so much an attempt to translate into architectural terms the main tenets of Boccioni's technical manifestos as an attempt to create a new world of architectural form beyond historicism. Sant'Elia did in empirical fashion what Gropius and Le Corbusier would do systematically: he looked at industrial architecture, and this, in turn, led him to a new aesthetic of vast unbroken surfaces, prismatic volumes, and bold silhouettes without any reference to the past. At least

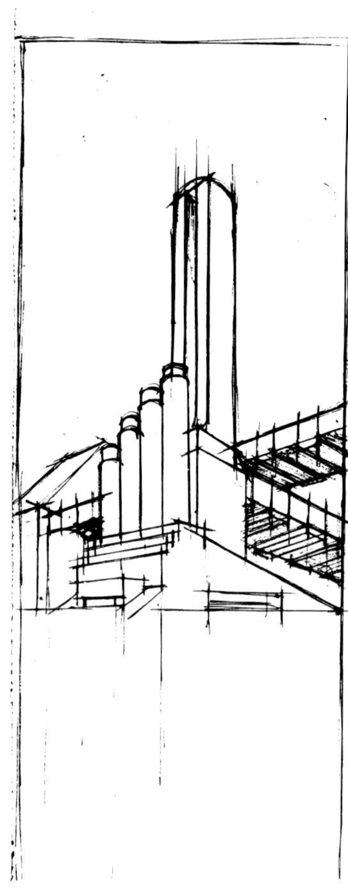

69. Antonio Sant'Elia. Industrial building, 1913. Musei Civici, Como.

70. American silos published by Gropius in the *Jahrbuch des Deutschen Werkbundes*, Jena, 1913.

one of his *dinamismi* can be traced directly to the famous illustration of an American silo published by Gropius in the *Werkbund Yearbook* of 1913 (figs. 69, 70).

As far as style is concerned, the main influence on the *dinamismi* is still Emil Hoppe. Sant'Elia's very manner of designing, with a low viewpoint and straight lines that overshoot the limits of the buildings, is reminiscent of Hoppe.[111] It is these lines that give the *dinamismi* the impression of modernity and speed, as if the view of the building were caught momentarily from a moving vehicle. There is an exciting new sense of movement in these sketches, which are a far cry from the heavy, static monumentalism of the drawings of 1912: "The very substitution of vertical and horizontal lines by oblique and elliptical ones is but a polemical and abstract consequence of substitution of a static aesthetic with an aesthetic of dynamism."[112]

But Hoppe gave Sant'Elia something more than dynamic, pathos-filled lines. His scaleless, monumental masses appealed strongly to the emotions of the spectator and were greatly influenced by the theories of *Einfühlung*.[113] In this, significantly enough, Hoppe came quite close to Boccioni. It was from them both that Sant'Elia learned about the underlying psychological component in the perception of space and thus came into contact with the rich, multifaceted psychological aesthetics of Einfühlung.[114]

THE INFLUENCE OF PSYCHOLOGY AND VISUAL THEORY

It has long been recognized that the development of artistic form in the beginning of the twentieth century was determined to a large extent by two opposing philosophical currents, Einfühlung, which advocated a psychological interpretation of style, and its seeming antipode, *Sichtbarkeit,* which held to a purely formalist conception of art. The conceptual antinomy between the two theories did not carry over into practice. Not even the theoreticians themselves could keep the best insights of the other camp from illuminating their work.[115]

Einfühlung (or empathy, as it was known in the English-speaking world), as theorized by Lipps and later by Wölfflin and Worringer, provided the theoretical underpinnings of Art Nouveau, while the theories of Sichtbarkeit (or pure visibility), put forth by Konrad Fiedler, Hans von Marées, Adolf von Hildebrand, and later Alois Riegl, gave the philosophical justification for the nonfigurative movements in art and architecture of the twentieth century: "Just as empathy is associated with Art Nouveau, so too the theory of pure visibility is considered the theoretical foundation of cubism, abstract art and rationalist architecture."[116]

At the turn of the century Einfühlung exerted great influence on both sides of the Atlantic. It was instrumental in bringing about a renewed interest in non-Western cultures, past and present, and also in the decorative arts. What it predicated was, after all, a subjective concept of beauty that varied from age to age and from individual to individual. The cultural relativism thus implied helped shift the focus in art history from the European and classical to other periods and other cultures, and from the fine arts to the decorative arts. It was not by chance that the appearance of the aesthetics of relativity coincided with the flourishing of the various *Werkbünde, Kunstgewerbemuseen, Werkstätten,* and *Künstlerkolonien,* which dedicated themselves to the task of producing applied arts. Einfühlung provided these ventures with a timely and challenging conceptual framework just as industrialization was erasing the last residues of craftsmanship from the market. Theories of empathy had such a galvanizing impact on artists and art historians of the time that one can speak of a "culture of Einfühlung" that pervaded the period.[117] Both Einfühlung and Sichtbarkeit were part of the great offensive against historicism that invested every area of culture.

The term Einfühlung was originally coined by Robert Vischer, but it was Theodor Lipps who gave it lasting expression with his work *Raumästhetik und geometrisch-optische Täuschungen* (Leipzig, 1897). According to Lipps's concept of empathy, aesthetic enjoyment is contingent on a physiopsychological response to artistic form. Human beings, in other words, project organic feelings and sensations onto the object of aesthetic contemplation: "Every act of aesthetic pleasure is ultimately based solely and simply on feeling;

even that which is given us by, among others, geometrical, architectural, tectonic, and ceramic lines and forms."[118]

Art historians were quick to grasp the far-reaching implications of this concept and to apply them to the history of art. One of the first scholars to adapt this idea to architecture was Heinrich Wölfflin in his dissertation of 1886, *Prolegomena zu einer Psychologie der Architektur.*[119] His psychological interpretation of style was based on the correspondence between architectural form and the bodily responses it evoked. Taking his cue from Lipps, Wölfflin tried to explain why architecture was able to convey different states of mind.

Wilhelm Worringer's *Abstraktion und Einfühlung,* first published in 1908 and translated into many languages, had an even greater impact.[120] It simplified and popularized both currents of thought, contrasting the recurrence of the organic in art with that of abstract geometrical form, which he considered a superior type of mental activity. The former reflected the human being's innate tendency to project his or her feelings onto the world of things, whereas the latter represented an attempt to overcome fear of the primal world and its diversity by imposing on it some sort of order.

Even though Einfühlung suggested an exciting new interpretative model for the history of art, most scholars nonetheless preferred to formulate "their *Grundbegriffe* on the sound and systematic knowledge of ancient art."[121] Architecture was invariably taken from the remote past, if it was brought into the picture at all. As a result the extraordinary impact of the theories of Einfühlung on contemporary architecture was overlooked for years. It was only in the 1960s, when Art Nouveau was no longer anathema, that a growing number of Italian scholars dedicated themselves to the study of the (now) obvious connection of Einfühlung in its varying formulations and the theories of Art Nouveau.[122] The very chronological coincidence of so many aesthetic theories based on empathy in the first years of the century, as well as the flowering of Art Nouveau, is revealing.

It was Henry van de Velde (1863–1957) who provided the most explicit link between Art Nouveau aesthetics and Einfühlung with his belief in "lines of force" as the prime vehicle for eliciting human emotions: "Line exerts an influence on every being not entirely devoid of sensibility, by means of the directions, proportions, and emphasis that it produces."[123] Architecture, too, influenced the spectator by means of its lines: "In a work of architecture this illusion of life expresses itself through the flexions, the different tensions of the line that invite us to participate in the play of functions, in the effort achieved by the elements of a building which support, weigh down, lift or evoke."[124] For van de Velde, the task of the modern architect was to free architecture from the meandering arabesque of naturalism, giving it instead bold sweeping lines that would evoke immediate human response.[125] Buildings, in other words, should convey a sense of mood, a *Stimmung.* It was just this organic quality that linked Art Nouveau to Einfühlung and distinguished it from the abstract formalism of Sichtbarkeit.

The implications of Einfühlung for architecture and city planning were immense.[126] Otto Wagner, chief architect of the city of Vienna, fell under the spell of both Einfühlung and Sichtbarkeit, no doubt because of his close contact with Vienna's famous school of art history: "The distinctions between *close* and *distant* vision, and *optic* and *haptic* vision, etc., taken from Fiedler, Hildebrand, Riegl and Wölfflin, were to be reflected in the reading of architectural space proposed by Otto Wagner."[127]

Wagner understood that the metropolis had brought about an irreversible psychological mutation: it affected the modes of vision and therefore implied a new beholder-subject. Motorized transportation, a prerequisite of the new urban scale, entailed a swiftly moving eye with aesthetic demands of its own. It now became necessary for the human eye to take in vast panoramas at a glance, and these could no longer be made up of highly detailed buildings that demanded a more contemplative attitude. "The modern eye," wrote Wagner, "has also lost the sense for a small, intimate scale; it has become accustomed to less varied images, to longer straight lines, to more expansive surfaces, to larger masses."[128] This new form of urban vision was no longer mediated by the sense of touch, as Jonathan Crary has shown.[129] A world of increasing abstraction was slowly coming into being, and architecture responded by simplifying facades and diminishing the richness of ornament and symbolism.

Otto Wagner was among the first to take speed into consideration in designing buildings and to tailor the aesthetic of the city to the needs of the new fast-moving subject, accommodating rapid changes in perspective and foreshortening. The car had rendered the time-honored "tactile" dimension, so important for Riegl, an anachronism. From this point on, architecture loses the richness of detail and ornament characteristic of close-range vision: henceforth the spectator's response to architectural form will be impressionistic, involving a swift scanning of the surfaces of the city without any regard for depth. The old capillary urban tissue with picturesque piazzas and meandering streets, dear to theoreticians like Camillo Sitte, was no longer possible or desirable. It was necessary to make city space intelligible to pedestrians and automobiles alike. Space and Time are no longer absolute categories, as in classical physics: the metropolis telescopes them into a new entity, Space-Time.[130]

Italians followed all these ideas with great interest. Beginning in 1905 a series of articles on Theodor Lipps, Johannes Volkelt, and August Schmarsow was published in Benedetto Croce's influential magazine *La Critica*.[131] It is hardly surprising, therefore, that an Italian avant-garde group, the futurists, should be among the greatest heirs to the theory of aesthetic delight.

Of all the Italian artists, none was more influenced by empathy than Boccioni.[132] His *stati d'animo*, *dinamismi*, and *linee-forza* are very much indebted to the theories of Einfühlung, which had gained common currency in Italy as well as in Germany and Austria. Toward the end of 1910 Boccioni had already given deep thought to the possibility of influencing the spectator through abstract means (lines, planes, colors) rather than by subject matter. The first record of his ideas along this line appears in the much-quoted letter to Nino Barbantini, director of Ca' Pesaro, the museum of modern art in Venice: "For me the ideal would be a painter who, wishing to evoke slumber, did not have recourse directly to a sleeping being (man, animal, etc.) but was capable of suggesting by means of lines and colors the idea of sleep, that is, universal sleep, beyond the contingencies of space and time."[133]

Boccioni continued to reflect on how to evoke certain responses in the spectator without having recourse to literal representation. One year later his thoughts on the matter had matured sufficiently to be presented in a manuscript that was to be of signal importance in artistic theory of the twentieth century. In this extraordinary document, later published as the preface to the first exhibition of the futurists in Paris, Boccioni presents his thoughts on abstract symbolism:

> One may remark, also, in our pictures spots, lines, zones of colour which do not correspond to any reality, but which, in accordance with a law of our interior mathematics, musically prepare and enhance the emotion of the spectator.
>
> We thus create a sort of emotive ambience, seeking by intuition the sympathies and the links which exist between the exterior (concrete) scene and the interior (abstract) emotion. Those lines, those spots, those zones of colour, apparently illogical and meaningless, are the mysterious keys to our pictures.[134]

Boccioni's ideal called for a closer connection between spectator and painting: colors and shapes had to reverberate in the spectator as in a sounding board, evoking the desired emotional response. To bind work and viewer more closely, the artist had to make use of certain dynamic lines that he termed "force-lines": "These are the *force-lines* that we must produce so that the work of art can be led back to true painting. We interpret nature by rendering these objects upon the canvas as the beginnings or the prolongations of the rhythms impressed upon our sensibility by these very objects."[135]

These lines became the vectors of Boccioni's psychophysiological symbolism, the mysterious wellsprings of the spectator's emotions. It was thanks to them that Boccioni arrived at the painting of stati d'animo, or states of mind. In a passage intended as a gloss on one of his most famous works, the triptych *The Farewells* (1911), Boccioni gives a brilliant exposition of his method:

> In the pictorial description of the various states of mind of a leave-taking, perpendicular lines, undulating and, as it were, worn out, clinging here and there to silhouettes of empty bodies, may well express languidness and discouragement.
>
> Confused and trepidating lines, either straight or curved, mingled with the outlined, hurried gestures of people calling one another, will express a sensation of chaotic excitement.
>
> On the other hand, horizontal lines, fleeting, rapid, and jerky, brutally cutting into half-lost profiles of faces or crumbling and rebounding fragments of landscape, will give the tumultuous feelings of persons going away.[136]

The same ideas appear in the *Manifesto of Futurist Sculpture* (April 11, 1912), in which Boccioni invokes the need for force-lines in sculpture. A year later Carrà published his *La pittura dei suoni rumori ed odori* (The Painting of Sounds, Noises, and Smells, 1913) in an attempt to correlate shapes and colors with emotions. Russolo was also working along similar lines in works like *Music* (1911–1912) and *Dynamism of an Automobile* (ca. 1912). As Boccioni explains in *Pittura sculptura futuriste,* "For every sensory emotion there exists an analogous color-form."[137] By 1913, the futurists were therefore trying to elaborate a new psychophysical syntax of abstract means that produced corresponding sensations, the states of mind, in the spectator.

What were Boccioni's sources? As to terminology, Boccioni's force-lines came, of course, from van de Velde's theories.[138] Vittore Grubicy de Dragon, the symbolist painter and art dealer, met van de Velde during his stay in Belgium, and Grubicy's art gallery in Milan was an important forum for modern art in Sant'Elia's day.[139] It is also possible that Boccioni came into contact with these theories in 1906 when he was in Munich, where Theodor Lipps lived. But a great part of Boccioni's ideas on Einfühlung, as well as those of Carrà and Russolo, came from the theoretical framework of symbolism, which had great impact on Milan's intelligentsia.

During his prefuturist days in Milan, around 1908, Boccioni had met Previati and was much impressed by his art and writings and with the possibility of conveying mood through light and color. It was probably through Previati that Boccioni was led to the work of Edvard Munch, which also involved states of mind: "It is noteworthy that Boccioni took from Munch, among other things, certain linear patterns [horizontal, perpendicular or curved] whose function is to express certain states of mind: he would later give theoretical shape to the corresponding concept, which is that of Einfühlung, in the introduction to the show of 1912."[140]

Sant'Elia could hardly ignore Boccioni's writings: both men moved in the same artistic circles in Milan and most likely met there in 1909, if not earlier. Although he did not read complex articles such as those published on Lipps and Volkelt in Croce's magazine, Sant'Elia was enormously susceptible to visual form in any medium. If some of his works therefore bear the unmistakable stamp of the psychological aesthetics of Einfühlung, this is due to his absorption of the Wagnerschule models, on one hand, and of Boccioni's art, on the other.

THE SAVINGS BANK OF VERONA

At about this time (1912) Sant'Elia opened his own architectural studio in the center of Milan, in Via San Raffaele. It was here, toward the end of 1913, that the famous drawings of the Città Nuova were begun. But he continued to work part-time for Arrigo Cantoni and for Giuseppe Boni, a well-known Milanese architect and professor at Brera.

During the second half of the year Sant'Elia participated in yet another competition with Cantoni, this time for the new headquarters of the Savings Bank of Verona. As head of a large studio, Cantoni handed many of the tasks over to the younger architects, overseeing the entire team more or less loosely. Tancredi Motta designed the plans, while the artist Leonardo Dudreville—Sant'Elia's old friend from Brera—did the perspectives in water-color and executed the figurative panels in the top story. Luigi Pellini was given the sections and the detailing.[141] According to Pellini's recollections many years later, the design of the facade and of the interior was entrusted to Sant'Elia, who thus played a much more promi-nent role in the project than he had in his previous collaboration with Cantoni.[142]

Cantoni was no old-fashioned academician. He had spent time in England, where he studied the Victorian Gothic, and then in Scotland, where he met Mackintosh. Milan still has several interesting buildings by Cantoni after the manner of the Scottish Secession. He was perhaps more sensitive than Sant'Elia to prevailing taste, as witnessed by his final entry for the Stazione Centrale of Milan, having discarded Sant'Elia's clearly superior project. If Cantoni did indeed assign significant portions of the design to Sant'Elia, because of the latter's recognized ability to create spectacular designs, he must have given detailed guidelines to his collaborators. After all, this was a competition that attracted international attention, owing to the historic importance of the square.

The new headquarters of the Savings Bank was to be situated in Verona's famous Piazza delle Erbe, a beautiful, elongated area built on the ruins of the old Roman Forum. The site proposed for the bank was then partially occupied by the old ghetto that began immediately behind the piazza. The competition was, in fact, part of an effort to modernize the center of Verona and make it more suitable for commerce and banking. The initiative gave rise almost immediately to a counterdemonstration by the city's conservationists, who claimed that although the three buildings to be torn down were hardly distinguished, they were part of the vital urban tissue of the old historic center.[143]

The Savings Bank as envisioned by Cantoni's studio is a picturesque neo-Gothic structure with secessionist touches (fig. 71). Because the site was uncommonly long, the facade was divided into three distinct parts of varying width, height, and cladding. The two extremities, with their complicated massing of turrets and chimneys, were treated almost like independent buildings. The main entrance, situated in the side adacent to the fourteenth-century Domus Mercatorum, was given greater prominence and height. Between the two sides, and in contrast to their rugged appearance, lies the central section, with walls of smooth white plaster and raised arches in the Venetian manner.

At the street corner, Cantoni and Sant'Elia boldly placed two arches meeting at right angles. They are crowned by a heavy balcony that also follows the ninety-degree angle of the street corner and is supported by corbels rising out of the keystones of the arches below. Thus the building is visually—and deliberately—undermined at its weakest point, that is, where the stress is greatest.[144]

It is hard to determine the exact part that Sant'Elia played in the overall design, because few of the original drawings have survived. As far as one can tell from photographs, most of the final drawings are in his hand, except for some of the watercolors by Dudre-

71. Antonio Sant'Elia for Arrigo Cantoni. Verona Savings Bank
(first version), 1913. *Emporium,* March 1915.

72. Antonio Sant'Elia. Preliminary sketch for the Verona Savings Bank(?) ca. 1913. Musei Civici, Como.

ville. Some of Sant'Elia's idiosyncrasies are easy to pick out, such as the stylized figures, the snakes, and the exuberant decoration. But the slender colonnettes, raised arches, and deep overhanging roofs, though rendered by Sant'Elia, were probably chosen by Cantoni. This sort of realism and fidelity to detail was hardly in keeping with Sant'Elia's ideas, all the more so since at this time he was already at work on the high-rise projects that would make him famous. Furthermore, a surviving drawing believed to be a preliminary sketch for this competition is not so overtly historicist (fig. 72). Although he never quite relinquished historicism, it was always streamlined and limited to what was compatible with Secessionlike draftsmanship.

There is a great contrast between the outside, which had to blend in harmoniously with the adjacent crenellated building, and the interior, which is all Secession (fig. 73). As would be expected, Cantoni allowed his architects greater freedom in the interior, where contextualism was unnecessary. The doorways are bordered by black trim, giving the walls the appearance of thin planes, as in the work of Hoffmann and the Wagnerschule in general. The interior in fact seems to be a liberal quotation from a sketch by Otto Prutscher published in *Der Architekt* in 1909.

The plan is a curious combination of Beaux-Arts elements disposed in an asymmetrical and often confusing way. Three monumental atria suggest a grandiose sequence but instead lead up to a series of non sequiturs. The itinerary suggested for the visitor is full of truncated vistas that do not dovetail. The plan was the work of his friend Tancredi Motta, and in spite of its obvious shortcomings, Sant'Elia would have occasion to remember it in his next project.

The competition had been announced in June 1913, but Cantoni's team worked on it mainly during the last months of the year and submitted their entry under the motto "Costruire" shortly before the December deadline. The public and press were largely in favor of Cantoni's entry, which was clearly the most audacious and colorful. Even though virtually all the critics singled it out for praise, they were not blind to its polemical stance:

> The project is not of the Veronese nor of the Italian type, and it reminds me of certain forms of modern Hungarian art. With its exotic modernity it would not blend well with our old cities,

73. Antonio Sant'Elia for Arrigo Cantoni. Verona Savings Bank, atrium (first version), 1913. Musei Civici, Como.

but whoever was able to conceive and design the project *Costruire* (and suffice it to recall the perspective of the magnificent corner entrance) is a real artist, and has produced a work that is absolutely original and beautiful. Aside from its wholly un-Veronese-like quality, I do not hesitate to declare it a masterpiece.[145]

From the very start the attitude of Cantoni's team toward the urban context had been irreverent. The program expressly called for a building inspired by the Middle Ages, the most glorious period of Veronese history. But, as the Cantoni group explained in an elegant secessionist booklet they published on the first version of the project they submitted, "This building must express decisively its function and its modern importance."[146] As for the urban tissue, they took a position vigorously in favor of the demolitionists calling for the clearance of the "miserabili case del ghetto."[147]

The final decision was not announced until April 16, 1914. Because none of the projects had taken into consideration Verona's historic traditions, the jury decided to hold a second competition among the five best projects, including Costruire. Commenting on the project by Cantoni's team, the jury regretted that "those violent foreign forms were not able to continue the historical traditions of the city of Verona with reverence."[148] Candidates were asked to resubmit entries more mindful of the historic context.

Costruire did not take the strictures of the jury very seriously and therefore stood little chance of winning. Their second version is slightly more traditional than the first (figs. 74,75), but the modifications were "almost invisible," as one indignant critic put it.[149] The controversial winner of this competition was the Roman architect G. B. Milani, whose conventional project was greeted with indifference by the public, while Costruire shared the third place with two other competitors.

In recent years critics have either ignored the Savings Bank project or criticized it violently because of its historicism.[150] Nevertheless, both versions of the project and the little publication are important in view of their chronological significance: they were roughly contemporaneous with Sant'Elia's "Messaggio" and with the Città Nuova. Giulio Ulisse Arata, the best-known architect to review the competition, summed up the final entry by Cantoni and Sant'Elia well: "This is not a modernism that differentiates itself too clearly from the Middle Ages, but it is a persuasive modernity: a new vision without being an incomprehensible machination of an all too abstract feeling. It is not, if you will, the result of a sincere emotion, but it is definitely the product of a refined sensibility."[151]

During the same time, Sant'Elia took part in a competition for the headquarters of the Association of Como Employees (Società dei Commessi di Como). First prize went to another architect, but Sant'Elia's original project has survived (fig. 76). The figurative panels and the black-and-white frames are very similar to those of the Verona Savings Bank. The entire work is situated squarely within the tradition of the Austrian Secession, particularly with regard to the treatment of the wall, reduced to so many panels bordered by a lively trim. But in this case Viennese influence was mediated by Italian architecture, more

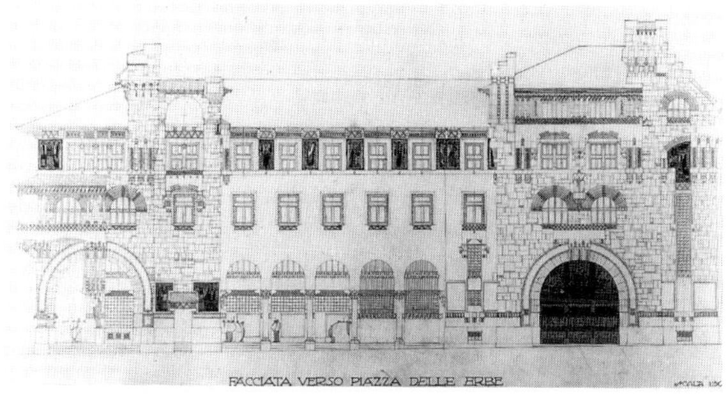

74. Antonio Sant'Elia. Verona Savings Bank (first version), 1914. Musei Civici, Como.

75. Antonio Sant'Elia. Verona Savings Bank, elevation (second version), 1914. *Emporium*, March 1915.

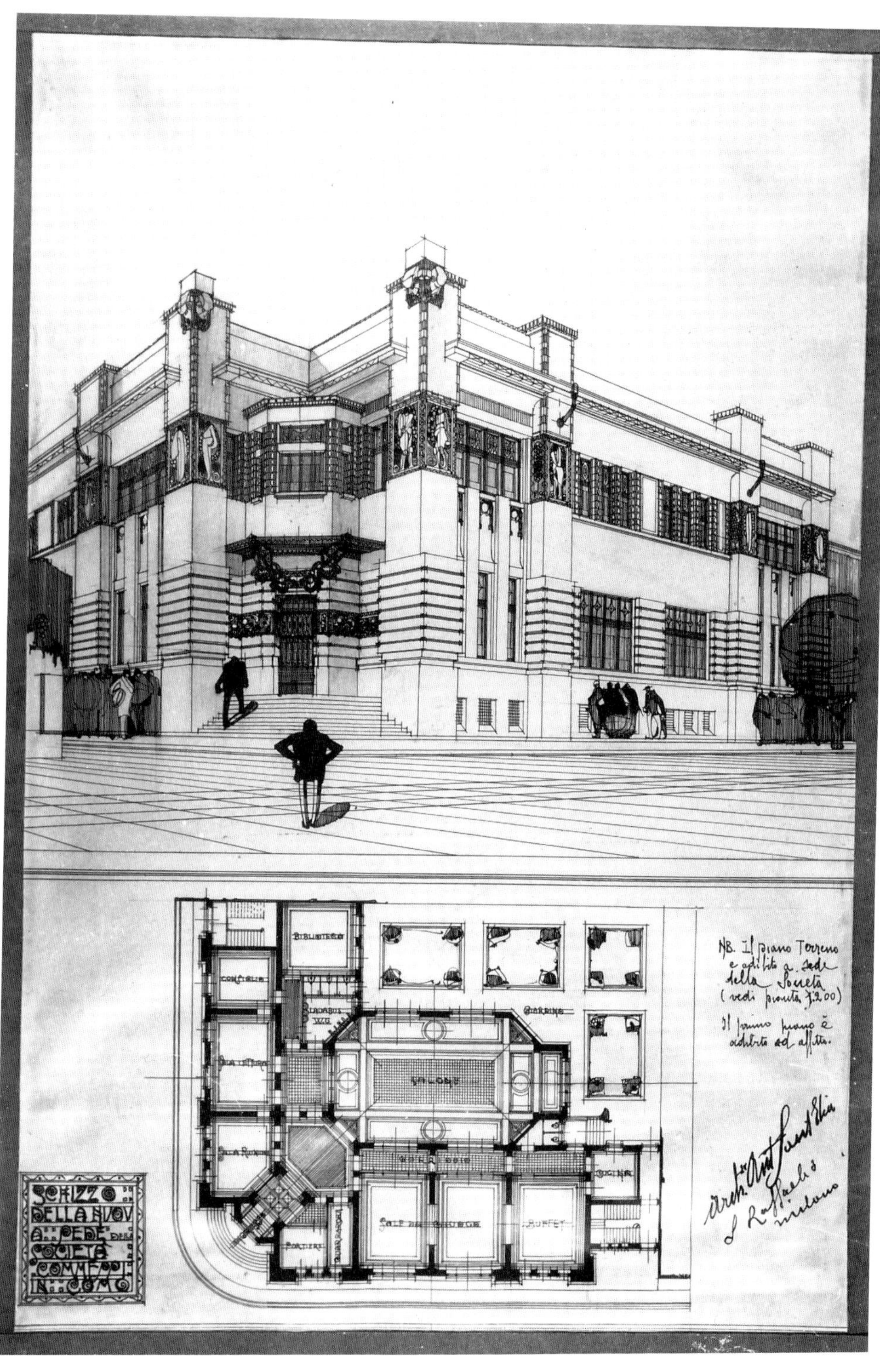

76. Antonio Sant'Elia. Headquarters of the Association of Como Employees, perspective and plan, 1913–1914. Musei Civici, Como.

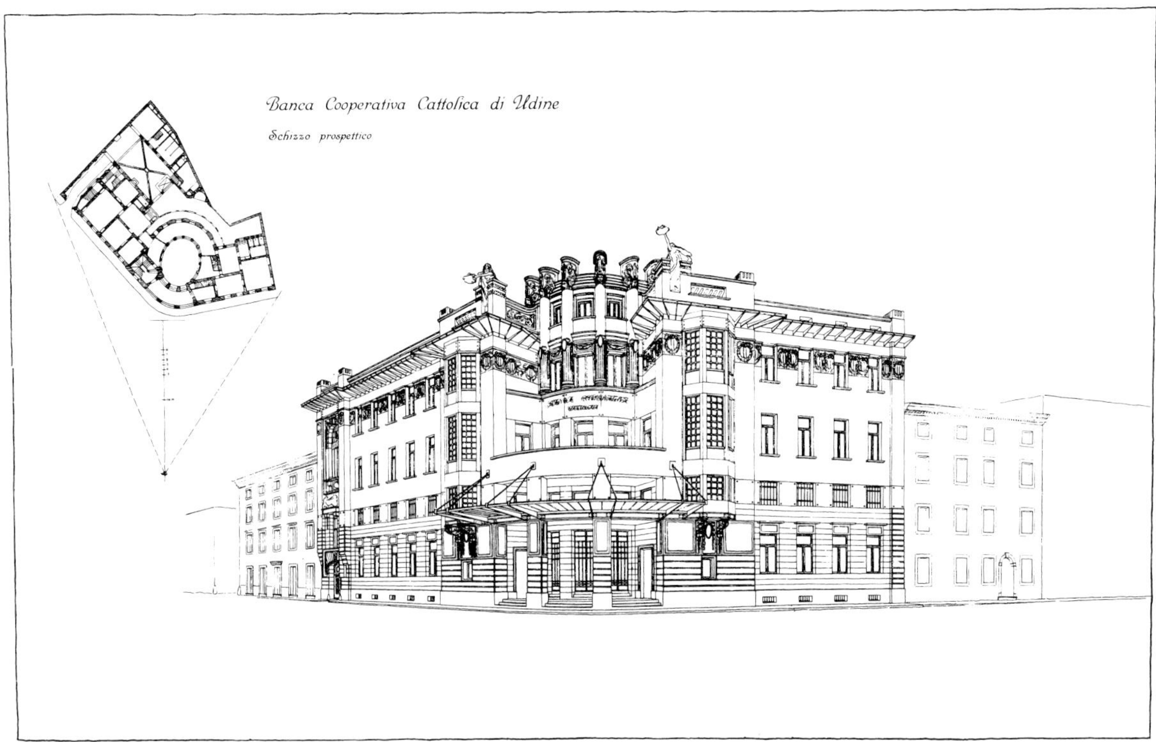

77. Raimondo D'Aronco. Banca Cooperativa Cattolica, Udine,
1907. Galleria d'Arte Moderna di Udine.

specifically, D'Aronco's Banca Cooperativa of 1907, at Udine (fig. 77). The compromise can be seen in the heavy, load-bearing appearance of the ground floor as opposed to the thin, panel-like treatment of the top part of the building.

It is characteristic of Sant'Elia that one of the most complete plans he left behind was lifted from Tancredi Motta's plan for the Savings Bank of Verona. Furthermore, Sant'Elia's was in contradiction with his elevation, which suggested a somewhat freer layout. As Bruno Zevi noted, "Extraordinary as [Sant'Elia] was when it came to destroying the volumetric box, he almost faltered when it came to rethinking spaces with originality."[152]

In December 1913, Sant'Elia was commissioned to design a tomb for the Caprotti family in the cemetery at Monza (fig. 78).[153] This is the only project, minor though it is, for which all plans, sections, elevations, and measurements are known (figs. 79–81). No doubt it was the success of Sant'Elia's entry in the competition for the local cemetery that led the Caprottis to seek him out.[154] Sant'Elia's vocabulary of flat planes with black borders is patently derived from the pages of Vienna's *Der Architekt*, which had featured a series of tombs by Hans Bolek, Emmanuel Margold, and Emil Hoppe, among others, a few years earlier.[155] Sketches for Klimt-like stained-glass panels, probably meant to be placed on the sides, have survived (fig. 82) but were not carried out in the final building.

78. Antonio Sant'Elia. Caprotti tomb, Monza, 1914. (Photo: Courtesy of Aldo Zana, Milan)

79. Antonio Sant'Elia. Caprotti tomb, preliminary sketch, 1914. Musei Civici, Como.

Very close to the Caprotti tomb in form and time was Sant'Elia's funeral monument to his father, Luigi Sant'Elia, who died on January 19, 1914. No definitive drawings are extant, but various preparatory sketches survive: the most accomplished of these shows a shift from the Secession-inspired Caprotti tomb, which Sant'Elia was finishing at the time, to a more conservative, Floreale-like design, greatly influenced by D'Aronco. Given the family's economic situation, the final project was much more modest. It seems that a simple tomb was erected, but it is not known if it was related wholly or in part to Sant'Elia's project.

One last project he designed at about this time shows the influence of Vienna: a lovely pavilion or kiosk, beautifully rendered in pen, ink, and watercolors, commissioned by the architect Giuseppe Boni (plate 8). Dated 1914 by its former owner, Tancredi Motta, this seductive little work is one of Sant'Elia's most successful Secessionist drawings.

The kiosk is a small elliptical building with a flat cantilevered roof. The windows consist of a continuous band of glass squares that neatly underscore the shape of the structure. On the long side, there is an aedicule, presumably for selling merchandise. The quiet simplicity of the lines, the near absence of decoration, and the prismatic shapes of the underly-

80. Antonio Sant'Elia. Caprotti tomb, perspective of the final project, 1914. (Holograph of lost original, courtesy of Banca Popolare di Lecco)

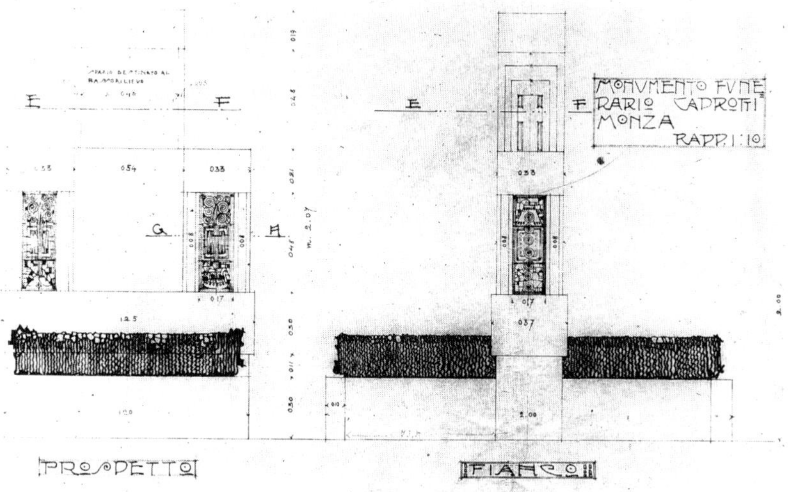

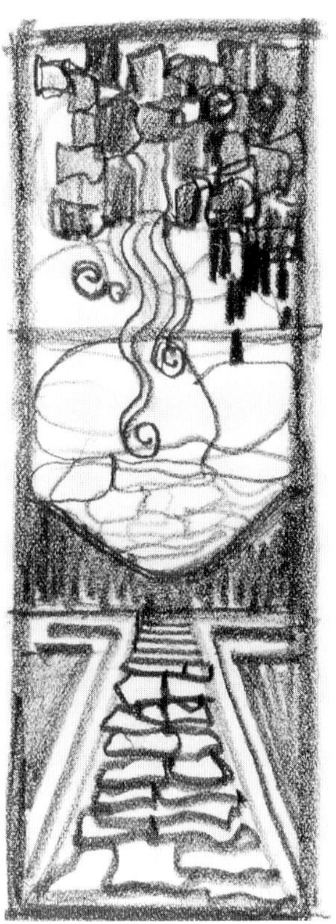

81. Antonio Sant'Elia. Caprotti tomb, front and side elevations, 1914. (Holograph of lost original, courtesy of Musei Civici, Como)

82. Antonio Sant'Elia. Sketches for a stained-glass panel, possibly for the Caprotti tomb, 1914. Musei Civici, Como.

ing solids all point once more to the pervasive influence of Otto Wagner, particularly his numerous projects for Vienna's Stadtbahn.

By the end of 1913 Sant'Elia's period of apprenticeship was over. If none of his competition projects had come to fruition, they had at least achieved a modest amount of success with the press and the public. His work in private studios and his competitions had broadened his cultural horizons, and his own projects, done in private and probably at night, free from the constraints of patrons, fulfilled him more and more.[156] At the end of the year, Sant'Elia decided to dedicate himself almost exclusively to his own work.

Four **Nuove Tendenze**

In 1914, his most prolific year, Sant'Elia reached the peak of his short life. The events that made him famous all took place within the brief span of March to July. In March, the final project for the Savings Bank was exhibited in Verona while in Milan the Associazione Architetti Lombardi opened its doors to the public. In May, "Nuove Tendenze," the most important show of his career, was inaugurated. At the same time he was campaigning actively on behalf of the socialists in his native town. On July 5 he was elected as a town councillor for the socialist opposition in Como. Six days later, on July 11, he published the *Manifesto of Futurist Architecture,* thus making public his adherence to the movement.

Sant'Elia also took part in a competition announced in February for a church in Salsomaggiore, near Parma, using, significantly, the pseudonym Utopia.[1] As one might expect, the church designs are executed in a much more conservative vein than his other work of the time (figs. 83–85, plate 9). In any case, Sant'Elia was eliminated in the first round of the competition, which was eventually won by Arata. The jury praised Sant'Elia's drawings but rejected his entry because it lacked plans, sections, and the written statement stipulated in the competition brief.[2]

Buildings of undeniable religious connotation, with apses, flying buttresses, and medievalizing statuary, remained a lifelong preoccupation, particularly in the last months of his life. Because Sant'Elia was not a believer, his religious works (churches, tombs, funerary chapels) tend to be quite secular. With the sole exception of the project for the cemetery at Monza—for which he followed the guidelines of the competition—there are no Christian symbols in Sant'Elia's work.[3] The religious purpose of his buildings is conveyed not by symbolism but by the customary architectural associations: apses, clerestories, flying buttresses, and twin towers on the facade. But Sant'Elia uses the various elements of traditional church design in a wholly unorthodox way, the main entrance sometimes being situated in the apse.[4]

The Salsomaggiore projects bring to mind one of the most famous Roman-

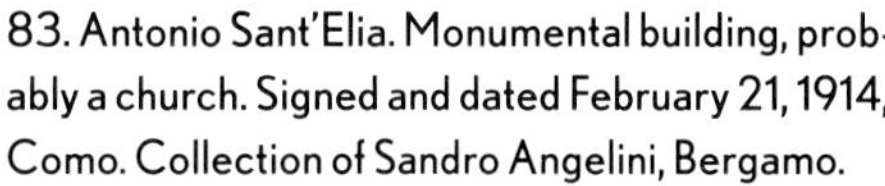

83. Antonio Sant'Elia. Monumental building, probably a church. Signed and dated February 21, 1914, Como. Collection of Sandro Angelini, Bergamo.

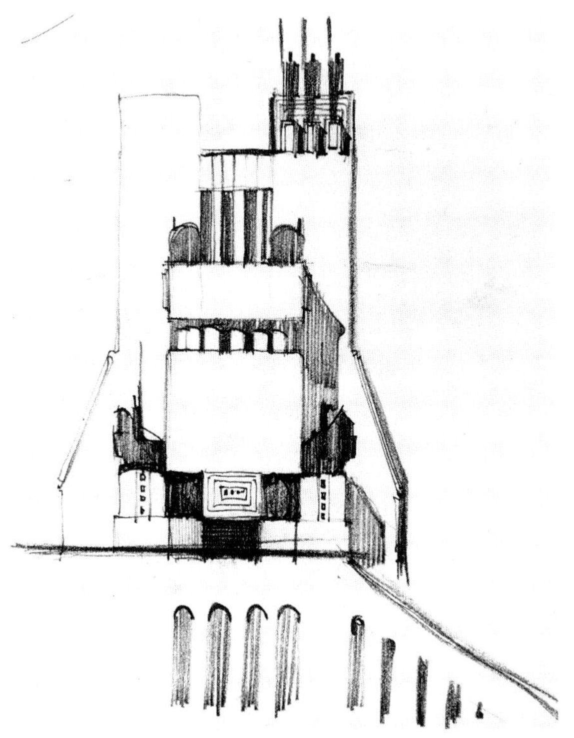

84. Antonio Sant'Elia. Monumental building (elevation of fig. 83), 1914. Musei Civici, Como.

esque monuments of Italy, the beautiful abbey church of St. Abbondio, in Como, which exercised a constant, if latent, influence on Sant'Elia (fig. 86). Its pure unadorned volumes and the stately disposition of its masses reappear not only in ostensibly religious designs such as these but also in secular projects.[5] An equally important source were Como's splendid Roman gateways, whose strong, lapidary profiles appear in some of Sant'Elia's works of this period (plates 10,11). Como remained an important source of inspiration for Sant'Elia, not only because many of his works were actually designed there but because many of its monuments reverberated through his sketches.

According to his friends Tancredi Motta and Luigi Pellini, Sant'Elia is also known to have taken part in a competition for small-scale villas on the Lido, in Venice.[6] No drawings survive, however, nor is the fact alluded to elsewhere. Sant'Elia's interest in villas was short-lived. It was preempted by the palazzi, the large-scale unit of the modern metropolis. The visionary bent to his personality could not be entirely satisfied with the quiet domesticity required by houses. Nevertheless, among the drawings of this period there are sketches for two villas, neither of them clearly dated nor otherwise identified, which may be related to the Lido competition.

In the first of these (fig. 87), Sant'Elia gave free rein to his imagination. Vaguely reminiscent of Mackintosh, the reticulated simplicity of the windows and the unconventional grouping of solids and voids of the massing are quite unusual, as is the bold cylindrical mass that acts as a linchpin to the composition.

The second villa has sometimes been said to reflect the influence of Frank Lloyd Wright (fig. 88).[7] Yet there is nothing in this sketch that Sant'Elia could not have gotten from the Liberty villas still fashionable in Italy at the time.[8] The flat roof came directly out of the Wagnerschule and its Italian followers, and already appears in Sant'Elia's first known project, cribbed unblushingly from Olbrich in 1908 (see fig. 6). And Wright himself, as Vincent Scully has shown, was very much influenced by Olbrich.[9] Moreover, Wright's early Prairie houses, published in Europe by Wasmuth in 1910, with their friendly, familiar horizontality and their insistent rootedness in nature, have nothing in common with Sant'Elia's work.[10] The second Wasmuth publication, *Ausgeführte Bauten* (1911), admittedly shows a different aspect of Wright—the machine-loving Wright, much more congenial to Sant'Elia. But there is no trace of this Wright in Sant'Elia's work either.[11]

85. Antonio Sant'Elia. Monumental building, 1914. Collection of Sandro Angelini, Bergamo.

86. Basilica of Santo Abbondio, ca. 1063–1095, Como. (Photo: Collection of the author)

87. Antonio Sant'Elia. Study for a villa. Dated February 22 (year illegible, 1914), Como. Musei Civici, Como.

88. Antonio Sant'Elia. Study for a villa, ca. 1914. Whereabouts unknown (lost at the International Exposition in Brussels in 1958). (Photo: Courtesy of Musei Civici, Como)

In February Sant'Elia took part in his first architectural exhibition, promoted by the Associazione Architetti Lombardi: the Prima Mostra Annuale della Federazione degli Architetti Italiani. Until then, the only works shown to the public (apart from the two published designs) were his competition projects, which had to conform to the requirements of the patrons. Although the exhibition did not attract much attention, Sant'Elia's presence in this heterogeneous but prestigious group was in itself an achievement, because the show included some of Italy's most famous modern architects, such as D'Aronco, Sommaruga, and Stacchini.[12]

On the whole, the exhibition was somewhat of a disappointment. With the exception of Sant'Elia's entries, the projects failed to live up to the expectations of the younger architects and critics. The public, declared Giulio Arata, one of the critics who reviewed the show, "needs an architecture subservient to the needs and demands of the modern life of our time, of building organisms stripped of that false and hybrid decorative aestheticism that invades the modern facade."[13] Instead, one was faced either with the tame, well-trodden paths of historicism or with the equally shopworn examples of the Liberty. Arata openly attacked the "archaeologists," above all Marcello Piacentini, later to become famous as Mussolini's most powerful architect. Although the critic had few kind words to say about the young Italian architects, Sant'Elia was spared his general condemnation: "Compared to his," Arata was later to write, "our entries seemed like dusty odds and ends taken down for the occasion from an old cupboard, or forgotten in a junkyard."[14]

The exhibition catalogue lists eleven drawings by Sant'Elia.[15] Four of these were published by Arata along with their respective titles. The first three are still linked to Sant'Elia's towering, crepuscular buildings of 1912 (figs. 89,90, plate 12). One of them (fig. 89), as Sant'Elia's caption makes clear, is a yet another project for Milan's railroad station and shows a colossal building shaped like a truncated pyramid. The representational aspect of this sketch is impressive. Powerful oblique buttresses shoulder the immense mass, which slopes down dramatically only to rise again in the form of two mighty pylons. Low dark vaults conjoin and brace the pylons in the center, while on either side of the main entrance they flare out unsupported, forming a marquee. Sant'Elia dramatizes the contrast between the oblique surfaces, possibly meant to be read as glass, and the towerlike verticals marking the entrance. One would have to wait for a Poelzig or a Berg for these powerful, clifflike masses with low squat openings. Expressionism—the need to impart emotion, or Stimmung, to the viewer—remained one of the wellsprings of Sant'Elia's work.

The skyscraper, on the other hand, is the earliest known sketch of the Città Nuova, and was clearly done after the others (fig. 91). Here the heavy masses have given way to a translucent shell held up by an exposed frame construction. The dinamismi, too, have been left behind. The new type of high-rise building demanded highly sophisticated circulation systems and a complexity of massing and elevation that far surpasses the elementary forms of 1913. Such buildings were opaque and monolithic, whereas Sant'Elia's skyscraper is transparent and reveals a clear differentiation between load-bearing supports and light partitions.

89. Antonio Sant'Elia. Sketch, new railroad station, Milan,
1913–1914. Signed "Schizzo. Nuova Stazione Milano."
Collection of Gianemilio Monti, Milan.

90. Antonio Sant'Elia. Church, 1913–1914. Collection of Gianemilio Monti, Milan.

91. Antonio Sant'Elia. Skyscraper, 1913–1914. Original drawing lost. (Photo: Collection of the author)

Meanwhile, Sant'Elia had begun to frequent one of the most interesting circles of the Milanese avant-garde. Among the numerous artists and architects who gravitated around the Academy of Brera was a group of students, all born in the 1880s, who were extremely dissatisfied with the lachrymose Verismo then in vogue in Milan and with the gloomy mysticism of the symbolists. They included Boccioni (who was never directly affiliated with the academy but frequented the milieu), Carrà, Russolo, Dudreville, Achille Funi, Mario Chiattone, Carlo Erba, and Giovanni Possamai. As early as 1909, therefore, Sant'Elia was in touch with Boccioni, Carrà, and Russolo, that is, before they joined Marinetti's movement.

As Carrà remarks in his autobiography, *La mia vita*, these young artists began to hold nightly discussions in the Caffè del Centro,[16] the Campari, the Cova, and several other gathering places.[17] Around 1909 this same group began to frequent the Famiglia Artistica, an antiestablishment association dedicated to the arts, music, and literature, then at the height of its fame.[18] At these nightly reunions, new trends from abroad were avidly discussed while the artistic conformity of Brera was attacked and abjured. "These gatherings," wrote Silvia Evangelisti, "would give birth to futurism and then to Nuove Tendenze which, a few years later, was to bring together all those who had been excluded from the futurist movement."[19] And indeed, on February 11, 1910, the *Manifesto of Futurist Painters* appeared, in the form of a flyer, heralding the official entry of Boccioni, Carrà, Russolo, Balla, and Severini into the futurist group.[20] From 1910 to 1914, the Milanese futurists (Boccioni, Carrà, and Russolo) took part in many of the shows organized by the Famiglia Artistica, exhibitions that were crucial for the development of modern art in Milan. Because the futurists did not have a show of their own until after World War I, it was at the Famiglia Artistica that the public got its first glimpse of their work.

The futurists burst upon the placid art world of Milan like a cataclysm. True, the Famiglia Artistica had opposed the city's artistic institutions, but it did so in ways that can hardly be described as radical, whereas the futurists' notorious theatrical performances, their virulent manifestos, and their political rallies ending in mass jailings shook the artistic establishment to the core. The repercussions in the art world were never-ending, and the blow dealt to the art scene should not be underestimated. Futurism polarized artistic debate in the prewar period in Italy to such an extent that academic circles became even more entrenched than before, while the more timid modern groups shrank fearfully from such extremes. By 1914, however, the futurists themselves had retreated somewhat from their previous positions of artistic intransigence. They had reached the peak of their originality in 1913. One year later Boccioni was placidly looking at Cézanne, and Carrà at Giotto.[21] It was only in politics that their virulence proceeded with undiminished fervor.

In the second half of 1913, several members of the Famiglia Artistica, including Sant'Elia, founded yet another artistic group, known as Nuove Tendenze.[22] It was characteristic of the spirit of moderation and caution that had set in as a reaction against futurism in Milan but also of the attenuated demands of the futurists themselves in 1914: "It is obvious that the extreme limit of their artistic propositions had already been reached in the futurist manifestos written between 1910 and 1913."[23] Nuove Tendenze was thus trying to chart a more conciliatory course. The proliferation of so many artistic groups and associations in the beginning of the century is indicative of the profound disillusionment with official art milieus.[24] Impatient with the artistic establishment, the young were eager to reach a new and wider public by means of channels not controlled by academic circles or by the usual patronage circuits.

Exactly when Nuove Tendenze was founded remains unclear. Ugo Nebbia, critic, art historian, and member of Milan's Soprintendenza ai Monumenti, and the artist Leonardo Dudreville were the founders of the new group, followed by the critics Decio Buffoni and Gustavo Macchi and the architect Giulio Ulisse Arata.[25] In fact, the embryonic nucleus already existed in the summer of 1913: the first mention of Nuove Tendenze appears in a letter dated August 20, 1913, from Dudreville to the painter Adriana Bisi-Fabbri, in which he asks if she would be willing to meet Nebbia with a view to joining the new association.[26] The group's first official document, however, is a pamphlet dated March 20, 1914, announcing their first exhibition to the public. By that time the roster of members was

92. Cover of the Nuove Tendenze catalogue, 1914. Beinecke Rare Book and Manuscript Library, Yale University.

complete: Giulio Ulisse Arata, Decio Buffoni, Mario Chiattone, Leonardo Dudreville, Carlo Erba, Achille Funi, Gustavo Macchi, Ugo Nebbia, Giovanni Possamai, and Antonio Sant'Elia.[27]

Nuove Tendenze opened its doors on May 20, 1914, in the showrooms of the Famiglia Artistica, in Via Agnello. Of the ten original members, three (Arata, Buffoni, Macchi) had defected, but Marcello Nizzoli, Alma Fidora, and Adriana Bisi-Fabbri had taken their places. The group was therefore made up of the painters Dudreville, Erba, Funi, Nizzoli, Bisi-Fabbri; of the architects Sant'Elia and Chiattone; the sculptor Possamai; and Alma Fidora, who contributed embroidery. About sixty works were distributed over four rooms, but the lion's share went to Sant'Elia, who exhibited sixteen projects (roughly one-quarter of the entire show).[28] The exhibition was accompanied by an elegant secessionist catalogue—a luxurious touch for the times—to which Nebbia, Dudreville, Erba, Funi, Possamai, and Sant'Elia contributed essays (fig. 92).

THE INFLUENCE OF FUTURISM

In his introduction, Ugo Nebbia cautiously takes his distance from futurism, without naming it, in order to underscore the attitude of moderation that characterized the new group.[29] Yet the connection between Nuove Tendenze and futurism is by now an established fact. The articles in the Nuove Tendenze catalogue and the works exhibited, as well as the history of the individual members, attest to the group's enormous debt to futurism, a debt readily acknowledged by most critics of the day, whether pro- or antifuturist. Margherita Sarfatti (1880–1961), a prominent art critic and fervid admirer of Sant'Elia, expressed the situation clearly: "Even without being counted as futurists, these young people have assimilated, each according to his own temperament, the lion's share of the new pictorial ideals that futurism has pioneered among us."[30] Giuseppe Carfagna, another reviewer, put it even more succinctly: "One wanted to give the impression of excluding futurism, [yet] in reality no one has ever been more futurist than this."[31]

But the most illuminating, if indignant, analysis of the relationship of Nuove Tendenze to futurism came from a futurist, Enrico Prampolini, who accused the members of Nuove Tendenze of plagiarism in a review of the show: "It is too bad that young people with a breath of audacity lack sufficient courage to declare themselves futurists openly, while recognizing the value of the latter and drawing from them the necessary sustenance."[32] Prampolini had cause for complaint. The leaflet that announced the show to the public was laid out like a futurist manifesto, with typographical variations in boldface;[33] and the wording was reminiscent of the open invitation written by the organizers of the Prima Esposizione d'Arte Libera in Milan.[34] Although not exclusively futurist, this exhibition, held in 1911, had been one of the first to show futurist works. In addition, it had been organized with the help of Nebbia, Boccioni, Carrà, and Russolo. Adriana Bisi-Fabbri had also taken part.

Leonardo Dudreville, the main organizer of the show, had exhibited with Boccioni at the Famiglia Artistica and had studied painting at Brera under Carrà's teacher, Cesare Tallone. A trip to Paris in 1907 led to Dudreville's acquaintance with Gino Severini, with whom he remained in touch for several years. And on April 21, just before the opening of Nuove Tendenze, Dudreville had been one of the executors of Luigi Russolo's *Intuonarumori* at the Teatro Dal Verme, in Milan. In 1910 Dudreville had even asked to become a member of the futurist movement but was turned down.[35]

Many of the paintings exhibited by Dudreville were distinctly futurist: "Dudreville," declared Raffaele Giolli in a preview of the show, "will exhibit some large paintings that will no doubt cause a lot of excitement . . . given their futurist audacity."[36] His four paintings dedicated to the four seasons (entitled *Stagioni*) were clearly related to Boccioni's stati d'animo and to his trilogy *The Farewells* (1911). Dudreville's *Everyday Domestic Quarrel* shows the interpenetration of people and objects characteristic of futurist art of 1913, particularly of Boccioni's theories on dynamism. Ugo Nebbia noted this clearly in his review of the exhibition: "[Dudreville's art] partakes of the arduous task of an art which, by means of rhythms, lines and color alone, seeks to evoke rather than to describe, not a given thing, nor a fact, but a state of mind, an emotion of a purely psychological nature."[37] These words could have been written by Boccioni himself—at least in 1912.

If Dudreville was influenced mainly by Boccioni, Funi shows greater affinity with Carrà.[38] Even his titles are futurist: *Woman, Car, Houses; Forms and Lights of a Nocturnal Street; Plastic and Chromatic Sensation of a Merry-Go-Round.* This affinity was soon ratified by the futurists themselves: after the show Funi joined the futurist movement with almost the same abruptness as Sant'Elia.

Carlo Erba's paintings for Nuove Tendenze have all been lost save one, *Carica di Cavalleria (moto in avanti),* which is known through old reproductions.[39] It is distinctly futurist,

as are his other surviving works. He, too, had met Boccioni, Carrà, Russolo, and Marinetti
in 1912. Just before the inauguration of Nuove Tendenze, Erba had asked to take part in the
first great show of futurist art in Italy, the Esposizione Libera Futurista Internazionale, held
in the spring of 1914 at the Galleria Sprovieri, in Rome, but he too was turned down.[40]

Marcello Nizzoli and Adriana Bisi-Fabbri also had close connections to the futurists.
The latter was, in fact, a second cousin of Boccioni's and had exhibited with him in 1911,
though her work does not show much futurist influence.[41] Nizzoli's paintings and embroi-
deries reveal the interpenetration of abstract form and chromatic analyses characteristic of
the futurists.[42] The exhibition entries of the anarchist sculptor Giovanni Possamai are lost,
and those known through old photographs are more Art Nouveau than futurist. But Possamai had studied and taught at Brera, and no doubt knew the futurist artists well.[43]

Even more revealing of the dependence of Nuove Tendenze on futurism were the catalogue entries, with their many paraphrases of the futurist manifestos, and also the use of
typographical characters of different size in boldface. So too was the format used by Dudreville and Sant'Elia, who wrote the two longest and most important essays in the catalogue, enumerating all their approvals and disapprovals.

With the exception of the short introduction by Ugo Nebbia, in which he tries to rec-
oncile modernism and moderation, all the other entries presuppose futurist precedents.
The essay by Leonardo Dudreville reveals great familiarity with Severini's *Le analogie plas-
tiche del dinamismo* and with Carrà's *La pittura dei suoni, rumori e odori*.[44] But he was primarily influenced by Boccioni's theories of stati d'animo: "In these [his paintings] I have
pinned down and executed graphically the synthesis of the state of mind caused by the
contact of my inner psychic individuality, with the outer life-ambiance that envelops me."[45]

Possamai, Funi, and Erba, who wrote the remaining essays, also fall back on futurist
ideas. Funi, possibly the most important painter of the group, used arguments in his own
catalogue entry that could almost serve as captions to some of Boccioni's paintings:
"A tram racing between the houses of a city, carries along with it everything that surrounds it; the cubes of the houses are dragged by that speeding line."[46]

Of course no one saw this better than the futurists. As Prampolini angrily remarked,
"Everything they declare in their manifestos and express in their work is false . . . because it
is not of their making; all that is daring and novel to be found there is taken from futurist
manifestos and works; and they plagiarize not only the ideas, but the very terminology."[47]
In short, all the members of Nuove Tendenze had had close ties with futurism, ties that
were to become even stronger after the exhibition closed its doors to the public. Of the
nine artists who were part of the group, three eventually joined the futurist movement:
Sant'Elia, Funi, and Dudreville. Furthermore, in June 1915, Erba, Funi, and Sant'Elia enrolled in the Lombard Battalion of Volunteer Cyclists, along with the futurists Marinetti,
Boccioni, Russolo, and Mario Sironi.[48]

Strangely enough, despite the obvious congruence of artistic goals, which contemporary critics were quick to grasp, the Nuove Tendenze artists pointedly refrained from men-
tioning the word *futurism*.[49] Nuove Tendenze eagerly accepted the futurists' artistic theory,
the wisdom of which seemed to them self-evident—they came, after all, from the same cul-

tural matrix in Milan. But they refused the programmatic, school-like character of the movement and especially its radical polemics and political pamphleteering. If their works of art and their essays followed those of the futurists so closely, they never pursued those ideas to their ultimate conclusions. Marinetti's attempt to bridge the gap between art and life by creating a futurist way of life was rejected by the more cautious Nuove Tendenze: "With regard to futurism, the program of Nuove Tendenze was that of defining a field of action that was avant-garde without being radical, not tied to collective rules of a movement, and based, rather, on free individual research."[50]

But Nuove Tendenze was not exclusively futurist. Its very moderation was un-futurist. If it looked toward the future, it also cast an eye backward, toward the recent past. The Austrian Secession had a great impact on the group, beginning with the layout and the graphics of the catalogue.[51] On the other hand, the urgent tone of the manifesto and the capitalized letters in boldface could also be found in Otto Wagner's *Modern Architecture,* first published in 1896. The poetics of Einfühlung, which were part of the theoretical foundations of Boccioni's *stati d'animo,* also played a certain role. Nuove Tendenze, in other words, was not just a pale reflex of futurism but a more complex phenomenon that reflected several aspects of the European avant-garde. This syncretism was characteristic of all Milanese avant-garde circles, with the exception of the futurists, who by that time had fully overcome their initial symbolist-secessionist period.

The only other architect in the group, Mario Chiattone, is a key figure in the understanding of Sant'Elia.[52] Young, wealthy, and well schooled, Chiattone had a thorough grounding in modern art. His father, Gabriele Chiattone, himself an artist and connoisseur of contemporary art, became one of the earliest patrons of Boccioni and Carrà.[53] Sant'Elia and the younger Chattione had met in 1909 at Brera, where both were studying architecture. Although three years younger than Sant'Elia, Chiattone was already an experienced painter and had helped organize an art show of *refusés* from the academy.[54] Between 1913 and 1914 they shared a studio in a building owned by Chiattone's father.[55] It was there that Sant'Elia consulted the much admired albums of the Wagnerschule and that their projects for the Nuove Tendenze exhibition were prepared. Several drawings, in fact, have been variously attributed to one or the other.[56] Chiattone had only recently turned to architecture, and the exhibition marked the first public showing of his work.

Only two of the three drawings Chiattone contributed to the exhibition are known (figs. 93,94). The most impressive of the these is the cityscape with sleek slabs seventy stories high—an urban landscape, like Sant'Elia's Città Nuova, unaccompanied by plans or sections (fig. 93). On the whole it was Chiattone, not Sant'Elia, who presented the most dazzling and, with the benefit of hindsight, the most prophetic vision of the modern metropolis. The treatment of the facades, particularly of the glass building with rounded corners, was the most innovative design of its kind until Mies van der Rohe's glass skyscrapers of 1919.[57] But although the verticalism is more pronounced and the antihistoricism more radical, this cityscape is less complex than Sant'Elia's. There is less emphasis on circulation, and the traffic levels are limited to two. Unlike the Città Nuova, it is situated on the waterfront, although water itself is not exploited for transportation.

93. Mario Chiattone. Metropolis, 1914. Published in the Nuove
Tendenze catalogue. Beinecke Rare Book and Manuscript
Library, Yale University.

Surprisingly enough, while Sant'Elia's projects were extolled for their modernity, Chiattone was all but ignored by the critics. Ugo Nebbia, the group's main spokesman, does not even mention Chiattone's name in his review of the show. Even Chiattone's apologists considered his projects more pictorial than architectural.[58] There is no doubt that his previous experience as a painter left its mark on his projects, but there is no reason to consider his approach any more pictorial than Sant'Elia's. Why Chiattone's contemporaries failed to notice him remains a mystery. The indifference of posterity is easier to explain. If Sant'Elia was remembered after his death, it was largely owing to his affiliation in the futurist movement; Marinetti saw to it that Sant'Elia's name and legend were kept alive. The placid Chiattone never joined the group and consequently "missed the hagiographical treatment that Marinetti gave to Sant'Elia."[59]

Although Chiattone was a close friend of many futurists, particularly of Boccioni, his work was not to their liking. Beautiful and oneiric in their own right, the vast, mysterious cathedrals he left behind are static and monumental and altogether lacking in the impetuous élan of the Città Nuova. Sant'Elia's love of diagonals and his deliberate distortion of the laws of perspective produce a spatial dynamism that is absent from Chiattone's more sober structures.[60] With the exception of his astonishing metropolis, nothing could be less futurist than Chiattone's remote, silent buildings. They partake of the same atmosphere of restoration that was later to characterize "Valori Plastici" and the "Novecento," Milan's two most important postwar artistic movements.[61] Like the painted architecture of Giorgio De Chirico, they seem rooted in the timeless immobility of the past.

Sant'Elia easily overshadowed the other members of Nuove Tendenze, and he was singled out for praise by most of the critics who reviewed the show. Both his drawings and his catalogue entry were a revelation, for although the public had been used to futurist art for some time—and would therefore not be shocked by the tamer variety produced by Nuove Tendenze—futurist architecture was new and unprecedented.

94. Mario Chiattone. Industrial building, 1914. Beinecke Rare Book and Manuscript Library, Yale University.

95. Antonio Sant'Elia. La Città Nuova, 1914. Published in the Nuove Tendenze catalogue. Beinecke Rare Book and Manuscript Library, Yale University.

96. Antonio Sant'Elia. Signed and inscribed "La Città Nuova, detail," 1914. Musei Civici, Como.

The catalogue lists sixteen drawings by Sant'Elia, divided under the following headings:

1. The Città Nuova (station for airplanes and trains)—one drawing.
2. The Città Nuova (details)—six drawings.
3. The Casa Nuova—one drawing.
4. Electric Plants—three drawings.
5. Architectural Sketches—five drawings.

One cannot identify all these entries accurately. Three were reproduced in the catalogue of the show (figs. 95–97), and the *Manifesto of Futurist Architecture,* published later that year, no doubt included drawings that had been on display (figs. 98–101). But the remainder can only be guessed. Various other drawings, designed with an accuracy hitherto unknown in Sant'Elia's personal work, may also have been exhibited (figs. 102,103, plates 13–15). And although there are more than sixteen drawings that seem to fit the exhibition standards, they were all part of the Nuove Tendenze series, whether they were actually on display or not. Be that as it may, these new works can be divided roughly into two groups, according to style and subject matter: the protorationalist Città Nuova and the more romantic power plants.

97. Antonio Sant'Elia. Signed and dated 1914, Como, and inscribed "La Città Nuova, detail." Published in the Nuove Tendenze catalogue. Original lost. Beinecke Rare Book and Manuscript Library, Yale University.

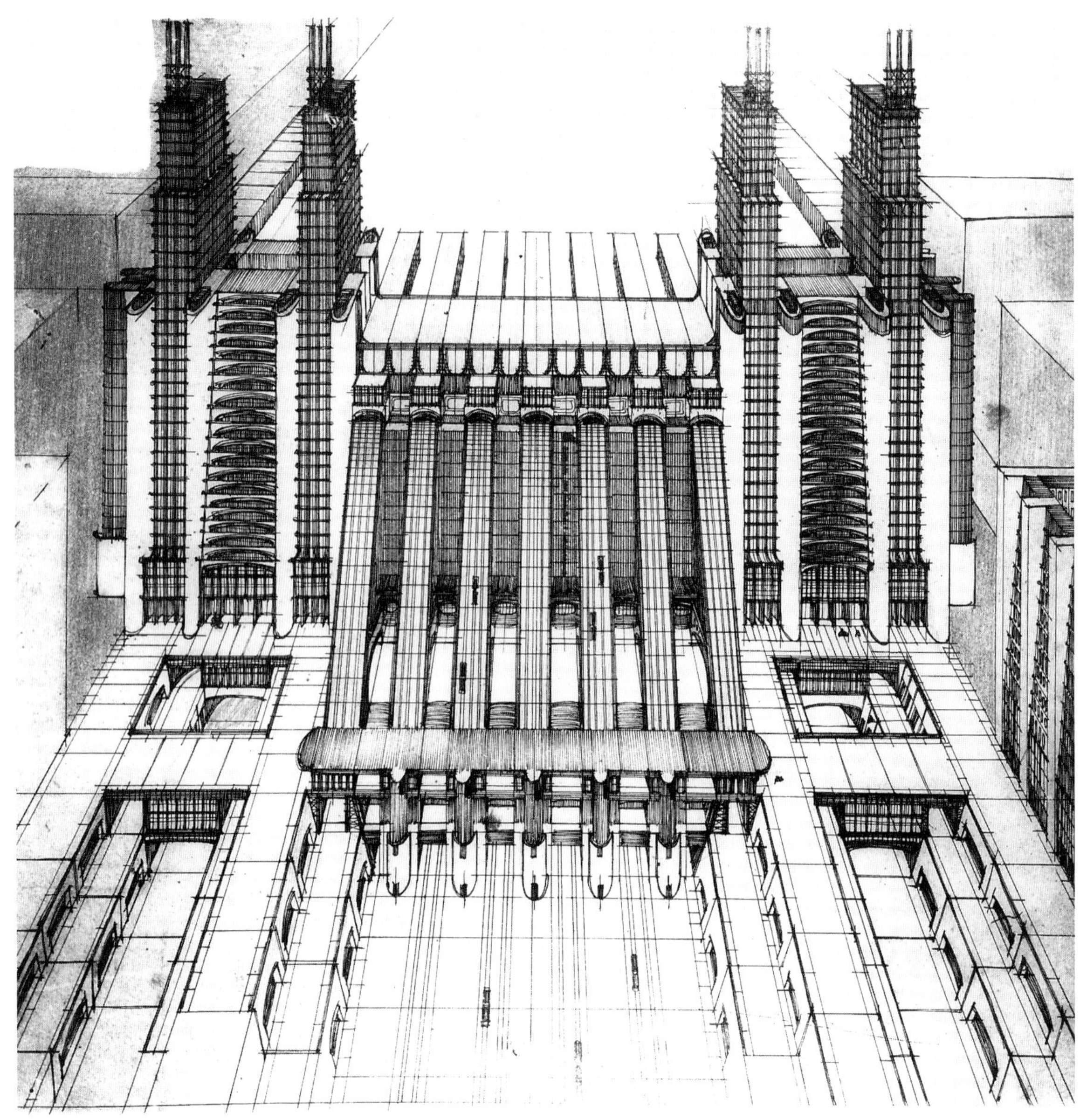

98. Antonio Sant'Elia. Station for airplanes and trains with funiculars and elevators on three street levels, 1914. Musei Civici, Como.

99. Antonio Sant'Elia. La Città Nuova, open-air street between setback apartment buildings, 1914. Collection of Paride Accetti, Milan.

100. Antonio Sant'Elia. La Città Nuova, 1914. Collection of Paride Accetti, Milan.

101. Antonio Sant'Elia. Setback high rise, 1914. Musei Civici, Como.

102. Antonio Sant'Elia. Setback high rise, 1914. Musei Civici, Como.

103. Antonio Sant'Elia. Monumental building. Signed and dated 1914. Whereabouts unknown (lost at the International Exposition in Brussels, 1958). (Photo: Courtesy of Musei Civici, Como)

The remarkable series of power plants constitutes one of the high points of Sant'Elia's oeuvre (plates 16–19). Power stations first appeared in his work in 1913, and Sant'Elia worked on them continuously after that. Probably no single event since unification had done as much for Italy—politically, economically, and psychologically—as the advent of electricity; it thus came to play an important role in the iconography of the visual arts and literature.[62] The enthusiasm of the futurists knew no bounds: "May the Kingdom of Electric Light finally come," they cried.[63] Boccioni had even painted a power plant in the background of his painting *Officine a Porta Romana* (1909).[64]

Sant'Elia had even more reason to be awed, coming as he did from Italy's lake region, where the nation's earliest hydroelectric complexes had been built. His native Como was surrounded by plants that were famous in his day, such as the Crespi plant, on the Adda (a tributary of Lake Como); the Edison, at Paderno (at the time Italy's largest power station); and those at Vizzola, Robbiate, and Castellanza.

Electricity was held in such high esteem that power stations were often given over to famous architects. Gaetano Moretti, Sant'Elia's teacher at Brera, was responsible for two celebrated plants that Sant'Elia undoubtedly had seen, Bolaffra and the neo-oriental Trezzo d'Adda (both built in 1905–1906). Because there was no architectural precedent for hydroelectric power stations, these buildings were among the most original in Italy and were greatly admired by the young.[65]

Initially, all enterprises of this sort were historicist. As vehement protests were raised against the new factories and power plants that were endangering the renowned beauty of the region, architects sought refuge in a romantic interpretation of industrial themes, disguising plants and factories as neo-Romanesque abbeys, medieval castles, and Renaissance villas.[66] These were carefully sited as if to stress the innocence of a landscape as yet unspoiled by industrialization. Not everything could be hidden, however, and the machinery was there for all to see, with its tubular, streamlined aesthetic. Sant'Elia retained the Romanticism inherent in these early power stations, including their relation to nature, while eschewing their historicism. At the same time he was to incorporate many of the traits of the existing industrial plants in his high-rise buildings and cityscapes.

Sant'Elia's hydroelectric plants form a striking contrast to his contemporaneous projects for the Città Nuova. Unlike his views of the modern metropolis, where everything is functional and machine-made, the power stations inspired him to greater heights of lyricism. Three of the power plants, executed slightly earlier than the Città Nuova, are dated February 25, March 15, and March 1 (plates 16,18,19, respectively). Whereas the sketches of the Città Nuova were strict drawing-board products achieved with the aid of ruler and compass, the *centrali elettriche* were designed freehand and done in loose, fluid lines and glowing color.[67] Sant'Elia used color as a landscape painter might, choosing a palette of greens, blues, mauves, and oranges drawn largely from the symbolist art of the day.

In the interest of poetic truth his perspective was slightly deformed: there was none of that perspectival clarity and rigor of the Città Nuova.[68] The smooth, sloping surfaces and colossal scale of the dams gave Sant'Elia the chance to work with the type of perspective most natural to him, the worm's-eye view.[69] In their towering monumentality, which dwarfs and awes the imaginary beholder, Sant'Elia's power stations bring to mind the beautiful dams envisioned by Hugh Ferriss many years later. Needless to say, no plans or sections were given. It was the overall image that was important: "In these cases the accent fell, therefore, not on the function of the building, but on its representation."[70]

Some of the power stations, interestingly, seem to be situated within a cityscape (plate 19). Italy's first power plant, Santa Radegonda, was in fact built in the center of Milan in 1883, but it was a modest structure. Sant'Elia's plants, by contrast are very close in scale and style to the illustrations of the Panama Canal by Joseph Pennel, a student of Whistler's.[71] Pennel's sketches, which became famous overnight, were republished in *The Studio* and *Emporium,* magazines that enjoyed a wide circulation in Italy. Before documentary newsreels or, much later, television became popular, there was a demand for the type of cinematic image that Pennel produced; he created dramatic and eye-catching illustrations, using all the tricks of the scenographer's trade. His heightened sense of drama, bold foreshortening, and the towering scale of his structures had enormous appeal for Sant'Elia, whose relative lack of academic schooling often made him more appreciative of magazine illustrations than of architectural projects. He was drawn to the most spectacular aspects of modern life, often bordering on science fiction and built to a scale out of all proportion with the urban environment.

With regard to perspective, profile, and color, Sant'Elia's power stations were an offshoot of his monumental buildings of 1912. The change from those moody nocturnes to the equally monumental power plants was no doubt influenced by his acquaintance with the futurists in the intervening years. But Sant'Elia did not rethink every aspect of his previous work, assigning a specific purpose to each part. He simply gave a new function to the old masses and added such modern trappings as high voltage wires, conduits, and elevators: "These projects are inevitably a throwback to 'objects' rather than 'processes': static, decorative entities, meaningless with regard to their buttresses, shorn of purpose and content."[72]

Sant'Elia was not a neophyte with regard to power plants. Both his training as a master builder and his brief stint as draftsman for the Villoresi Canal (later incorporated into Italy's largest electric industry, the Lombarda) must have given him some insights as to the functioning of a hydroelectric plant. But his reaction to these marvels of modern science and technology that were springing up daily around his native land was more like a joyous ode of rapture than an architectural transcription.[73] These power stations were Sant'Elia's equivalent of Marinetti's numerous paeans to modern power plants: "Through a network of metal cables the double power of Mediterranean and Adriatic ascends to the crests of the Apennines to concentrate in great cages of iron and crystal . . . enormous nerve centers in the mountainous spine of Italy. . . . Many millions of kilowatts are distributed, broadcast in fertilising abundance, but governed by switches under the fingers of the engineers. Engineers who pass their days in high-tension chambers where 100,000 volts shimmer between great bays of glass."[74]

In spite of Sant'Elia's obvious enthusiasm for the modern metropolis, a very different subtext runs through his power plants. It is difficult to overlook the fact that many of Sant'Elia's drawings reveal a hidden yearning for emotions that nature alone could provide. It was just this anxious and unconfessed relation to nature that was the mainstay of Einfühlung. True, one of the most salient features of the Città Nuova is the absolute absence of nature, and even in his hydroelectric plants, water itself is never visible. However, as nature began to disappear from the horizons of the city dwellers, it found its way, unbidden and unnoticed, into many works of art. The industrial city became, paradoxically, the last repository of Romanticism. Like the skyscrapers designed by Hugh Ferriss many years later, Sant'Elia's buildings take on the scale, the atmosphere, and all the attributes of the sublime.[75]

A vestigial Sturm und Drang still lingers in these power stations. The constant use of the worm's-eye view and the hidden naturalism of his color conspire to cast the beholder in a position not unlike that used by, say, Caspar David Friedrich: the human figure is overwhelmed by the greater forces of nature. One can perhaps be pardoned for seeing Sant'Elia as an architectural Friedrich of the industrial age and the power stations as tropes for the sublime. In these projects, which rise like sheer cliffs above the spectator, in a perpetual evasion of feasibility, there beats the heart of a modern Romantic. Sant'Elia was, in fact, a *vedutista* of the modern industrial world, looking for the past in the future.

THE CITTÀ NUOVA

The Città Nuova, the other group of sketches shown at Nuove Tendenze, represents the summa of Sant'Elia's work. Here one can already find the main characteristics of what would later become the International Style: the post-and-lintel tectonics, the thinness of the facade reduced to a membrane, the high degree of abstraction, and a total rejection of history in urbanism as well as architecture. Although its assessment by later historians, whether favorable or unfavorable, has tended to be clouded by political sectarianism, this remains an extraordinary and revolutionary work. In it Sant'Elia brought together all his previous experience as master builder, draftsman, and professional architect. The appearance of the Città Nuova in May 1914 comes as a surprise, because it differs significantly from the drawings exhibited two months earlier at the show of Lombard architecture. The latter, judging from the four examples known to us, are rough sketches tossed off in a day and jotted down freehand, with little or no detailing.

In the Città Nuova, however, Sant'Elia reaches a degree of precision and control over pen and ink unrivaled in his earlier work. The sketches are large—larger than anything he had done before. Subject matter is allowed to determine style: with few exceptions (fig. 95, plates 13,14), color and curves are abolished as concessions to the picturesque. All the other drawings of the series are in black and white, and the hard-edged, machinelike precision thus achieved helps underscore the idea of brisk efficiency of the modern metropolis. Although he had been a poor student of perspective at Brera, with the Città Nuova Sant'-Elia showed that he had mastered the craft magnificently. In these drawings he rarely forced the laws of perspective as he did in his earlier work, where he makes the third dimension recede too suddenly, as in theater design.

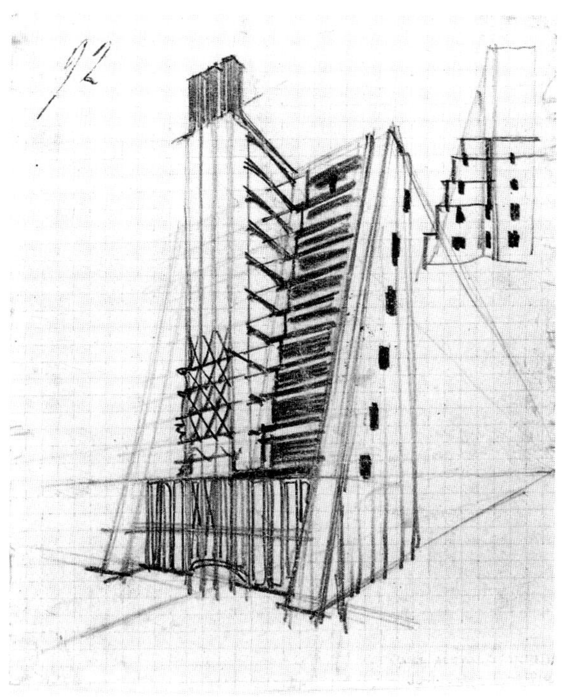

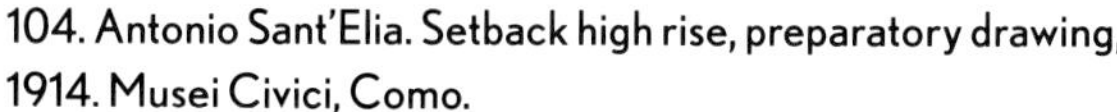

104. Antonio Sant'Elia. Setback high rise, preparatory drawing, 1914. Musei Civici, Como.

105. Antonio Sant'Elia. Setback high rise, preparatory drawing, 1914. Musei Civici, Como.

Some of the drawings are signed and have an elementary caption, which was unusual for Sant'Elia.[76] None of them is dated. In general Sant'Elia signed and dated only sketches that were the product of a day's work; these are the fruit of constant and meticulous reworking. The first known project of the Città Nuova is the lost skyscraper exhibited at the show of Lombard architecture (fig. 91). Probably executed toward the end of February, it does not yet reveal the ascetic rigor of the Città Nuova drawings. These last therefore seem to have been done between the end of March, when the Lombard exhibition closed, and May 20, when Nuove Tendenze opened. The praise Sant'Elia received for his entries in the first show may help explain the increasing self-confidence one finds in his work thereafter.

Sant'Elia lavished great care on the drawings of the Città Nuova. For almost each of the final projects, a series of preparatory sketches have come down to us, showing every stage of the process (figs. 101,104,105). The finished product rarely departed from the thumbnail sketch, or did so only in minor details. Once the definitive form of a project was reached, usually in soft pencil, Sant'Elia went over the lines using ink, ruler, and tracing paper, so that the slight variations produced by freehand were eliminated.[77] The chisel-edge exactness of these drawings has none of that textured look of the painterly works in color. In any case, the drawing-board style of the Città Nuova appeared rather abruptly in Sant'-Elia's work and disappeared just as suddenly, after Nuove Tendenze closed its doors.

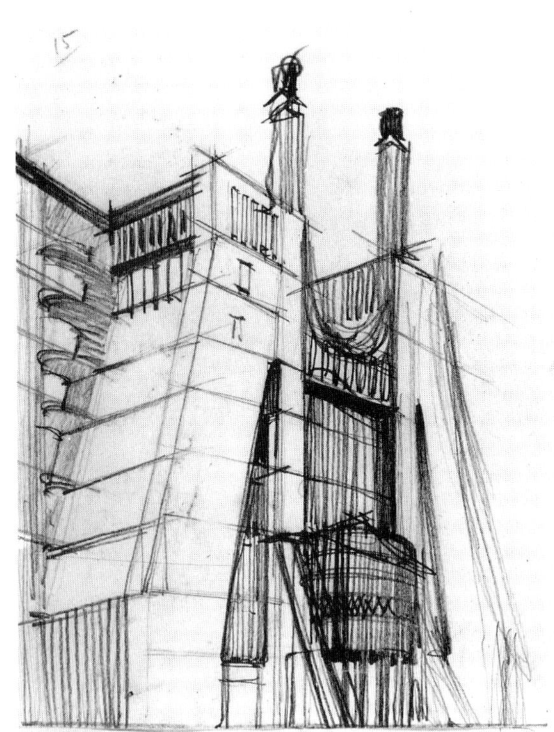

106. Antonio Sant'Elia. Setbacks placed back-to-back, forming an interior street, 1914. Musei Civici, Como.

The basic unit of Sant'Elia's New City is the "Casa a Gradinata," or, as it was originally called in the Nuove Tendenze catalogue, the "Casa Nuova,"[78] the setback high-rise building with a separate tower to house the elevators (figs. 101,102). The latter is connected to the main part of the building by means of bridges that increase in span from the ground upward. There are variations of this theme; sometimes it appears back-to-back with another identical building to which it is connected by parabolic arches in reinforced concrete so that one building abuts another (figs. 99,106,107). The space between the two symmetrically placed buildings is transformed into an interior street spanned by arches. Presumably shops and offices are located within, as in Mengoni's famous Galleria Vittorio Emanuele, in Milan.[79] Inner streets were not new, of course. They had already been used extensively in late nineteenth-century ferrovitreous architecture and were extremely popular in Italy. From the arches are hung the side facades—vast sheets of iron and glass with deep overhangs above the entrance. One of the sketches of the New City, known only through old photographs, shows a section and a small perspective of the interior galleria (fig. 108).

In a more economical version, the same buildings appear face-to-face, and the elevator shaft is situated in between (fig. 99). Through each story runs a corridor, open on one side and extending the length of the facade. Passageways connect these corridors to the service shaft in the center. In this case an open-air pedestrian street is formed below. Sant'Elia thus provides for both horizontal and vertical circulation within his buildings. These closed or open-air corridors are the only streets to be found within the Città Nuova. Outside the buildings, the street as such has ceased to exist.

One wonders if the tradition of socialist utopias had anything to do with the Città Nuova. A strong literary precedent for Sant'Elia's setbacks can be found, albeit in a decidedly antiurban setting, in Charles Fourier's description of the "rues-galeries" of his phalanstery: "The gallery-street . . . is situated on the second floor. It cannot be adapted to the ground floor, which must be pierced at several points by arches for motor vehicles. . . . The gallery-streets of a Phalanx cannot be lit from both sides; each adheres to one of the main buildings; all these buildings have a double row of rooms, one row being lit by the part facing the countryside, and the other by the gallery-street."[80] Whether Sant'Elia knew of Fourier's description—so different from the canonic illustrations of the phalanstery—is a matter of conjecture, but the parallels are striking and should give one pause, especially in view of his affiliation with the Socialist Party at the time. The Città Nuova exudes the same millenarian fervor and the same belief in the existence of an urban model that would solve all social contradictions.

The pyramidal profiles of the stepped-back buildings anticipate the shape of the American ziggurat skyscraper. Each apartment receives light and air, all the more so because the streets of the Città Nuova are not narrow, as in New York, but are stretched out

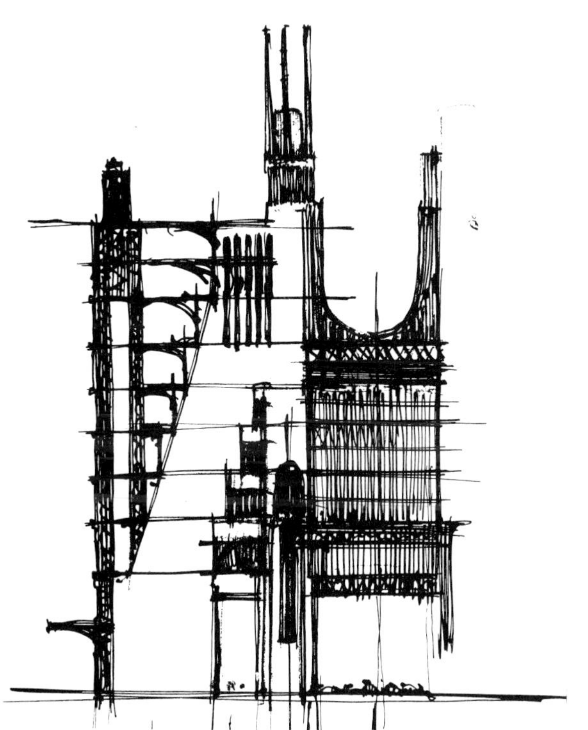

107. Antonio Sant'Elia. Setback, section, 1914. Collection of Kenneth Walker, New York.

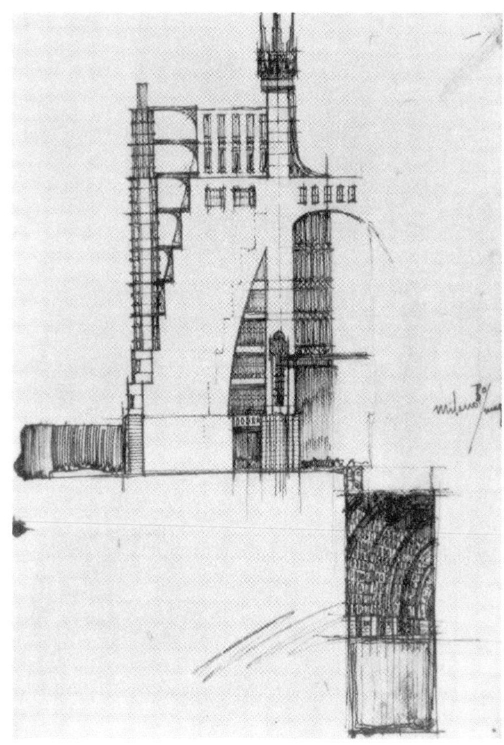

108. Antonio Sant'Elia. Setback, section, and perspective of galleria. Dated May 30, Milan. Whereabouts unknown (lost at the International Exposition in Brussels, 1958). (Photo: Collection of the author)

like broad valleys between the high-rise buildings on either side. This canyonlike image is encapsulated in smaller scale inside Sant'Elia's buildings, where an interior street is flanked on either side by internal facades ten to fifteen stories high and spanned by catwalks and elevated pedestrian streets (fig. 99).

Sant'Elia offered an ingenious solution to the elevator problem: he was possibly the first to house elevators in a separate structure and to treat them as "autonomous channels of vertical traffic."[81] Reyner Banham correctly points out that Sant'Elia may have been influenced by the elevators used on the shores of Lake Como to carry passengers from the landing stages below to the chalets on the mountain tops.[82] Since the end of the century Como's famous lake region had been setting in place a new infrastructure to accommodate a burgeoning tourism industry. The erection of hotels and villas high in the mountains entailed a complex communications network that transformed the traditional landscape: elevators and funiculars were constructed to link travelers with cars, trains, and ferries below. Sant'Elia's own little Villa Elisi was connected to Como by a funicular, which had popularized a new way of viewing the landscape—from above.[83] One is reminded of Marinetti's *Technical Manifesto of Futurist Literature* (1912): "Looking at objects from a new point of view, no longer from in front or behind, but from above—that is to say, foreshortened—I was able to break the old logical shackles of the plumb-lines of the old understanding."[84]

There were also precedents in industrial architecture, mainly in factories and warehouses, which Sant'Elia was bound to have seen in the outskirts of Milan.[85] See-through elevator shafts (whether of iron or concrete) located outside buildings were not unknown in a city that had pioneered the manufacture of elevators in Italy.[86] From buildings like these Sant'Elia learned to articulate structure in a revolutionary way (fig. 91): only in industrial architecture were steel or iron girders exposed on the exterior.

Sant'Elia introduced another innovative feature in the setback high rises: his distinctive roofs, which are flat and relatively small because the buildings taper toward the top. They have become terraces to be used for various purposes: lighthouses, radio-transmitting equipment, or illuminated advertisements (fig. 102). As Banham remarked, Sant'Elia was breaking new ground by making the advertisement an integral part of the design of the building.[87] The co-option of commercial propaganda techniques for artistic purposes was, of course, a well-known strategy of the futurists.[88]

Unlike Boccioni and Marinetti, who often spoke of the beauty of steel in their manifestos, Sant'Elia never wavered from his appreciation of iron, advocating its use in conjunction with prestressed concrete, even for buildings of dizzying heights.[89] Although Italy was notoriously deficient in the production of steel, Sant'Elia's stubborn attachment to iron is an example of his anachronistic and Romantic approach to modern technology, an approach that betrays his secessionist roots.[90] Iron, of course, was a great favorite with Milan's Liberty architects, and Sant'Elia himself used it prodigally in his early projects. During the competition for Milan's new train station he had learned to explore its structural qualities, using it in conjunction with glass so as to permit larger spans. After that he began to favor iron for its structural rather than decorative properties, though the latter never disappeared entirely from his work. He seems not to have noticed that it was not used structurally except at small scale.

Concrete was a different case. Since the end of the nineteenth century, prestressed concrete had been replacing steel in the building industry because it permitted a free plan unencumbered by vertical supports. But it was customarily hidden from view, as in Sommaruga's Palazzo Castiglioni, where the ferroconcrete Hennebique system had been used and then covered over with caryatids, leaves, and flowers of "artificial stone" (cement). Curiously enough, the only reference to concrete in previous futurist manifestos was a negative one: "Let's call a halt to the speculative architecture of the reinforced-concrete contractors."[91] As Wolfgang Pehnt has observed, the futurists never accepted architecture as the reflection of function and technique alone but sought, in Sant'Elia's words, to "project the world of the spirit into the world of things."[92]

As an architect, Sant'Elia realized that concrete was the key to the future. Nevertheless, he has occasionally been faulted for an incomplete understanding of the properties of concrete and their implications for architecture. The persistence of massive flying buttresses in Sant'Elia's work shows that he considered concrete a stylistic element rather than a structural fact. In other words, he had not grasped the fundamental difference between cement and concrete. Likewise, he has often been criticized for an imperfect understanding of the skeleton frame: his walls are often articulated in a rigid way, as if they were load-bearing.[93]

Setbacks, the pièce de résistance of the Città Nuova, first appeared tentatively in Sant'-Elia's work early in 1914 (fig. 91). They are probably indebted to the discussions on stepped-back skyscrapers that took place in the United States during the 1890s.[94] But the main source was undoubtedly the work of the French architect Henri Sauvage (1873–1932) and his partner, Charles Sarazin, who designed a series of stepped-back buildings for workers as early as 1909, if not before.[95] Not until 1912 did they have the opportunity to use these ideas in the celebrated apartments on Rue Vavin, in Paris (fig. 109). First exhibited at the Salon d'Automne in 1913, this building was apparently not published until March 1914, just before the Nuove Tendenze show.[96] Soon after, they began a more complex stepped-back apartment building on Rue des Amiraux, the completion of which was delayed until 1922 because of the war. Since they also used stepped-back buildings back-to-back, large spaces with zenithal lighting are created inside, which are set aside for public use.[97] Here a certain debt to Sant'Elia's Città Nuova seems entirely plausible. Certainly these later stepped-back buildings gain in visual and structural clarity: the service shafts are no longer divided into segments that bind three or four stories together but shoot upward from the ground as they do in Sant'Elia's designs.

Sant'Elia's acquaintance with the earlier work of Sauvage has been documented. In conversation with Jörn-Peter Schmidt-Thomsen, Dudreville remembered that one evening at a café in Milan, Sant'Elia had enthusiastically shown him an illustration of a French setback taken from an Italian periodical.[98] Although Dudreville could no longer recall the title of the periodical in question, Sant'Elia's debt to Sauvage is borne out by a section that undoubtedly represents the apartments on Rue Vavin (fig. 110).[99] The receding stages form duplexes, as in photographs of the actual flats, while the abbreviated section to the left is based on the drawing published in *L'Illustration*. Sant'Elia rarely concerned himself with sections, but in this case he was probably encouraged to work out the details on his own, prompted by the unusual example of Rue Vavin.[100]

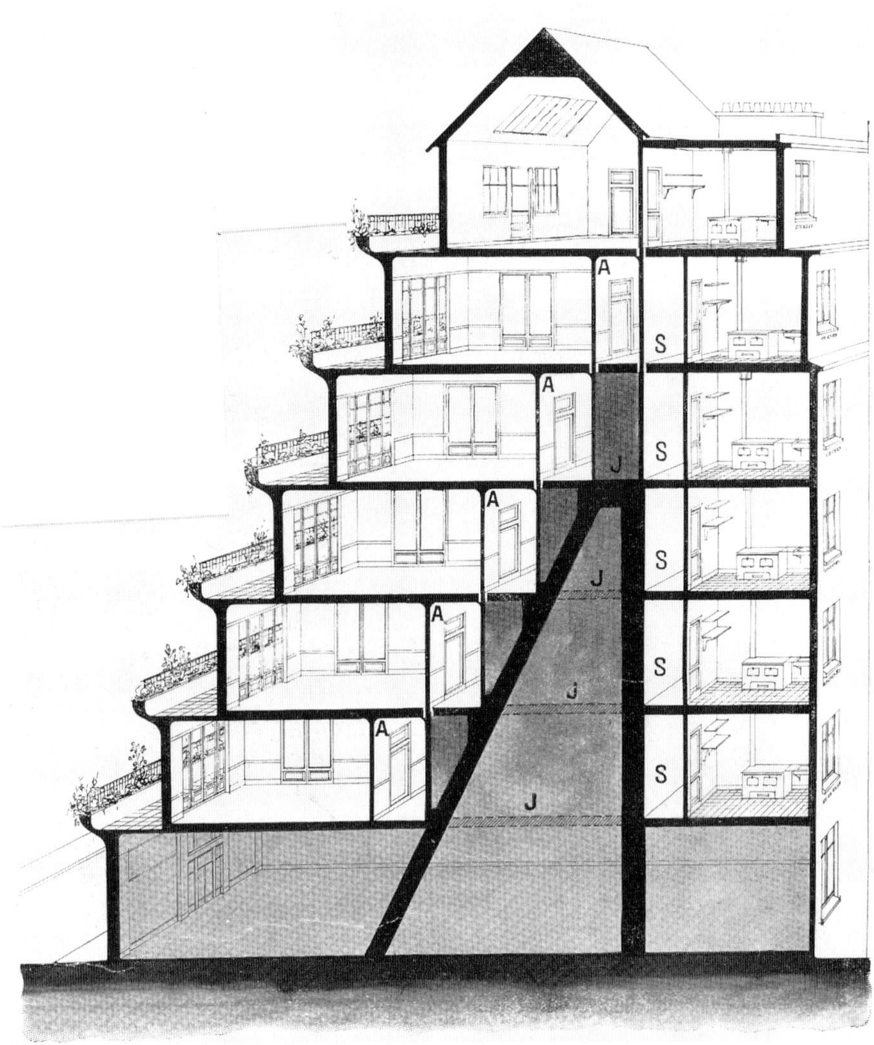

109. Henri Sauvage and Charles Sarazin. Maison à gradins,
1913–1914. *L'Illustration*, March 21, 1914.

Also in 1913, *Der Architekt* published another setback design, a monumental project
by Adolf Loos for a warehouse in Alexandria.[101] The first four or five stories are articulated
by a giant Ionic order, and the receding stages begin only beyond the capitals. However, the
more down-to-earth projects by Sauvage are closer to those of Sant'Elia than is the ponderous monumentality of Adolf Loos. In fact, it is Loos who may owe a debt to Sant'Elia
(via Sauvage) in his designs of 1923, where the setbacks appear back-to-back.

The most famous project of the Città Nuova shows different types of stepped-back
buildings combined into a complex superstructure that spreads out its tentacles to encom-

pass the many-layered urban tissue: streets for pedestrians, high- and low-speed traffic lanes, overpasses, and bridges (fig. 96). It is a magnificent paean to the modern metropolis. The attention paid to metropolitan traffic and circulation is the most remarkable and innovative feature of the Città Nuova. Sant'Elia clearly focused on this point with an eye to the future: at the time, Milan was still served mainly by horse-drawn vehicles, and automobiles were scarce and slow (figs. 111,112). Iron catwalks, overpasses, and viaducts intersect the buildings, so that there is no separation between city and infrastructure: two systems, habitation and circulation, are perfectly integrated.

In his attempt to accommodate the greatest number of vehicles in as little space as possible, Sant'Elia consigned traffic to three superimposed layers, as explained in the caption published in the *Manifesto of Futurist Architecture:* there are overpasses for pedestrians, roads for automobiles, and tracks for tramways. Traffic lanes are thus typologically differentiated according to vehicle and speed.[102] Furthermore, pedestrian and vehicular traffic are kept to carefully circumscribed areas; there is none of the intermingling of individual and machine that occurs in modern cities. The stratification of urban soil into different planes of reference for automobiles and pedestrians was introduced by several planners and illustrators in the beginning of the century.[103]

Given the basic configuration of Sant'Elia's city—an artificial canyon flanked by

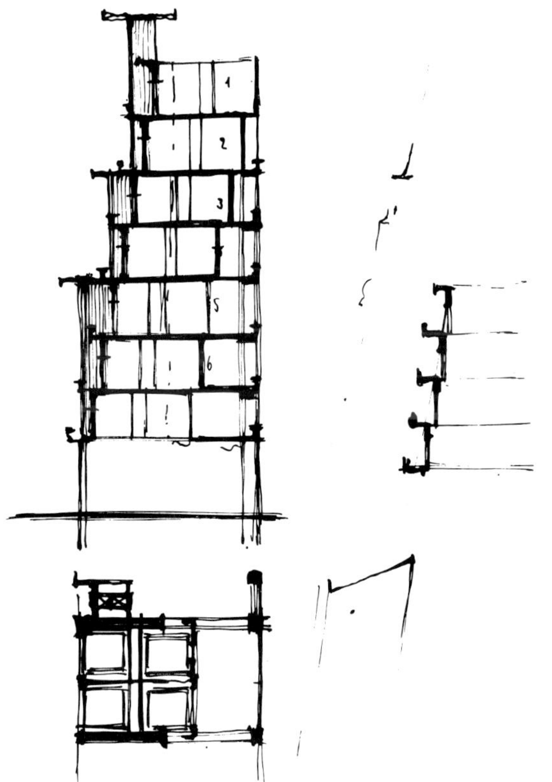

110. Antonio Sant'Elia. Setback, section, 1914. Musei Civici, Como.

111. Milan at the turn of the century: Corso Vittorio Emanuele. (Photo: Courtesy of the Archivio Fotografico Castello Sforzesco, Milan)

112. A 1914 Fiat, the embodiment of speed at that time. (Photo: Courtesy of the Archivio Fotografico Castello Sforzesco, Milan)

artificial mountains—bridges and overpasses were the only means of getting from one side to the other. As highways and traffic lanes grew in complexity, they came to play an increasingly important role, both in the Città Nuova and the power stations. Bridges, of course, had figured prominently in the iconography of futurism since the first manifesto (1909): "We shall sing of . . . bridges bestriding rivers like giant gymnasts," Marinetti had exclaimed.[104] But they had to be modern. Nothing so irritated the futurists as the picturesque little hunchback bridges of Venice: "Let us raise to the skies the impressive geometry of metal bridges and of factories crowned with smoke in order to abolish the cascading curves of the old architecture."[105]

Otto Wagner's projects for Vienna, built and unbuilt, were important precedents for Sant'Elia. From Wagner's iron bridges, shouldered by powerful masonry pylons, Sant'Elia learned how to exploit the contrast between stone and iron, between the monolithic masonry and the criss-crossed girders that served to lighten the load visually as well as structurally. In this particular case, as Siegfried Giedion pointed out, Sant'Elia borrowed heavily from Wagner's project for the Ferdinandsbrücke (1905), where street, bridge, and railway are brought together in a multistoried structure (fig. 113).[106] Once more we see Sant'Elia assimilating the theories of Gottfried Semper—whose work he probably ignored—

through the agency of Otto Wagner's projects. It was Semper, as Wagner well knew, who insisted on a clear differentiation between load and support and who advocated the use of stone piers for the vertical supports and of iron girders (which were visually "lighter") for the horizontal ones.[107]

Nevertheless, Sant'Elia's bridges are never purely utilitarian: he made use of them at the slightest provocation, out of the sheer pleasure of designing these slender, springy structures stretched taut across his thoroughfares. Often redundant, their slow, elastic curve served as a foil to the gridlike geometry of his skyscrapers.[108] In this Sant'Elia was closer to the futurists than to Wagner, who used them sparingly, given their cost and the technical difficulties they entailed (considerations that never seem to have bothered Sant'Elia). But Wagner's influence was paramount: many of his Stadtbahn stations for Vienna are situated on the second or third story of the building, permitting traffic to flow undisturbed below, like the stations at Alser Strasse or Währingerstrasse, both of the late 1890s.[109]

But there was also a Milanese precedent for this design, the project for the colossal Albergo Tre Croci, which Giuseppe Sommaruga was erecting during those very years in nearby Varese (fig. 114). This dramatic building (1908–1911) has been rightly hailed as Sommaruga's most futurist work.[110] Perched on the top of a steep mountain that dominated the surroundings, the hotel was linked to the valley below by means of a cable car and a road for automobiles that cut right through the building. The dynamic movement

113. Otto Wagner. Project for the Ferdinandsbrücke, Vienna, 1905. Historisches Museum der Stadt Wien.

114. Giuseppe Sommaruga. Final project for the Albergo Tre Croci, Varese, 1908–1911. (Photo: Collection of the author)

with which it turns on its axis to span the approach road, and the connection to the valley by means of the funicular, bear more than a passing resemblance to Sant'Elia's project. As Nicoletti remarked, "Sommaruga probably offered something more to the young Sant'Elia: his conception of architecture as an egocentric, exclusive, and all-encompassing event."[111]

Sant'Elia's attitude toward technology was ambivalent, as his statuary shows.[112] He usually liked to embellish the definitive versions of his works with some neomedieval extravaganza—usually a knight on horseback. It is characteristic of his mythical grasp of modern life that there should be three such horse-and-rider groups, much stylized, and one motorized vehicle in this well-known drawing of the Città Nuova (fig. 96). Boccioni likewise preferred horses to automobiles in his paintings—although in his work they appear as the correlative of energy, dynamism, and the vital drive behind all living things.[113] Those of Sant'Elia are static, heavy, and monumental, an anachronistic survival from a previous phase of his intellectual development that has been allowed to persist out of season, as it were.

On the upper level, a lone inhabitant, streamlined to near abstraction like all Sant'-Elia's figures, walks about—one of the few denizens in the entire series. The absence of human figures in the Città Nuova denotes not so much the loneliness of the urban dweller as the difficulty of judging proportions, that is, the physical relationship between the individual and the building. Scale is always ambiguous in Sant'Elia's work.

Indeed in the New City, scale itself precluded details and small dimensions altogether, and the human figure was one of the first casualties. Sant'Elia took great delight in designing the elegant, fashionably dressed men and women that people all his other work. But when dealing with the modern metropolis he, like other futurists, was led to efface the individual from his drawings.[114] The modern city—as opposed to the capitals of the nineteenth century—swallowed up the individual in its immensity. There was no place in the futurist megalopolis for Baudelaire's *flâneur* and his inseparable counterpart, the boulevard. Even crowds vanished, as scale and modern transportation contributed to the disappearance of the pedestrian.[115]

A comparison of the preparatory sketches and the final drawings shows that the former were more spontaneous, less gratuitous (figs. 115,116). There is a greater congruence between the structural forces at play and the representation of those forces on the facade. That the walls are not load-bearing is made clear by the long mullions dividing the glass longitudinally, thereby reducing the facade to a mere partition. In the final rendering the skeletal construction of the building is obvious, but the new function of the facade is less clear (fig. 96).

Another glimpse of the Città Nuova, published in the *Manifesto of Futurist Architecture* in 1914, shows setbacks overlooking a broad urban valley made up of four superimposed road levels (fig. 100). In the dematerialization of the envelope and the crystal-like clarity of the glass shell, the architecture brings to mind the work of Mies van der Rohe. Although pedestrians are able to reach the lower strata reserved for automobiles by means of elevators, they are usually consigned to the upper levels, where malls and *gallerie* (interior streets) are laid out for their use. Like Sauvage before him, Sant'Elia has turned his back on the *rue-corridor,* that is, the street as container.[116] Others had abolished it before, but only in connection with garden cities or utopias—not in urban centers with high-rise buildings.[117] In this Sant'Elia differed from the early futurists, who celebrated the street and its main inhabitant, the crowd.

Piazzas, like streets, had always been treated as closed spaces in the past. According to time-honored custom, city squares in Italy were in fact *salotti pubblici,* in the manner so admired by Camillo Sitte, and marked a caesura in the urban tissue. In the Città Nuova there are no such stops: the fast tempo of the metropolis is never-ending. In spite of the broad circulation deck in the upper level, this is not a city for pedestrians, or even crowds, and one can ill conceive stopping somewhere to rest or even taking a walk.

As the buildings grow in height, so the many-layered streets grow in depth: "The street . . . will no longer stretch out like a doormat at ground level but will plunge into the earth by means of several stories."[118] What is surprising about this project is the contrast between the vast scale of the circulation routes and the feeble density implied by the buildings. The various road levels imply a much higher demographic density than is actually the case, since the buildings rarely reach beyond fourteen or fifteen stories. This hypertrophy of transportation facilities is what Ragghianti termed Sant'Elia's obsession with circulation, which expresses itself "vertically, horizontally and at times even obliquely and elliptically. Traffic channels penetrate everywhere, and are the only structures that have been determined. The rest (the interior and the functions and divisions of the buildings, the articulation of the residential spaces and of the services, etc.) remains wholly undefined. . . . What

115. Antonio Sant'Elia. La Città Nuova, preparatory
study, 1914. Musei Civici, Como.

116. Antonio Sant'Elia. La Città Nuova, preparatory study,
1914. Musei Civici, Como.

else does the Città Nuova do other than circulate?"[119] And how, one might ask, does this impressive infrastructure affect the concept of urban dwelling? As Sanford Kwinter remarks, "The blatant interference of forms, violently splitting and passing through one another, could logically be translated internally it seems only by introducing the most vertiginous disjunctions and intermittence to their lived space."[120]

Equally famous is the design of a colossal station for trains and airplanes, with funiculars and elevators linking the three different street levels (fig. 98). It too was published in the *Manifesto of Futurist Architecture.* Proportions are truly pharaonic: for Sant'Elia modernity coincided with monumentality. As the perspective drawing of this station makes clear (plate 13), Sant'Elia incorporated into his design various features from his preparatory sketches for Milan's train station, such as the vast, sloping facade, the two-pronged profile of the main building, and the broad, transversal *galleria* that runs breadthways under the building. But there is a new emphasis on structural clarity. The facade is particularly striking, rushing downward like a glass waterfall, interrupted only by the moving strips of the conveyor belts.

Although only two years had passed since the competition for the Milan train station, Sant'Elia has come a long way under the tutelary influence of futurism. In the earlier drawing (plate 13), the symbolist roots of his work are evident in the low, dark entrance to the cavernous lobby. Rituals and ceremonies are incumbent in such a station: there, too, parting was such sweet sorrow. One is reminded of Boccioni's celebrated triptych *The Farewells,* which attempts to capture the various emotions of those who leave by train and those who stay behind. Here, on the other hand, the accent is on the technological machinery that both revolutionized and trivialized travel. As Marinetti once said, "We collaborate with Technology in order to destroy the old poetry of distance and of savage loneliness, the exquisite nostalgia of departures that we replace with the tragic lyricism of ubiquity and omnipresent speed."[121]

The nerve center of this vast nexus of communications systems is a cyclopean building overlooking a series of interlocking highways and railway tracks. It reflects, Giedion once remarked, "the futuristic delight in intersecting streams of movement."[122] Elevators and funiculars connect the various strata and carry the passengers from the lower to the upper decks. On the roof an airstrip stretches out, hemmed in by two pairs of towers. On either side of the broad highway, stepped-back buildings tower above the deep urban canyon.

It is possible that the numerous transportation systems in this drawing, all moving simultaneously in different directions, were also meant to evoke the multifarious cacophony of city sounds. Urban noise, after all, played an important role in futurism: "We cross a great modern capital with our ears more attentive than our eyes," wrote Luigi Russolo.[123] One month before the opening of the Nuove Tendenze, Russolo presented three of his notorious pieces at the Teatro Dal Verme in Milan, two of which were called, significantly, *Awakening of a City* and *Convention of Automobiles and Airplanes.* It is highly probable that Sant'Elia was present at Russolo's concert, since it included the active collaboration of their common friend, Leonardo Dudreville.

Like most of Sant'Elia's projects, the buildings of the Città Nuova and the power stations are both pyramidal. His syntax is singularly repetitive. Whatever the building type, the basic outlines and structural elements are virtually interchangeable: "Sant'Elia remains a prey to certain volumetric traits, to a predetermined formal idiom that variously associates pylons, pilasters, terraces with ramps or stairways, towers for the elevators."[124] At times, the morphology for one building can be found in the preparatory sketches for another building with an entirely different purpose.[125] In the case of the Città Nuova station, the basic form was borrowed from a power station at Paderno d'Adda, in his native Lombardy (fig. 117). Although the sloping facades had been used before, notably in his projects for train stations, the diagonal movement of the seven parallel conveyor belts was suggested to him by the conduits of the hydroelectric plants.

Sant'Elia exploits the visual impact of vehicular movement and makes it an integral part of his architecture. Because the architecture and the circulatory channels are so enmeshed that they cannot be separated, the architectural facades themselves "move" as trains cut through the station, elevators swarm up the glass shafts, and funiculars hoist passenger cabins across the diagonal slant of the facade, introducing a multiplicity of points of view. As Paolo Portoghesi astutely notes, Sant'Elia is interested not so much in a kinetic architecture as he is in making use of the predictable flow of vehicles in order to bring a certain animation to his architecture: "The multi-level city is less a rational solution to

117. Guido Semenza. Power station at Paderno d'Adda, plan, 1898. (Photo: Collection of the author)

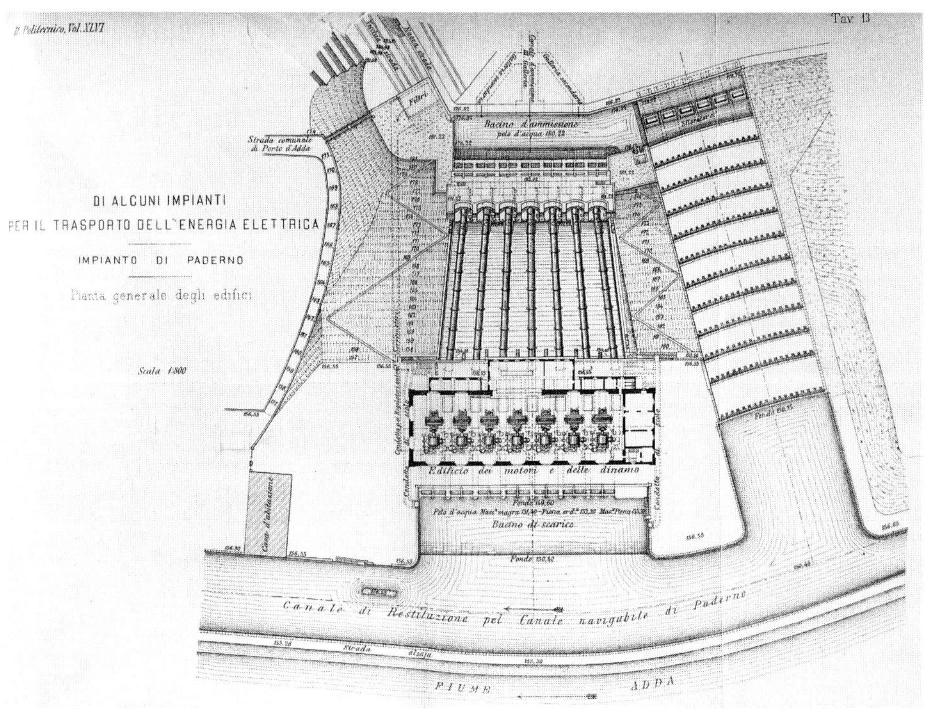

functional problems than the contemplation of a complex machinery in which traffic assumes a role analogous to that of water in a fountain."[126]

Ironically, despite the attention given to circulation, vehicles themselves are seldom shown in the Città Nuova. For all Sant'Elia's talk about speed, there is not a single automobile in his work. Trams and trains appear in this project, but they are seen from above and are so reduced in size as to appear like flat black rectangles. They are wholly deprived of the dynamism with which Sant'Elia's architecture is imbued. His love of machines and technology was veined with a certain distrust. Futurists were generally reluctant to commit to paint and canvas the monsters of steel and smoke that played such a seminal role in their written work. It was easy enough to evoke an automobile in poetry, where one could dwell upon its attributes—strength, speed, dynamism—but showing it figuratively was another matter altogether. With no precedent in art, the beauty that Marinetti had once called superior to that of the *Victory of Samothrace* eluded their grasp.

This resistance was, perhaps, inevitable, since speed dissolves form into a cometlike image. The best renderings of automobiles by the futurists were those that rejected the static appearance of the vehicle and chose to dwell instead on the impression of velocity, such as Balla's numerous studies of cars or Russolo's famous *Dynamism of an Automobile.*[127] In some of his preparatory sketches Sant'Elia manages to convey the idea of speed by means of lines of force, even though the vehicles themselves are invisible. But he loses this impression of immediacy when he works with ruler and compass. Just as a racing horse has twenty legs rather than four, according to Boccioni's celebrated *Technical Manifesto of Futurist Painting,* so too a speeding car can be caught only fleetingly by the shutter of the eye, by means of the lines it leaves behind.

Airplanes make their first appearance within Sant'Elia's oeuvre in these studies. The purpose of the airstrip is made unambiguously clear by the caption that Sant'Elia inscribed (and misspelled) just beneath the title: "Station for airplanes and trains."[128] Even in the preparatory sketches, awkward, cross-shaped marks could be seen on the upper deck that serves as an airstrip (figs. 118,119). In the perspective, an equally maladroit, birdlike machine hovers overhead (plate 13). As with the trams and funiculars of the elevation, Sant'Elia was not capable of suggesting the idea of flight, let alone of speed, and the airplane appears as if stuck to the sky.

Flight had been an important staple of futurist iconography ever since the first programmatic manifesto of 1909, in which Marinetti spoke of "the gliding flight of airplanes." Boccioni had reproduced one, with mixed success, in an early prefuturist drawing of 1907 ("Beata Solitudo–Sola Beatitudo").[129] Paolo Buzzi's volume of poetry *Aeroplani, canti alati* had appeared in 1909; five years later Marinetti's *Monoplano del Papa* was published.[130] References to aviation were legion in the work of the futurists, for whom the airborne pilot was a new Icarus, the embodiment of their heroic, vitalist aspirations in the modern world. Yet airplanes were also part of the industrial horizon of Sant'Elia's everyday life, particularly in his native province, where the Caproni corporation manufactured aircraft.

Sant'Elia's mechanized vision of the new human environment is also greatly influenced by the utopian arcadias sung by Marinetti and Boccioni. In the early days, the futurists vented their iconoclastic wrath primarily against art and architecture, that is, against history: "Destroy," shouted Marinetti in the first founding manifesto, "destroy without pity the venerated cities!"[131] With time, the target of their hostility shifted from culture to nature. Hatred of nature was in part a reaction to the crepuscular atmosphere and contemplative attitude toward landscape typical of Italy's decadent writers, such as D'Annunzio. This shift is especially evident in Boccioni's book *Pittura scultura futuriste (dinamismo plastico),* published shortly before the Nuove Tendenze exhibition. And indeed, Sant'Elia's metropolis shares many analogies with Boccioni's evocation of the new, mechanized environment, in particular with the chapter entitled "Against Landscape and Old-Fashioned Aesthetics." "We futurists," wrote Boccioni, "detest the countryside, the peace of the woods, the murmur of the brook."[132] In lieu of the old, familiar, pastoral landmarks, Boccioni proposed an entirely industrialized scenario as the ideal setting for modern life: "Landscape is

118. Antonio Sant'Elia. Station for airplanes and trains, 1914. Musei Civici, Como.

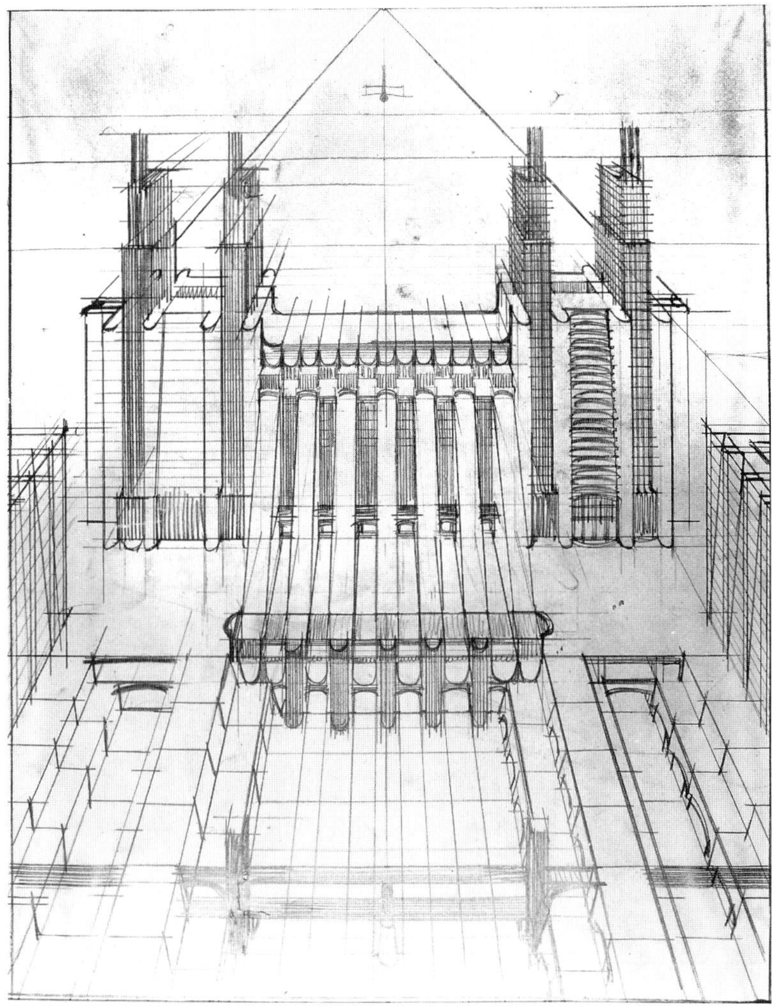

119. Antonio Sant'Elia. Station for airplanes and trains, preparatory sketch, 1914. Musei Civici, Como.

possible everywhere: in the marbles of palaces, the smooth cement of houses, the asphalt of highways, the long corridors of hotels with their mysterious numbered doors where soft rugs spread their tracks; in the white enameled rooms of the clinics, in the methodical hum of busy machines . . ."[133]

In time, the futurists began to mechanize the human being as well. In a manifesto addressed to performers of futurist plays, Marinetti instructed the performers to dehumanize the voice and the face completely, to make use of geometric gestures and to neutralize and petrify the voice.[134] Human flesh itself, he added elsewhere, "forgetting the burgeoning irregularity of trees, seeks to resemble the steel that surrounds it."[135]

The genesis of these projects is extremely complex, and numerous sources have been suggested. Alberto Sartoris pointed out many years ago that there was a "patent parallelism" between Sant'Elia's multilevel Città Nuova and Leonardo da Vinci's city sketches of Codex B (circa 1490).[136] Leonardo produced two different models: one for a fluvial city, where transportation is effected by means of boats, the porticoed streets above being reserved for pedestrians; and another with two superimposed circulation networks, a higher level for "gentil omini," and a lower one for transportation, services, and plebeians.[137] Sant'Elia may have heard of these works at Brera, particularly since Leonardo clearly states that the river of the fluvial city is the Ticino, which flows near Milan.[138] But Leonardo's farsighted ideas of the fifteenth century had little to offer Sant'Elia in terms of modern needs and technology.

Eugène Hénard's proposals for Paris (ca. 1910), another significant precedent, may also have been known to Sant'Elia.[139] But Hénard's superimposed streets were far removed from the requirements of modernity and speed that Sant'Elia saw as characteristic of the modern metropolis. More interesting were Charles Lamb's designs for a many-layered city (1908), where vehicular traffic was relegated to the lower levels, while pedestrians were consigned to elevated streets.[140] Immensely successful, Lamb's designs reappeared, unacknowledged, in *King's Dream of New York,* also of 1908, rendered by Harry Petit for the publisher Moses King, with its catwalks flung hundreds of feet above street level (fig.

120. Cover of *King's Dream of New York,* by Harry M. Petit, 1908. (Photo: Courtesy of Yale Slides and Photographs Collection)

121. Antonio Sant'Elia. La Città Nuova, preparatory study, 1914. Musei Civici, Como.

122. Reed, Stem, Warren, and Wetmore. Grand Central Station, section, 1912. *L'Illustrazione Italiana*, February 1, 1913.

120).[141] One drawing by Sant'Elia seems to imply knowledge of *King's Dream of New York* (fig. 121).

Although American publications featuring designs such as Lamb's were easily available in Milan, the idea of superimposed traffic networks was driven home more forcefully in 1913, when the influential Milanese magazine *L'Illustrazione Italiana* published a cutaway section of New York's Grand Central Station (fig. 122) by Reed, Stem, Warren and Wetmore.[142] The inauguration of Grand Central Station attracted worldwide attention owing to the masterful solution given to such intricate problems. The section, which shows a complex assemblage of train tracks, pedestrian ramps, and elevated streets situated at various levels, was much more likely to fire Sant'Elia's imagination than the cruder schemes that appeared sporadically in the Italian press.

A few months later, an unsigned variant of Lamb's ideas for New York (fig. 123) was again published in *L'Illustrazione Italiana*.[143] The conceptual similarities with Sant'Elia's projects for the Città Nuova are inescapable (figs. 96,98,100).[144] Both show a broad central avenue, flanked by tall buildings, extending all the way to the horizon. Vehicular traffic occupies the lower levels in the center, while pedestrian streets are situated to the sides of the upper levels. Access from one side to the other is achieved by means of bridges, and from the lower to the upper levels by means of escalators and stairways. Both drawings are rendered according to one-point perspective and bird's-eye view. As is so often the case with Sant'Elia, the debt to other sources is more evident in the preparatory sketch: he liberates himself progressively as he reelaborates his initial drawing.

Far less satisfying to the eye, but closer to home—and therefore more lasting in effect—were the various town-planning schemes for Milan that Sant'Elia had occasion to see when working for the city administration. In the past Sant'Elia has all too often been compared exclusively with foreign architects, such as Wagner and Le Corbusier, by scholars who simply ignored what was going on in Milan.[145] It is important, however, to situate Sant'Elia within the context of local politics and problems: he was always profoundly responsive to what was going on in Milan. In the last decades of the nineteenth century, the new industrial bourgeoisie had begun to change the morphology of the city by introducing new transportation systems and new building types for the expanding metropolis, both of which introduced a new scale into the city fabric. Not only the topography of the city had

123. "The Circulation of the Future and the Cloudscrapers of New York." *L'Illustrazione Italiana,* August 31, 1913.

changed but also the inhabitants' perception of it; the town-country relationship of the past had been replaced by that of the town-periphery and tentacular sprawl.

Two local projects in particular caught Sant'Elia's attention. In 1907 the engineer Emilio Belloni designed the Corso d'Italia (fig. 124), an immense and monotonous highway 260 feet wide that was to extend in a straight line from the Duomo to the Ticino River nineteen miles away.[146] Belloni's concept was an awkward and inorganic adaptation of the Linear City by Arturo Soria y Mata.[147] Traffic was differentiated according to vehicle and speed: express lanes were situated below, and slow-moving local traffic above. This project even had its futuristic side: electricity, gas, water, pneumatic post, and telegraphs were to run along the highway on cable. So, too, were heating, ventilation, and even a vacuum-cleaning system.[148] In Milan futurism was, so to speak, in the air.

The Corso d'Italia was a naive technocratic solution to the urgent problem of opening up the historic center in a city grown fearfully large in a short time. In his attempt to answer Milan's real and urgent needs, Belloni entirely overlooked the fact that his project involved the destruction of hundreds of historic buildings and the relocation of thousands of inhabitants. Not only was its exalted scalelessness out of proportion with the surrounding urban tissue, but it was also to link two terminal points that were not significant in terms of either production or marketing—the Duomo and the Ticino River. Thus the fact that the Corso d'Italia was to have a transportation capacity of fifty-thousand people per hour was meaningless. And yet, as Bossaglia has observed, "This is the atmosphere in which the approximative dreams of Sant'Elia took shape, an atmosphere largely prophetic of the orgy of projects that characterized the fascist era."[149]

The Corso d'Italia was published in 1909 in *Le Case Popolari e le Città-Giardino*, a magazine Sant'Elia knew well because it had published his second project. Belloni entrusted the perspective to the young architect and illustrator Mario Stroppa (known by his nom de plume, Marius).[150] A master at perspective, Marius specialized in architectural renderings in bird's-eye view. From the Corso d'Italia Sant'Elia retained the idea of leaving the lowest traffic levels open to air and light, unlike the American models, where traffic was consigned to superimposed levels strictly parallel to one another and consequently closed off from above.

A year later a far more interesting scheme for Milan caught Sant'Elia's imagination. In 1908 the engineer Evaristo Stefini drew up a plan for a linear city that linked Milan to Sesto San Giovanni (fig. 125), the main industrial district north of the city.[151] Like Belloni's Corso d'Italia, it too was an offshoot of Arturo Soria y Mata's seminal *Linear City*. The main focus of the project was a central highway that was divided symmetrically into ten lanes for pedestrians, vehicles of medium speed, horseback riding, automobiles, and express trains. Over- and underpasses linked the two sides. It was also crossed at right angles by the Martesana Canal, a marvel of Lombard engineering, and by two railroad lines, which connected the industrial city to Milan and the rest of Europe. On either side of the highway, an uninterrupted strip of land was reserved for low-density housing: the green city. Beyond this tranquil residential area, another strip of land was allotted to industries and collective services.

This was the first plan to take into account what was rapidly becoming the main axis of development of the city—the area northeast of Milan, hence its name, Quartiere Indus-

124. Emilio Belloni. Corso d'Italia, 1907. Drawing by Marius (Mario Stroppa). *Le Case Popolari e le Città-Giardino,* 1909–1910.

125. Evaristo Stefini. Quartiere Industriale Nord Milano, 1908.
Drawing by Marius. *Le Case Popolari e le Città-Giardino,*
1909–1910.

triale Nord Milano. Not only were new industries to be concentrated along this axis, but because of the railroads it was also supposed to be situated in a privileged position with regard to export and marketing. The project implied a new urban vision that no longer coincided with the compact, concentric city that grew in organic rings around the historic core. Stefini's proposal deliberately tried to break the old monocentric hold of the city center. And unlike the plans for the Corso d'Italia, the site proposed for the project was free of historical remains and did not involve demolition.

Once more it was Marius who was responsible for the masterful perspective of the Quartiere Industriale Nord Milano. By deliberately selecting a high point of view and one-point perspective, Marius managed to convey the idea of speed and of a swiftly moving eye, as if the spectator were in a plane high above the road: "Interpreting the innovative characteristics of the project with a markedly dynamic image, [Marius] seemed to anticipate many analogies with the poetics of futurism and with Sant'Elia's subsequent urban metaphors."[152] Sant'Elia was quick to grasp the advantages of such a strategy: it is no accident that his only documented use of one-point perspective appears precisely in his station for trains and airplanes, where he borrows so heavily from Marius.[153]

Sant'Elia had not forgotten the drawing of New York published in *L'Illustrazione Italiana* (fig. 123), but he learned from Marius to adjust the angle of vision slightly so that the whole scene was quite symmetrical. He also shifted the point of view so as to give a greater impression of height and speed, although in this case he does not succeed as well as Marius. Sant'Elia usually conveyed the idea of speed by forcing the perspective in the manner of theater designers; here, however, the few trams that can be seen appear dwarfed and curiously static. If Sant'Elia borrowed the overall image, he rejected the idea of the low-density garden city. Like other futurists, he abhorred the homespun, static concept of the garden city and its antiurban slant.

Plate 11. Antonio Sant'Elia. Monumental building, 1914.
Musei Civici, Como.

Plate 12. Antonio Sant'Elia. Power station, 1913–1914.
Musei Civici, Como.

Schizzo per la Città Nuova
Stazione Aeroplani e Treni —

Plate 14 . Antonio Sant'Elia. La Città Nuova, 1914.
Collection of Paride Accetti, Milan.

Plate 13. (*opposite*) Antonio Sant'Elia. La Città Nuova: Station
for airplanes and trains, 1914. Private collection.

Plate 15. Antonio Sant'Elia. Power station. Dated
October 27, 1913, Milan. Musei Civici, Como.

Plate 16. Antonio Sant'Elia. Power station. Dated February 25, 1914, Como. Collection of Paride Accetti, Milan.

Plate 17. Antonio Sant'Elia. Power station, 1914. Collection of
Paride Accetti, Milan.

Plate 18. Antonio Sant'Elia. Power station. Dated March 15, 1914, Milan, and initialed. Collection of Paride Accetti, Milan.

Plate 19. Antonio Sant'Elia. Power station. Dated March 1, 1914, Milan, and initialed. Collection of Paride Accetti, Milan.

Plate 20. Antonio Sant'Elia. Study for a church, ca. 1915. Musei Civici, Como.

Plate 21. Antonio Sant'Elia. Study for a church(?), 1915. Musei
Civici, Como.

Thus Sant'Elia's Città Nuova was anchored in the new projects drawn up by Milan's captains of industry. Their optimism with regard to the future expressed itself in projects whose avant-garde antihistoricism was an important source of inspiration to him. The authors felt, no doubt, that they were on the brink of a revolution in transportation, and in their eagerness to discern its outlines, they lost sight of feasibility and soared into utopian realms.

SKYSCRAPER STORY

Sant'Elia was also looking to America, more specifically, to New York and its skyscrapers. Not New York as it actually was—Manhattan slowly reaching for the skies—but a New York projected impatiently into the future, the New York of popular illustrators, with skies crowded by zeppelins and soaring towers. True, Manhattan had captured the imagination of Europeans with Daniel Burnham's Flatiron Building (1902), Napoleon Le Brun's Metropolitan Life Tower (1909), and Cass Gilbert's recently finished Woolworth Building (1913), published enthusiastically by *L'Illustrazione Italiana*.[154] This interest in America was not accidental: *L'Illustrazione Italiana* was the mouthpiece of the dreams and aspirations of Milan's entrepreneurial bourgeoisie, who looked to the United States for inspiration and saw in the modern metropolis the locus of their work and profit.

Yet in Sant'Elia's eyes all those fine soaring structures were tainted by historicism. Even the science-fiction illustrators used an old idiom to clothe what was essentially a modern creation, born of the needs and technological means of the twentieth century. As Lewis Mumford put it so eloquently, "The mask of American architecture was frozen; the face was dead, the very skyscrapers were born old."[155]

Sant'Elia eagerly accepted the skyscraper as a new building type but impatiently rejected its historicism—the tripartite division into base, shaft, and capital, and its neo-Gothic or neoclassical overlay.[156] He was attracted to its verticality precisely because he saw in it a rejection of history, a break with the European—that is, horizontal—city.[157] Yet he remained conditioned by the historic cities, as the feeble height of his buildings shows. New York had over one dozen skyscrapers that were much taller than Sant'Elia's modest high-rises. Psychologically, no doubt, he still cast his projects in a scale that was consonant with that of the old European city, where the maximum height rarely exceeded six stories. In height and scale, at least, a certain vestigial historicism still resonates in Sant'Elia's metropolis.

But New York offered Sant'Elia much more than a viable new typology. It provided him an urban "ready-made" onto which he projected his dreams for the Città Nuova. He adopted the new setting with all the stock features added by popular illustrators: a stratified traffic network, catwalks and bridges at soaring heights, airborne means of transportation. Although he never referred to his setbacks as skyscrapers, there is no doubt that he regarded them as such. The futurists were avid admirers of America, which they considered to be the very embodiment of technological progress. Boccioni speaks of "the need to americanize ourselves by entering the all-consuming vortex of modernity through its crowds, automobiles, telegraphs, noises, screeching, violence, cruelty, cynicism, and unrelenting competitiveness; in short, the exaltation of all the savage anti-artistic aspects of our age."[158] Yet Sant'Elia's decision to emulate America was not an easy one.[159] Skyscrapers were unusual in Italian architecture, both with regard to scale and typology.[160] As a type, the skyscraper was associated exclusively with America and, ironically, with a lack of history. Although its decoration was made up of columns, pediments, gargoyles, and caryatids, it had no Vitruvian or Renaissance pedigree. In addition, in the eyes of Europeans it was linked with escalating land prices and ruthless speculation, which had not yet reached the fearful fiscal heights in Europe that they had in New York or Chicago.

The buildings of the Città Nuova may look somewhat stunted beside their New York counterparts, but for the Italy of Sant'Elia's day they were vertiginous. A contemporary and clamorous example in Milan illustrates what little chance Sant'Elia's projects had of being received with anything but contempt. In a much-publicized case in 1909, the well-known architect Achille Manfredini designed a "skyscraper" to be erected near the city center (fig. 126). Although the project came to naught, it triggered a heated debate in the pages of Italy's leading periodicals, a debate that is indicative of prevailing attitudes toward the skyscraper. The hostility with which it was greeted is surprising even today, insofar as the skyscraper in question was only fourteen stories high and neo-Baroque in style. Furthermore, it was to be built in an area that had just been cleared for redevelopment because of the absence of historic buildings.

126. Achille Manfredini. Project for a skyscraper, 1909.
(Photo: Collection of the author)

Manfredini's project, significantly dubbed an "americanata" by the press (the suffix "ata" is pejorative), elicited the most venomous and xenophobic of reactions. The authoritative *Corriere della Sera,* Italy's leading periodical, served as a forum for the debate. Its editors made no secret as to where they stood: "Cities that are not like American ones, which have no past, should try as much as possible to preserve their characteristics, which constitute their greatest attraction."[161]

Luigi Broggi, one of Milan's most successful eclectic architects, spoke up in defense of the "cloudscraper." Curiously enough, even he thought the New York examples were utterly devoid of aesthetic merit, no doubt because not historicist enough: "Why must we think that we will build ugly things as they do in America? Let us not forget that there the absence of beauty prevails, not only in the 'cloudscrapers' but also in buildings of average height: it is a characteristic of the country. Here it is otherwise—we are in the land of beauty."[162] He was answered by Luca Beltrami, the doyen of Italy's architectural establishment, who exclaimed indignantly that "although the building was beautiful in itself, it would be a disgrace for the entire context, just as a woman's hair, so interesting in its given place, does not please me in the soup."[163]

The detractors won the day.[164] The architectural magazine *La Casa,* which had published Sant'Elia's first project, heaved a sigh of epistolary relief: "Let the Americans erect edifices of hundreds of stories on their soil devoid of history, and scrape their foggy sky as much as they wish. But let not the skies of Italy—the Lord be praised—be contaminated!"[165] And thus, the first skyscraper in the history of Italian architecture was rejected as an aberration.[166]

But Sant'Elia challenged an even more important dogma of Milanese town planning and politics, one sanctioned by time and capital—the traditional street. Unlike the American skyscraper, which was a self-contained structure, the Città Nuova was inseparable from the urban tissue to which it was connected.[167] Sant'Elia deliberately ignored the contemporary trend, in Milan as elsewhere, toward greater subdivision of the land. By the end of the nineteenth century, land division had been institutionalized in Milan as the guiding force behind town planning. Because height was determined by the need to respect the traditional historic skyline and the size of the plot by the market value of each square foot, the module of the Italian city was inevitably the small, five- or six-story apartment building: "The dream of a new Milan made up of vast isolated buildings . . . found an unsurmountable obstacle in the obsession with profit and speculation."[168]

Nevertheless, the picture of the Città Nuova that Sant'Elia left behind remains incomplete and fragmentary. He gives no indication as to the facade of his buildings when arranged face-to-face (fig. 99), nor of the rear facade of the free-standing ones (fig. 101). No plans and only a handful of rudimentary sections of the Casa Nuova have come down to us (figs. 107,108). The fact that one of them (fig. 108) is dated May 30—after the opening of Nuove Tendenze—is significant: perhaps they were undertaken in answer to queries or criticisms concerning the absence of plans or sections in the show. At any rate, Sant'Elia used the sections in question to explore the connection of the elevator shafts to the main part of the building and to discover how to link two buildings back-to-back.

Although in his previous buildings and even in the power stations Sant'Elia had conceived of his projects as impenetrable masses, he now thought of them as thin envelopes—at least to judge from the exteriors. If one examines the rare sections, however, one realizes that there was still no distinctive inside space corresponding to the "Casa a Gradinata." In section, the actual interior space of the receding stages is treated as an undifferentiated whole. His thoughts on the matter never really crystallized beyond the vaguest of notions, content as he was to design exteriors.[169] His interior spaces seem always to be dominated by symmetry and axial planning: "All the lexical elements—volumes, openings, itineraries—are gathered along a main axis according to specular symmetry."[170]

THE URBAN ENVIRONMENT

Sant'Elia did not leave a plan of the Città Nuova, or of the Casa Nuova, nor did he fully envisage it as a whole. His thoughts on the subject must be extrapolated from the drawings shown at Nuove Tendenze and later republished in the *Manifesto of Futurist Architecture.* He must, of course, have had a rough idea of the layout of the streets. Judging from the most complete drawings of the Città Nuova, this plan was orthogonal, or at any rate linear.[171] The same symmetry and axial planning that is characteristic of his architecture reappears in his town planning. On the other hand, the space of the Città Nuova is isotropic: it has "no inside or outside, no center and no periphery."[172]

Sant'Elia's urbanism was as antihistoric as his architecture. He conceived his city as an entirely new entity arising *ex novo* from the ground, without having to compromise with any remains of the past. But it is not only the historic urban fabric that is absent: there is not so much as a blade of grass in Sant'Elia's metropolis, nor are the natural surroundings even hinted at. Topography is entirely artificial. This elision of nature was a passing concession to the futurists and their love of all things mechanical: after this brief interlude Sant'-Elia was to return to the hidden naturalism of his mystical monuments.

In this double rejection of nature and history Sant'Elia went further than anyone else had gone before him. His was a radical break with all known models of town planning. Like other futurists, he turned his back on the idea of the garden city, so dear to English and German town planners who refused the metropolis. Not by accident did Marinetti inveigh against the ignoble "gardens cities" [*sic*][173] in his manifesto against English art. Sant'-Elia also refused the picturesque neomedieval urbanism advocated by Camillo Sitte, as well as the horizontal model proposed in Wagner's *Moderne Architektur* (1896). He likewise refused the historicism of the Americans while eagerly accepting the vertical solution to city planning they proposed. Yet one has only to compare his work to the achievements of Tony Garnier and Otto Wagner to see the immense gap that separates his drawings of the Città Nuova from actual all-encompassing works of modern urbanism.

Garnier's Cité Industrielle, designed in 1901 but not published until 1917, was the first comprehensive town-planning scheme of the new century. In spite of its structural and technological innovations and the care that Garnier devoted to each part, his Cité remains the old garden city given a superb new setting. Wagner's *Moderne Architektur* had a much greater impact, as did his seminal work as chief architect of Vienna. Wagner went far beyond Garnier in his vision of a truly metropolitan atmosphere for his city. In spirit, if nothing else, Wagner clung to the same urban ideology later put forth by the futurists.

In contrast to these two architects—not to mention Le Corbusier, who was roughly the same age—Sant'Elia had very little to offer by way of urbanism and city planning: a few drawings and passing remarks in his "Messaggio." Yet to compare him unfavorably to his near-contemporaries is to misunderstand the true nature of his contribution: "These critical interpretations are based on a misconception of the scope of the projects characteristic of Sant'Elia, which is not that of urbanism but of architecture on an urban (or rather metropolitan) scale."[174] The truth is that Sant'Elia was not a patient student of urbanism and town planning in the manner of Garnier or Le Corbusier. In spite of the importance given to circulation, Sant'Elia was more concerned with a pictorial view of the city—that is, with an image that was more architectural than urbanistic.[175]

One must remember, too, that Sant'Elia's experience as an architect was conditioned in part by a poor education, which sporadic competitions and part-time work in architectural studios could not rectify. In consequence, his knowledge of urbanism was not the fruit of systematic research but of improvised, fitful borrowings from sources encountered by chance: "Obviously, the educational evolution of Sant'Elia is not like the rigorous one of Le Corbusier (which took place during those very years); it does not proceed, in other words, from a foundation of rational synthesis which virtually brings together and fashions into a final architectural formula the analysis of all the valid experiments of the past and of the present."[176]

Sant'Elia was less interested in the latest theories of contemporary architecture than he was in the popular culture and pseudoscientific literature of the day, that is, in the visual ready-mades, half-utopian, half-prophetic, so common in magazine illustrations of the time. In his day the young "modernolaters" (as Marinetti was fond of calling them) pored over machinery catalogues and advertisements for modern technology with the same enthusiasm that earlier generations had looked at fine prints. Mario Chiattone, who shared a studio with Sant'Elia at the time, "carefully studied silos, plants, ships, battleships, American skyscrapers and metal bridges . . . as well as construction problems imposed by the machine and mechanization."[177] For Sant'Elia these exciting new sources held greater promise for the future than did architectural books or periodicals. The latter, however, would have afforded him a more disciplined and realistic approach to architecture. Science fiction only nourished the utopian side of his work, as his catalogue essay for Nuove Tendenze shows, with its elevators that swarm up the facades "like serpents of iron and glass," its high-rises that loom "on the brink of a tumultuous abyss," and its streets that "plunge into the earth." The real source of these futuristic images, Ragghianti observed, does not lie in architectural theory but in science fiction.[178]

Yet science fiction helped create a certain climate of euphoria and admiration for modernity that did much to popularize ideas that were rapidly becoming realities, such as skyscrapers and steel frames. The writings of Jules Verne, H. G. Wells, and Edward Bellamy were very popular in Italy and inspired a host of imitators. Among Italian writers of science fiction, the most important was the Piedmontese Mario Morasso, who had frequently collaborated in Marinetti's magazine *Poesia*. A fervid believer in the unlimited progress of science and technology, Morasso was a crucial predecessor of the futurists within Italy itself.[179]

Sant'Elia's dependence on visual culture, corroborated by eyewitness reports, accounts for the fragmentary nature of his vision of the city: we are left with scenographic views, truncated images of a larger whole that was never fully conceptualized.[180] Without plans, sections, or even complete elevations, the Città Nuova is little more than a Potemkin village, an impressive array of facades: "Even in its geometric presentation, we are always dealing with scenic 'vedute,' with shells deprived of a proper articulation, and not only with regard to interiors but to the exteriors themselves, of which only the perspective is given. Sant'Elia is a modern Bibbiena who does not design living organisms but volumes and surfaces that exhaust themselves in their external appearance, in spectacle."[181]

Perhaps the greatest innovation of the Città Nuova is the successful merging of architecture and urban infrastructure: the buildings have no formal autonomy but must be read in conjunction with the traffic lanes, viaducts, and overpasses from which they are inseparable. This shift of interest from the isolated building to the urban environment is due in great part to Sant'Elia's contact with futurism, the source of the optimistic faith in the urban ideology as opposed to the *Grossstadtpessimismus* then rampant in England and, above all, in Germany.[182] The metropolis was the aim and the setting of all futurist art.[183] The crowd, rather than the individual, was the futurist subject par excellence and the addressee of all the futurist manifestos: "We shall sing of great crowds galvanized by labor, pleasure or unrest."[184] Not the fashionable, pleasure-seeking crowd of the Impressionists, exuding joie de vivre and given to leisure and hedonistic pursuits, but a nameless, faceless (and in Sant'Elia's case, invisible) army of technocrats that in the eyes of the futurists was to pull Italy out of its passéist lethargy and reconquer, thanks to science and technology, the privileged position it had held in the past. And indeed, the streamlined aesthetics of his buildings, along with their new urban environment, constituted Sant'Elia's attempt to address the needs of the nascent *Massenpsychologie.*

Nevertheless crowds themselves are never visible in Sant'Elia, as they are in the paintings of his futurist friends. Only the buildings, the roads, and the vehicles imply their existence. The very fact that the Città Nuova was built ex novo creates a gap between the views of Sant'Elia and those of the futurist painters. Poets and writers such as Marinetti and Paolo Buzzi might conjure up visions of an entirely new world, but Boccioni, Balla, Carrà, and Russolo never quite severed their links to the existing historical city—at least in their paintings. In spite of their artistic and iconographic revolution, something of the old flâneur still lingers in their work.

Sant'Elia, however, went further in destroying the old order and in presenting an entirely new environment. He thus shares with many writers and designers of science fiction the portrayal of the metropolis as a place of emptiness, occupied only by racing vehicles. Shorn of historical trappings, his vast new city engulfs the tiny individuals who fade away into an abstraction. This manifest absence of the crowd and the disintegration of the traditional street is precisely what sets Sant'Elia's vision apart from the unanimist approach of the other futurists, for whom the urban environment and the crowd form an inseparable whole.[185]

If the Città Nuova as a whole is reminiscent of futurism in general, its details point specifically to Boccioni. Older than Sant'Elia by six years, Boccioni was also the most articulate of the futurist artists and the one best able to translate his art into words. After his successful foray into sculpture (like architecture, a three-dimensional art), his work was bound to have even more relevance for Sant'Elia. Boccioni's *Technical Manifesto of Futurist Sculpture* (1912), where his revolutionary ideas are codified, probably represents the most far-ranging body of ideas that futurism left behind. Its impact on Sant'Elia can be felt both in his drawings of the Città Nuova and in his own essay on futurist architecture.[186] Boccioni, as the text shows, was no longer interested in painting states of mind but in creating a "style of movement." Greatly influenced by the synthetic cubism of Picasso and Braque— but also anxious to go beyond it—Boccioni tried to adapt the futurist theories of dynamic interpenetration of planes to the realm of sculpture. The new sculpture was no longer to remain isolated and aloof from its environment but was to enclose its surroundings within itself:

> In sculpture as in painting one can generate renewal only by seeking THE STYLE OF MOVEMENT, that is, by rendering systematically and definitively as a synthesis that which impressionism gave in a fragmentary, accidental, and hence, analytical way. And this systematization of the vibration of light and the interpenetration of planes will produce futurist sculpture, the grounding of which will be architectural, not only in the sense of the construction of masses, but also in the sense that the sculptural block will include the architectural elements of THE SCULPTURAL MILIEU in which the subject lives.[187]

Architecture thus assumes a tremendous importance for futurism. Because the seat of all futurist activity was the metropolis, the streets and the buildings constituted the environment that was to be incorporated within the object according to the celebrated formula: "Let us break open the figure and enclose in it its environment."[188] With the publication of Boccioni's *Technical Manifesto of Futurist Sculpture,* architecture began to replace music as the ideal model for futurist art.[189] Boccioni's *Manifesto of Futurist Architecture,* discovered unexpectedly in 1971, reveals how sensitive he was to the forms and rhythms of the metropolis and how instrumental it was in shaping his ideas on art, sculpture, and, ultimately, architecture itself:

> We have said that in painting we shall put the viewer at the center of the picture, making him the center of emotion rather than a mere spectator. The architectural environment of the city is also being radically transformed. We live in a spiral of architectural forces. In the past, construction unfolded in the sense of a sequence of panoramas: one house after the other, one street after the other. Now we see around us the beginnings of an architectural environment that develops in every direction from the luminous basements of the large department stores, from the many levels of tunnels of the underground railways to the powerful upward thrust of American skyscrapers.[190]

Nevertheless there are significant differences between the ideas of Boccioni and those of Sant'Elia. In his polemic against cubism, Boccioni tried to give a dynamic representation of movement not through anecdote (subject matter)—though many of his works show cyclists, football players, and horsemen—but by plastic means alone.

Although many scholars have mentioned the importance of kinesis in the Città Nuova, Bruno Zevi correctly points out that Sant'Elia gives a static representation of movement, as compared to the other futurists.[191] In architecture, the idea of motion could be evoked by two different ways. The first, which was external to the work of art, consisted in the cars, trams, and escalators that move through the architecture. The other was inherent in the figurative means themselves by way of empathy, as in Sant'Elia's dinamismi: the architectural notation suggests movement because of the use of quick, nervous strokes.[192] This latter type of dynamism was, of course, the aim of Boccioni's art up to 1913, admirably expressed in the *Technical Manifesto of Futurist Painting.* In the ambitious projects of the Città Nuova, on the other hand, the lines are arrested in the motionless precision of Sant'Elia's graphics. This is very different from an architecture that is in itself kinetic, such as Vladimir Tatlin's Monument to the Third International (1920).

Sant'Elia understood that the transition from small city to metropolis also entailed a shift in psychological perception and that the metropolis had in fact enlarged and enriched the individual's "psychic field."[193] The vast, changed dimensions of the city demanded a revision of the figurative codes of architecture and urbanism. Accordingly, Sant'Elia simplifies and standardizes his architectural idiom. Historicism is abolished. The windows are kept to the simplest reticulated pattern, and the architectural composition is dominated by the bold, sweeping verticals of the elevator shafts. Horizontally it is linked by powerful viaducts and overpasses. These are all forms that are not distorted by speed and that register easily from a distance. From a strictly urbanistic point of view, speed itself demanded the straight line.

Five The Manifesto of Futurist Architecture

The drawings of the Città Nuova were not the only contributions Sant'Elia made to the history of architecture. The catalogue of Nuove Tendenze also included an important essay by him, untitled, like the other written entries, but now universally known as the "Messaggio."[1] Curiously enough, this text did not arouse much enthusiasm at the time; none of the critics who were so favorably impressed by Sant'Elia's projects in that show had much to say about it. And yet it is a remarkable piece of work, perhaps the most original architectural text to have been published since Adolf Loos's *Ornament and Crime* of 1908.

Like all the other catalogue entries of Nuove Tendenze, the "Messaggio" was shot through with futurist art theory, although the words *futurist* and *futurism* did not appear. But his text went well beyond theirs in the variety and scope of futurist ideas it conveyed. The actual format of the "Messaggio" is very close to that of the futurist manifestos, particularly to those associated with Boccioni: a prologue containing the thesis, followed by an enumeration of his objections and beliefs.[2]

All the main topics touched upon were familiar items on the futurist agenda. The opening lines introduce the sorry state of the profession, which the "Messaggio," like other futurist manifestos, sets out to combat: the problem of modern architecture, writes Sant'Elia, "is not a question of finding new moldings, new frames for windows and doors, of replacing columns, pilasters, and corbels with caryatids, flies, or frogs."[3] He then brings up the theme of antihistoricism, a staple of futurist art theory: "This architecture cannot naturally be subject to any law of historic continuity. It must be new, as our state of mind and the contingencies of our historic moment are new." Hatred of the past was a statutory part of every futurist manifesto: "Our task," declared Boccioni, "is to destroy four centuries of Italian tradition."[4] In rejecting the expression of historical continuity, however, Sant'Elia was taking more than a generic stand against tradition; he was specifically opposing the evolutionary view of architecture epitomized by Camillo Boito, which still dominated academic circles, particularly at Brera.

Sant'Elia claimed that a new form-creating process had come to take the place of the old historic styles. In modern times the placid flow of stylistic evolution had been arrested by the advent of iron and prestressed concrete, and this had brought about an irreversible change of direction: "Modern construction materials and our scientific notions do not lend themselves to the discipline of historical styles, and are the main cause of the grotesque aspect of the fashionable buildings in which one tries to obtain the heavy curve of the arch and the massive appearance of marble from the lightness, the superb slenderness of the beam and the fragility of reinforced concrete." Similar ideas appear in Boccioni's unpublished manifesto of architecture: "In the enslavement to old styles we find the threadbare and vulgar archaeological habits that give rise to building fetishism."[5] Otto Wagner had said essentially the same thing with different words: "All modern creations must correspond to the new materials and demands of the present if they are to suit modern man."[6]

Marinetti's ideas also reverberate throughout the essay as, for example, in the apologia of new building types that appears in the "Messaggio": "We feel we are no longer the men of cathedrals and meeting halls, but of grand hotels, railway stations, vast highways, colossal harbors, covered markets, luminous arcades, straight lines, and salutary demolitions." Sant'Elia's proud, exalted optimism is very close in tone and imagery to Marinetti's beautiful ode to modern typologies in the founding manifesto of futurism:

> We shall sing of the great crowds galvanized by labor, pleasure or unrest: of the many-colored and polyphonic tides of revolution in the modern capitals; we shall sing of the vibrating nocturnal fervor of the arsenals and the building yards ablaze with violent electric moons; of swollen railway stations, avid for smoking serpents; of factories hung from the clouds by means of the twisted arabesques of their smoke; of bridges bestriding rivers like giant gymnasts . . . : of bold steamboats scouting the horizons, of broad-chested locomotives pawing the tracks like huge steel horses bridled with pipes, and the gliding flight of airplanes.[7]

Sant'Elia reserved his most inspired lines for the image of the modern city, which was the most utopian part of his text: "We must invent and rebuild *ex novo* the modern city like an immense tumultuous building yard, agile, mobile, dynamic in all its parts, and the modern house like a gigantic machine." Yet even here, as Maurizio Calvesi shrewdly remarked, the images of the city that Sant'Elia evokes—and that he later reiterates in the *Manifesto*—are inspired by Boccioni's urban paintings, such as *The City Rises* (1910–1911), *Forces of a Street* (1912), or *The Street Enters the House* (1911).[8] The paintings of the industrial periphery of Milan, complete with its workers and chimney stacks, its tools and vehicles, had a profound impact on Sant'Elia. For Boccioni, the futurist city is perennially in the process of being rebuilt, a process aptly evoked by Sant'Elia's image of the "tumultuous building yard," with its exaltation of urban labor as well as urban change.[9] Nothing expresses so vividly the transient, ever-changing nature of the metropolis as the ubiquitous scaffoldings of futurist iconography: "Nothing is more beautiful," wrote Marinetti, "than the scaffolding of a house under construction—the scaffolding symbolizes our burning passion for the transformation [le devenir] of things."[10]

Sant'Elia believed that modern architecture should make use of all the new materials that technology had placed at its disposal and in such a way that they were clearly expressed in the overall form: "The house of cement, glass, iron, stripped of painting and sculpture, enriched solely with the inherent beauty of its lines and its relief, extraordinarily ugly in its mechanical simplicity . . . must rise on the brink of a tumultuous abyss." This was an extension of Boccioni's call for a new dynamic sculpture in which the use of new materials had a twofold purpose: to help give a sense of kinesis to sculpture and to produce different sensations in the spectator, thereby increasing the emotional potential of the work of art.[11] Inspired by the synthetic cubism of Picasso and Braque, who first introduced prosaic materials and ready-mades into their art, Boccioni had tried to expand the range of response of the spectators. According to his *Manifesto of Futurist Sculpture*, "even twenty different materials can be used in the same work with the aim of producing a plastic emotion. To enumerate but a few: glass, wood, cardboard, iron, cement, horsehair, leather, textiles, mirrors, electric lights, etc."[12] The point is made even clearer in Boccioni's *Manifesto of Architecture:* "It is necessary to ennoble construction materials, and time-saving ones par excellence (iron wood brick prestressed concrete) while keeping alive their characteristics."[13] Like Sant'Elia, Boccioni thought that modern buildings should not only be made up of modern materials but also be expressive of the fact. Structural elements, in other words, should be frankly exposed rather than hidden.

The parallels continue. When describing the new architecture of the future, Sant'Elia calls for nothing less than a tabula rasa of traditional syntax: "We must begin by doing away with monuments, sidewalks, porticoes, steps, by sinking streets and piazzas, raising the level of the city." Giovanni Papini had said as much in his essay "Contro Firenze passatista," in which he complained about the city's stifling old-fashioned atmosphere and advocated "knock[ing] down the petrous stage sets of our stubborn anachronisms, to widen roads, to renew our life."[14]

There is no doubt, however, that Boccioni's ideas predominate, particularly in the conclusion, where Sant'Elia lays down his creed. Indeed, one could say that Boccioni's most important ideas were being systematically adapted to architecture. This last section follows closely the canonic formula of the futurist manifestos: the disapprovals and affirmations are divided into two almost symmetrical groups. The vocabulary, no less than the form, is similar to that used in the *Technical Manifesto of Futurist Painting* (1910), a collaborative effort believed to have been written by Boccioni.[15] Where the latter had introduced his concluding statements with "We combat" and "We proclaim," respectively, Sant'Elia used "I oppose" and "I declare."

In the first objection raised in the conclusion, Sant'Elia opposes imitation of different styles and nationalities ("fashionable architecture of every country and every kind"), a complaint previously voiced by Boccioni in his *Technical Manifesto of Futurist Painting,* and even more forcefully in *Pittura scultura futuriste (dinamismo plastico),* where he had inveighed against submission to ancient styles and to foreign influence.[16]

The second objection also has a clear futurist prototype. Carrà's injunction against the "stupid obsession with the solemn, the toga-clad, the serene, the hieratic, the mummified"[17] is translated by Sant'Elia into architectural terms: "classical, solemn, hieratic, scenographic . . . architecture."

Another objection raised by Sant'Elia, the rejection of static forms, is basically a transposition of Boccioni's concept of "dinamismo plastico." Sant'Elia called for an audacious architecture that eschewed weighty, ponderous monuments and all forms that contributed to the impression of immovable masses: "perpendicular and horizontal lines, cubical and pyramidal forms that are static, grave, oppressive, and wholly incompatible with our ultranew sensibility."

Various manifestos contain almost identical words. In "The Painting of Sounds, Noises and Smells," Carrà criticizes "the use of the pure horizontal, of the pure vertical, and of all dead lines" and also "the cube, the pyramid and all static forms."[18] This rejection of cubical and pyramidal forms was part of futurism's critique of the cubist conception of art, which was considered utterly devoid of dynamism.[19]

Boccioni, too, returns to this point more than once. In his preface to the first show of futurist sculpture in Paris (1913), he had called for a new kind of sculpture based on an architectural organization of space: "Architecture is to sculpture what composition is to painting."[20] He goes on to explain, however, that this architectural scaffolding underlying modern sculpture was new and unconventional, and no longer pyramidal, like architecture of the past.[21] He is even more explicit in his *Manifesto of Architecture:* "The cube the pyramid the rectangle within which, as a rule, the building is enclosed, must be suppressed: these maintain the architectural form in immobility."[22]

Sant'Elia's condemnation of ornament in the concluding section of the "Messaggio" also derives from Boccioni: "Decoration, as something overlaid or appended to architecture, is absurd. . . . The decorative value of a truly modern architecture depends exclusively on the use and original orchestration of rough, naked, or violently colored materials." The original source was, as Calvesi pointed out, Boccioni's revolutionary *Technical Manifesto of Futurist Sculpture:* "Thus transparent planes, glass, metal strips, wire, electric lamps, external or internal, may indicate the planes, tendencies, tones and semi-tones of a new reality. Thus a new intuitive use of the color white, grey, black, can heighten the emotional impact of the surfaces while the hue of a colored plane will accentuate violently the abstract meaning of the artifact!"[23]

The revolt against ornament—traditionally associated with women—played an important role in the search for a modern architecture, and it is precisely this aspect of Sant'Elia's text that has earned him a severe reprimand on the part of feminist critics in recent years: "The scorn for decoration epitomizes the machismo expressed by Le Corbusier, Gabo, Pevsner and Marinetti–Sant'Elia. Their belligerence may take the form of an appeal to the machine aesthetic: the machine is idolized as a tool and symbol of progress, and technological progress is equated with streamlined art."[24]

Sant'Elia had been trying to liberate himself from decoration for some time. There is an increasing trend toward abstraction in his work, from the weighty masses of 1912 to the larval futurism of the dinamismi (1913) and finally to the Città Nuova. One wonders, however, if Sant'Elia's crusade against ornament—at least as expressed in the "Messaggio"— may not also reflect Marinetti's theories on the new futurist syntax. In his revolutionary call for novel forms of writing, Marinetti had couched his language in strikingly visual terms: "I therefore encouraged the futurists to destroy and ridicule garlands, palms, haloes, elaborate cornices, the stoles and cerements, all the historic props and the romantic *bric-à-brac* that constitutes a great part of all the poetry up to our time."[25] More specifically, Sant'-Elia's rejection of decoration is very similar, mutatis mutandis, to Marinetti's abolition of the adjective as a cloying, excessive element to be jettisoned at all costs: "One must abolish the adjective, so that the naked noun may preserve its essential color. The adjective, partaking in itself of the nature of nuance, is incompatible with our dynamic vision, because it implies a pause, a meditation."[26]

Finally, the last point raised by Sant'Elia in the "Messaggio" was unabashedly futurist and partly inspired by Boccioni himself: "Just as the ancients took their artistic inspiration from the elements of nature, so too must we—[who are] materially and spiritually artificial—find our inspiration in the elements of the new mechanical world that we have created." Boccioni and his friends, Banham noted, had written very similar lines in the *Manifesto of Futurist Painting:* "Just as our ancestors drew artistic inspiration from the religious atmosphere that weighed upon their souls, so too must we draw our own inspiration from the tangible miracles of contemporary life."[27]

In drafting his text Sant'Elia, unlike the other artists of Nuove Tendenze, made use of the first person plural—except for the conclusion—thus making the "Messaggio" conform to the canonic format of futurist manifestos. In these, more often than not the result of a collaborative effort, the individuality of each member of the group was swallowed up in the collective subject.[28] Indeed the destruction of the "I" was officially decreed in the *Technical Manifesto of Futurist Literature,* itself a joint undertaking, inevitably dominated by Marinetti: "[One must] destroy the 'I' in literature, that is, destroy all psychology. Man, entirely spoilt by libraries and museums, subjected to a terrifying logic and wisdom, is no longer of any interest. We must thus abolish him in literature and finally replace him with matter."[29]

In short, if the other catalogue entries were influenced by futurism, Sant'Elia's could be said to be particularly so. The ideas, the rhetoric, and the very format were borrowed from futurism. Fragments of various manifestos are embedded in the text: "a good two-thirds of the 'Messaggio,'" wrote Maurizio Calvesi, "are thus developed, plotted, and often paraphrased according to suggestions by Boccioni, Carrà, Marinetti. . . . Which is to say that it was already an entirely futurist text."[30]

Yet Sant'Elia's "Messaggio" was much more than an anthology of futurist ideas. It was also an intensely personal document with many original contributions to architectural theory. Unlike Marinetti, Boccioni, and the others, Sant'Elia was never exclusively a futurist. Futurism had great influence on his work before he joined the movement, though not, strangely enough, after he had done so. In any case, it was only one of the many intellectual strands that shaped his cultural makeup, though perhaps it was the most important one.

Traces of his prefuturist days are also present, as when Sant'Elia exclaims that "elevators must swarm up the facades like serpents of iron and glass." Since the first manifesto serpents had appeared often in futurist texts, as metaphors for modern technology. Sant'-Elia himself had repeatedly used snakes in his Liberty days (figs. 16–18). In casting this imagery in the symbolist vocabulary of their early days, the futurists reveal, once more, a certain fear of technology, as if they hesitated to accept it on its own terms without zoomorphic attributes.

Another example of nonfuturist sources in the "Messaggio" appears in the stratification of the traffic system: "The street will no longer stretch out like a doormat at ground level but will plunge into the earth by means of several stories that will bring together the traffic of the metropolis and be connected by metal catwalks and swift-moving conveyor belts." This recalls the *Technical Manifesto of Futurist Painting:* "A street soaked by rain and illuminated by electric lamps will plunge to the very center of the earth."[31] Once again, the words may be reminiscent of Boccioni or even of Mario Morasso, but the image they evoke owes little to futurism. These words conjure up glimpses of the semi-utopian New York of King's Dream, Richard Rummel, and H. Wiley Corbett.

Such is the case in the most revolutionary part of the "Messaggio": "Everything must be revolutionized. . . . It is necessary to exploit the roofs, utilize the basements, play down the importance of the facade." Here we find bold, original ideas that were later to reappear with far greater clarity in the International Style, notably in the work of Le Corbusier: the terrace roof, the utilization of the ground floor (or at least the basement), the devaluation of the facade (and, consequently, the end of the *rue-corridor*). Similarly, when Sant'Elia says that we must rebuild the modern house "like a gigantic machine," he was anticipating Le Corbusier's "machine à habiter," as Edoardo Persico pointed out many years ago.[32] However, Sant'Elia was neither the first nor the last to come up with this idea: the more one scrutinizes the history of architecture, the more traces of machines à habiter one finds. "The building," wrote Wagner's pupil Karl Maria Kerndle, "must function like a perfectly constructed machine; it must in its installation be on the level of the wagon-lits."[33] Many of the ideas in the "Messaggio" were in fact popularizations of cherished tenets of the Wagnerschule.

The positivist assumptions underlying many of Sant'Elia's statements in the "Messaggio" have often been noted. Truth to materials had been a commonplace in architectural discourse since the nineteenth century, while the call for new materials in architecture, the importance of the machine imagery, and the need to draw inspiration from modern life rather than from immutable styles of the past, were all part of the intellectual baggage of the European avant-garde of the day. As Banham observed, "The basic strategic device of the *Messaggio* is to accept as true the main historical concepts of the nineteenth-century Rationalists and Academics—such as the political and social causation of superficial stylistic changes, the unchanging nature of the fundamentals of the architectural art."[34] These are ideas that Sant'Elia had been familiar with since his student days: the academy of Brera left traces in his theory as well as in his drawings.

In fact, a certain naive technological determinism pervades Sant'Elia's text. For years, he claimed, architecture had been dominated by tradition, but the advent of new construction methods and materials such as iron (Sant'Elia never mentions steel) and concrete would automatically bring about a new architecture, that is, "an architecture that finds its raison d'être exclusively in the special conditions of modern life."[35] Consequently familiarity with modern technology should lead to a renewal of architecture: "The problem of modern architecture [must be solved] . . . by strokes of genius, and equipped exclusively with a scientific and technical know-how." And yet Sant'Elia was no rigid technocrat. He endowed his imaginary machine-made metropolis with mythical attributes of speed and omnipotence, characteristic of the uninformed. Technology was not, Argan reminds us, an article of faith to which he adhered blindly: "Sant'Elia is not therefore the founder or the apostle of a new aesthetic of positivism, but he who intuited most profoundly the ideal possibilities of the new architecture."[36] And he quotes Sant'Elia's words to that effect: "Real architecture is not . . . an arid combination of practicality and utility, but remains art, that is, synthesis, expression."[37]

The poetics of Einfühlung also make a brief appearance in the "Messaggio," as when Sant'Elia claims that our architecture must be new just as our states of mind are new. So does Expressionism. As Tafuri has pointed out, Sant'Elia's ideas about urban space as a reflection of changing technologies is a common theme in expressionist theories and can be found, for example, in the writings of Paul Scheerbart, Bruno Taut, and the *Gläserne Kette.*[38]

The numerous contradictions between the "Messaggio" and his own architecture, particularly the Città Nuova, have often been noted. Sant'Elia's repeated attacks on monumentality are not consonant with his projects ("We have in fact lost the sense of the monumental, the massive, the static"). Neither then, nor later, would Sant'Elia lose the feeling for ponderous masses that he inherited from the architecture of the Italian *Ottocento.* Likewise when he denounces the use of "perpendicular and horizontal lines," one is astonished at how few lines of the Città Nuova are *not* perpendicular or horizontal.[39] Even more surprising is his opposition to the "cubical and pyramidal forms that are static, grave, oppressive" when virtually all his architecture tends to the pyramidal.

As for historicism and decoration, which he attacks with less virulence only than Adolf Loos, at the very moment the "Messaggio" was being drafted, his project for the Verona Savings Bank, with all its medieval trappings, was being shown to the public (fig. 71). It is true that this work was the result of collaboration and that the competition brief specifically called for a historicist solution. Nevertheless, one might add that his decoration, which after 1913 was limited primarily to statuary, was almost invariably drawn from the Middle Ages—a reminder of the pervasive influence of academicism that outlasted Sant'Elia's apprenticeship at Brera.

A certain discrepancy between theory and practice was not unusual in architectural manifestos of the twentieth century or even earlier.[40] Unlike art, architecture demanded time, money, and private or public patronage in order to be built, and the tone of most manifestos of architecture was almost inevitably prophetic or utopian. It should be remembered, moreover, that the Città Nuova and the "Messaggio" represent different moments in Sant'Elia's development.[41] The drawings are generally earlier and cannot therefore embody principles that had not yet taken shape. The same gap between theory and practice is to be found, for example, in Boccioni's technical manifestos and in his paintings; the theory was always in advance of the art itself: "No one had realized that it would be approximately like trying to read the works that Boccioni was painting in 1910 ('Portrait of a Lady,' 'Maestra di scena,' 'Mourning,' and even 'The City Rises') in precise relation to the propositions of the contemporary 'Technical Manifesto.'"[42]

But in Sant'Elia's case there is another explanation for the contradictions between the "Messaggio" and the Città Nuova. The main sources of the "Messaggio" were literary and artistic rather than architectural. Years ago Francesco Tentori concluded that Sant'Elia's projects did not reveal the technological expertise and mastery of modern materials called for in his theory.[43] Maurizio Calvesi then showed how the modern materials advocated by Sant'Elia (cement, glass, iron) were in fact the same as those recommended by Boccioni in his manifestos; how the literary image of the modern city "like an immense, tumultuous building yard" took its inspiration from Boccioni's paintings of 1911–1912; and finally how a great part of the "Messaggio" was compiled from various manifestos, particularly those written by Boccioni. Calvesi rightly concludes that the significance of the "Messaggio" within the history of architecture "is comparable to that which the first 'Technical Manifesto' of the futurists has vis-à-vis the history of painting: it is a text, in other words, in which the 'negations' are worth more than the 'affirmations.'"[44]

Just as his drawings had been influenced by popular illustrations and the sometimes pedestrian projects of local city planners rather than by the theoretical work of specialists, so too was his theory nurtured primarily by fiery slogans and catchwords from futurist manifestos, seasoned here and there with traces of his academic education and tinged, however slightly, with the poetics of Einfühlung. In spite of the undeniable originality and audacity of the text, its sources impose severe limitations on the contents: "Evidently what the Messaggio conveys is a naive myth of the machine, still soaked in the literature and optimism of the nineteenth century with regard to the new totems of modern technology."[45] Like his projects, the "Messaggio" reveals an improvised shortcut to modernity that bypassed the realm of the architectural, as if the renewal of architecture could be brought about by fiat, as in Boccioni's technical manifestos of painting and sculpture. What was at stake in Boccioni's work was a new type of figuration—the assemblage of forms on canvas—and the gap between theory and practice was easy to bridge: "Sant'Elia conceived these leitmotivs in terms of images, and translated them into the figurative sensibility of the lexicon within his grasp: of an idiom, that is, based on the secessionist culture from which it attempted to extricate itself thanks precisely to the impetus of Marinetti's lyricism."[46]

A close analysis of the "Messaggio" reveals the profound ambiguity of Sant'Elia's concept of modernity: behind the unbridled enthusiasm for the marvels of the modern world, there lurks a certain naive awe of progress, a cautious distance from technology masterfully analyzed by Manfredo Tafuri. Tafuri has shown how in the early years of the century many of the European avant-gardes remained faithful to the mimetic principle of representation of the outside world, which he called "machine naturalism": instead of imitating nature, they imitated the new technological nature made by man.[47] For Sant'Elia this process of substitution of one nature by another had begun in 1912, when he replaced the natural setting of his early works by an all-encompassing architectural environment. In the following year, however, contact with the futurists led him to erase from his architecture every trace of the sublime, every line, shape, or color that might evoke a landscape. The massive funereal structures were replaced by a modern metropolis where form was guided solely by iron, concrete, and the geometric severity of the machine aesthetic. It is worth quoting Tafuri's passage in full in order to grasp the fundamental process at work here:

> But, faced by this *new nature of artificial "things,"* used as basic material for their artistic work, they still behave with a mentality anchored to the principle of *mimesis.*
>
> Industrial *things* take the place of Classical Nature, of the Illuminist cult of man, and even Reason: they are the result of the pitiless logic of Capital that has destroyed, paradoxically, the faith in anthropomorphism. In this sense they are *new nature.* And it is in this sense that Marinetti, Sant'Elia, Picabia, Marcel Duchamp, Ladovsky and Melnikov look at it for new emotional occasions, trying to *reproduce* it in a completely new way.[48]

Caught between the dying gasps of Romanticism and the rapidly advancing technological revolution, the young artists stood awe-struck before their new environment, much as their forebears had in the face of the mountains and lakes surrounding them, and they carried over intact from a previous age their mandate as faithful transcribers of their world. They therefore saw the new nature of technological reality as a source of immutable, timeless values from which they could draw sustenance for their art.[49]

THE REAPPEARANCE OF THE "MESSAGGIO"

Original as it was, the "Messaggio" failed to create much of a stir in Milan's architectural circles, where it was eclipsed by the drawings Sant'Elia did for the same show. On June 10, 1914, Nuove Tendenze closed its doors to the public. Then, unexpectedly, his *Manifesto of Futurist Architecture* appeared, in two slightly different versions: as a flyer dated July 11, 1914 (fig. 127), and again in the August issue of *Lacerba,* the official mouthpiece of the futurist movement.[50] This time his writing caused a sensation. Overshadowed by the new text and its massive publicity apparatus, the "Messaggio" sank quietly into oblivion, its existence forgotten by all but a handful of artists and critics. It did not come to light again until June 1956, when it was republished in an obscure magazine in Lugano by the Swiss architect Giovanni Bernasconi, a close friend of Mario Chiattone, who probably lent him a copy of the Nuove Tendenze catalogue.[51]

Its reappearance sent tremors throughout the art-historical world: "Jesus and Mary! Compared to the 'Manifesto,' [the 'Messaggio'] lacks the entire first part contained in the latter. . . . Furthermore the word 'new,' referring to *architecture, house* or *building,* takes the place of *futurist*—a word that Marinetti was to replace diabolically no less than nine times—and a few complete phrases or parts of phrases are here different from the way in which Marinetti later put it, with the complicity of Cinti and the signature of Sant'Elia."[52] The famous *Manifesto of Futurist Architecture,* for years considered Sant'Elia's only theoretical work and the basis of his reputation as a futurist, turned out to be a reworked version of a long-forgotten essay published in the catalogue of Nuove Tendenze—before he joined the futurist movement. At the time the implications seemed staggering. The absence of any

L'ARCHITETTURA FUTURISTA

Manifesto

LA CITTÀ FUTURISTA. — Stazione d'aeroplani e treni ferroviari, con funicolari e ascensori, su 3 piani stradali.

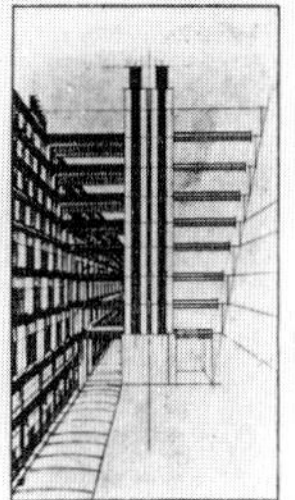

LA CITTÀ FUTURISTA. — Via secondaria per pedoni, con ascensori nel mezzo.

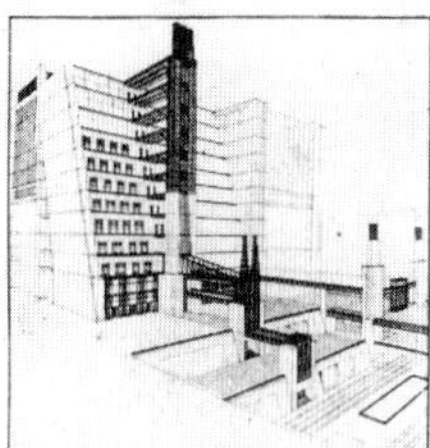

LA CITTÀ FUTURISTA. — Casa a gradinata con ascensori dai 4 piani stradali.

LA CITTÀ FUTURISTA. — Ponte a 3 piani comunicanti per mezzo d'ascensori.

Antonio Sant'Elia.
architetto

DIREZIONE DEL MOVIMENTO FUTURISTA: Corso Venezia, 61 - MILANO

Dopo il 700 non è più esistita nessuna architettura. Un balordo miscuglio dei più vari elementi di stile, usato a mascherare lo scheletro della casa moderna, è chiamato architettura moderna. La bellezza nuova del cemento e del ferro vien profanata con la sovrapposizione di carnevalesche incrostazioni decorative, che non sono giustificate nè dalle necessità costruttive, nè dal nostro gusto, e traggono origine dalle antichità egiziana, indiana o bizantina, e da quello sbalorditivo fiorire di idiozie e di impotenza che prese il nome di *neo-classicismo*.

In Italia si accolgono codeste ruffianerie architettoniche, e si gabella la rapace incapacità straniera per geniale invenzione, per architettura nuovissima. I giovani architetti italiani (quelli che attingono originalità dalla clandestina compulsazione di pubblicazioni d'arte) sfoggiano i loro talenti nei quartieri nuovi delle nostre città, ove una giocanda insalata di colonnine ogivali, di foglione seicentesche, di archiacuti gotici, di pilastri egiziani, di volute rococò, di putti quattrocenteschi, di cariatidi rigonfie, tien luogo, seriamente, di stile, ed arieggia con presunzione al monumentale. Il caleidoscopico apparire e riapparire di forme, il moltiplicarsi delle macchine, l'accrescersi quotidiano dei bisogni imposti dalla rapidità delle comunicazioni, dall'agglomeramento degli uomini, dall'igiene e da cento altri fenomeni della vita moderna, non danno alcuna perplessità a codesti sedicenti rinnovatori dell'architettura. Essi perseverano cocciuti con le regole di Vitruvio, del Vignola e del Sansovino e con qualche pubblicazioncella di architettura tedesca alla mano, a ristampare l'immagine dell'imbecillità secolare sulle nostre città, che dovrebbero essere l'immediata e fedele proiezione di noi stessi.

Così quest'arte espressiva e sintetica è diventata nelle loro mani una vacua esercitazione stilistica, un rimuginamento di formule malamente accozzate a camuffare da edificio moderno il solito bussolotto passatista di mattone e di pietra. Come se noi, accumulatori e generatori di movimento, coi nostri prolungamenti meccanici, col rumore e colla velocità della nostra vita, potessimo vivere nelle stesse case, nelle stesse strade costruite pei loro bisogni dagli uomini di quattro, cinque, sei, secoli fa.

Questa è la suprema imbecillità dell'architettura moderna che si ripete per la complicità mercantile delle accademie, domicilii coatti dell'intelligenza, ove si costringono i giovani all'onanistica ricopiatura di modelli classici, invece di spalancare la loro mente alla ricerca dei limiti e alla soluzione del nuovo e imperioso problema: **la casa e la città futurista.** La casa e la città spiritualmente e materialmente nostre, nelle quali il nostro tumulto possa svolgersi senza parere un grottesco anacronismo.

Il problema dell'architettura futurista non è un problema di rimaneggiamento lineare. Non si tratta di trovare nuove sagome, nuove marginature di finestre e di porte, di sostituire colonne, pilastri, mensole con cariatidi, mosconi, rane; non si tratta di lasciare la facciata a mattone nudo, o di intonacarla, o di rivestirla di pietra, nè di determinare differenze formali tra l'edificio nuovo e quello vecchio; ma di creare di sana pianta la casa futurista, di costruirla con ogni risorsa della scienza e della tecnica, appagando signorilmente ogni esigenza del nostro costume e del nostro spirito, calpestando quanto è grottesco, pesante e antiestetico con noi (tradizione, stile, estetica, proporzione) determinando nuove forme, nuove linee, una nuova armonia di profili e di volumi, un'architettura che abbia la sua ragione di essere solo nelle condizioni speciali della vita moderna, e la sua rispondenza come valore estetico nella nostra sensibilità. Quest'architettura non può essere soggetta a nessuna legge di continuità storica. Deve essere nuova come è nuovo il nostro stato d'animo.

L'arte di costruire ha potuto evolversi nel tempo e passare da uno stile all'altro mantenendo inalterati i caratteri generali dell'architettura, perchè nella storia sono frequenti i mutamenti di moda e quelli determinati dall'avvicendarsi dei convincimenti religiosi e degli ordinamenti politici; ma sono rarissime quelle cause di profondo mutamento nelle condizioni dell'ambiente che scardinano e rinnovano, come la scoperta di leggi naturali, il perfezionamento dei mezzi meccanici, l'uso razionale e scientifico del materiale.

Nella vita moderna il processo di conseguente svolgimento stilistico nell'architettura si arresta. **L'architettura si stacca dalla tradizione. Si ricomincia da capo per forza.**

Il calcolo sulla resistenza dei materiali, l'uso del cemento armato e del ferro escludono l'architettura intesa nel senso classico e tradizionale. I materiali moderni da costruzione e le nostre nozioni scientifiche, non si prestano assolutamente alla disciplina degli stili storici, e sono la causa principale dell'aspetto grottesco delle costruzioni «alla moda» nelle quali si vorrebbe ottenere dalla leggerezza, dalla snellezza superba della *poutrelle* e dalla fragilità del cemento armato, la curva pesante dell'arco e l'aspetto massiccio del marmo.

La formidabile antitesi tra il mondo moderno e quello antico è determinata da tutto quello che prima non c'era. Nella nostra vita sono entrati elementi di cui gli antichi non hanno neppure sospettata la possibilità; si sono determinate contingenze materiali e si sono rivelati atteggiamenti dello spirito che si ripercuotono in mille effetti; primo fra tutti la formazione di un nuovo ideale di bellezza ancora oscuro ed embrionale, ma di cui già sente il fascino anche la folla. Abbiamo perduto il senso del monumentale, del pesante, dello statico, ed abbiamo arricchita la nostra sensibilità del **gusto del leggero, del pratico, dell'effimero e del veloce.** Sentiamo di non essere più gli uomini delle cattedrali, dei palazzi, degli arengari; ma dei grandi alberghi, delle stazioni ferroviarie, delle strade immense, dei porti colossali, dei mercati coperti, delle gallerie luminose, dei rettifili, degli sventramenti salutari.

Noi dobbiamo inventare e rifabbricare la città futurista simile ad un immenso cantiere tumultuante, agile, mobile, dinamico in ogni sua parte, e la casa futurista simile ad una macchina gigantesca. Gli ascensori non debbono rincantucciarsi come vermi solitari nei vani delle scale; ma le scale, divenute inutili, devono essere abolite e gli ascensori devono inerpicarsi, come serpenti di ferro e di vetro, lungo le facciate. La casa di cemento, di vetro, di ferro, senza pittura e senza scultura, ricca soltanto della bellezza congenita alle sue linee e ai suoi rilievi, straordinariamente *brutta* nella sua meccanica semplicità, alta e larga quanto più è necessario, e non quanto è prescritto dalla legge municipale, deve sorgere sull'orlo di un abisso tumultuante: la strada, la quale non si stenderà più come un soppedaneo al livello delle portinerie, ma si sprofonderà nella terra per parecchi piani, che accoglieranno il traffico metropolitano e saranno congiunti, per i transiti necessari, da passerelle metalliche e da velocissimi *tapis roulants*.

Bisogna abolire il decorativo. Bisogna risolvere il problema dell'architettura futurista non più rubacchiando da fotografie della Cina, della Persia e del Giappone, non più imbecillendo sulle regole di Vitruvio, ma a colpi di genio, e armati di una esperienza scientifica e tecnica. Tutto deve essere rivoluzionato. Bisogna sfruttare i tetti, utilizzare i sotterranei, diminuire l'importanza delle facciate, trapiantare i problemi del buon gusto dal campo della sagometta, del capitelluccio, del portoncino, in quello più ampio dei **grandi aggruppamenti di masse,** della **vasta disposizione delle piante.** Finiamola coll'architettura monumentale funebre commemorativa. Buttiamo all'aria monumenti, marciapiedi, porticati, gradinate, sprofondiamo le strade e le piazze, inalziamo il livello delle città.

IO COMBATTO E DISPREZZO:

1. Tutta la pseudo-architettura d'avanguardia, austriaca, ungherese, tedesca e americana;

2. Tutta l'architettura classica, solenne, ieratica, scenografica, decorativa, monumentale, leggiadra, piacevole;

3. L'imbalsamazione, la ricostruzione, la riproduzione dei monumenti e palazzi antichi;

4. — Le linee perpendicolari e orizzontali, le forme cubiche e piramidali che sono statiche, gravi, opprimenti ed assolutamente fuori dalla nostra nuovissima sensibilità;

5. L'uso di materiali massicci, voluminosi, duraturi, antiquati, costosi.

E PROCLAMO:

1. Che l'architettura futurista è l'architettura del calcolo, dell'audacia temeraria e della semplicità; l'architettura del cemento armato, del ferro, del vetro, del cartone, della fibra tessile e di tutti quei surrogati al legno, alla pietra e al mattone che permettono di ottenere il massimo della elasticità e della leggerezza;

2. — Che l'architettura futurista non è per questo un'arida combinazione di praticità e di utilità, ma rimane arte, cioè sintesi, espressione;

3. — Che le linee oblique e quelle ellittiche sono dinamiche, per la loro stessa natura hanno una potenza emotiva mille volte superiore a quella delle perpendicolari e delle orizzontali, e che non vi può essere un'architettura dinamicamente integratrice all'infuori di esse;

4. — Che la decorazione, come qualche cosa di sovrapposto all'architettura, è un assurdo, e che **soltanto dall'uso e dalla disposizione originale del materiale greggio o nudo o violentemente colorato, dipende il valore decorativo dell'architettura futurista.**

5. — Che, come gli antichi trassero l'ispirazione dell'arte dagli elementi della natura, noi — materialmente e spiritualmente artificiali — dobbiamo trovare quell'ispirazione negli elementi del nuovissimo mondo meccanico che abbiamo creato, di cui l'architettura deve essere la più bella espressione, la sintesi più completa, l'integrazione artistica più efficace;

6. — L'architettura come arte di disporre le forme degli edifici secondo criteri prestabiliti è finita;

7. — Per architettura si deve intendere lo sforzo di armonizzare con libertà e con grande audacia, l'ambiente con l'uomo, cioè rendere il mondo delle cose una proiezione diretta del mondo dello spirito;

8. — Da un'architettura così concepita non può nascere nessuna abitudine plastica e lineare, perchè i caratteri fondamentali dell'architettura futurista saranno la caducità e la transitorietà. **Le case dureranno meno di noi. Ogni generazione dovrà fabbricarsi la sua città.** Questo costante rinnovamento dell'ambiente architettonico contribuirà alla vittoria del **Futurismo,** che già si afferma con le **Parole in libertà, il Dinamismo plastico, la Musica senza quadratura e l'Arte dei rumori,** e pel quale lottiamo senza tregua contro la vigliaccheria passatista.

Antonio Sant'Elia.
architetto

MILANO, 11 Luglio 1914.

DIREZIONE DEL MOVIMENTO FUTURISTA: Corso Venezia, 61 - MILANO

LA CITTÀ FUTURISTA. — Casamento con ascensori esterni, galleria, passaggio coperto, su 3 piani stradali (linea tramviaria, strada per automobili, passerella metallica) fari e telegrafia senza fili.

LA CITTÀ FUTURISTA. — Casa a gradinata, con ascensori esterni.

127. *Manifesto of Futurist Architecture,* July 11, 1914. (Photo: Collection of the author)

reference to futurism in the earlier text and its unquestioned authenticity begged the question: Had Sant'Elia really been a futurist or, as many then claimed in light of the recent discovery, was he an innocent victim of Marinetti and his circle, who adulterated the "Messaggio" without his permission?

Doubts concerning the true author of the manifesto had first appeared in 1943, when Carrà, in his autobiography, claimed that Marinetti and his secretary, Decio Cinti, had had a hand in the drafting of the manifesto.[53] At the time, this passage went by almost unnoticed, but after the republication of the "Messaggio," it was accepted by many as evidence of Marinetti's unauthorized appropriation of Sant'Elia's text.

The history of this text—of its vicissitudes and resurrections—is extremely complex and informative of the influence of politics on historiography. Both the eclipse and the reappearance of the "Messaggio" were determined by the rising and waning reputations of futurism and fascism. The oblivion to which the "Messaggio" fell prey did not come about naturally. There were, after all, various copies of the Nuove Tendenze catalogue lying about, including one at the Museo Civico, in Como, where most of Sant'Elia's drawings were kept.[54] But the futurists, or rather Marinetti, did everything he could to eradicate the memory of the earlier text.[55] It is not by accident that the "Messaggio" came to light forty-two years after the original date of publication: during the postwar decade Italian futurism was seen as little more than an offshoot of fascism. The movement was thought of as morally suspect, if not wholly immoral, and Sant'Elia, who died before fascism came into being, was considered guilty by association.[56] For this reason, his nonfuturist works began to attract much attention, which in turn led to the rediscovery of documents that had been forgotten or even deliberately concealed for ideological reasons.[57] The rediscovery of the "Messaggio" gave many scholars the hope of wresting him from futurism and thus, by implication, from fascism. "By disqualifying him as a futurist," wrote Bruno Zevi, "we redefine him as an artist and as a man."[58]

The reemergence of the "Messaggio" led to one of the most Byzantine—and pointless—architectural disputes of the century. On one side stood the fervid defenders of Sant'-Elia's futurism, centered mainly around Reyner Banham and *Architectural Review*. On the other stood those who just as staunchly sought to prove that Sant'Elia had never been a futurist and that Marinetti had doctored the "Messaggio" behind his back. This faction was championed primarily by Bruno Zevi, who directed his campaign from the pages of *L'Architettura* and the Italian weekly *L'Espresso,* where he was editor of the architectural page. Also part of this second group was Chiattone's friend Giovanni Bernasconi, who vigorously defended Sant'Elia's reputation from any taint of futurism. Originally occasioned by the republication of the "Messaggio," the debate soon became charged with political overtones, for what was at stake was much more than Sant'Elia's appurtenance to futurism. The history of the document and the attendant political undercurrents help explain the polemic tone, indeed the tribunician zeal, with which some scholars embarked upon the exegesis of the two texts.

Any attempt to discover the truth must begin with a study of the essay itself. The manifesto differs from the "Messaggio" in various ways, none of which involve serious discrepancies of meaning. The new version follows the tripartite futurist formula (exordium, central nucleus, programmatic finale) even more closely than the original. Accordingly, the exordium and the conclusion are given greater prominence: four introductory paragraphs were added at the beginning and as many programmatic points at the end. Minor changes were effected throughout the text. The words "modern" and "new," for example, were replaced eight times by "futurist" and once by "futurism." On the whole the tone of the manifesto is more aggressive, seasoned with such provocative phrases as "onanistic copies of classical models" or "bewildering array of idiocies or impotence," neither of which appeared in the "Messaggio."[59] The latter did not, in other words, show the "exhibitionism of content" characteristic of futurist manifestos.[60]

The aim of the four initial paragraphs is to provide a polemic and technical prologue with which all futurist manifestos began and which was lacking in the "Messaggio."[61] From the very first phrase—"No architecture has existed since 1700" (*Archivi*, 81)—the debt to Boccioni is clear. In the first *Manifesto of Futurist Painting*, conceived primarily by Boccioni, a similar passage occurs: "We are nauseated by the vile sloth which compels our artists, from the 16th century on, to make their living out of a constant exploitation of ancient glories."[62]

Part of the addenda was in fact a reelaboration of ideas already expressed in the "Messaggio," resulting in a certain amount of redundancy. Sant'Elia was in essence continuing to challenge the validity of historicist codes and decoration in modern times: "The new beauty of cement and iron is profaned by the superimposition of tawdry decorative incrustations that can be justified neither by structural necessity nor by our taste" (ibid.). Sant'Elia's criticism was not limited to historicist architecture but took on urbanism as well, that is, the layout of the old historical city ("as if we . . . could live in the same houses, the same streets, built for the needs of the men of four, five, six centuries ago").

Of the new ideas enunciated in the first part of the manifesto, none represent a radical departure from the "Messaggio." "In Italy such architectural prostitutions are welcomed, and rapacious foreign incompetence is taken for brilliant invention." Here one finds a theme dear to Boccioni and Marinetti—and hitherto extraneous to Sant'Elia—the idea of the "primato italiano," the unquestioned superiority of Italian over foreign achievement. It reappears in the polemic against academicism, revealed in a new anti-German innuendo that was absent from the "Messaggio": "[Academics] remain stubbornly attached to the rules of Vitruvius, Vignola and Sansovino, with some minor publication of German architecture in hand." This increasing opposition to foreign influence, veined with xenophobia, was characteristic of the jingoist mood prevalent in Italy at the onset of World War I. Various manifestos by Marinetti, Boccioni, and Carrà carried similar tirades.[63]

In the central part of the manifesto only one change was of any consequence—the addition of the words "ephemeral" and "swift" to a phrase that remained otherwise unchanged: "We have lost the sense of the monumental, the massive, the static, and we have enriched our sensibility with the taste for THE LIGHT, THE PRACTICAL, THE EPHEMERAL AND THE SWIFT." Calvesi has suggested that these words show Marinetti's heavy editorial hand, since both notions are recurrent in his writings.[64]

The main differences between the "Messaggio" and the manifesto occur in the conclusion, which is once again divided into positive and negative statements. In the first objection, the generic condemnation of trendy architecture ("fashionable architecture of every country and every kind") has been replaced by a more specific and aggressive injunction against "all the pseudo-architecture of the Austrian, Hungarian and American avant-garde" (*Archivi,* 84). So blatant is the contrast between this statement and Sant'Elia's own drawings that it has often been quoted as evidence of Marinetti's authorship. On the surface, the phrase seems innocuous enough: one of the main targets of the manifesto was unquestionably the Secession, from which Sant'Elia was trying to free himself, with varying degrees of success. As Chiattone later declared, "We wanted to extricate ourselves from the 'Wagnerschule' whence we came, but only in order to go beyond it."[65]

Furthermore, attacks against the Secession are not rare in futurist manifestos. By and large all its painters, Carrà excepted, had gone through a secessionist phase. But when they joined the futurist movement, recantation became practically mandatory. Nationalism and cultural self-sufficiency came to be almost synonymous with futurism. Boccioni, whose Art Nouveau phase had been particularly strong, had no qualms about denouncing his former source of inspiration. In his *Technical Manifesto of Futurist Painting,* he declared, "We combat the false claims to the future put forward by the Secessionists and by the Independentists, the new academicists of every nation."[66]

Yet if one takes into account the political context in which the text was written, the phrase takes on quite a different meaning: the words are a reflection of the mounting tension that followed the assassination of Archduke Franz Ferdinand of Hapsburg at Sarajevo, on June 28, 1914.[67] Hostility against Austria flared anew. Although the "Messaggio" had opposed modish architecture from foreign countries rather vaguely, "in the Manifesto the attack was limited essentially to those lands that had been allies of Italy in the Triple Alliance since 1884."[68]

War was imminent. Marinetti returned immediately from London, where he had been lecturing on futurism. This was the chance that the futurists had been waiting for, convinced as they were of the cathartic value of war ("Guerra sola igiene del mondo"). Old structures would be swept away, and new creative forces, hitherto unknown, would be unleashed. The Libyan campaign had but whetted their appetite. Now the chances of pitting themselves against Austria, Italy's historical archenemy ("il nemico secolare"), brought them hope. During the next few months, Marinetti was to attempt to convert *Lacerba* into a political weapon aimed chiefly at preparing Italy for war.[69]

For the socialists, it was a different matter: they were still unconditionally committed to peace. (Mussolini's about-face, which split the party, dates from October 1914.) Sant'Elia, who had been elected alderman in Como on the socialist ticket, could hardly have subscribed to a view that ran counter to the express policy of his party. There is no doubt that the passage against the Austro-Hungarian avant-garde constitutes an interpolation by Marinetti. Sant'Elia had no reason either personally or professionally to state such a view—even allowing for the normal discrepancy between theory and practice that was common in architectural manifestos. In this case, as in so many others, Sant'Elia's architectural critique was overridden by the political views of the futurists.[70] Be that as it may, the manifesto is a crucial text for architecture, whether or not it was written wholly or in part by Sant'Elia, and it must be judged on its own merits, irrespective of the identity of the author.

Marinetti's intervention would also explain the inclusion of America ("Pseudo-architettura americana") in the general condemnation of foreign architecture. Although Sant'Elia might conceivably have opposed American architecture because of the historicism inherent in its most audacious creations, it is more plausible to see in it, as Schmidt-Thomsen has done, yet another nationalistic gesture of Marinetti, an affirmation of Italy's cultural hegemony.[71] Sant'Elia owed too much to America to renounce categorically such a source of inspiration.

The next important change appears in the third statement, which is entirely new: "Oblique and elliptical lines are dynamic, and by their very nature possess an emotional power one thousand times greater than that of perpendiculars and horizontals; there cannot be a dynamic, all-encompassing architecture without them" (*Archivi,* 84). This too is believed to be an interpolation, since there are relatively few oblique and elliptical lines in Sant'Elia's work. The source for this particular passage can be found in Carrà's manifesto "The Painting of Sounds, Noises, and Smells," where he mentions oblique lines, as well as "the sphere, the ellipse that rotates, the inverted cone, the spiral and all dynamic forms."[72] Yet this statement is not in contradiction with the "Messaggio." On the contrary, it completes and clarifies the passage in which Sant'Elia objects to perpendicular and horizontal lines as being grave and oppressive.[73] The possibility of heightening human emotion by purely graphic means is an idea that harks back to Einfühlung and to Boccioni's theory of the *stati d'animo.* This is implied elsewhere in the manifesto, where Sant'Elia says that architecture should "transform the world of things into a direct projection of the world of the spirit" (*Archivi,* 85).

None of the changes discussed hitherto actually challenge the text of the "Messaggio" in a substantive way. Not so the closing statement, which Sant'Elia is reported to have disavowed, at least in private: "The fundamental characteristics of futurist architecture will be obsolescence and transience. [OUR] HOUSES WILL NOT LAST AS LONG AS WE SHALL. EACH GENERATION WILL HAVE TO BUILD ITS OWN CITY" (ibid.). Ephemeral architecture was a popular concept among futurists as a whole—and with Marinetti in particular—long before it appeared in the *Manifesto of Futurist Architecture.*[74] In Carrà's aforementioned manifesto, he had called for a dynamic architecture that changed according to states of mind: "We are thinking, by contrast, of an architecture similar to the dynamic musical one created by the futurist musician Pratella. A kinetic architecture of clouds and smoke in the wind, and of metallic constructions when experienced in a violent and chaotic state of mind."[75] Boccioni had been less utopian in his unpublished manifesto, claiming that "the dynamic needs of modern life will necessarily create an architecture susceptible to evolving."[76] But it was primarily Marinetti who made this idea a fundamental part of his aesthetics. "The masterpiece should disappear together with its author,"[77] he exclaimed in a celebrated passage written, significantly, after the "Messaggio" was published but before the

Manifesto of Futurist Architecture had appeared in print. Ironically, Marinetti was to give lasting expression to this concept of transient architecture, in a play written years later, *Ricostruire l'Italia con l'architettura futurista Sant'Elia.*[78] Moreover, for Marinetti's interpolation of this controversial point, we have Sant'Elia's own testimony, recorded by two witnesses.

According to Carrà's autobiography, he had mentioned Sant'Elia's name to Marinetti, who regretted that all the arts except architecture were represented within futurism. As a result, Marinetti immediately asked Carrà to invite Sant'Elia to join the futurist movement. But Sant'Elia, when informed of the proposal, dismissed the whole thing with a burst of laughter. Later, however, he changed his mind, for Carrà had duly impressed upon him the advantages of such a move.[79] After a few days, continues Carrà, Sant'Elia finally agreed to join the group and was introduced to Marinetti at his home in Corso Venezia. Carrà, Boccioni, Russolo, and Decio Cinti were also present. Not long after this initial meeting, Sant'-Elia showed Carrà some sheets of paper on which he had jotted down his ideas on modern architecture. These notes contained—or so it is believed—the *Futurist Manifesto* (or the "Messaggio") in embryo.

However, continues Carrà, shortly after the publication of the manifesto, the two men met in Milan's Galleria Vittorio Emanuele. Pointing to the eighth and last statement Sant'Elia is reported to have said laughing: "Don't attribute this nonsense to me. You know that I believe exactly the opposite." These phrases, he claimed, had been inserted into the text by Cinti and Marinetti, "who had always favored paradoxes, well aware of their effect in proclamations of this sort." And Carrà adds that Sant'Elia could not possibly approve of such ideas because "like every true artist he aspired to a solid and powerful architecture, capable of challenging the centuries."[80]

Carrà, of course, was hardly a reliable witness. An apostate of futurism, he had broken with the futurists definitively just before World War I, and during the following years he drifted over to the static metaphysics of the Novecento—to the enemy camp, so to speak.[81] Furthermore his memory serves him badly. Architecture had indeed been represented within the movement: both Prampolini and Boccioni had written manifestos of architecture, as Marinetti had to have known.

Although Carrà's story should be accepted with reservations, we need not discredit it entirely: it is still the most important testimony available. Moreover, with regard to Marinetti's editorializing on this specific point, his declaration is confirmed by Aldo Carpi De' Resmini, a former colleague of Sant'Elia at Brera who later rose to become director of the academy. He too claims to have met Sant'Elia shortly after the publication of the manifesto and to have expressed his astonishment at some of the statements in the text, statements he knew to be foreign to Sant'Elia's way of thinking. Sant'Elia answered that the futurists, or rather Marinetti, had been so insistent on publishing the manifesto that he had ended up accepting "but that the manipulation to adapt it to the futurist manner was not his but Marinetti's."[82] There is no reason to doubt, therefore, that Marinetti was responsible for at least part of the addenda to the manifesto. The question is, was this done with or without Sant'Elia's permission?

Various scholars have undertaken a careful analysis and comparison of the two texts to determine Marinetti's role in the writing of the manifesto. In the process, all available documents were studied, and all surviving members of Sant'Elia's circle were interviewed, including founders of Nuove Tendenze (Mario Chiattone, Leonardo Dudreville, Ugo Nebbia), the futurists (Carlo Carrà, Luigi Russolo, Virgilio Marchi), old colleagues from Brera (Anselmo Bucci, Aldo Carpi De' Resmini), those associated with the Milanese artistic milieu (the critics Decio Buffoni and Mario Buggelli, the painter Amaldi), and even veterans of World War I who had known Sant'Elia in the trenches (Alfredo Jeri and Antonio Giovesi).

Ironically, the result of all this scholarly investigation was that the authorship of the "Messaggio"—hitherto unassailable—was called into question. In 1956, at the height of the controversy, the writer and critic Leonardo Borgese wrote a letter to the Roman weekly *L'Espresso,* then the forum of the debate over Sant'Elia's adherence to futurism. "It seems strange," exclaimed Borgese, "that no one ever thought of asking Ugo Nebbia, who was a friend of Sant'Elia, and who has passed for years and years as the true author of the famous Manifesto."[83]

Questioned on the matter, Nebbia replied that he had indeed lent Sant'Elia a hand with regard to the drafting of the text but that the text in question was the "Messaggio," not the manifesto: "For the first exhibition of this group [Nuove Tendenze] . . . I had tried to get the participating artists to express their own ideas in the catalogue. Which is what Dudreville, Erba, Funi, and Possamai did, and naturally Sant'Elia, to whom I tried only to give a hand without modifying the important ideas which he was communicating to me and with which I was in perfect agreement."[84]

Nebbia was a cultivated, well-read art historian and critic and an inspector of Milan's historical landmarks.[85] Although he did not meet Marinetti until after World War I, he is known to have become acquainted with Boccioni in 1911, when the two men took part in the Prima Esposizione d'Arte Libera in Milan. Nebbia was no farsighted critic fighting in defense of modernity. As his preface to the Nuove Tendenze catalogue shows, he favored a cautious avant-garde that did not reject the past, and he shunned the ostentatious violence of the futurists. Whoever wrote or ideated the "Messaggio," on the other hand, was perfectly conversant with futurist theory and with the manifestos. Nebbia cannot have been responsible for this, not because he was not well read but because he was not so inclined.[86] Yet, as he himself stated, he had tried to lend Sant'Elia a hand without interfering with his ideas. That the contents of the "Messaggio" are so different from Nebbia's own moderate views is proof of how faithfully he carried out his task.

Far from dispelling doubts, Nebbia's words only added to the mass of conflicting information, for although no one seriously questioned his credibility, one month earlier the critic Mario Buggelli, another acquaintance of Sant'Elia's, had come forward claiming to have had a hand in the writing. A lively and polemic journalist, great friend of the futurists, and "discoverer" of local talent, he was notorious for his mordant wit and irreverent pen. Buggelli's collaboration is known mainly through secondary sources: he confessed to Aldo

Carpi De' Resmini, then director of the academy of Brera, that he had helped Sant'Elia write the text.[87]

Unfortunately, Buggelli's recorded statements on the matter are rather cryptic. In a letter to *L'Espresso* written in November 1956, Buggelli made the astonishing statement that the "Messaggio" did not exist: "No one will ever be able to prove the falsehood of that document because it does not exist. I repeat: it does not exist. I affirm it most categorically and stake my word of honor on this affirmation. When one assumes the existence of a 'messaggio' by Sant'Elia as opposed to the 'Manifesto of Futurist Architecture' signed by him, one is stating an untruth."[88] Buggelli promised to say more on the matter, about which he claimed to know more than anyone else. But the exchange with Zevi became so stormy that Buggelli refused to speak out again and eventually took his secret to his grave.[89] This unfortunate quarrel regrettably deprived posterity of some crucial information, for, in addition to having known all the futurists personally, Buggelli took part in the same regiment as they in World War I and no doubt had some interesting things to say. At the time, his delphic words about the nonexistence of the "Messaggio" were dismissed as the ravings of an old man, but a few years later various scholars were prepared to give them due attention.

We are left, therefore, with two witnesses, both equally trustworthy, one of whom claims to have compiled the "Messaggio," while the other states, just as categorically, that there is no such thing as the "Messaggio" and that he helped Sant'Elia write the manifesto—which, as we know, was heavily edited by Marinetti. Marinetti's own testimony is of little help in this case because of his conflicting accounts of how and when Sant'Elia joined the futurist movement: on different occasions he gave the date as 1910, 1911, 1912, and 1913.[90]

Nebbia, Buggelli, and Marinetti are not the only ones whose help must be taken into consideration when judging the "Messaggio" and the manifesto. In 1971 an unpublished manifesto of architecture by Boccioni was unexpectedly discovered and published by Zeno Birolli.[91] Like Sant'Elia's "Messaggio," it too created a great deal of excitement when it appeared for the first time. The text is a model of clarity and farsightedness, and one wonders why such an impressive document was not made public earlier.

Technically speaking, Sant'Elia's was not the first, perhaps not even the second, manifesto of futurist architecture to be written. In January 1914 the young Enrico Prampolini had published the second part of his architectural manifesto "Futurist Architecture Too . . . and What Is It?"[92] Although Prampolini was already a futurist in good standing with other members of the group, this architectural manifesto seems to be the spontaneous outburst, unofficial and unauthorized, of a newcomer to the movement. It never received the ultimate futurist accolade—republication in their official organ, *Lacerba.* Because it is known that Marinetti was eager to have architects in the movement, Crispolti has suggested, plausibly enough, that Boccioni's manifesto was an official attempt to answer Prampolini's unauthorized one.[93] Boccioni's text is not dated, but there is reason to believe that it was written sometime after March 1914 but before the Nuove Tendenze show, that is, shortly before publication of the "Messaggio."[94]

Unlike that of Prampolini, Boccioni's manifesto bears a marked resemblance to the ideas contained in the "Messaggio," and Birolli suggests the existence of a close relationship between the two texts.[95] It contains all the topics cherished by Sant'Elia and the futurists: the fight against decoration and historicism, the beauty of new materials and exposed construction, opposition to foreign fashions in architecture, and, above all, the stati d'animo. On the other hand, many parts deal with subjects that are not found in the "Messaggio" nor in the manifesto, whereas those parts that are close to Sant'Elia can also be found in Boccioni's other writings. This has led some scholars to doubt the existence of any connection between the two essays.[96] Be that as it may, any account of Sant'Elia's two texts must henceforth take Boccioni's manifesto into consideration.

Before turning to the role played by this ever-growing cast of candidates—Nebbia, Buggelli, Boccioni, and Marinetti—it is necessary to determine the chronological sequence of Sant'Elia's two texts. When were they written? And which came first, the "Messaggio" or the manifesto? The identity of Sant'Elia's coeditors is contingent on the question of dates. If the manifesto is the earlier of the two, then it is quite possible that Marinetti had something to do with the "Messaggio" as well.

Various scholars have suggested that there may have been a sort of Ur-text at the onset, written in concert with the futurists and from which both the "Messaggio" and the manifesto derive. In other words, we are dealing not with two separate documents but with two interdependent versions stemming from the same source.

Ivo Tagliaventi was the first to propose, without going into details, that because both texts were futurist, Sant'Elia might have entered into an agreement with the futurists before Nuove Tendenze. He implies that Sant'Elia then excised every explicit reference to the movement in his essay, in order not to alienate fellow members of the group: "The 'Manifesto' is not a bowdlerized version of the 'Messaggio' but . . . the latter is an excerpt and an adaptation of the former for the *Exhibition of Nuove Tendenze*."[97] The "Messaggio," in other words, was extracted from the manifesto like Eve from Adam's rib.

This thesis was put forth more forcefully by Alberto Longatti. Comparing the opening lines of both texts, he says of the "Messaggio": "The discourse seems to be truncated, it opens too abruptly with an assertive phrase 'The problem of modern architecture is not a question of rearranging lines,' which seems to be the conclusion of an argument [enunciated] previously and either not made explicit here, or else erased."[98] The missing introduction, he claims, can be found in the four initial paragraphs to the manifesto. These dovetail so smoothly with the beginning of the "Messaggio" that in his view we must be dealing with a single text from which an excerpt—the "Messaggio"—was extracted for publication in Nuove Tendenze.

According to Longatti, the first meeting between Sant'Elia and the futurists mentioned by Carrà took place, unbeknownst to the other members of Nuove Tendenze, before the exhibition, when Sant'Elia was still preparing his projects and catalogue entry. The manifesto was thus written in concert with Marinetti and the futurists but with the aid of Buggelli. Then, either because they agreed to postpone publication until after the Nuove Tendenze show or because they never really reached an agreement, Sant'Elia published the text—or at least an excerpt—in the catalogue of Nuove Tendenze. Only after the exhibition did he come to an understanding with the futurists, at which point the unabridged version appeared in print. This would explain, in his view, why Buggelli claimed that there was no such thing as a "Messaggio" as distinct from the manifesto. Although published earlier, the "Messaggio" was really just a part of the Ur-text (the manifesto).

This theory has its problems, not the least of which is an implication of rather unethical behavior on the part of Sant'Elia—an assumption one is reluctant to make without the necessary evidence—namely, that Sant'Elia kept silent about his agreement with the futurists in order not to jeopardize his much-needed participation in the Nuove Tendenze exhibition.[99] Furthermore, it fails to provide an adequate explanation for the resemblance between Boccioni's manifesto and Sant'Elia's "Messaggio."

Chronology is a crucial part of the problem. In his version of the facts Carrà does not mention dates. He just gives an idea of the sequence of events: "a few days" after he went to see Sant'Elia on Marinetti's behalf, Sant'Elia finally decided to join the group, and again "a few days" after the meeting with Marinetti, Sant'Elia showed him a "mucchietto di fogli" (handful of sheets), which according to Carrà contained the germ of the manifesto. He does not tell us how much time elapsed between the drafting and the actual publication of the manifesto but telescopes the whole episode into a matter of days. Although one should beware of attaching too literal an interpretation to Carrà's words, written almost thirty years after the events, there is no doubt that his is the most detailed account that has come down to us. Furthermore, Carrà volunteered the information long before the issue became charged with political overtones. If he is correct, Marinetti met Sant'Elia after the Nuove Tendenze show, when the "Messaggio," drafted with the help of Nebbia and possibly Buggelli, was already published. The mucchietto di fogli was probably the typescript of the "Messaggio."

In fact, the pace of events was such as to make a meeting with Marinetti before Nuove Tendenze highly unlikely. Marinetti, Boccioni, and Carrà were away during the weeks preceding May 20, the publication date of the "Messaggio." In February Marinetti was touring Russia and Germany. He returned in March and at the end of April left again for London, whence he returned unexpectedly on June 30, after the assassination at Sarajevo. However, on July 11—date of the *Manifesto of Futurist Architecture*—Carrà had still not been informed of Marinetti's presence in Milan, as can be seen from a letter he wrote to Severini.[100] Therefore, the meeting with Marinetti mentioned by Carrà in his autobiography can hardly have taken place before July 11. Sant'Elia, too, was busy in the first days of the month, campaigning on behalf of the socialists for the municipal elections at Como, which took place on July 5. Apart from this futurist rhythm of events, there were internecine quarrels within the group. In March Carrà had a quarrel with Boccioni and subsequently sent his resignation (later rescinded) to Marinetti.

Moreover, as Schmidt-Thomsen points out,[101] had the "Messaggio" been available to Marinetti before publication, it is highly unlikely that he would have relinquished such an important work (that is, a potential manifesto) and allowed it to be emasculated by the substitution of innocuous words such as "new" and "modern" for "futurism" and "futurist." He would not have ceded it to a group that, to his well-tutored eyes, must have inevitably seemed—Sant'Elia excepted—a provincial and parochial enterprise living off the crumbs that fell from the futurist table. Erba and Dudreville, it should be remembered, had both been turned down for membership in the movement because their work was not considered sufficiently challenging.

Surviving members of Nuove Tendenze have also put Sant'Elia's meeting with Marinetti after the show. Dudreville, for example, stated categorically that "it is all too clear that Sant'Elia became a 'futurist' when he accepted Marinetti's offer, after the exhibition of 'Nuove Tendenze' at the *Famiglia Artistica*."[102] Of the same opinion was Carlo Accetti, a lawyer from Como who knew Sant'Elia during those years and who later amassed the best collection of drawings by Sant'Elia in private hands.[103]

Finally, Prampolini's indignant accusation of plagiarism leveled against Nuove Tendenze in June is incomprehensible if Sant'Elia was already a member, official or not, since Prampolini was already on close terms with the futurists. Moreover, although many questions remain to be answered, there is no doubt that the internal logic of the facts gains in clarity if one accepts this order of events. Seen after the manifesto, the "Messaggio" appears to be a falling off, a truncated torso. But if it comes before the manifesto, there seems to be a logical progression from one to the other.

Who, then, helped Sant'Elia write the "Messaggio"? At this point it is probably impossible to identify the exact contribution of Nebbia, Buggelli, Boccioni, Marinetti, and Cinti, since all the eye-witness accounts conflict. In the entire history of architecture, few texts are as baffling and controversial as these two overlapping versions. The very difficulty in identifying Sant'Elia's helpers is revealing, because many, if not most, of the futurist manifestos are known to be the fruit of corporate authorship. As Calvesi has said, "The futurism of Boccioni, of Carrà, Balla and also that of Sant'Elia . . . was the sum total of their individual personalities, with the common denominator Marinetti."[104]

In spite of differing opinions as to who helped draft the "Messaggio" and the manifesto, no one doubts that Sant'Elia needed help. His friends and acquaintances declared almost unanimously that the wording of both texts was beyond his scope.[105] As Dudreville remarks, "Speaking with him at length and in detail, while he [Dudreville] examined some essay that Sant'Elia had brought, he was immediately convinced of finding himself face-to-face with a vivaceous, independent and original intelligence . . . although Sant'Elia revealed an obvious lack of preparation with regard to culture of a general nature."[106]

Such evidence of his writing as exists bears this out. The grades Sant'Elia received on various exams reveal his lack of writing ability. A few captions and a handful of postcards, almost all written from the front, are all that survive in his hand, and even these show an occasional spelling mistake. Because the bulk of his drawings is extant, one can safely assume that this paucity of written documents was due not to the accident of survival but to his reluctance and inability to write.

This is not to say that the two texts did not reflect Sant'Elia's way of thinking: whether he was helped by Nebbia, Buggelli, Marinetti, or Boccioni—Cinti helped only with minor editing—the ideas expressed therein were his own. Half-remembered snatches of the futurist manifestos no doubt stuck in his mind, and he was definitely capable of transcribing them, however imperfectly. On the other hand, the help he received from his friends, voluntary and involuntary, inevitably went beyond simple editorial assistance.[107] Rhetorical turns of phrase and metaphors did not come easily to him, and in polishing his style his helpers gave the wording a twist that probably exceeded Sant'Elia's original intentions. Dudreville, who knew all the protagonists well, has probably left the best conclusion to be drawn from the current state of scholarship:

> Now, this text was not actually written by Sant'Elia (who was a young man endowed with a bright and quick intelligence, but almost no literary culture, and at any rate too lazy and little inclined to things of the sort), nor is it known with certainty who penned it. I myself would not be able to state it with precision because, since it was clear *to all* at the time that Sant'Elia was not the author, some attributed it to Buggelli, others to Nebbia. In any case the issue seems to me immaterial since the ideas of the "Messaggio" were, without any doubt, the ideas of Sant'Elia, which we all knew very well.[108]

Disagreements concern mainly the authorship of the manifesto, more precisely, the beginning and end.[109] Were the opening paragraphs and the conclusion added wholly or in part by Marinetti? And was this achieved with or without Sant'Elia's permission? Opinions are split into two well-defined camps: those who believe that Sant'Elia joined futurism out of opportunism (and suffered Marinetti to change his "Messaggio" at will) and those who believe that he was co-opted against his wish (in which case Marinetti doctored the "Messaggio").

Few scholars today seriously believe that Marinetti tampered with the text behind Sant'Elia's back. That, at any rate, was the initial reaction to the "Messaggio" when it reappeared in 1956, after an eclipse of forty-two years.[110] Basing their position on Carrà's revelations, along with the blatant discrepancies between the two texts, these earlier critics dismissed the manifesto as a fabrication by Marinetti, regardless of its intrinsic merits. This was also the opinion of some members of Nuove Tendenze, who had been profoundly shocked with Sant'Elia's defection and with the appearance of the *Manifesto of Futurist Architecture*. Both Nebbia and Chiattone thought that Sant'Elia had been an unwilling victim of Marinetti: "And presumably, once his consent had been wearily extracted from him, Marinetti then re-elaborated the Messaggio behind his back; Sant'Elia, furthermore, did not write."[111]

It is difficult to believe that Sant'Elia would have supinely ceded the "Messaggio" to Marinetti so that the latter could tailor it to his wishes, bringing it in line with the more militant tenor of the futurist manifestos. Sant'Elia must have been responsible for at least part of the addenda, pending editorial assistance, authorized and unauthorized, from Marinetti and Cinti. In any case, he never disclaimed the document, or even parts of it, in public. Although the text was seasoned with characteristic Marinettianisms ("onanistic copies of classical styles," "coercive prisonhouse of intelligence"), one should remember that these were part of the jargon of the times. Virgilio Marchi, a latter-day futurist and architect, summed up the situation very well:

> Apart from the fact that it is inconceivable that an artist of great talent like Sant'Elia remained a prey to a manifesto carrying his signature without being informed, one must remember that at

a time of intense and effervescent discussions and enthusiasm provoked by the motive center Marinetti, there came into being a language, a vocabulary with a multiplicity of nuances, and a dialectic that was common to every branch of that revolutionary activity. It is hardly strange, therefore, that side by side with expressions then in vogue in the professional sphere (such as "architectural prostitutions" etc.), there were modes and idioms of typically Marinettian inspiration. One might say that the words were in the air.[112]

Besides, if Marinetti had actually written the "Messaggio," why did he not cosign it as he did with so many others?[113] It is more likely that the text he helped draft was the manifesto: no doubt he convinced Sant'Elia to accept phrases that the latter questioned but that had the shock value so essential to a futurist manifesto. And if Marinetti did not cosign the manifesto, in which he obviously had a hand, it may have been because it was too similar to the "Messaggio," which had already appeared in print over Sant'Elia's signature.

Marinetti's participation, as we have seen, is supported by the statements of Carrà, Carpi De' Resmini, Chiattone, Nebbia, and most of the critics. Cinti's collaboration turns up almost as insistently as Marinetti's: "Who retouched the original 'messaggio'?" asks Dudreville. "Not, surely, Nebbia," he continues, "nor even, perhaps, Buggelli. It was probably Cinti who, as everyone knew, was charged with tasks of this type within Marinetti's group."[114] Accetti concurs, adding that Sant'Elia entrusted the polishing of the text to Decio Cinti, "who, contemplative and elusive as he was, corrected the prose of Marinetti and his companions."[115]

Boccioni, too, may have had something to do with Sant'Elia's text, because it was mainly his ideas that served as a source of inspiration for both the "Messaggio" and the manifesto. Nevertheless, if parts of the manifesto were rewritten by Marinetti and Sant'Elia, Boccioni's ideas are more likely to be found unadulterated in the "Messaggio." "It is certain," wrote Birolli, "that of the two variants of S. Elia [sic], Boccioni is closer to the first [the "Messaggio"] as one can see by comparing individual topics and passages."[116]

BOCCIONI'S MANIFESTO

And what about Boccioni's manifesto? Was it written before Sant'Elia's "Messaggio"—in which case it may have had some influence on that text—or did it postdate it? Most critics incline toward the first alternative. Had the "Messaggio" appeared before Boccioni's manifesto, Boccioni "would hardly have ignored or failed to refer to a text by the architect Sant'Elia."[117] Because Marinetti was eager to enlist architects in his movement,[118] it is possible that, given Boccioni's great interest in the matter, he asked him to draw up a manifesto of futurist architecture.[119] Certainly no one was more qualified. As both his art and his writings reveal, Boccioni was very up-to-date with architectural developments in Milan, particularly in the industrial periphery: "The large popular housing blocks with their spareness and simple decoration in white-solid and black-void are much closer to the reality of the bourgeois villa or apartment building."[120] In addition Boccioni had known other architects for years; it was Sant'Elia's modernist work that appealed to him. It would therefore be curious indeed if the two had not exchanged thoughts on a subject that was of vital importance to them both. Boccioni's far-ranging culture and theoretical sharpness no doubt inspired and influenced Sant'Elia, while the latter's drawings, which had already received considerable acclaim at the exhibition of Lombard architects, must have had some impact on Boccioni.

Various passages in Boccioni anticipate the functionalism later advocated in Le Corbusier's *Vers une architecture:* "A surgical instrument, a ship, a car, a train station, enclose in their design a necessity of life that creates a pattern of voids and solids, of lines and planes of equilibrium, and of equations by means of which a new architectural emotion bursts forth."[121] These exciting new assets, Boccioni complains, were entirely ignored by contemporary architects and town planners, who continued to be guided solely by the means and methods of the past. There is much truth to Ezio Godoli's assertion that the tendency in recent criticism to study Boccioni's text exclusively in relation to Sant'Elia's has led to a general underestimation of Boccioni's manifesto.[122]

The most innovative part of his manifesto deals with the need to revolutionize the exterior of the building, which was still based on antiquated and academic notions of symmetry and decorum: "Thus the facade of a house must descend, rise, take itself apart, recede, jut out, according to the strength of the demands put upon it by the [interior] spaces. It is the exterior that the architect must sacrifice to the interior, as in painting and sculpture. And since the exterior is always traditional, the new exterior, fruit of the triumph of the interior, will inevitably give birth to the new architectural line."[123] In audacity and originality, this passage has no equal in contemporary writings on architecture and seems to prefigure some of the bolder conceptions of De Stijl.[124] Sant'Elia's "Messaggio" had also stressed the need to "play down the importance of the facades." But Boccioni went beyond that. His experience in art led him to break open the contours of forms and volumes and prepared him to see that the same would eventually happen to architecture, the sister art that could seldom remain divorced from contemporary trends in painting and sculpture.

Moreover, Boccioni's ideas on architecture, as revealed in this manifesto, transcend the technological determinism that Tafuri had identified in Sant'Elia, for whom the use of new materials such as concrete and iron would "necessarily" produce a new architectural idiom. As Godoli has observed, "In Boccioni's notion of the architectural one finds an intellectual posture that surpasses the evolutionism of a positivist nature such as one finds in Sant'Elia's *Messaggio* in which he [Sant'Elia] insists on the correlation between the renewal of architectural language and the use of new building materials."[125] Boccioni, in other words, frees architecture from the need of imitating technological reality. The new materials are a means, not an end; and the form-giving process in architecture must retain its autonomy.

Why was Boccioni's manifesto never published? Possibly, as many have suggested, because the "Messaggio" had appeared in print before Boccioni had time to publish his text. Accompanied by the drawings of the Città Nuova, Sant'Elia's work was far more aggressive than Boccioni's and almost more futurist in form and tone: the prophetic takes precedence over the explanatory. Because the movement needed an architect as much, if not more, than it needed an architectural manifesto, Sant'Elia was invited—possibly even pressured—to join the group. The two men seem to have enjoyed a cordial relationship, although Boccioni's abhorrence of newcomers to the movement—in contrast to Marinetti's more catholic disposition—was well known. If he put aside his own text, he may not have done so voluntarily. In any event, after the publication of the "Messaggio" Boccioni's manifesto had become redundant and was shelved accordingly.[126]

We are thus left with two overlapping texts and three candidates who claim to have worded one or the other: Nebbia, Buggelli, and Marinetti. Neither of the texts was actually written by Sant'Elia, although the ideas represented therein are his own. Both are therefore partly apocryphal.[127]

THE POLITICS OF THE MANIFESTO

The publication of the manifesto also poses some difficult problems. It was published in Milan as a flyer dated July 11, 1914. On August 1, 1914, it also appeared in the official organ of the movement, the Florentine magazine *Lacerba.* This last date is emblematic, for on that day Germany declared war on Russia: World War I had begun.[128] It was the last important manifesto to be published by the futurists. To be sure, they continued to produce manifestos well into the 1940s, but after 1914 their momentum was spent: Carrà had already resigned, and Boccioni's work could no longer be described as futurist. The very center of the movement was shifting from Milan to Rome, where younger men like Prampolini and Bragaglia, as well as the older Balla, were challenging the fine arts–oriented hegemony of Boccioni and Carrà in favor of a broader range of futurist activity encompassing the decorative arts.

Marinetti supervised the publication of Sant'Elia's manifesto with unusual care, anticipating that this issue would prove particularly popular.[129] He oversaw all the details personally and arranged for publicity posters announcing the publication of the forthcoming work.

There are minor discrepancies—though no fundamental ones—between the Milanese and the Florentine versions. By and large the clearest text is the one published in Milan, which is supposedly earlier. Basing his conclusions on a philological comparison of the two versions and on documentary evidence, Bernasconi suggests that Marinetti antedated the Milanese flyer, which he believes was published only after the *Lacerba* version came out in print.[130]

There is some evidence that other manifestos may have been antedated in order to make them coincide with the eleventh of the month—a hallowed date in futurist numerology. This is believed to be the case with the *Manifesto of Futurist Painting,* officially dated February 11, 1910, but actually written later in the month.[131] The usual procedure was publication in the form of a flyer on the canonical eleventh of the month, followed by republication, often with minor alterations, in *Lacerba.* As the deadline for the eleventh could not always be met, the pamphlet version was sometimes antedated.

Bernasconi bases his claim on three letters, two written by Marinetti and one by Carrà.

In the first of two letters written to Ardengo Soffici concerning Sant'Elia's manifesto—and dated July 21, 1914—Marinetti writes:

> Please order from Vallecchi an advertisement in very large characters of the MANIFESTO OF FU-TURIST ARCHITECTURE by Antonio Sant'Elia in the usual poster format that he sends to the newsstands.
>
> There are many people in Milan and all over Italy who are waiting for our views on architecture.[132]

This last phrase would hardly make sense if the first version of the manifesto had already been launched in Milan on July 11.[133] In the second letter to Soffici (dated July 23, 1914), Marinetti adds a cryptic phrase to the effect that he is sending him Sant'Elia's manifesto.[134] Since no other futurist manifesto was in the offing, Bernasconi claims that this could refer only to the version of the manifesto published separately as a flyer.

Additional evidence can be found in the letter written by Carrà to Severini on July 11, 1914 (the purported date of the manifesto), which shows that on that day Carrà was still unaware of Marinetti's unexpected return from London.[135] There is no mention of a new futurist manifesto. The first futurist document to mention Sant'Elia's name is Marinetti's letter to Soffici of July 21, 1914. This would lead us to assume that the first official meeting between Sant'Elia and the futurists, and the subsequent drafting of the manifesto, occurred between July 11 and July 21.

Bernasconi ingeniously links the information contained in these letters to the slight discrepancies between Sant'Elia's texts and to the rapidly deteriorating political situation. On July 23 the Austro-Hungarian empire sent Serbia an ultimatum in reprisal for the assassination of the Hapsburg heir at Sarajevo. Italy's entry into the war was only a question of time. On the same day Marinetti sent Soffici Sant'Elia's manifesto for publication in *Lacerba,* that is, the revised form of the "Messaggio" to which he added, among other things, the lines: "I despise and combat . . . all the pseudo-architecture of the avant-garde—Austrian, Hungarian, and American." On August 1, Germany declared war on Russia, and two days later on France. Once more Marinetti retouched the manifesto in response to the new political situation, with a view to publishing it as a flyer: he inverted the initial words of the conclusion, changing them from "I despise and combat" to "I combat and despise," and added the adjective "tedesca" (German) to the list of undesirable influences from foreign countries (*Archivi,* 84).[136] Sant'Elia's manifesto thus gives Marinetti's untiring "interventismo" yet another outlet. Marinetti himself, who republished Sant'Elia's manifesto often, invariably used the version published as a flyer.

This was not the only case in which a politically neutral manifesto was transformed into a document with pointed references to interventionism. On May 20, 1914, Balla's *Le vêtement masculin futuriste* (Futurist Manifesto of Male Attire) was published in France as a flyer. A few months later, on September 11, it was republished under the title *Il vestito antineutrale* (The Antineutral Suit). Although signed by Balla alone, Marinetti had in fact transformed it into a manifesto with strong political overtones.[137]

The appearance of Sant'Elia's manifesto so soon after the exhibition came as a total surprise to fellow members of Nuove Tendenze, who had not been informed of his conversion to futurism. Four decades later Dudreville still smouldered, recalling the offhand way in which he had been informed of the about-face by a third party, the journalist Filippo Quaglia: "Sant'Elia is leaving you: he is going over to the futurists. Marinetti and Boccioni offered him membership in the futurist group and he accepted. Someone has already written the manifesto, which will be published as soon as possible."[138]

This was a tremendous blow to Dudreville, both personally and professionally. The exhibition had been such a success that it had been invited to tour various Italian cities, including Sant'Elia's hometown, and even Switzerland. Como, in fact, had offered nothing less than its famous Palazzo Comunale for the event. All this came to an end, however, with Sant'Elia's departure, and Dudreville had no choice but to turn down these tantalizing offers. In fact, Sant'Elia's departure, later to be followed by that of Achille Funi, destroyed the group: Nuove Tendenze never recuperated from the loss of its most dazzling member.

To a certain extent all the "New Tendents" had been influenced by futurism, as had probably all of Milan's avant-garde, but to go from that position to open militancy in the notorious group was a large step, which Sant'Elia's acquaintances unanimously ascribed to opportunism. Dudreville, who had failed to mellow with the passage of time, was adamant: "Furthermore, Sant'Elia had his ideas to champion, and to achieve this he placed them at the service of futurism, just as he would have consigned them to the cubists, the expressionists or, indifferently, to any other group that offered him the greatest probability of success."[139] One should remember, nevertheless, that Dudreville put his ideas "at the service of futurism" even earlier than Sant'Elia but was turned down, and as a result his views were probably jaundiced by envy.

Unfortunately, one cannot wholly erase the taint of opportunism from Sant'Elia's reputation: Dudreville's words were confirmed by virtually all the friends of Sant'Elia who were interviewed in later years. Arata was equally candid: "His thirst for celebrity and his goal of a radical reform of architecture had led him to embrace futurism."[140] Chiattone, Sant'Elia's old friend, and Carpi De' Resmini likewise spoke of his hope of at last being able to accomplish something through an association with the futurists, despite their differences of opinion.[141] Carrà, as we have seen, had declared that he had tried to bait Sant'Elia by holding out promises of work and fame, adding that it was precisely these last two considerations that had finally persuaded Sant'Elia.[142]

Faced with a stagnant and unimaginative patronage that provided little incentive to young architects and no opportunity for self-expression, Sant'Elia must have hoped that an association with the futurists would give him needed exposure and thus open a few doors. Marinetti was a wealthy man, with a genius for publicity, and his generosity toward fellow futurists was proverbial. Sant'Elia could not possibly have agreed with all their tenets, particularly with regard to politics, but his venality (if such it was) was mixed with a sincere admiration for their art, whose influence on his own work dates back to 1913—long before he was invited to join the movement.[143]

Strangely enough there was almost no reaction to the manifesto in the press. At the time it went by relatively unheeded in the flurry of events that precipitated World War I.

Apart from one or two passing remarks in marginal journals, the only review of that time appeared in *Pagine d'Arte,* one of Italy's best magazines on modern art.[144] Written by his sometime friend Giulio Arata, this article was actually a scathing attack—virtually the only negative one Sant'Elia received within his lifetime: "Futurist activity has closed its circle. This cephalopodous mollusk began to set its tentacles in motion, first grabbing poetry, then painting, with a third it grasped music. Then, after a pause of a year or so, it put a fourth in motion in order to attract sculpture within its orbit, and finally, after one more pause, it bestirred itself with one last effort to introduce into its digestive apparatus the last prey: architecture."[145] The virulence with which Arata assailed the manifesto was all the more surprising in view of the enthusiasm he had shown in reviewing Sant'Elia's work for the exhibition of Lombard architecture earlier that year.[146]

Arata, in fact, had an ax to grind. He had been one of the most prestigious members of Nuove Tendenze, but sometime before the beginning of the show he dropped out altogether. It is strange that, after having announced his membership in the press, he should have abandoned a group with whose eclectic modernism he had so much in common; and stranger still that he had not reviewed Nuove Tendenze, since he was partly responsible for the architectural rubric in *Pagine d'Arte* and *Vita d'Arte.*[147] After all, despite his caustic review of Sant'Elia's manifesto, six months later we find him once again praising his projects in print, during the Verona competition. His animosity to futurism is easier to explain; the key lies in the following cryptic passage of his review: "Antonio Sant'Elia with a rapid transition passed through opposite camps in architecture: after a brief period of work on Egyptian, Italian, and Byzantine antiquity, he became a member . . . of the Nuove Tendenze group, the right wing of futurism; today, driven, perhaps, by loftier dreams, he has passed over to the extreme revolutionary left wing of art."[148]

Much has been written about Arata's description of Nuove Tendenze as the "right wing of futurism" and of futurism as the "extreme revolutionary left wing of art." These phrases cannot possibly be taken as statements of political fact. Nuove Tendenze was more temperate than futurism artistically but hardly so politically. Sant'Elia was a socialist, Giovanni Possamai an anarchist. Carlo Erba had been in contact with anarchist circles in Milan. Gustavo Macchi, possibly the most erudite member of the group, had spent some time in Germany and was well versed in Marx, Nietzsche, and Schopenhauer.[149]

Arata's violent opposition to the futurists revolves around their belief in art as a form of militancy. For him futurism represented the prostitution of art at the service of extra-artistic (that is, political) goals.[150] In a series of articles written in *Pagine d'Arte,* Arata defends the idea of the modern artist as an apolitical, autonomous figure under the protection of a benign and paternal state that cares for his well-being in exchange for his neutrality. This was, of course, anathema to the futurists, who saw themselves as part of a revolutionary ferment bent on transforming existing structures, whether political or aesthetic. Arata was wrong, therefore, in asserting that Sant'Elia was moving from the right wing to the left. If anything, Sant'Elia was moving in the opposite direction, because the shift from Nuove Tendenze to futurism was less radical than that between the Socialist Party to futurism.

At the time of republication of the "Messaggio" much was made of the differences between the two texts for reasons that were largely political. The greater the gap between the nonfuturist and politically innocent "Messaggio," and the futurist (that is, pre-fascist) manifesto, the more easily could the blame be shifted onto Marinetti, who, it was believed, had adulterated the "Messaggio" behind Sant'Elia's back. The manifesto was therefore regarded with suspicion and treated with the utmost rigor.[151]

At the other extreme, Reyner Banham, who saw in futurism one of the forerunners of what he called the Modern Movement, always tended to downplay the "Messaggio" precisely because it was not futurist enough and could therefore not be used as one of the underpinnings of the International Style. "A sentiment like 'Le case dureranno meno di noi' anticipates Le Corbusier as exactly as do some of his drawings (e.g.: those for the Stazione Centrale), and the Messaggio remains, deprived of passages like this, a provincial and retrospective text when compared to the Manifesto."[152]

Posterity has been more clement toward Sant'Elia's "Messaggio," though hardly more scholarly.[153] Now that Sant'Elia's nonfuturist works have been rehabilitated, it has received increasing attention. Although it too was drafted with the help of others, it is undeniably closer to Sant'Elia's intentions than the manifesto.[154]

Yet the manifesto is the document by which Sant'Elia's ideas on architecture became known to the world, at least until 1956, when the "Messaggio" was rediscovered.[155] And whether or not Sant'Elia agreed with them, the fact remains that some of the most celebrated slogans of the text are the result of Marinetti's inspired emendations. Today scholarship has rightly focused on the essential similarity between the "Messaggio" and the manifesto. They must be considered as two equally valid versions of the same document.[156] Impressed by the futurists' impassioned love of modernity and by their triumphalist rhetoric, and perhaps by the millenarian fervor of the socialists, Sant'Elia gave verbal form to his vague ideas on architecture for the metropolis. And yet his text provided a beautiful rallying cry, a banner under which disparate minds could recognize themselves. Perhaps its very elusiveness helped make it so.

Six   The Late Work

After his election as town councillor in July 1914, Sant'Elia received a few commissions in Como as a result of his new status. In autumn, he was asked to provide designs for two elementary schools. Plans for the first of these, the Francesco Baracca School, on Via Brambilla, had been  approved several years earlier but had to be altered for technical reasons. Sant'Elia was responsible for the facade decorations alone, and his designs were carried out with modifications after the war. As with his other commissions, his style changed to accommodate the tastes of the patron, in this case the city of Como. In consequence he exchanged the radical modernity of the Città Nuova for the traditional wreaths and cartouches in *sgrafitto* that had festooned Como's palazzi for centuries. The building was a three-story mass that Sant'Elia articulated in a rather conventional way, reserving rustication for the ground floor and unifying the upper floors by means of a giant order of pilasters, covered by thin, vinelike decoration (figs. 128,129). Only in the design of the gateway to the precincts did he allow himself some distant echoes of the Secession (fig. 130). The design for the other elementary school was less pedestrian, but it was never built (fig. 131).

His only other work in Como, like the others a modest project, was the facade decoration for a house on Via Cesare Cantù, where his father had his hairdressing salon for many years (fig. 132). Sant'Elia had been a schoolmate of the landlord's son and apparently supervised the work in person from the scaffolding.[1] Once more Sant'Elia fell back on the time-honored tradition of the local town houses: neo-Renaissance swags, wreaths, and leafy bowers in reddish sgrafitto. Carried out with minor changes from the drawing, this facade is one of the rare surviving projects by Sant'Elia.

When it came to his hometown, with its quaint little streets and placid palazzi with faded frescoes, the man who had only a few months earlier called for the "abolition of the decorative" and heaped scorn on the "foglione seicenteschi" (seventeenth-century acanthus leaves) was using those same foglione with loving care, out of respect for local tradition. It is noteworthy that during these very days

128. *below* Antonio Sant'Elia. Primary school in Via Brambilla, elevation, 1914–1915. (Holograph of lost original, courtesy of Musei Civici, Como)

129. Antonio Sant'Elia. Primary school in Via Brambilla, detail, 1914–1915. (Holograph of lost original, courtesy of Musei Civici, Como)

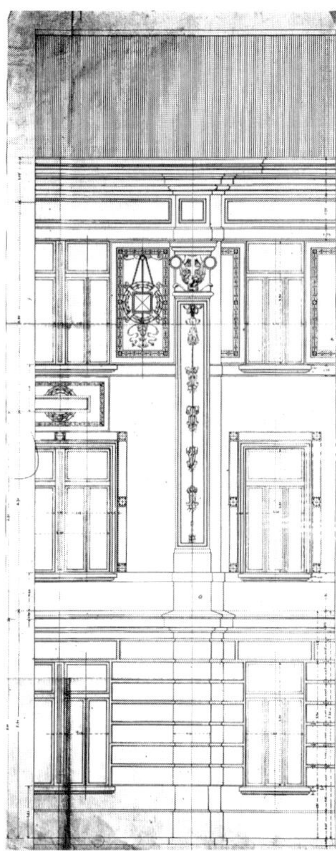

Sant'Elia was hard at work on the Verona Savings Bank, where he flouted the historicist prerequisites stipulated by the competition, diluting them with large doses of modernity. In Como he permitted himself no such license. The triangular frieze below the roof, which also appears in his project for Verona, is the only muted reference to the Secession.

Like the Villa Elisi, these minor projects in Como had also been left out of the canon, although isolated voices now and then would recall their existence. But it is works like these that are crucial to the understanding of a revolutionary young architect like Sant'Elia, caught in the great divide between tradition and modernity. As a rule, compromise was the lot of any young Italian architect with modernist velleities. But these repeated compromises also point to contradictions, hesitations, and a lingering attachment to the tradition from which he was desperately trying to free himself. When it came to his personal surroundings (the famous Red House on Via Senato, where the most important futurist manifestos were written), even Marinetti chose, instead of tubular steel, opulent oriental rugs, damask curtains, and dusky lamps—the sort of bric-a-brac in which a D'Annunzio or even a Des Esseintes would have been at home.[2]

After joining the futurists Sant'Elia collaborated with them on the cover of a book of poetry by Luciano Folgore.[3] The words of the title, *Ponti sull'oceano,* curve obligingly over the blue ground of the cover (fig. 133). Marinetti, who carefully supervised the publications of all official members of his movement, seems to have been instrumental in the choice of the design.[4] In a letter to Folgore dated July 24, 1914, he wrote of the cover: "The drawing by Sant'Elia aims precisely at rendering (as far as possible) the immensity of the ocean beneath the arches of your bridges."[5]

In Sant'Elia's cover the word no longer expresses its denotative function by abstract signs alone but assumes a pictorial function, as in Apollinaire's contemporary *Calligrammes,* themselves much influenced by Marinetti's experiments with *parole in libertà* (words in freedom).[6] In *Destruction of Syntax,* his manifesto of 1913, Marinetti outlined his revolution in syntax, punctuation, and orthography: words could be shortened, lengthened, or modified to increase their emotional impact.[7] A radical overhauling of traditional typography was essential to drive home the explosive charge of *paroliberismo;* characters of

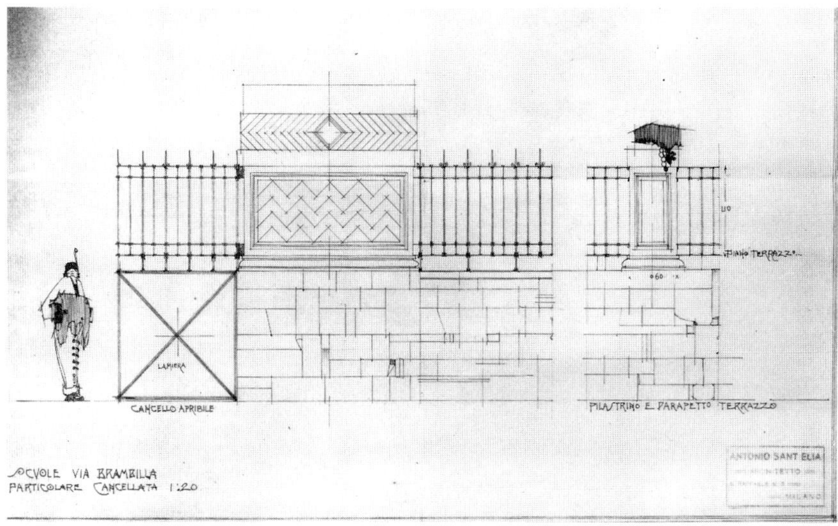

130. Antonio Sant'Elia. Primary school, detail of entrance gate, 1914–1915. (Holograph of lost original, courtesy of Musei Civici, Como)

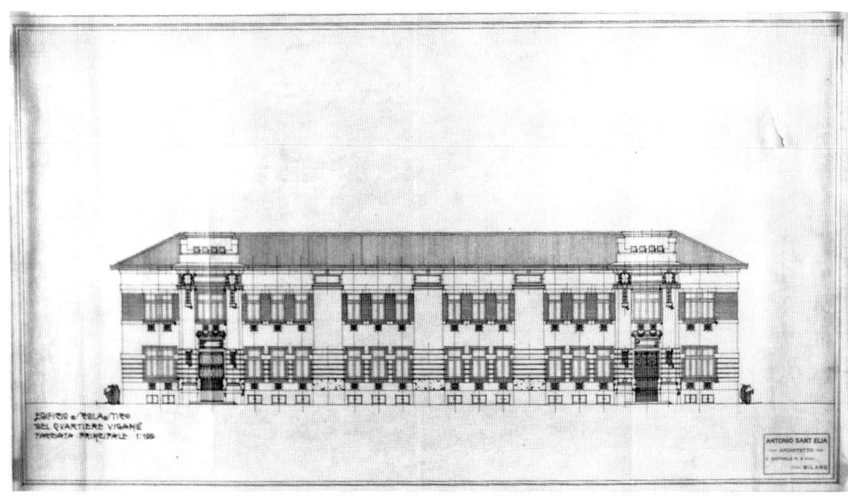

131. Antonio Sant'Elia. Facade of the primary school in the Viganò–San Giuseppe district, 1914–1915. Musei Civici, Como.

132. Antonio Sant'Elia. Facade decoration for a town house carried out in Via Cesare Cantù, Como, 1915. Collection of Riccardo Belluschi, Como.

133. Antonio Sant'Elia. Cover of Luciano Folgore's book *Ponti sull'oceano,* 1914. Beinecke Rare Book and Manuscript Library, Yale University.

different shapes, colors, and sizes were no longer to remain anchored to an invisible horizontal line but were arranged dynamically on the page. One of the first futurists who chose to follow Marinetti along this path was Luciano Folgore. Sant'Elia thus made a significant jump from the moderate goals of Nuove Tendenze to the radical frontier of the avant-garde. This modest undertaking was the only project Sant'Elia ever carried out in collaboration with the futurists and was to have no sequel.

Soon after his official entry into the futurist movement, which brought with it instant recognition, his career as an architect came to a standstill. He continued to work at the studio of Arrigo Cantoni until December 1914 or January 1915, when the second version of the Verona Savings Bank was due. But except for a few sketches and the projects for Como, Sant'Elia's personal production ground to a halt for almost an entire year. In 1915, shortly before going off to war, he again produced a handful of drawings, but these were very different from the bold modernity of the Città Nuova. On October 10, 1916, Sant'Elia was killed in action while storming Austrian positions in northern Italy. The drawings of the Città Nuova, executed just before Sant'Elia joined the futurist movement, were therefore virtually his last, except for the dozen or so produced early in 1915. What could have caused this caesura?

POLITICS AND IDEOLOGY

Sant'Elia's psychological situation was far from easy. His official entry into the futurist circle took place soon after the notorious Settimana Rossa (Red Week), an antimilitarist, antinationalist insurrection that spread throughout Italy between June 7 and 14, 1914. Barricades were set up in all the major cities, and workers and students rioted everywhere, especially in Milan. Although the demonstrations represented a more or less spontaneous outburst of popular feeling against established order, they received strong support from the socialists, particularly in the pages of their powerful organ, *L'Avanti!* edited, at the time, by the young Benito Mussolini. The disorders provoked by Red Week horrified the forces of the Right and triggered a serious counteroffensive led primarily by the Nationalist Party, to whom Marinetti had given his support earlier that year.[8] By the end of June 1914, therefore, Marinetti and Sant'Elia were already on opposite sides of the political fence.

More important, Sant'Elia gave his formal allegiance to futurism soon after he won a seat in Como's municipal council. His election on July 5, 1914, as a town councillor for the socialist opposition was not a landslide victory: Sant'Elia was second to last in the number of votes, and the socialists were in the minority.[9] Yet his victory was not unimportant either, for it established him in the public eye as a militant party member.[10] The facts of Sant'Elia's political life in Como—what little we know of it—are disappointing. According to the minutes of the municipal council, during the seven monthly sessions he attended Sant'Elia is not recorded as having spoken once, not even when the new master plan of Como was under discussion. He seems to have been as inarticulate in public as he was on paper. His contribution was limited to the projects for the two primary schools discussed earlier. At any rate his career as a politician ended when he went off to war in June 1915.

Marinetti, on the other hand, was already widely known for his right-wing sympathies and his virulent antisocialism: "We profess," he had written in an open letter published in *Lacerba,* "an ultraviolent anticlerical and antisocialist nationalism."[11] The avowed pacifism of the socialists, so vocal during the Libyan war of 1911 and now again as World War I appeared on the horizon, was anathema to Marinetti, who believed strongly in the regenerative powers of war. And yet it had not always been thus. Marinetti's political views, at least initially, were developed within the ambit of anarcho-syndicalism and under the aegis of Georges Sorel's theories—that vast breeding ground of both left- and right-wing ideologies.[12] He had in fact made several overtures to workers' organizations, many of which had responded warmly.[13] Nevertheless, over the years his impassioned nationalism led him to seek alliances increasingly on the right. After the Libyan campaign his political stance had begun to crystallize around the twin poles of nationalism and war.

The same can be said for the remaining members of the group, all of whom had once had cordial dealings with the Italian Left. Carrà had frequented anarchist circles early in his career, a fact brilliantly evoked by his powerful painting of the funeral of the anarchist Galli (1911). He was well versed in Marx, Kropotkin, Max Stirner, and the Italian marxists.[14] Russolo, who would later emigrate rather than side with the fascists, had also translated his political sympathies into paintings, particularly in his depictions of the dismal chimney stacks and factories of the Milanese periphery. Boccioni and Severini had begun their careers in Rome, where, under the tutelage of Balla, they were drawn into the orbit of the left-wing circles of the capital. It was there, wrote Severini in his autobiography, that they became acquainted with the works of Marx, Engels, Bakunin, and the Italian syndicalist Arturo Labriola.[15] Paintings such as Balla's *The Day of the Worker* (1904) and *Bankruptcy* (1902) or Boccioni's *Labor* (1910–1911; later renamed *The City Rises*) and *Stonecutters* attest to the seriousness of their concern. Boccioni, when asked to become a member of the group in 1911, had expressed doubts concerning the compatibility between his own left-wing sympathies at the time and Marinetti's right-wing stance.[16] After joining Marinetti, however, all the early futurists were drawn to the Right, even though they never reached a political consensus. Slowly, social themes fade from their work. The turning point can be situated around October 1913, when the *Programma Politico Futurista*, with its explicit, avowed antisocialism, was published in *Lacerba* over the signatures of Marinetti, Boccioni, Carrà, and Russolo.

The entire issue of the politics of futurism must be treated with caution: one cannot hope to do justice to the extreme complexity of the problem in a few lines; the purpose here is not to give a full account of futurist ideology but to outline some aspects that may have affected Sant'Elia. There is no doubt that he joined the futurist movement precisely when Marinetti's saber rattling was diametrically opposed to the official position of his own party. If Marinetti's political profile had been somewhat ambiguous in the past, by July 1914 his position was clear. Conflict was bound to arise between Sant'Elia's loyalty to socialism and the antisocialist militancy of Marinetti. Sant'Elia's ideological contradictions played no small part in the accusations of opportunism that were leveled at him when he joined the futurist movement.

He was not alone in his dilemma. In a sense the Italian intelligentsia as a whole was undergoing a deep crisis during those very months.[17] Italy was greatly shaken when the Great Powers declared war on one another toward the end of July 1914. The tragic lessons of the Libyan war were still fresh in their minds. Most Italians were committed to neutrality. Parliament knew it could wrest more concessions from Austria by remaining neutral, and Italian Catholics refused to take up arms against Catholic Austria. The army itself was opposed to war, well aware of just how weak its position was. Even more intransigent was the Socialist Party, which adamantly refused to lend its support to a war that would only serve to advance the cause of militarism and capitalism.[18] However, the futurists, the syndicalists, and the incipient Nationalist Party rallied around the interventionist cause, seeing in the conflict a chance to restore Italy to the role of a great power, and they made up in activism and belligerence what they lacked in numbers.

The clash between interventionists and neutralists worsened toward the end of the year. Old, unfulfilled dreams of epic grandeur, lying fallow since the days of Garibaldi and Mazzini, sprang up with renewed ardor. Neutrality stirred up memories of the Risorgimento *mancato,* that unfinished epos which still lacked a crowning feat. The nation began to feel an unappeasable thirst for heroic deeds that would bring to a glorious end the historic mission of the Risorgimento. Now a perfect cause presented itself. Italy longed to reconquer its natural frontiers, the Italian-speaking *terre irredente* of Trentino and Alto Adige. Only then could unification be considered truly complete. Anti-Austrian sentiment ran high.

In this atmosphere of intense political turmoil, the futurists organized various demonstrations in favor of intervention, first in Milan and later all over Italy. Only war, they believed, could shake the nation out of its passéist lethargy and bring about a truly modern society. In September, while the battle of the Marne was raging in France, they burned several Austrian flags in the Piazza del Duomo and in the galleria, following which they were briefly incarcerated.[19] Art itself became politicized. On September 11, Balla launched his manifesto *The Antineutral Suit.* A few days later, on September 20, the manifesto *Sintesi futurista della guerra* was published, signed by Marinetti, Boccioni, Carrà, Russolo, and Piatti. Balilla Pratella, the futurist musician, composed "Hymn to War." In December the futurists took active part in the demonstrations staged at the university in Rome. During the first months of 1915 Balla began the famous series of tricolor paintings, pushing his interventionism one step further, while Carrà published his *Guerrapittura* (War Painting). Sant'Elia alone of the futurists did not participate in the campaign.

The Socialist Party itself was racked with pleas to support intervention. Younger members, in particular, felt torn between loyalty to the party and loyalty to the country. On October 20, Mussolini unexpectedly asked the party to abandon its position of neutrality. The motion was not passed, and on November 24, 1914, he was formally expelled from the Milanese section of the Italian Socialist Party. Nevertheless, the escalation of the conflict produced severe strains on the party, and a sizable minority broke away to follow Mussolini.

The Mussolini who left to form his own party was not yet the fascist dictator of later years. At this point he still considered himself a socialist, as can be seen from the newspaper he founded after his expulsion, *Il Popolo d'Italia,* subtitled "Quotidiano Socialista." But he was already veering to the Right. Not surprisingly, he was drawn into an alliance with Marinetti, who had been one of the first to organize interventionist demonstrations.[20] In April 1915, in the course of one of these, Mussolini, Marinetti, and Balla were all arrested.[21] Mussolini was also on excellent terms with Boccioni. As he wrote in a letter to the futurist poet Paolo Buzzi, "Boccioni will have told you—if he ever spoke of me—that all my sympathies—even in the domain of art—are with the innovators and the destroyers: with the 'futurists.'"[22]

Thus the lines were not at all sharply drawn, particularly for a political neophyte such as Sant'Elia, who saw a considerable number of fellow socialists side with Mussolini. In addition he saw his new futurist friends—Marinetti, Boccioni, Russolo, and Balla (whom he knew by name only)—join forces with the fiery ex-spokesman of the Socialist Party. Interventionism made deep inroads within the Left as well as the Right.

Moreover, as an aspiring young modernist, Sant'Elia cannot have felt too comfortable within the ranks of the socialists: with regard to art, at least, the taste of the party ran to the pious, lachrymose Verismo, with its spectral workers, its consumptive women, its soup kitchens—all rendered with a scrupulous fidelity of detail that would have pleased a Zola. Boccioni had already complained bitterly about "a public that speaks of revolution, of strikes, of spiritism, of the radio and wants to serve at the table of aesthetics the patina of the sixteenth century."[23]

By the second half of 1914, therefore, Sant'Elia was a man undergoing a deep personal crisis, having embraced, almost concomitantly, organizations with opposing ideologies: futurism and socialism. He seems to have had a certain gift for ideological accommodation. In this he reveals an aspect of the characteristic *trasformismo* of Italian politics: the chameleonlike ability to switch politics according to expediency.

THE LAST SKETCHES

Sant'Elia's political trasformismo was matched by his malleability in matters of art, as his late works show.[24] Sometime in the first months of 1915 he embarked on a series of drawings that bear an unmistakable resemblance to cult buildings (figs. 134–140; plates 20, 21). These sketches, surprisingly conservative, reveal such a radical change in style that one would be tempted to assign them to 1912 were it not for the distinct date of 1915 on both of them (figs. 136,139).

Sant'Elia's late work is hardly what one would expect after the modernist pyrotechnics of the Città Nuova. Mass and monumentality return. Although he clearly differentiates between partitions and load-bearing structures in his setbacks, the emphasis here is on load and gravity. The separate parts of the building have coalesced into an agglutinated mass. The change in style would have been startling enough in itself. As it is, it was also iconographic: power plants and skyscrapers have given way to temples. Even the Gothic arch, hitherto absent in his work, makes an appearance (plate 20). A greater contrast can scarcely be imagined than between the graphic style of these static, funereal masses and the futurist drawings of the Città Nuova, with their cult of modernity and speed.

About one dozen sketches can be safely attributed to this period. They must have been executed between January and June of 1915, when Sant'Elia went off to war. These drawings can be divided roughly into two overlapping groups, both of which represent a throwback to Sant'Elia's angst-ridden work of 1912. One of them, fairly traditional in perspective, is strongly reminiscent of his expressionist works, whereas the other, slightly more unusual, brings to mind the decorative idiom of the Secession. It is hard to establish a chronological sequence between the two sets of drawings. The very appearance of such *retardataire* works after the Città Nuova should caution us against taking an evolutionary view of Sant'Elia's oeuvre, that is, putting the more conservative works first.

The expressionist temples are fairly uniform in design (figs. 134–136, plates 20,21). Sant'Elia has taken over the main elements of traditional church architecture and reassembled them in his own way, adding Art Nouveau touches here and there. As in his early work, color is once again used to evoke mood, and Sant'Elia returns to his symbolist palette of blues, mauves, and purples. In the most accomplished of these drawings, beautifully executed in pen and watercolor, a massive nave, tall and tapering upward, rises above a seemingly endless flight of stairs (plate 21). It is shouldered by colossal buttresses whose purpose is purely symbolic. Directly below, dwarfed by the scale and massiveness of the exterior, lies the low and inconspicuous entrance. Once again Sant'Elia all but ignored interior space, as the disproportionate scale and virtual lack of lighting shows. Iconography, used sparingly, is rather secular and consists of the usual statues of prancing horses, lancers, and angels, stylized to near abstraction.

The other group of drawings consists of variations on a secessionist theme—a pyramidal structure, square or rectangular in plan and triangular in section (figs. 137–140). Once more the inspiration is distinctly Viennese, as in figure 140, where Sant'Elia borrowed the elevation from Wagner's project for the Interimkirche of 1905 (fig. 141).

134. Antonio Sant'Elia. Study for a church, 1915. Musei Civici, Como.

135. Antonio Sant'Elia. Study for a church, ca. 1915. Musei civici, Como.

136. Antonio Sant'Elia. Study for a church. Signed with initials
and dated 1915. Musei Civici, Como.

137. Antonio Sant'Elia. Study for a church, 1915. Musei Civici, Como.

138. Antonio Sant'Elia. Study for a church, 1915. Musei Civici, Como.

Sant'Elia's almost incantatory fascination with the works of Wagner and his students points to the pervasive element of nostalgia that characterizes his work, a deep yearning for the past that even the brief interlude of the Città Nuova could not exorcise. He was, after all, returning to Viennese projects of ten years earlier—an anachronism with regard to the contemporary architecture of his day.

Unlike the smooth, dematerialized planes of the Città Nuova, the temples have a rugged texture: the nervous hatched lines seem to point to structural notation, indicating ashlar or perhaps cut stone. This predilection for weighty, load-bearing structures reveals the essence of Sant'Elia: an expressionist temperament overlaid with Viennese formalism. He never abandoned the Milanese tradition, according to which mass was considered the necessary support onto which the trappings of modernity could be grafted.

In one of the most original sketches of this group, the colossal nave is linked to the entrance by means of a low, tunnel-like passageway flanked by tall, tapering pylons (fig. 138). A small dome, perched on a cube, intersects the pitched roof, which slopes down to the ground. The buttresses have been eliminated, but the sheer love of mass and weight, used for psychological as well as visual effect, remains. Interlocking solids like this had interested Sant'Elia since 1913 (fig. 61). Yet even here the debt to the Wagnerschule makes itself felt. Similar churches, triangular in elevation, can be found in a project by Josef Plečnik, published in 1906–1907, and in Raimondo D'Aronco's project for a funeral chapel at Mantua.[25]

139. Antonio Sant'Elia. Study for a church. Dated 1915. Musei Civici, Como.

140. Antonio Sant'Elia. Study for a church, 1915. Musei Civici, Como.

141. Otto Wagner, Interimkirche, perspective, 1905. Historisches Museum der Stadt Wien.

Churches had appeared in his drawings briefly a year earlier, when he entered the competition for the Duomo at Salsomaggiore (figs. 83–85). They too were conservative, but they were not the fruit of personal choice. Furthermore, although the earlier ones conform to more traditional standards of church design, these have been streamlined and the overall effect is decidedly "moderne." The later ones, with their tall, tapering silhouettes and funereal *tenebrismo,* take their inspiration from symbolist art and funerary architecture. The very change in draftsmanship—Sant'Elia worked freehand rather than with a ruler—and the introduction of ominous, somber colors reintroduce the theme of the sublime, that is, the anticity.

The reappearance of these enigmatic cult buildings within his oeuvre marks the beginning of a period of involution, almost a revival, because they were in blatant contradiction to his own "Messaggio," not to mention futurist ideology, according to which *cattedralismo* was a serious offense.[26] What could have occasioned this retrenchment just as he was beginning to make himself known? And was this drastic shift in mood, color, and building type merely the expression of an inner crisis, or did it also reflect a widespread cultural trend?

In fact the futurist movement as a whole—Marinetti excepted—was undergoing a moment of introspection. Boccioni had abandoned his path-breaking experiments in dynamic form and had gone back to Cézanne.[27] Carrà retreated even further in time and was meditating on the art of Giotto and Uccello.[28] Russolo too refused the stimulating asperities of his earlier work and returned to figuration after 1915.[29] All three, therefore, abandoned the challenging experimentalism of the dinamismo plastico. Obviously, the much maligned museums and traditions were being revisited, at least in spirit. The truth is that Sant'Elia joined futurism as its first and most brilliant phase was coming to an end. Its brief tenure as one of the most original and innovative avant-garde groups of the century was almost over, and it had little to offer him beyond the outward signs of its own deep and disquieting crisis.

Although Sant'Elia's entries for the Lombard Architects and the Nuove Tendenze exhibition were very much influenced by futurism, they had in fact been completed before he formally joined the group in July 1914. After becoming a member, Sant'Elia did not produce any specifically futurist works, other than the cover of Folgore's book, but instead retreated, not unlike Boccioni and Carrà, into his past. He never exhibited with the futurists within his lifetime.[30]

WAR

Meanwhile, as pro-interventionist feeling in Italy reached a high-water mark, the futurists stepped up their campaign in support of war. In May 1915 (known thereafter as Maggio Glorioso), ten months after the outbreak of the conflict, massive demonstrations all over Italy showed that at least part of the nation favored intervention on the side of the Entente (that is, against their former partners of the Triple Alliance).[31] Finally, on May 24, 1915, the government opted for war.

And Sant'Elia? Years later, when the surviving elements of the movement had passed over into the ranks of fascism, Marinetti and the futurists liked to stress Sant'Elia's heroic participation as a volunteer in the Great War. Nevertheless, the sources are unclear. In his memoirs, written many years after the fact, Dudreville stated that on the day Italy declared war, Sant'Elia filled the galleria "with his curses against the government, the fatherland, and the war . . . swearing like a Turk."[32] Dudreville adds that he was joined in his invectives by the young anarchist sculptor Giovanni Possamai, another member of Nuove Tendenze. According to Giovanni Bernasconi, an old acquaintance of Chiattone's, Sant'Elia already occupied a peripheral position with regard to the futurists at the time: "Traumatized by futurist violence he ceased drawing, sought refuge in the house of the Chiattone family, and nothing more was heard of him."[33]

Sant'Elia's opposition to war is confirmed in an open letter by the journalist and fellow socialist Marco Ramperti. The latter took issue with the critic Margherita Sarfatti, who had described Sant'Elia in an article as a "socialista interventista." Sant'Elia, wrote Ramperti, "had always been disdainfully opposed to war. He grappled with it in his mind; faced it, in effect, as a volunteer, but only out of love for novelty and danger; to be [counted] among

those who risked and those who died. This he loved and sought, with the lyric impetuous-
ness of a twenty-year-old artist."[34] Sarfatti, however, had known Sant'Elia very well: she had
been a strong supporter of his work, and Sant'Elia had given her some of his finest drawings (plate 13).[35] Furthermore, she had been a socialist herself and had been rent by the
same temptations with regard to conflict.

Marinetti agreed with Sarfatti. In a letter to Ramperti, he wrote: "It is true that the
great Sant'Elia was initially opposed to war. However, stimulated by the love of novelty and
danger, which constitutes the essence of futurism, he was immediately influenced by the
patriotic ardor of us futurists, particularly that of Russolo and Funi."[36]

Sant'Elia has left differing accounts of his position on the issue. In one of his rare
handwritten documents, a postcard to the sculptor Gerolamo Fontana, dated July 23, 1915,
he writes: "Courage my friend, I too shall soon leave with great enthusiasm. I heard from
your father that you have left for the front and down deep I was happy because we artists
are more congenial than the others. But I hope with all my heart that you will return un-
scathed. I was called up on the 1st of June, and I too hope to be in the front within one
month. I shall write you in more detail in a few days."[37] It would seem, therefore, that although he was originally opposed to war, Sant'Elia let himself be won over by the interventionists. Perhaps he came to share the futurists' belief in the redemptive powers of war, as
did so many socialists. The conviction that war would bring about the downfall of the old
corrupt order and hasten social revolution exercised such a powerful attraction that even
the Left let itself be lured into temptation. Furthermore the Battaglione Lombardo Volontari Ciclisti, in which Sant'Elia served during the first months of the conflict, was the only
corps of volunteers in the Italian army, and one wonders how Sant'Elia could possibly have
been drafted.[38] On the contrary, his wish to stay together with the other futurists was obvious from the start.

It is possible, too, that something of the voluntarist *Lebensphilosophie* of early futurism, and of Boccioni in particular, had some influence on Sant'Elia. Their insistence on the
anarchic elitist action of the individual was at odds with the mass society of the modern
metropolis they celebrated. The Nietzschean, vitalist roots of futurism entailed the cult of
danger and heroism for its own sake, and war offered them the possibility of acting out this
dramatic role. Although they sang of great crowds "galvanized by labor" they always tried
to extricate themselves from the leveling threat of the masses.

Be that as it may, registrations opened in May. The futurists Marinetti, Boccioni, Russolo, Piatti, Sironi, and Sant'Elia all signed up together, along with Erba, Funi, and Possamai from Nuove Tendenze, and the journalist Mario Buggelli. A host of other artists and
literati from Milan also joined. The raucous jingoism unleashed by the declaration of war
produced a mood of general euphoria. On June 3, the Lombard regiment was ordered to
Gallarate, where the volunteers were billeted while awaiting special training (fig. 142). The
futurists went to great lengths to make their presence felt as a compact group within the
regiment, choosing to stay together in one large room.[39]

In July, just before being transferred to the front, the soldiers organized two charity
evenings at the local theater in support of the men drafted from Gallarate. The futurists

142. The futurists at war. From left to right, Marinetti, Boccioni, Sant'Elia, Piatti, and Funi at Gallarate, 1915. (Photo: Courtesy of Archivio Fotografico Castello Sforzesco, Milan)

took active part in the proceedings, as both actors and artists. As the only architect of the group, Sant'Elia was in charge of decorations and divided the task among his fellow artists. According to Russolo's recollections, these consisted of two long friezes appended to the balconies and one large cardboard panel above the entrance featuring futurist portraits of various officers and soldiers of the regiment.[40]

On July 21, the Lombard regiment returned briefly to Milan, where it was given a triumphal welcome as the soldiers paraded through the city (fig. 143).[41] There they were joined by Marinetti, who had just had a hernia operation. From Milan the volunteers were sent to Peschiera, on the shores of Lake Garda, in order to receive further training as *alpini* (mountain troops). At their new headquarters, they were kept inactive for weeks, enduring torrid summer weather and terrible sanitary conditions. From the numerous letters and articles written from the old fort where they were quartered, one can reconstruct the atmosphere of youthful impatience and excitement produced by the proximity to the theater of war (fig. 144). The writer and painter Anselmo Bucci, a close friend of Sant'Elia's, has left a colorful picture of futurist life in the old fort at Garda: "In that singular column of soldiers that included Marinetti, Boccioni, Sant'Elia, Erba, Russolo, Funi, Sironi, Piatti, strange and violent quarrels broke out when the name of Cézanne—known, at the time, to us alone—was bandied back and forth almost as if he were an officer, a soldier, a mule."[42]

Nevertheless, when they were finally sent to the front, at an altitude of thirty-five hundred feet, they were hardly prepared in either training or matériel. After all their paeans to modernity and technology, it is ironic to picture the futurists going off to war together, armed with bicyles and anachronistic weapons. In a series of articles written from the front, Marinetti recounted with his usual bravado the adventures of the futurists in the midst of the Lombard regiment of volunteers.[43] His optimism was premature. Because of the difficulties encountered at the front, the regiment was dissolved in November of that year. An effective defense of Italian positions—not to mention an attack—could not be improvised by a group of earnest and heroic but ill-prepared and nonprofessional soldiers. By the end of the year a more realistic estimate of the situation had come to take the place of extravagant hopes: "The myth of a Risorgimento type of war crumbled, revealing the tragic reality of a war of attrition in the trenches."[44] On December 1, shortly before disbanding, the Lombard regiment of volunteers marched together for the last time in the center of Milan, heads down, as if conquered, after which they were officially dismissed and ordered to join different regiments.[45]

On January 15, 1916, shortly after the futurists' return from the front, the manifesto *L'orgoglio italiano* was published, signed by Marinetti, Boccioni, Russolo, Sironi, Piatti, and Sant'Elia.[46] Written in all probability by Marinetti alone, this manifesto recounts in fulsome tones the feats of the futurists at war, in particular the taking of the Austrian position at Dosso Cassina in October. The themes were not new. Marinetti's delusions of Italian supremacy had been heard with monotonous regularity since the days of the Libyan war: "We ascertained that the Italians, under the genial leadership of Cadorna, were able to improvise in a few months the first artillery in the world, and conquer continuously during the most terrifying and difficult war that was ever waged." But as war fever mounted, the mystique of violence reached unprecedented heights: "The Italian who does not boldly declare himself proud of being Italian and convinced that Italy is destined to dominate the world with the creative genius of its art and the power of its peerless army—deserves to be slapped, punched, and shot in the spine." Marinetti's rodomontades notwithstanding, the

143. The Lombard Regiment of Volunteer Cyclists parading through Milan, 1915. (Photo: Courtesy of Archivio Fotografico Castello Sforzesco, Milan)

144. Sant'Elia, Boccioni, and Marinetti (from left to right) in the war zone, 1915. (Photo: Courtesy of Archivio Fotografico Castello Sforzesco, Milan)

"peerless army" of volunteers was disbanded before the manifesto was even published. The refrain "slapped, punched, and shot in the spine," which recurs throughout the text with incantatory insistence, reads almost like a blueprint for the fascist *squadrismo* of the postwar years. And indeed the idea of shooting one's enemies in the spine ("fucilate nella schiena") comes directly from a speech made by Mussolini that same year: "As for me I am more and more firmly convinced that it is necessary, for the good of Italy, to shoot in the spine [fucilare nella schiena], and I mean *shoot*, some half a dozen congressmen, and to send at least a couple of ex-ministers to jail."[47] The relationship between Mussolini and the futurists at this early stage has either been ignored by those who refuse to seek explanations beyond the preserves of art or stressed unduly by those who see in futurism nothing but a precocious form of fascism.

If Sant'Elia's ideological acrobatics were startling before, the about-face represented by his connection to the manifesto far exceeds all previous contradictions. The main butts of the tract were old liberal neutralists like Benedetto Croce and Giovanni Giolitti or socialists like Claudio Treves, Enrico Ferri, and Filippo Turati, all of whom are named in the text. It is hard to believe that Sant'Elia would have gone along with the blatant antisocialist polemic and the violent language in which it was couched. Perhaps he got carried away by the siege mentality that reigned in the trenches.[48] But it is more likely that Marinetti concocted the entire thing on his own. After all, the style is unmistakably Marinettian, and the text was published only after their regiment had been dissolved.[49] If Sant'Elia did indeed sign the manifesto of his own free will, the fact is revealing of the superficial way he absorbed, and then discarded, different ideologies, both political and artistic. At any rate, whether or not Sant'Elia agreed with the manifesto, he does not seem to have been unduly troubled by it, since a few months later all the futurists were in the regular army again, though in different regiments.

In the beginning of 1916 Sant'Elia was conscripted and sent to the front once again, this time as part of the 225th Regimento Ambrosiano of the Third Army, which was stationed on the Carso, a barren limestone wilderness situated at an altitude of several hundred feet (fig. 145). He was now an officer, having been promoted to the rank of *sottotenente* (second lieutenant) for his service with the Lombard regiment of volunteers. Perhaps after the first sobering experience of war, Sant'Elia reconsidered and returned to the front only because ordered to do so. This change of heart would explain the discrepancy of opinions concerning his attitude to the war.[50] In the last known document by Sant'Elia, a postcard to his mother written from the front and dated June 30, 1916, he scribbled the terse note: "Dear Mother, I am well. It is not true that I volunteered. Kisses, Antonio."[51]

Sant'Elia's brave conduct in the war was extolled even within his lifetime. In June he was wounded at Monte Zebio as he assumed command of his platoon, after its two commanding officers had been hit. His wounds had barely been dressed when he returned to the front to face enemy fire. For this feat he was cited for bravery and awarded the silver medal of valor.

During the autumn, General Luigi Cadorna, commander-in-chief of the Italian army, launched three new offensives along the Isonzo River on the Carso.[52] All three were cut

145. Second Lieutenant Antonio Sant'Elia at Monfalcone, 1916. (Photo: Collection of the author)

short by lack of ammunition and heavy casualties, aggravated by torrential rains. At about this time Sant'Elia was transferred to the Arezzo brigade at Monfalcone, about sixteen miles northwest of Trieste. It was there that his last project was built, a cemetery for his regiment. Ironically, he was one of the first to be buried in it. Commissioned by Sant'Elia's commanding officer (named, appropriately enough, Napoleone Fochetti), the cemetery was to include numerous tombs positioned according to strict army protocol.[53] Because of the desperate circumstances the plans had to be finished quickly. Italian soldiers were being served to the enemy as cannon fodder owing to Cadorna's misunderstanding of the situation and to the general lack of preparation by the Third Army. Sant'Elia's regiment had just lost 330 men in the Altopiano, and the wounded numbered close to 1,000.[54] They were fighting an enemy superior to them in numbers, training, and matériel. In addition, the Italian front was one of the most dangerous of World War I: it ran almost exclusively through mountainous zones, and the Austrians held higher ground everywhere. On the Italian side everything ran out: food, ammunition, human lives.

None of the drawings for the cemetery have survived, save for a reproduction of the main building (fig. 146). Known only through old photographs and a newspaper clipping, Sant'Elia's project is a monument rather than a chapel, possibly a cenotaph to be erected in front of the burial grounds. It shares many characteristics of Sant'Elia's religious buildings:

146. Antonio Sant'Elia. Cemetery of the Arezzo Brigade at Monfalcone, 1916 (destroyed). (Photo: Courtesy of Musei Civici, Como)

the rigorous symmetry of the facade, the twin towers reminiscent, once more, of the Romanesque church of St. Abbondio, and the massive structure.

Designs for some of the individual tombs are known only through vague descriptions by his contemporaries. According to his friend Alfredo Jeri, who served in the same regiment, Sant'Elia had also designed a tomb with a heavy stone cross. He was so pleased with this particular grave that he jokingly remarked that he himself might inaugurate it.[55] It is also said that, with his customary zeal, Sant'Elia even included a tomb inscribed with the name of General Fochetti.[56]

Construction of the cemetery was entrusted to the *capomastro* Nino Dabbusi, a lieutenant in the brigade who was also a member of the Famiglia Artistica. He had just begun to survey the initial building stages when Sant'Elia was mortally wounded, on October 10, 1916. Interviewed a few days after Sant'Elia's death, Dabbusi praised his heroism but had little to say about the surviving plans.[57] It is not known whether Sant'Elia's project was carried out faithfully, because the cemetery was destroyed in June 1917.

On his tomb the following epitaph was inscribed, composed by a comrade-in-arms:

> To the Second Lieutenant Antonio Sant'Elia
> War Volunteer
> Who died a Holy Death for Italy
> Facing the Hated Secular Foe
>
> Of His Artistic Daimon
> This Cemetery which now shelters him
> Was the Last Creation.

He was twenty-eight years old.

  # Epilogue: The Myth of Sant'Elia and Fascist Historiography

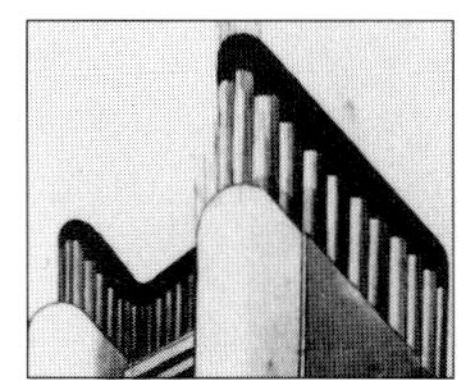

The story of Sant'Elia does not end with his death, however, for years later he was to suffer a curious resurrection. On October 23, 1921, five years after his death, his body was transferred from Monfalcone to the main cemetery in Como, where it was buried with full honors. Although the ceremony was organized by the local authorities, the proceedings were dominated by the fascists. After a religious service, the long funeral procession made its way to the cemetery. It included various military organizations: *alpini*, *arditi* (shock troops), and all the local *fasci* (fascist militias) with their respective banners. At the head of the procession four horses pulled a hearse festooned with flowers. The coffin was covered by a wreath given by the Squadra d'Azione Fascista Antonio Sant'Elia, a fascist militia named after the young architect.

At the cemetery, representatives of political, artistic, and military circles delivered speeches before a vast throng. The futurist Luigi Russolo gave a dramatic oration. A member of the Socialist Party also managed to speak, despite violent opposition from the fascists.[1] This event, which took place one full year before the fascists' official accession to power, marked the beginning of a process that would continue for more than two decades: the gradual association of Sant'Elia with various rites and rituals of the Fascist Party.

For the next six or seven years, however, there is little mention of Sant'Elia other than sporadic articles in the local press and a few distant echoes abroad. Then, in the late 1920s and early 1930s, one witnesses a veritable apotheosis. Numerous exhibitions featured his work prominently. An entire room was devoted to his projects at the Fifth Triennale, held in Milan in 1933, where his work was shown alongside the architecture of Le Corbusier, Loos, Mies, and Gropius. Every important Italian critic praised the Città Nuova: Giulio Carlo Argan, Edoardo Persico, Pietro Maria Bardi, Giuseppe Terragni, Alberto Sartoris, and even archconservatives like Ugo Ojetti and Telesio Interlandi. In his native Lombardy many towns dedicated a street or a square to his memory.[2]

What were the reasons behind this unexpected rise to fame so many years after

Sant'Elia's death? As a soldier he had fought bravely, even heroically—but there were better examples at hand. As a socialist he was ill-suited to become a paragon worthy of emulation by the fascists. As an architect he had left behind very little, and Como could easily boast of first-rate architects such as Terragni, Pietro Lingeri, and Cesare Cattaneo, who were ardent fascists as well.

The answer perhaps lies in the complex and ambiguous cultural policy of the regime. For a short period many of the futurists and rationalists believed that fascism was actively engaged in supporting modern art and architecture. The cultural apparatus of the party was entrusted to the so-called left-wing fascists, such as Giuseppe Bottai, who were sympathetic to the avant-garde.[3] Mussolini himself, in one of his sibylline utterances on art, the famous speech delivered at the Academy of Fine Arts at Perugia in 1926, had declared that "without art there is no civilization." Therefore, "we must create, otherwise we shall be battening on an old patrimony; we must create the new art of our time, the art of fascism."[4]

To the young modernists, words like these spelled the beginning of a new era. After fifty years of political and cultural stagnation, Italy once more had a strong government such as the great leaders of the Risorgimento had called for. Thus, in the late 1920s and early 1930s modernists of all persuasions multiplied their efforts to secure Mussolini's patronage for modern art, confident that the Duce would indeed throw his lot in with the avant-garde and choose modernity as the official artistic idiom of the regime. A great part of the Italian intelligentsia let itself be lured by this illusion.[5]

A STYLE FOR FASCIST ITALY

Of all the arts, it was of course architecture that stood most to gain from a possible association of modernism and fascism. Consequently, it was the architects who were most active in campaigning for official recognition. Their hopes were not entirely unfounded. The cultural policy of the regime crystallized slowly, and on numerous occasions, particularly during the first decade of fascist rule, Mussolini markedly favored modern architecture.[6]

This hope opened up vistas of unlimited progress for Italy's young architects. Indeed, to them Italy promised to be a new Russia, despite the difference in ideology. There, if only for a short time, futurist and constructivist art was used to convey official Soviet propaganda, as Marinetti noted with pride:

> I am glad to know that the Russian futurists are all bolshevik, and that futurist art was, for some time, a state art in Russia. Russian cities, during the last May Day celebration, were decorated by futurist painters.
>
> The trains of Lenin were painted externally with dynamic colored forms very similar to those of Boccioni, Balla and Russolo. This does credit to Lenin and gladdens us as a personal victory.[7]

It was precisely this equation of modernism and bolshevism that troubled an important sector of the Italian intelligentsia, which was violently opposed to modernism under any form. In their eyes modernity seemed to stand for a violent overthrow of the established order, of the forms and associations that had sufficed for centuries. Futurism was often castigated for its supposedly subversive origins. In Russia, wrote Giuseppe Prezzolini,

"Bolshevism and Futurism were allies. . . . The two revolutions, the two antihistories, joined forces. Both want to destroy the past and to rebuild everything on new foundations of an industrial type. The factory was the fountainhead of the political ideas of the bolsheviks, just as it was the source of inspiration of futurist art." And he concludes that "Italian fascism cannot accept the destructive program of Futurism; rather, in conformity with its *Italian* logic, it should restore the values that are opposed to Futurism."[8] Ardengo Soffici agreed: "We have already seen how this futurist tendency is precisely that which is followed and glorified, logically, by Russian bolshevism; and this should be sufficient to demonstrate that not even this [tendency] can be the one which best serves the general aims of fascism."[9]

Rationalism, the Italian equivalent of the International Style, fared no better. Foreign influence, a liability in view of the increasing xenophobia of fascism, took on the added irritants of a possible connection to Weimar and Russia—a serious offense for those who believed that fascism had come to save Italy from just such revolutions. From the early 1930s on, the rationalists were often accused of being bolshevik, Jewish, or masonic. "Just as Judaism plays such a major role in Bolshevism," wrote Marcello Piacentini after the second exhibition of the Italian Rationalist Movement (MIAR) in 1931, "so too in the Rationalist movement, it is the Gropiuses and the Mendelsohns who man the barricades."[10] Giuseppe Pensabene, an admirer of Sant'Elia, published an editorial against all Jews active in Italian architecture, such as the modernists Eugenio Faludi, Arrigo Bonfiglioli, and Gino Levi-Montalcini.[11]

Italy, however, was not Germany. At no time did the avant-garde disappear entirely from the scene. Nor was modern architecture ever relegated exclusively to industrial or utilitarian structures. Even in the late 1930s, when the regime inclined more and more toward a neo-imperial style based on the monuments of ancient Rome, the rationalists still received important commissions from the government, as, for example, Terragni's project for the Danteum, approved by Mussolini in person in 1938, though never built.

However, this relative pluralism is apparent only in hindsight. For contemporaries with the example of Germany before their eyes, nothing was less certain than artistic freedom. On the contrary, the avant-garde felt it needed an Italian pedigree for the International Style, with which to defend themselves against repeated accusations of *Kulturbolschewismus*.[12] It was imperative to establish once and for all the Italian roots of modern architecture. Sant'Elia perfectly suited their purpose. He had, so to speak, unimpeachable credentials: his modernist projects had unquestionably been designed before those of the International Style, and he had died a hero's death fighting for the liberation of Trieste and the terre irredente.[13] Hence the large number of shows, conferences, and articles dedicated to his work in the 1930s. That his work was not, properly speaking, the source of inspiration for the Italian rationalists went by unmentioned, save for a few lucid critics.

Nevertheless, modernism did not constitute a homogeneous front. Two groups jockeyed for power in an attempt to attract Mussolini's attention: the rationalists, ardent supporters of the International Style, centered mainly around Milan's dynamic young architects and critics, such as Giuseppe Terragni, Giuseppe Pagano, Edoardo Persico, Pietro

Maria Bardi; and neofuturists like Fortunato Depero, Enrico Prampolini, and Fillia (Luigi Colombo), led by the indefatigable Marinetti.

In the early 1930s the quarrel between rationalists and futurists assumed the form of an equivocal concept of "lyricism," which the futurists found to be lacking in the work of the rationalists.[14] The futurists criticized their modernist confrères for introducing gelid, Teutonic elements into the solar world of the Mediterranean. What was lacking in rationalism was the impetuous creativity of the Latin temperament—the lyricism that they saw in the work of Sant'Elia.[15] Conversely, the rationalists accused the futurists of being scenographers whose lyricism functioned well on paper but could not be translated into architecture.[16]

They were not far wrong. Although rationalism could boast some of Italy's most promising young architects, with a certain amount of work to their credit, futurism had no architects other than the dead Sant'Elia, whose works remained unbuilt. Various architects at one time or other called themselves futurists—Alberto Sartoris, Guido Fiorini, and Angiolo Mazzoni, for example—but their work had little or nothing to do with the tenets of the movement. Others, like Fortunato Depero, Enrico Prampolini, or Fillia, were really artists whose architecture was limited to temporary exhibition buildings, theater design, or interior decoration. Both camps, however, constantly invoked Sant'Elia's name to validate their claims.

Although the architectural profession as a whole had already been organized along corporate lines—in keeping with Mussolini's corporate state—architects were still free to choose their styles, though not their ideology. What both rationalists and futurists sought was nothing less than an official state architecture, a style that would be compulsory for all the buildings erected by the regime. Each of the competing factions hoped that its own characteristic style would be the exclusive representative of fascism in architecture. What was at stake was the monopoly on the regime's cultural expression, the creation, in other words, of an official fascist aesthetic. In itself this plea for a unified style was not new: both the fear of foreign influence and the bid for a state art had preoccupied the Italian intelligentsia since the Risorgimento.

In a series of articles published in 1931, the art critic Pietro Maria Bardi,[17] one of the main exponents of Italian rationalism, asked the government to establish clear formal rules to be enforced in all the projects of the regime: "The State has every interest in controlling the delicate question of architecture, according to a dictatorial and unifying criterion, in order to assign general guidelines to all its building activities."[18] Carlo Belli, another young rationalist, was even more direct: "We wish to give a fascist physiognomy to the architecture of our era. To put it more bluntly, we want a State Architecture."[19] The rationalists' effort on behalf of an architectural monopoly on the regime culminated in Bardi's famous *Rapporto sull'Architettura*, presented to Mussolini at the inauguration of the second exhibition of rationalist architecture in Rome.[20] There he argued at length that if fascism needed an unambiguous architectural physiognomy with which to erect the public works of the regime, this could be no other than rationalism. Sant'Elia's role as a pioneer was constantly stressed: "Let us go back to the beginning of this creative enterprise: to Sant'Elia who, with characteristic Italian audacity, arrested the direction of an architecture headed for the cemetery."[21]

Futurism was not far behind with respect to state architecture. *Futurismo,* the magazine of the futurists, was virtually dedicated to this goal. In one of the first issues, Mino Somenzi, the editor, declares that "a totalitarian regime such as ours, personified by the capabilities and will power of a 'single man' [Mussolini] has an indispensable need for an artistic dictatorship consonant with its own superb political ascension."[22] Somenzi goes on to propose the creation of a Department of Fascist Art, to be presided over by the Duce, which would be responsible for all projects of a visual nature, "from postage stamps to master plans."[23]

This stance does not sound too different from the rationalists'. But there is an escalation of violence in the vocabulary of the futurists. Marinetti speaks of the "militarization of creative fantasy,"[24] while Walter Bartoli calls for a "paramilitary *imposition* of a fascist art."[25] Writing for the magazine *Nuovo Futurismo,* Anselmo Ghezzi proposes a "totalitarian regimentation of artists in the trade union." And he adds: "To consider the artist as a 'free' agent par excellence, to whom everything is permitted, is a harmful and passéist 'forma mentis.' No, under a fascist regime even the artist must assume a well-defined characteristic: he is the spiritual standard-bearer of the Nation, and as such must feel, more than any other, perhaps, the need for a rigid discipline and a perfect regimentation."[26] But the futurists were not content with advocating state intervention in matters of architectural style. They also prescribed the one kind of architecture that was worthy of representing the regime: "If we want to create a fascist architecture there is but one path to be followed: the one outlined by Sant'Elia."[27]

Two men alone had the courage to speak the truth. In 1930, the young Giulio Carlo Argan published a brilliant essay that constitutes the first scholarly work written on Sant'-Elia.[28] Because of his refusal to deal with practical issues, wrote Argan, Sant'Elia's conception of a futurist city "remains a conception in a void: poetic activity rather than poetry . . . ideology and psychology of architecture rather than architecture."[29] He was followed three years later by the critic Edoardo Persico, who was reacting against the Sant'Elia show organized by Prampolini at the Fifth Triennale. "The futurist architect San'Elia [sic]," read the inscription in the room devoted to Sant'Elia, "was the precursor of architectural renewal all over the world." In his rebuttal Persico wrote with implacable clarity: "Truth has it otherwise. . . . In a show such as this, organized by the Triennale, equivocations and falsifications cannot be tolerated, even if committed out of love or charity for one's country."[30]

The two factions went about their business very differently. On the side of the rationalists the statutory nod to Sant'Elia was purely a question of political expediency: if they paid lip service to his genius, there were no intemperate flights of fancy. They were inspired not by his dazzling drawings but by the more sober works of Le Corbusier, Mies van der Rohe, Mendelsohn, and by ideas that Sant'Elia had never dreamed of, such as standardization and the *existenz minimum.* Yet they, too, cautiously invoked Sant'Elia as the limpid, Latin source of their architecture, the predecessor of the great masters of the International Style.[31]

The same cannot be said for the futurists, whose uncritical glorification of Sant'Elia could not come about without a deliberate distortion of the truth. The portrait of Sant'Elia left behind by their uninformed panegyrics is more than overdrawn: it is to a great extent fictitious. Over the years they carefully edited his life and work in an attempt to make him more palatable to the fascist propaganda apparatus, creating a new persona for Sant'Elia, one more suited to the tenor of the times. Although they organized several exhibitions of his drawings, they made public only those works that served to advance the cause of futurism. Sant'Elia's secessionist roots were never mentioned again, in part because they were associated with the hated Austrian enemy, in part because they were naturalist or historicist, and hence representational.

Even more biased were the numerous articles that the futurists devoted to Sant'Elia's works, which always put forth exaggerated claims with regard to his role in the history of modern architecture: "The Italian futurism and dynamism of Antonio Sant'Elia are the foundation stones of the new architecture. They influenced profoundly and unequivocally all architectural theories in the world, which are none other than logical and national offshoots of Santelian architecture."[32] To enhance Sant'Elia's stature, his most obvious shortcomings were passed over in silence, particularly the lack of plans and sections—a perpetual stumbling block for his apologists.[33] The idea that Sant'Elia was the "inventor" of modern architecture and urbanism was a common theme in futurist periodicals, reflecting the superficial knowledge of architecture of most members of the group.[34]

THE LEGEND

But Sant'Elia could not function as a suitable figurehead for modern architecture without being virtually transformed into a fascist. Various adjustments had to be made to achieve this end. First, there was the troublesome problem of Sant'Elia's political past. Rather than ignore the fact altogether, Marinetti found it expedient to gloss over Sant'Elia's activities as a socialist. Even though Sant'Elia had died as a loyal member of the Socialist Party, indeed as an official representative elected by universal suffrage, Marinetti implied that he had already left the party at the time of his death: "An ex-socialist, interventionism had wrested him from the humanitarian, pacifist, internationalist theories. From socialism, moreover, he had taken only the need for renewal, and had always remained tuned to the great dreams of art."[35] Although Marinetti does not say it, the analogy with Mussolini, another ex-socialist wrested from interventionism, was quite obvious.[36]

But even this distortion was not sufficient. To make a fascist out of Sant'Elia, it was necessary to resurrect his death, which had been overshadowed by the heavy toll of casualties during World War I. Death in battle was a crucial tenet of fascist hagiography, and the heroism with which Sant'Elia had sacrificed his life to the fatherland had to be made known. His second burial, in 1921, official as it was, had been a purely local affair, prompted by local piety and military pride. Indeed, it became customary when writing on Sant'Elia to dwell at length upon his heroic death, which gave, so to speak, the stamp of official sanction to his modernism.[37]

Anecdotes of varying authenticity have come down to us concerning his end. Here too futurist imagination supplied the lacunae left by history. Many years after his death, when Sant'Elia had become instrumental as an ideological alibi for modern architecture in Italy, his last words, supposedly uttered just before dying, were suddenly remembered: "Men, tonight we shall sleep either in Trieste or in paradise with the heroes." The phrase was too good to be wasted. It became famous instantly, like a popular ditty, and was published repeatedly with minor variations.[38] Although Sant'Elia was indeed killed in the offensive against Trieste, the inclusion of this city was not casual: it played an important role in futurist iconography as the very symbol of Italy's "unredeemed territories," and numerous manifestos were dedicated to it. "You are," wrote Marinetti to the Triestini, "the purpureal and violent countenance of Italy set toward the enemy."[39]

Of the several reports of Sant'Elia's end, written by friends and comrades-at-arms, none relates these words.[40] On the contrary, the phrase appears suspiciously late—at least a decade after Sant'Elia's death—in various articles written or inspired by Marinetti, who was not present when Sant'Elia died. The first official account of his death by the futurists was published in 1916 in the form of a manifesto, "La morte gloriosa del futurista Sant'Elia." It included a letter by Sant'Elia's fellow soldier Adolfo Cotronei, who worked for the *Corriere della Sera,* and another by Lieutenant Antonio Giovesi. According to Giovesi, Sant'Elia's last words were: "Storm troopers, my boys, we are headed toward victory, toward Trieste . . . forward everyone!"[41] These were the words that later served as a basis for Marinetti's contribution to the legend.

No effort was spared by the self-appointed mythographers of the regime in rendering Sant'Elia a suitable addition to the fascist pantheon. In 1933, for example, a small booklet on Sant'Elia appeared in the series "Breviaries of Martyrs and Heroes," under the joint authorship of Marinetti and Mario Del Bello.[42] The title of the collection is significant. "Martyrs" and "heroes" could refer to Catholics as well as to fascists: the ambiguity was intentional. Fascism aspired to be a secular religion complete with hymns, rituals, and martyrs. Religion had become an important attribute of the true fascist in the 1930s, and the anticlericalism of the 1920s was a thing of the past.[43] The tone of the little book is frankly hagiographic: "Religiously, yea, religiously must we contemplate the drawings and read Sant'Elia's Manifesto, for from these has sprung the universal architectural revolution with its many rationalisms: Le Corbusier, Mallet-Stevens, etc."[44] Elsewhere Del Bello had attempted to add a halo of sainthood to the pious oleograph devised by Marinetti: "Kneeling over his grave, let us bow our heads in reverence."[45]

By the mid-1930s, Sant'Elia's transformation into a fascist hero was virtually an accomplished fact.[46] He had been endowed with heroism, vitality, and a sacrificial death, crucial prerequisites of the new role models of the regime. He became, as it were, a precursor to the legendary arditi, who had formed the original nucleus of fascism and to which various futurists had belonged. Many people who never gave a second thought to architecture admired Sant'Elia for his heroism, endlessly extolled in so many publications. In an often-quoted remark, Vittorio Mussolini, the Duce's oldest son, declared: "In matters of modernity we young people must follow the words of the patriot, soldier and futurist Antonio

Sant'Elia, who died on the battlefield, as stated in his celebrated manifesto."[47] The connection forged between Sant'Elia and fascism was not limited to Italians. Theo van Doesburg, who was close to Prampolini at the time, wrote a glowing article linking fascist dictatorship and futurist ideas, citing Sant'Elia frequently.[48]

The majority of articles on Sant'Elia published by the futurists appeared in their own magazines. A large number of these were founded between 1930 and 1935, with the aim of presenting futurism as the style most suited to represent the regime: *La Città Futurista, La Città Nuova, Futurismo, Nuovo Futurismo, Oggi e Domani, Stile Futurista.*[49] Within these pages the postwar futurists tried to define futurist architecture, which they saw as embodying all the characteristics of fascist ideology. Sant'Elia understandably occupied a prominent place in these publications. In fact, the term "architettura Sant'Elia" was often used as a synonym for modern architecture *tout court.*[50]

The most important of these publishing ventures from the architectural point of view was *Futurismo,* founded in 1932 in Rome and later known as *Sant'Elia* and then *Artecrazia.* *Futurismo* was one of the keystones of the merger between futurism and fascism attempted by Marinetti and his friends. The headlines of one of the first issues read: "Fascists, be futurist in art."[51] Sant'Elia was presented as the initiator of all modern architecture and urbanism. Not only were Gropius and Le Corbusier, among others, presented as futurists and disciples of Sant'Elia, but some of their articles, pirated from other sources, were republished without permission.[52] The general level of the articles was low—foreign names, for example, were often misspelled. Marinetti was more concerned at this point with swelling the ranks of the movement than with artistic consistency.[53]

Sporting a new title in 1933, *Sant'Elia* tried to rally support for futurism by launching the Movimento Italiano Sant'Elia: "With the aim of organizing the nascent fascist aspirations against the invasion of 'styles' that do not correspond to the lyric demands of the climate and temperament . . . of our race, ultra-Italian architects, engineers, painters . . . and builders, wish above all to defend the primacy and the historic originality of the creative Italian genius . . . by initiating the Sant'Elia Movement."[54] Jibes at their rationalist foes were frequent. "Architects!" proclaimed the front page, "'Novecento' or 'rationalism' are anti-Italian expressions. Subjugate the world with Italian pride and lyricism to the original fascist style: that of Sant'Elia."[55] But the movement was doomed: Sant'Elia had become well known, at least in certain circles, but not sufficiently so to garner enthusiasts for a nebulous cause. Soon the magazine took on the more appropriate title *Artecrazia.* Throughout these avatars, one notes the downward trajectory of futurism as a serious avant-garde movement. Reduced to a marginal role in Italian culture, the members of the group exhausted themselves in loud proclamations of support for the regime in a vain attempt to convince an increasingly distant Mussolini of the political importance of their group.[56]

In an effort to lend more credence to futurist architecture, the editors tried to forge links with the forces of production, that is, the world of industrialists and entrepreneurs who were busy providing services for Mussolini's Rome. Publicity for construction materials had appeared occasionally in the magazine, but from October 1933 on, *Sant'Elia* openly published propaganda for "linoleum Sant'Elia," "Sant'Elia ceramics," "Sant'Elia furniture," and even "Sant'Elia stones and marbles." "Sant'Elia Materials" became, in fact, a special rubric under which firms could use the famous name to advertise their products.[57] This publication, whose name was intended as homage to the man, thus ended in his reification as a commodity.[58] His name had become a mere label, a sort of warranty that gave modernity in architecture the trademark of *italianità*.

POSTHUMOUS BUILDINGS

By far the most ambitious initiatives planned by the futurists to celebrate Sant'Elia's work were the "Onoranze a Sant'Elia," held in Como in 1930. These were officious events, led by the tireless Marinetti and produced under the double aegis of futurism and fascism. In a flyer put out by the organizing committee, and probably written by Marinetti himself, Sant'Elia is closely associated with the regime: "Not only is Antonio Sant'Elia a cause for pride for the town of Como, but he also represents one of the greatest glories of Fascist Italy, since it is thanks to Sant'Elia that all the architecture that characterizes the civilization of the century bears the absolute stamp of the Italian genius."[59]

The "Onoranze" consisted of an exhibition of ninety-five drawings by Sant'Elia—the largest ever held—curated by Marinetti and Escodamè, which was to travel to Milan and Rome afterward. Mussolini granted his personal patronage to the show, and fascist dignitaries of the highest echelons, such as Giuseppe Bottai and Araldo Di Crollalanza, lent their support to the venture, as did the National Trade Union of Fascist Architects. Heads of all the local and regional fascist organizations were present at the inauguration on September 14, 1930, along with various army officers (the army claimed Sant'Elia for its own, too). Marinetti's dramatic opening speech presented the public with a mythical Sant'Elia whose work gave birth to "the great architectural revolution" that later produced Le Corbusier, Theo van Doesburg, and Robert Mallet-Stevens (Marinetti invariably used these three men as examples).[60]

In spite of the magnitude of the event, the proceedings would be of scant interest for the history of architecture were it not for the fact that one of Sant'Elia's projects was actually erected posthumously in response to an unexpected suggestion made by Marinetti during the "Onoranze." Ever since the end of the war the local authorities had been searching for a suitable design for a war memorial to the soldiers who had died in World War I. What better plan, commented Marinetti at the closing ceremonies, than to adopt a project by one of Como's most illustrious sons, himself a hero and victim of that war?[61]

Sant'Elia's projects, of course, were rarely accompanied by plans or sections, nor were they drawn to scale. Furthermore, most of his sketches are unspecified as to their purpose. Nevertheless, so secure was Sant'Elia's growing reputation that one of his projects was chosen for the monument, winning over highly polished designs by Terragni and Lingeri.[62] The drawing in question, picked by Marinetti and Prampolini, consisted of a relatively small building of uncertain function (plate 10). It has been called both a cathedral and an electric plant. Terragni himself, perhaps mistaking Sant'Elia's extended lines for high-voltage wires, took it for a "centrale elettrica."[63]

Prampolini, who often dabbled in architecture, was asked to provide all the plans, sections, and detailing needed for construction. Basing his work on Sant'Elia's drawing, Prampolini redesigned the building, remaining relatively faithful to the original except for the crowning features, where he gave free reign to his imagination (fig. 147). The side windows and the lateral entrances to the high podium were eliminated, as were the statues on both sides of the main entrance. Crystal columns ten feet high were to cap the structure: in the daytime they would reflect the sunlight, while at night they would emit colored light. These innovations, absent in Sant'Elia's sketch, were characteristic of Prampolini's work in theater design, particularly with lighting and scenography.

But Prampolini was not an architect, and the complex problems that arose soon taxed his meager knowledge of the profession. He owed his appointment exclusively to Marinetti's prestige as a trusted intellectual of the regime. Eventually both Marinetti and Prampolini ceded their positions, pressured by the local authorities who were anxious to have the entire project finished once and for all. Thus in 1931 the execution of the monument was assigned to Terragni, whose own two projects had been shelved by the town hall.[64]

By this time the foundations of prestressed concrete had been poured. Terragni quickly executed detailed plans of the interior, which was to house a crypt, staircases, two elevator shafts, and a votive chapel with the names of the six hundred dead chiseled on its walls—all of which had been omitted in Prampolini's unprofessional approach. Dozens of

147. Enrico Prampolini. Study for the Como War Memorial, based on a sketch by Sant'Elia, 1930–1931. (Photo: Courtesy of Terragni Foundation, Como)

148. Giuseppe Terragni. The Como War Memorial, preparatory study, 1931–1932. Terragni Foundation, Como.

superb, carefully rendered drawings attest to the seriousness and high standards that Terragni brought to his task (fig. 148).[65]

The result is, of necessity, a compromise. The monument has an air of solidity and even of tradition about it. Needless to say, it bears hardly any resemblance to Sant'Elia's work of any period, or even to Terragni's, and is more expressive of the elegant taste of Milan's Novecento. Flanked on either side by a semicircle of cypress trees, its restrained, marmoreal monumentality would not look amiss in, say, Mussolini's Rome. Sant'Elia's apocryphal last words are inscribed on the side of the monument facing the waters of Lake Como: "Men, tonight we shall sleep either in Trieste or in paradise with the heroes."

The inauguration, which took place on November 4, 1933, was once more the occasion for an immense fascist pageant, ending in a triumphal tribute to Sant'Elia. The futurists were conspicuously absent, given their fiasco in attempting to erect the monument. Because the memorial was dedicated to the soldiers who died in World War I, the unveiling was made to coincide with the fifteenth anniversary of the victory against the Austrians. The entire ceremony, however, was transformed into a showcase for the military prowess of the fascists. Fascist associations and paramilitary groups paraded in full regalia before the monument. Every fascist dignitary extolled Sant'Elia in his speech, including the bishop of Como, who, after praising "l'eroico Sant'Elia" and "Il Duce," concluded by enthusiastically invoking the "providential and historical event of the kiss of peace between Church and State."[66] The ceremony ended with the Blackshirts goose-stepping all the way to the main cemetery to lay flowers on Sant'Elia's tomb.

One year later—not content with the formidable difficulties caused by the Como War

Memorial—the futurists attempted yet again to build another of Sant'Elia's projects. In 1932, the Partito Nazionale Fascista announced the competition for their central headquarters, the Palazzo del Littorio, to be erected on the newly finished Via dei Fori Imperiali in Rome. This was the most important commission yet announced by the regime.[67] Once more the futurists exhorted the authorities to choose a sketch from among Sant'Elia's most visionary projects: "We futurists, faithful interpreters of the great art of Sant'Elia, propose to build the 'Casa del Fascio' and its connected buildings by realizing his prophetic architectural dream, choosing from among his most typical projects those which are more consonant with our aims."[68] The futurists cannot have been taken too seriously, given their amateurish approach to architecture. When faced with serious commissions or competitions, they met the challenge with rhetoric: the grand gesture, the histrionic posturing, was their response.

Yet the posthumous cult of which Sant'Elia was the object was not the preserve of a handful of uninformed panegyrists. A few years later, in 1936, another plan to build a Casa Littoria according to Sant'Elia's sketches was put forth, this time by no less a figure than Ezra Pound. In an article published in the newspaper *Il Mare* (Genoa), Pound suggests the creation of an arts center in Rapallo, to be built after one of Sant'Elia's designs. Its purpose, Pound explained, was to convey the essence of the fascist regime: "A *Casa Littoria* in Rapallo could easily contain at least one library accessible to foreigners, either dilettantes or tourists, to help them understand the new Italy. This building, if inspired by a project of Sant'Elia, would open the eyes and probably the mind to the contemporaneous [situation] of the nation."[69] Immediately afterward Pound wrote to Marinetti, asking him to lend his support to the idea.[70] Marinetti responded enthusiastically: "Today more than ever, after the great imperial victory, architecture must have the henceforth indispensable geometric splendor ideated by Antonio Sant'Elia, shot in the forehead at Monfalcone for a greater Italy." (Mussolini had proclaimed Italy an empire in 1936.) "Therefore," he adds, with his revolutionary grammar and syntax, "to inveigh once more against our triumphant architectural revolution is vain and not at all imperial. Glory to Antonio Sant'Elia glory to fascist Italy so well architectured by Benito Mussolini."[71]

Perhaps the poets' poet and the gifted but somewhat provincial architect from Como do not make such an unlikely pair. "Better mendacities than the classics in paraphrase" is an apt gloss on the "Messaggio," couched of course in an eloquence unknown to Sant'Elia. Or perhaps Pound saw in him another Henri Gaudier-Brzeska, that other young promise whose career was cut short by an early death in World War I.

Pound was not the only serious poet to take an interest in Sant'Elia. A passage from the manifesto had already been paraphrased, unacknowledged, by Italy's greatest living poet, Gabriele D'Annunzio.[72] In the charter for the city of Fiume, conquered from Austria by D'Annunzio and his legionnaires, there is a chapter prescribing the architectural guidelines for the new "redeemed" Italian city. Although the charter (written in 1920) is largely believed to be the work of the Italian syndicalist Alceste De Ambris, head of the Fiume cabinet, a few passages, including the one on architecture, are by D'Annunzio: "Convinced that a nation cannot but have the architecture that the strength of its bones and the nobility of its brow deserve, we consider encouraging and helping entrepreneurs and builders to understand that the new materials—iron, glass, cement—ask only to be put to use harmoniously in the new architecture."[73] The analogy is vague, but the anachronistic reference to iron rather than steel clearly points to Sant'Elia.[74] Conversely, Sant'Elia's "D'Annunzianesimo" has not gone unnoticed—the exalted lyricism bordering on rhetoric that one finds in his work.[75]

SANT'ELIA AND ANTI-SEMITISM

But Sant'Elia's name was yet to be used for far more equivocal purposes. Hitler's accession to power had no doubt strengthened the anti-Semitic elements in Italian politics, though these were limited, at least initially, to isolated, marginalized groups, such as those gathered around notorious anti-Semites like Giovanni Preziosi, Telesio Interlandi, and Roberto Farinacci. But after the proclamation of the axis in November 1936, the ties between Italy and Germany became stronger, and Germany's policy toward the Jews became a question of state policy in Italy.

On July 14, 1938, the "Manifesto of Italian Racism" was published. Supposedly written by a group of anonymous "scientists" of the regime, it was in fact the work of Mussolini himself, who thus appeared to ground his racial policies on science. The manifesto was followed, on October 7 of the same year, by the "Carta della Razza," the charter of race, forbidding Italian subjects to marry non-Aryans. One month later the racial laws were promulgated.[76] Distinguished Jews, many of whom held positions of power within the regime, were dismissed from their posts and had their property confiscated. Emboldened by the train of events, publications like *Quadrivio, Il Tevere,* and *La Difesa della Razza* stepped up their attacks against all aspects of modernity they viewed as emanations of a generic Jewish spirit.[77]

Anti-Semitism was not limited to the old guard. Rationalists and futurists also had a brush with it in an attempt to defend modern art from accusations of Jewish influence. This time Sant'Elia's Aryan stock was invoked in order to legitimize rationalist architecture: "italianità" in itself was no longer sufficient to vouchsafe a certain amount of protection for modern art. In an article published in *Artecrazia,* Prampolini's brother Vittorio Orazi wrote: "We claim, in contrast to every accusation of foreign provenance or of Jewish influence, *that rationalist architecture is the brilliant ideation of an Aryan Italian—the futurist Antonio Sant'Elia. . . .* [Rationalism has] therefore an Italian origin by no means influenced by Semites. (Le Corbusier, prince of architects and, in a certain way, codifier of rationalist architecture, is Aryan.)"[78]

Some of Italy's most important modernists were to lend their name to initiatives such as this. On August 8, 1938, Terragni and Sartoris sent an open letter to the editor of Como's leading newspaper, *La Provincia di Como,* addressing the alleged "Jewishness" of modern art and architecture. Although not published there, the letter was accepted a few months later in the Roman magazine *Origini.* In order to prove the Aryan origins of rationalism, the authors listed the leading nations of the West, followed by the name of the founding father of modern art in each country:

> The movement for modern architecture was created by Antonio Sant'Elia;
>
> in Argentina, [it was created] by Alessandro Bustillo, who is not Jewish;
>
> in Australia, by Raymond MacGrath, who is not Jewish;
>
> in Austria, by Otto Wagner, who was not Jewish;
>
> in Albania, by the Ragazzi brothers, who are not Jewish;
>
> in Belgium, by Victor Bourgeois, who is not Jewish;
>
> in Czechoslovakia, by Jan Kotera and Adolf Loos, who were not Jewish.[79]

With the refrain "who is not Jewish," the letter reads very much like a futurist manifesto. Once again Sant'Elia is mobilized in defense of modernity, but this time he was made to endorse not only fascism but anti-Semitism as well.

Another version of this manifesto was published in the last issue of *Artecrazia*.[80] This issue, which included vehement protests against the retrograde right wing of the regime, was impounded by the authorities, who closed the magazine for good. Marinetti's position with regard to anti-Semitism was complex and ambivalent. Mino Somenzi, the editor, was himself Jewish and curated the entire issue, the purpose of which—however improbable this may now seem to us—was to show that what the ferocious forces of reaction abhorred was modernism tout court, the Jewish question being just a pretext.

Earlier that year, in November, the violently reactionary daily *Il Tevere*, directed by Telesio Interlandi, had published an anthology on degenerate art in Italy. He was trying to organize an Italian version of the *entartete Kunst* (degenerate art) exhibition held in Munich the previous year. Interlandi then proposed (unsuccessfully) a referendum against modern art, which he considered Jewish and bolshevik, in the magazine *Quadrivio*, which he also directed.[81] Toward the end of 1938, in response to these acts of provocation, Marinetti and Somenzi organized demonstrations in both Como and Rome and produced the polemic issue of *Artecrazia* (fig. 149).[82] But even bearing in mind the precarious position of the modernists of all persuasions in 1938, the motivations that prompted Marinetti to republish this text are highly questionable. After all, the manifesto was originally written in August, *before* Interlandi's more recent crusades against degenerate art.

Late in 1940, Sant'Elia's name was exhumed one last time. In view of the increasingly violent attacks against modernism, Marinetti tried to create a common front of artists and architects, the Gruppo Primordiali Futuristi Sant'Elia. Members included Terragni, Lingeri, Nizzoli, Sartoris, and Prampolini.[83] But it was too late for last-ditch efforts of this sort, and in any case Sant'Elia's name was not strong enough to be used as a bulwark against the rising tides of reaction.

Ironically, Sant'Elia—the most modern of Italian architects—rode out the storm: he had been transformed into a fascist hero of impeccable credentials. At the height of this unofficial *Kulturkampf* Interlandi himself singles him out from the general blame attaching to modernism: "The architecture of Sant'Elia . . . has nothing to do with the squalid buildings with which 'modern' architects regale us with admirable untimeliness. Marinetti

149. Conference held in honor of Sant'Elia in Terragni's Casa del Fascio, Como, November 1938. Bazzi's painting *The Death of Sant'Elia* is in the background. Beinecke Rare Book and Manuscript Library, Yale University.

knows that the architecture we combat is of communist and Jewish inspiration, and is re-pugnant to our nature and to our genius."[84]

It has been claimed that by constantly praising the regime Marinetti gave an ideologi-cal shelter to modern art in Italy, thus preserving it from the destruction suffered by the avant-garde in Germany. This is not the place to discuss whether the aging futurists, led by the beribboned Marinetti and reduced to a position of political conformism, still consti-tuted an avant-garde. What is beyond dispute is Marinetti's use of Sant'Elia's work to fur-ther his strategy of yoking futurism to fascism.[85]

Sant'Elia's posthumous popularity reached its peak in the first half of the 1930s. Poems and songs, not to mention paintings, plays, and sketches, were dedicated to his memory. Nonetheless, one should not exaggerate Sant'Elia's importance. Although his rep-utation undoubtedly overflowed the narrow confines of futurism, he remained a vague and elusive figurehead, a stick figure that Marinetti harnessed whenever necessary to shore up his cause. The purpose of this excursus is not to do justice to the extraordinary complexity of architecture under Mussolini, so well covered by others, but to analyze the ideological role Sant'Elia was made to play during that period.

After World War II, one might have thought that Sant'Elia's second lease on life was at an end. After all, his legend, as propagated by the futurists, had outlived its political usefulness. But the apologists of futurism were followed, albeit for different reasons, by those of the International Style. It was primarily Reyner Banham who saw himself as Sant'Elia's champion, bent as he was on tracing the genealogy of the International Style. "Even though he left behind no completed buildings he was a pioneer of the International Style, and the first to conceive the planning of cities as fully three-dimensional structures, and his position in the family-tree of the Modern Movement is thus assured."[86]

Drawing uncritically on Marinetti's fulsome articles and on the inflated accounts of the futurists, Banham magnified Sant'Elia's modest record: "Put the two together [the drawings and the "Messaggio"] and you have a body of architectural ideas that raises serious questions about the originality of Le Corbusier and Mies van der Rohe and Gropius."[87] The lack of plans, sections, and even elevations—a serious threat to the reputation of an architect hailed as a pioneer of the International Style—was explained away as the result of loss and dispersal: "The evidence of Sant'Elia's abilities has, I suspect, simply been lost in the inevitable attrition of time."[88] The influence of Art Nouveau was downplayed, and only the rationalist or protorationalist aspects of Sant'Elia's work were deemed worthy of attention: "By the time Sant'Elia evolved this undecorated style of his own, he was out of direct touch with Vienna—if he had ever been in touch at all."[89] Thanks to these works, Sant'Elia continued to appear as a unique, prophetic individual far in advance of his time—a voice crying in the architectural wilderness. Because most of the material on Sant'Elia was in Italian museums and libraries, foreign scholars relied heavily on Banham's work and thus inadvertently helped perpetuate many of the myths launched during the fascist period.

In Italy, where the ups and downs of Sant'Elia's reputation were always motivated by political considerations, such unreserved admiration was quite rare. Fascism had left deep scars that the postwar years did nothing to mitigate. Given the enthusiastic endorsement of Mussolini's regime by most futurists, futurism as a whole was equated with protofascism, and Sant'Elia's achievements were harshly judged. "I do not believe," declared Carlo Ragghianti, "that the actual projects of Sant'Elia have been treated with sufficient severity."[90] Hence the vehemence with which some scholars tried to extricate Sant'Elia from the futurist movement, by claiming that the manifesto had been retouched by Marinetti behind Sant'Elia's back. "By disqualifying him as a futurist," wrote Bruno Zevi, "we redefine him as an artist and as a man."[91]

In the mid-1950s the magazine *L'Architettura* published a series of articles dedicated to Sant'Elia.[92] Written by Leonardo Mariani, the first of these reproduces a series of unpublished drawings the author claimed to have discovered. In fact, these sketches had always been in the museum at Como, as was common knowledge, and many had appeared in print before.[93] Moreover, Mariani appended purely arbitrary captions to the drawings (identifying buildings as hangars, aeronautical observatories, garages, cinemas), which were aimed at enhancing the modernist aspect of the projects. In an attempt to fill in some unfortunate lacunae in Sant'Elia's work, he published two more batches of "inediti," containing plans, sections, and urban projects. For the most part these consisted of obvious forgeries, designed after the manner of Sant'Elia but executed in a clumsy way. A detail of the project for Milan's railroad station was even blown up and published under the title "Milan 2000"—a title that has subsequently found its way into numerous publications, although it is a pure fabrication. Given the paucity of scholarly works on Sant'Elia at the time, no one seems to have protested.[94] In spite of the singular limitations of these sketches—the casual scribbling of a poor draftsman—serious critics accepted them as genuine.[95] Clearly, we are still in the futurist tradition of uninformed, propagandistic eulogies, unsupported by serious research.

Over the past few years a vast literature on Sant'Elia has accumulated, and there is no longer any justification for seeing his achievements through the distorting lens of fascist historiography. When all is said and done, he remains an elusive figure whose life is known to us only in its broad outlines. Two world wars and the taciturn nature of Sant'Elia have conspired to deprive us of much important information regarding his life and work.[96] No more than thirty or so lines of his handwriting have come down to us, almost all from postcards sent from the front to friends and family.

Tall, freckled, and redheaded, Sant'Elia cut a striking figure in Milan's bohemian circles, with his dapper black cape and rakish hat (frontispiece). "A redder man . . . was there never," wrote the artist and writer Anselmo Bucci, "a futurist dissonance of reds."[97] Indeed, Sant'Elia was so proud of his flaming red hair that he stubbornly refused to have it cut according to army regulations. He alone, amid his close-shaven comrades, managed to save his incandescent scalp. A fashionable men's clothing store in Milan was responsible for his elegant attire, seeing in the dashing young man an ideal model for its creations.[98] His chain-smoking, accompanied by the inevitable cough of the inveterate smoker, and the ever-present cigarette welded to his lower lip were affectionately remembered by all his old friends.

It is unnecessary to dwell once again on Sant'Elia's inadequate schooling, architectural or otherwise. His relative freedom from academic conventions may have accounted for the freshness of his vision, but his weak grounding in technical matters as well as his perennial difficulty in expressing himself imposed severe limitations on that vision. What is unusual in Sant'Elia is the discrepancy between his extraordinary talent as a designer and the elementary, schoolboy notions of tectonics that were largely improvised. He never felt the need to palliate his obvious shortcomings, so often pointed out by contemporary critics.

Sant'Elia's executed works are modest and do not reveal more than a competent master builder: the Villa Elisi, now entirely rebuilt, the Caprotti tomb at Monza, and the little cemetery at Monfalcone, destroyed during World War I. The rare plans and sections that have come down to us, mostly taken from other sources, are quite pedestrian and reveal an iconoclast more in word than in deed. Sant'Elia simply did not think in terms of interior space.[99] He was an image maker, a facade-oriented architect who thought of his buildings in terms of invertebrate monoliths. The very fact that almost all the existing plans were done before 1914, which is precisely when he began his modernist works, only proves that the Città Nuova represented for its creator a new style rather than a revolutionary way of thinking about space.

ARCHITETTURA UT PICTURE

Sant'Elia's pictorial approach to architecture has often been noted: "architettura *ut pictura*," Ragghianti called it.[100] He had a feeling for surfaces, for the tactile quality of the image, and for the graphic means employed to produce it. His use of perspective combined with the worm's-eye view gave him the dramatic recession that so heightened the emotional tenor of his work. In his perspectives, no surface was parallel to the picture plane, which was intersected by only one of the corners of the project; he multiplied the vanishing points, thus offering different readings of the same image. Perspectival drawings, however, were an evasion from the Beaux-Arts system, which rested on a clear connection between plans, sections, and elevations.[101] Sant'Elia's architecture, therefore, depended on two opposing systems that were never welded into a coherent whole. His vision remained two-dimensional: when he tried to translate it into a third, it became conventional, if not downright banal. In Sant'Elia the painter took over where the architect faltered.[102]

In the past, Italy's Liberty architects have often been criticized for having assimilated the various currents of Art Nouveau in a very superficial way—as a cosmetic operation, an adjectival aesthetic with which to clothe the facades of the expanding metropolis.[103] Sant'Elia was no exception. The Secession came to him as a purely figurative phenomenon, as did futurism a few years later.

This pattern reveals a trait that has always disconcerted critics: Sant'Elia's evolution, cut short by an untimely death, does not follow a one-way trajectory, from the florid excesses of the Liberty to the austere threshold of the International Style, according to the evolutionary fallacy of the Modern Movement. There was not, in other words, a "before" and an "after" futurism in his work: all these currents coexist concomitantly—the Liberty, expressionism, modernism.[104]

There was nothing exceptional about this. Bound to tradition by the conservative taste of their patrons, all young Italian architects had as a rule to give up their modernist leanings when working for the state or the more traditional strata of society. On the other hand, in work executed for their private use, they gave free rein to their imagination. They were, so to speak, bilingual. The same trait can be found in Central Europe, although for different reasons: "This corollary to the curvilinear Art Nouveau, the rectilinear Modern Movement, represents the other architectural tendency around 1900. It emphasizes flat, undecorated surfaces, sharp edges, and the straight line. . . . What is most remarkable is that the two different form-languages are often used simultaneously by a single artist."[105] Sant'Elia's conversion to modernity did not alter this process. It did not dislodge the Secession from his oeuvre, however much he may have censured it in his manifesto.

Sant'Elia was saddled between two worlds and two centuries. Brought up in an atmosphere of intense historicism, he never quite abandoned his faith in the past. To profess the perfervid faith in modernity of a Boccioni or a Marinetti, it was necessary to travel, to read, to follow, as they did, what their counterparts were doing in France, Germany, and England. Restricted to the landlocked horizons of Milan, Sant'Elia had no such opportunities. He could only waver back and forth uncertainly between past and future.

THE LONG DRAWN-OUT DRAMA OF THE RISORGIMENTO

Like all other futurists, Sant'Elia basked in the heroic afterglow left behind by the Risorgimento.[106] The unfulfilled promises left behind by the great nineteenth-century movement of unification was the fertile ground in which the fears and frustrations of a nation could germinate. The pessimism and inferiority complex engendered by a belated and deceptive Risorgimento had its effects on architecture. Sant'Elia's work is an excellent illustration of the contradictions of Italian society at the beginning of the century, torn between the internationalist demands of the modern age and the nationalist aspirations of unified Italy. The exalted forms of his architecture served as an escape valve for the grandiose expectations of the recent past, expectations that could not find an outlet in the limiting conditions of the present. "In this sense," wrote Carlo Cresti, "the drawings of the New City may be considered grandiose images of a celebratory architecture, suitable to illustrate after the fact and with all the eulogistic requisites, the last episode of the long drawn-out drama of the Risorgimento."[107]

Several scholars have called attention to the psychological roots of Italian architecture at the turn of the century: "Precisely for this reason, futurist architecture, which developed to a large extent from the premises of Sant'Elia, is conceived without any consideration to concrete practical demands, with a view to psychological needs: and its most important contribution is not properly speaking architectural but essentially scenographic."[108] The heavy, haunting masses that one finds in Italian architecture at the time, so little geared to any functional purpose, can be traced back, at least in part, to historical and political conditions common to the whole nation. This tendency toward the mystical and the monumental translated into form vague emotional yearnings rather than strictly architectural needs. But because Sant'Elia's means and motivations were not, strictly speaking, architectural, his massive buildings could never tackle concrete problems either in architecture or in urbanism.

Utopia itself, which played such an important role in Sant'Elia's work, was not unrelated to Italy's political and economic situation. Utopias, Nicoletti has shown, usually appear in times of uncertainty and frustration: "Concentrating their interest on the emotional value of form, these utopists avoided the exploration of urban problems and, above all, the definition of any design method. . . . In contrast to Le Corbusier's social dream, they produced a merely formalistic Utopia detached from the social dialectic of their time."[109] The gap between the heroic aspirations of the Risorgimento and the grim realities of unified Italy was immense. Sant'Elia's answer was to bypass the disheartening conditions of the present and to design his architecture in the future tense.

Ultimately, none of these factors—the cultural handicaps caused by a tardy Risorgimento, the insular situation of Italy's schools of architecture, the backwardness of the housing industry—explain Sant'Elia, though all of them surely affected him, as well as other young architects of his generation. Sant'Elia was not a passive tool in the hands of circumstances attending his birth. He made choices all along, and in studying Sant'Elia's work one is struck less by what he saw and read than by what he did not. His ignorance of—and indifference to—the contemporary works of Frank Lloyd Wright, Hendrik Petrus Berlage, Walter Gropius, and Peter Behrens cannot be overlooked. What is astonishing is that even with the lack of such invaluable stimuli, it was Sant'Elia who produced what was by far the most modern cityscape of the day. There is much truth to Bruno Zevi's celebrated remark that "only men who lived in an industrially underdeveloped country could dream of a house 'on the brink of a tumultuous abyss.'"[110]

In spite of the futurists' vehement claims to the contrary, Sant'Elia was not the founding father of modern architecture, in Italy or elsewhere. If one must be oedipal about such matters and come up with a father for modern architecture in Italy, that would certainly be Terragni. Sant'Elia's influence was limited largely to a vague and emotional revolt against the past.

None of this need be adverse criticism, however. Sant'Elia has been criticized repeatedly for his unprofessional approach to architecture, but a negative judgment such as this necessarily predicates his having been an architect to begin with. But if one considers him as a draftsman in the manner of, say, Hugh Ferriss, then the qualities of his work are unprecedented and exceptional.[111] Social relevance and structural propriety were not the goals of his work. Sant'Elia was an architect neither by profession—he received, after all, a degree in *disegno architettonico*—nor by inclination. Faced with a humiliating present, he had no option, or so he thought, but to dream his way out of the impasse, and so regain in the impalpable realm of his imagination the epic dimensions of the Risorgimento.

Appendix 1

Sant'Elia contributed the following untitled essay to the Nuove Tendenze catalogue. In the 1950s it became known as the "Messaggio."

The problem of modern architecture is not a problem of rearranging lines.

It is not a question of finding new moldings, new frames for windows and doors, of replacing columns, pilasters, and corbels with caryatids, flies, or frogs; it is not a case of leaving the facade of exposed brick, plastering it, or cladding it with stone; in short, it is not a case of determining formal differences between the new building and the old but of creating the newly built house from a sound plan with all the resources of science and technology, richly fulfilling every demand of our habits and our spirit, treading asunder all that is grotesque, heavy, and antithetical to us (tradition, style, aesthetics, proportions), determining new forms, new lines, a new harmony of profiles and volumes, an architecture that finds its raison d'être exclusively in the special conditions of modern life, and its relation as an aesthetic value in our sensibility.

This architecture cannot naturally be subject to any law of historic continuity. It must be new, as our state of mind and the contingencies of our historic moment are new.

The art of building was able to evolve through the ages and pass from one style to another, preserving unaltered the general characteristics of architecture, because in history changes of fashion are as frequent as those determined by the shifts in religious convictions and the succession of political systems; but those causes of radical transformation in the conditions of the environment that bring about change and renewal are extremely rare, such as the discovery of natural laws, the improvement of technical means, the rational and scientific use of materials.

In modern life the process of consecutive stylistic development in architecture has been arrested. **Architecture takes its distance from tradition and of necessity begins all over again.**

Calculations of the resistance of the materials and the use of reinforced concrete and iron rule out "architecture" understood in the classical and traditional sense. Modern construction materials and our scientific notions do not lend themselves to the discipline of historical styles, and are the main cause of the grotesque aspect of the fashionable buildings in which one tries to obtain the heavy curve of the arch and the massive appearance of marble from the lightness, the superb slenderness of the beam, and the fragility of reinforced concrete.

The formidable antithesis of the modern and the ancient world is determined by all that did not exist before. Elements whose existence the ancients never suspected have entered our lives. Material contingencies were determined and spiritual attitudes revealed that have repercussions in a thousand ways, first and foremost the formation of a new ideal of beauty as yet obscure and embryonic but for which even the crowd feels the fascination. We have in fact lost the sense of the monumental, the massive, the static, and we have enriched our sensibility with a taste for the light and the practical. We feel we are no longer the men of cathedrals and meeting halls but of grand hotels, railway stations, vast highways, colossal harbors, covered markets, luminous arcades, straight lines, and salutary demolitions.

We must invent and rebuild *ex novo* the modern city like an immense, tumultuous building yard, agile, mobile, dynamic in all its parts, and the modern house like a gigantic machine. Elevators must not huddle in stairwells like solitary worms, rather staircases—now rendered useless—must be abolished, and elevators must swarm up the facades like serpents of iron and glass. The house of cement, glass, iron, stripped of painting and sculpture, enriched solely with the inherent beauty of its lines and its relief, extraordinarily ugly in its mechanical simplicity, as tall and as wide as it need be rather than as prescribed by municipal law, must rise on the brink of a tumultuous abyss: the street will no longer stretch out like a doormat at ground level but will plunge into the earth by means of several stories that will bring together the traffic of the metropolis and be connected by metal catwalks and swift-moving conveyor belts for necessary displacements.

For these reasons I affirm that we must abolish the monumental and the decorative; that we must solve the problem of modern architecture not by cribbing from photographs of China, Persia, or Japan, nor by rhapsodizing foolishly over the rules of Vitruvius, but by strokes of genius, and equipped exclusively with scientific and technical know-how; that everything must be revolutionized, that it is necessary to exploit the roofs, utilize the basements, play down the importance of the facade, to transfer problems of good taste from the sphere of little moldings, pretty capitals, and sweet little gateways to the broader sphere of a bold orchestration of masses and the audacious disposition of plans. The days of monumental funereal and celebratory architecture are over. Architecture must be something better and more vital, and in order to obtain this extra something we must begin by doing away with monuments, sidewalks, porticoes, steps, by sinking streets and piazzas, raising the level of the city, and rearranging the crust of the earth in order to render it at last a servant to our every need, our every whim.

And I oppose:

Fashionable architecture of every country and of every kind;

Classical, solemn, hieratic, scenographic, decorative, monumental, graceful, and pleasing architecture;

Embalming, rebuilding, reproducing monuments;

Perpendicular and horizontal lines, cubical and pyramidal forms that are static, grave, oppressive, and wholly incompatible with our ultra-new sensibility;

The use of massive, voluminous, lasting, antiquated, and costly materials that are not consonant with modern culture and technical expertise as a whole.

And I declare:

That the new architecture is the architecture of cold calculation, of fearless audacity, and of simplicity; the architecture of reinforced concrete, of iron, glass, cardboard, textiles, and all those surrogates of wood, stone, and brick that allow us to obtain the maximum elasticity and lightness;

That real architecture is not for these reasons an arid combination of practicality and utility, but remains art, that is, synthesis, expression;

That decoration, as something overlaid or appended to architecture, is absurd, and that the decorative value of a truly modern architecture depends exclusively on the use and original orchestration of rough, naked, or violently colored materials.

And finally I declare that, just as the ancients took their artistic inspiration from the elements of nature, so too must we—[who are] materially and spiritually artificial—find our inspiration in the elements of the new mechanical world that we have created, of which architecture must be the most beautiful expression, the most complete synthesis, the most effective artistic integration.

Antonio Sant'Elia

Appendix 2

FREQUENTLY CITED MANIFESTOS

Marinetti, F. T., "Fondazione e manifesto del futurismo," *Le Figaro,* February 20, 1909, rpt. in *Archivi,* pp. 15–19.

Boccioni, Carrà, Russolo, Balla, Severini, *Manifesto dei pittori futuristi,* February 11, 1910, rpt. in *Archivi,* pp. 63–65.

Boccioni, Carrà, Russolo, Balla, Severini, *La pittura futurista: Manifesto tecnico,* April 11, 1910, rpt. in *Archivi,* pp. 65–67.

Boccioni, *La scultura futurista,* April 11, 1912, rpt. in *Archivi,* pp. 67–72.

Marinetti, *Distruzione della sintassi—Immaginazione senza fili—Parole in libertà,* May 11, 1913, rpt. in *Teoria e invenzione futurista,* pp. 57–70.

Carrà, *La pittura dei suoni, rumori e odori,* August 11, 1913, rpt. in *Archivi,* pp. 73–76.

Prampolini, "Anche l'architettura futurista . . . E che è?" *Il Piccolo Giornale d'Italia,* January 29–30, 1914, rpt. in Crispolti, *Ricostruzione futurista dell'universo,* pp. 82–87.

Boccioni, "Architettura futurista. Manifesto," published posthumously (ca. 1914) in *Altri inediti e apparati critici,* pp. 38–40.

Sant'Elia, *L'architettura futurista,* July 11, 1914, rpt. in *Archivi,* pp. 81–85.

Marinetti, Boccioni, Russolo, Sant'Elia, Sironi, Piatti, *L'orgoglio italiano,* January 1915, rpt. in *Archivi,* pp. 32–34.

Notes

Unless otherwise noted, all translations are my own.

CHAPTER 1: BIRTH OF A NATION

1 The unification of Italy took place in 1861, when the Regno d'Italia was proclaimed under the aegis of Victor Emmanuel II. Venice, however, remained an Austrian enclave until 1866, and Rome a papal state until 1870.

2 Massimo D'Azeglio, quoted in Edgar Holt, *The Making of Italy, 1815–1870*, New York, 1971, p. 258.

3 Johann Gottfried Herder, Johann Gottlieb Fichte, and Alexander von Humboldt in particular maintained that language alone determined national consciousness and that, consequently, the geographical limits of a state should coincide with linguistic barriers. See Tullio De Mauro, *Storia linguistica dell'Italia unità*, Bari, 1974, pp. 1–2.

4 Alberto Asor Rosa, "Creazione e assestamento dello Stato Unitario (1860–1887)," in *Storia d'Italia dall'Unità a oggi*, vol. 4, bk. 2, Turin, 1975, p. 840.

5 De Mauro, *Storia linguistica*, p. 91.

6 Ugo Monneret de Villard, *Opere di architettura moderna*, Milan, 1909, p. 5.

7 Ibid.

8 G. Lavini, "L'architettura nazionale," *Architettura Italiana*, November 1911, p. 13.

9 Monneret de Villard, *Opere di architettura moderna*, p. 13.

10 Camillo Boito, *Architettura del medio evo in Italia*, Milan, 1880, p. xxvi.

11 Franco Borsi, *L'architettura dell'Unità d'Italia*, Florence, 1966, p. 74.

12 On Boito, see Maria Antonietta Crippa, "Boito e l'architettura dell'Italia unita," in C. Boito, *Il nuovo e l'antico in architettura*, Milan, 1989, pp. xi–xlv; Liliana Grassi, *Camillo Boito*, Milan, 1959; Bruno Zevi, *Architettura e storiografia*, Venice, 1950, pp. 24–33. For Boito's activity as a literary figure see Benedetto Croce, "Camillo Boito," in *La letteratura della nuova Italia*, vol. 5, Bari, 1939, pp. 325–330; and also E. Giachery, "Camillo Boito," in *Dizionario biografico degli italiani*, Rome, 1969, vol. 11, pp. 237–242.

13 Carroll L. Meeks, *Italian Architecture, 1750–1914*, New Haven, 1966, p. 208.

14 See Franco Bernabei, *Pietro Selvatico nella critica e nella storia delle arti figurative dell'ottocento*, Vicenza, 1974.

15 For the introduction of Froebel to Italy, see the article traditionally ascribed to Selvatico and signed with the pseudonym "Y": "I giardini dell'infanza di Federico Froebel," *Il Politecnico* (Milan), vol. 15, 1862, pp. 290–301.

16 Vincenzo Fontana, *Il nuovo paesaggio dell'Italia giolittiana*, Bari, 1981, p. 6.

17 V. Fontana, "La scuola speciale di architettura (1875–1915)," in *Il Politecnico di Milano, 1863–1914*, Milan, 1981, p. 232. Fontana compares Boito's role to that of Verdi rather than Manzoni, but the principle is the same.

18 Boito, *Architettura del medio evo in Italia*, p. xxix. It is interesting that Ruskin, too, uses language as an analogy to architecture. See *The Seven Lamps of Architecture*, London, 1849, pp. 190–191.

19 Boito, *Architettura del medio evo in Italia*, pp. xxvii–xxviii.

20 Ibid., pp. xxx–xxxi.

21 On eclecticism, see Luciano Patetta, *L'architettura dell'eclettismo*, Milan, 1975; and Paolo Portoghesi, *L'eclettismo a Roma, 1870–1922*, Rome, n.d. (1968?).

22 See Franco Borsi, *L'architettura dell'Unità d'Italia*. See also Eberhard Schroeter, "Rome's First National State Architecture: The *Palazzo delle Finanze*," in *Art and Architecture in the Service of Politics*, ed. H. Millon and L. Nochlin, Cambridge, Mass., 1978, 128–149.

23 An exception was the unsigned article calling for a return to Baroque architecture (in 1912!): "Why not return to the Baroque?" the author asks; "this is obviously the national style since it spread over the entire peninsula. The state, which must continuously build schools, public buildings, barracks, should impose this style to the Civil Engineers as a norm to be obeyed; private enterprise would not fail to follow, and thus the National Architectural Style would finally be constituted." "Per un'architettura ufficiale italiana," *L'artista moderno*, Turin, 1912, p. 106.

24 Eclecticism was based, by tacit agreement, on a code of sorts: "In public buildings and in churches, the Renaissance [style] predominated; in buildings dedicated to cure and in seaside resorts, the Roman-Pompeian; in villas and town houses, the Italian eighteenth century or French rococo; in railroad stations, the French cosmopolitan Baroque." L. Angelini, "Concorsi d'architet-

tura in Italia," *Emporium*, January 1916, p. 48.

25 "What we claim, if we revive again the formal world of the Renaissance, if from it we wish to newly create the national German style, is more than a claim of aesthetic insight and historical judgement, it is a challenge from the whole spiritual course of the German nation, it is a summons of art, of the mighty history of recent years, a call of the Fatherland." J. Lessing, "Die Renaissance im heutigen Kunstgewerbe," Berlin, 1877, quoted in John Heskett, *Design in Germany, 1870–1918*, London, 1986, p. 18.

26 Ruskin, *The Seven Lamps of Architecture*, pp. 189–192.

27 Pasquale Villari, "Lettere meridionali," quoted in Manfredi Nicoletti, *L'architettura Liberty in Italia*, Bari, 1978, p. 22.

28 For the most useful works related to the Italian Art Nouveau scene, see Robert Schmutzler, *Art Nouveau*, New York, 1964; Stephan Tschudi Madsen, *Sources of Art Nouveau*, Oslo, 1956; Nikolaus Pevsner, *Pioneers of Modern Design*, Harmondsworth, 1987.

29 S. Tschudi Madsen, *Art Nouveau*, New York, 1967, p. 138.

30 See Meeks, *Italian Architecture*, p. 425.

31 For the emergence of an accepted designation of the Art Nouveau phenomenon in Italy, see Tschudi Madsen, *Art Nouveau*, pp. 26–29; Rossana Bossaglia, *Il Liberty in Italia*, Milan, 1968, pp. 12–16. See also Alison Adburgham, *Liberty's: A Biography of a Shop*, London, 1975.

32 Luca Beltrami, distinguished architect, writer, and senator, apparently used it for the first time in an article of 1901, where he mentions the "floreale detto Liberty." Bossaglia, *Il Liberty in Italia*, p. 15.

33 For the influence of the Liberty on music and literature, see Fortunato Bellonzi, *Mostra del Liberty italiano*, Milan 1972, pp. 13–28; Glauco Viazzi and Vanni Scheiwiller, eds., *Poeti simbolisti e Liberty in Italia*, Milan, 1967.

34 Nikolaus Pevsner, *The Sources of Modern Architecture and Design*, New York, 1968, p. 40.

35 Bossaglia, *Il Liberty in Italia*, p. 28.

36 As Marco Rosci stated, "Whereas democracy tends to borrow its internationalist vocation from the theory and praxis of the supranational class solidarity of workers' movements, the numerous aristocratic ideologies tend more and more to ground themselves on the foundations of the 'national traditions.'" "Arte e industria nell'età giolittiana," *L'Italia Liberty*, Milan, 1973, p. 38.

37 Ibid., pp. 51, 58. For illustrations, see Lara-Vinca Masini, *Art Nouveau*, Florence, 1976, p. 316.

38 See Marco Rosci, "Arte e industria nell'età giolittiana," pp. 28–51, for a correlation between the Liberty and the Italian economy under Giolitti.

39 "It [the Floreale] was accepted by the 'free lancers' of industrial initiative, by the Lombard or Piedmontese entrepreneur who in his sentimental positivism adopted within the private sphere of his firms or of his home that vocabulary he saw in use as an expression of 'progress' in the European circles with which he was accustomed to deal." Renato De Fusco, *Il floreale a Napoli*, Naples, 1959, p. 19.

40 The one admittedly clamorous exception was Basile's addition to the Parliament in Rome, the Palazzo Montecitorio.

41 The first translation of Ruskin did not appear until 1897, when Italy was already coming to terms with Art Nouveau. For Ruskin's enormous influence in Italy, see Enrico Thovez, "La colpa del insegnamento del disegno," *Arte Decorativa Moderna*, 1902, 75–80, 82ff. See also A. Melani, "L'esposizione d'arte decorativa odierna in Torino," *Arte Italiana Decorativa e Industriale*, August 1902, pp. 63–68.

42 The influential Luca Beltrami referred to them disdainfully as "vegetarian . . . iconoclasts." Quoted in Paola Barocchi, ed., *Testimonianze e polemiche figurative in Italia: Dal divisionismo al novecento*, Florence, 1974, p. 188.

43 For international exhibitions, see Walter Benjamin, "Grandville, or the World Exhibitions," in *Charles Baudelaire: A Lyric Poet in the Era of High Capitalism*, London, 1983, pp. 164–166; Wolfgang Friebe, *Buildings of the World Exhibitions*, Leipzig, 1985; Peter Greenhalgh, *Ephemeral Vistas: The Expositions Universelles, Great Exhibitions, and World's Fairs, 1851–1939*, New York, 1988.

44 *L'Arte Decorativa Moderna*, January 1902, quoted in De Fusco, *Il floreale a Napoli*, pp. 20–21.

45 Giulio Carlo Argan, *Studi e note*, Rome, 1955, p. 281.

46 *Prima esposizione internazionale d'arte decorativa moderna*, Turin, 1902, p. 11.

47 Nicoletti, *L'architettura Liberty*, p. 107.

48 Ibid., p. 115.

49 M. Nicoletti, "Art Nouveau in Italy," in *The Anti-Rationalists*, ed. J. M. Richards and Nikolaus Pevsner, London, 1973, p. 42.

50 G. Beltrami, "L'arte nuova all'esposizione di Torino," *La Lettura*, July 1902, p. 606.

51 On D'Aronco, see L. Carloni and E. Valeriani, *Rai-*

mondo D'Aronco, disegni d'architettura, Rome, 1980; M. Nicoletti, *D'Aronco e l'architettura Liberty*, Bari, 1982; *Atti del congresso internazionale di studi su "Raimondo D'Aronco e il suo tempo*," Udine, 1982; *D'Aronco, architetto*, Milan, 1982; Francesco Tentori, *Raimondo D'Aronco dai suoi libri e dai suoi schizzi*, Milan, 1982.

52 On D'Aronco's work in Istanbul, see David Gebhard, "Raimondo D'Aronco e l'Art Nouveau in Turchia," *Architettura. Cronache e Storia* (hereafter cited as *L'Architettura*), December 1966, pp. 550–554; January 1967, pp. 620–624; February 1967, pp. 690–694; March 1967, pp. 760–764.

53 Joseph Olbrich, quoted in De Fusco, *Il floreale a Napoli*, p. 17. See also Roger Marx, "L'exposition internationale d'art décoratif à Turin," *Gazette des Beaux-Arts*, December 1902, p. 506.

54 Quoted by Fritz Wärndorfer, one of the founders of the *Wiener Werkstätte*, in a letter to the Austrian architect Josef Hoffmann: see Edward Sekler, "Mackintosh and Vienna," in *The Anti-Rationalists*, p. 140.

55 Giulia Veronesi, *Joseph Maria Olbrich*, Milan, 1948, p. 27.

56 See A. Frizzi, "L'edificio per la mostra degli automobili," pp. 289–304, and E. Guidetti, "L'impianto elettrico per 'l'Armonia dei colori' sulla facciata dell'edificio per la mostra degli automobili," pp. 305–310, both in *L'Ingegneria Civile e le Arti Industriali*, 1902, vol. 28.

CHAPTER 2: THE EARLY YEARS

1 Nino Torlaschi, "Ricordo di Sant'Elia," *Il Gagliardetto* (Como), October 10, 1935, p. 3. Sant'Elia continued to take part in athletic competitions even after his move to Milan.

2 See *Ottantesimo anniversario della scuola d'arti e mestieri "G. Castellini*," Como, 1963; see also Emilio Guicciardi, "Riconoscenza e gloria per Antonio Sant'Elia architetto futurista ed eroe," *La Martinella di Milano*, October 1958, pp. 523–525.

3 The subject of the written exam also survives and gives an idea of the level of the school: "Roof truss of the Polonceau type, or of the counterfixed type in wood and iron."

4 This famous term was coined by Napoleone Colajanni in *L'Italia nel 1898*, Milan, 1898, p. 28.

5 Antonello Negri, "La città della produzione," in *Boccioni a Milano*, ed. Guido Ballo, Milan, 1982, p. 77. For information on the Milanese factories, see also Giovanni Stracca, "Il Politecnico e il processo di industrializ-

zazione della Lombardia," in *Il Politecnico di Milano*, pp. 166–227.

6 A. Asor Rosa, "Creazione e assestamento dello Stato Unitario (1860–1887)," pp. 958, 959.

7 On the Villoresi, see V. Fontana, *Il nuovo paesaggio*, pp. 120–122; Etienne Dalmasso, *Milan: Capitale économique de l'Italie*, Paris, 1971, pp. 68–70.

8 Maurizio Grandi and Attilio Pracchi, *Milano: Guida all'architettura moderna*, Bologna, 1980; the first figure is quoted on p. 39, and the other two are cited on p. 95.

9 According to the industrial census of 1911, 20 percent of Italy's blue-collar workers lived in Milan. A. Molinari and A. Visconti, *Milano: Storia arte scienza economia servizi pubblici statistica amministrazione*, Milan, 1926, p. 115.

10 On public housing sponsored by the Comune di Milano, see M. Grandi and A. Pracchi, *Milano: Guida all'architettura moderna*, pp. 111–135; L. Tilly, *The Working Class in Milan, 1881–1911*, Ann Arbor, 1973, pp. 209–309. For the public dormitories see *Milano nel 1906*, Milan, 1906, pp. 249–258.

11 Ornella Selvafolta, "La città dei servizi," in *Boccioni a Milano*, p. 82.

12 Cesare Beruto, quoted in Giuseppe De Finetti, *Milano: Costruzione di una città*, Milan, 1969, p. 197. In Italian the biological analogy is stronger because both plant and plan are rendered by the same word (*pianta*).

13 Renato Airoldi, "La Milano dell'ingegner Beruto," *Casabella*, October–November 1979, p. 12.

14 "Studio per villa: Disegni inviatici dal signor Antonio Sant'Elia—Milano," *La Casa* (Rome), 1909, pp. 10–11.

15 Only reproductions survive. See Carlo Cresti, "Intorno a due disegni quasi sconosciuti di Antonio Sant'Elia," *Necropoli*, December 1972, pp. 45–50.

16 "In short, we feel that the detailing of this decoration and of the interior design have not been studied in depth, and do not correspond to the quality and beauty of the exterior." See "Studio per villa," p. 11.

17 *Deutsche Kunst und Dekoration*, May 1900. See also Enrico Thovez, "Olbrich e la colonia di Darmstadt," *La Lettura*, January 1902, p. 7.

18 Loredana Compagnin and Maria Luisa Mazzola, "La nascita delle scuole superiori di architettura in Italia," in *Il razionalismo e l'architettura in Italia durante il fascismo*, ed. S. Danesi and L. Patetta, Venice, 1976, p. 194; see also V. Fontana, "La scuola speciale di architettura (1865–1915)," in *Il Politecnico di Milano*, pp. 228–246.

19 F. Lori, *Storia del Politecnico*, Milan, 1941, p. 77.

20 It should be remembered that the Liberty was never ad-

mitted in the schools of architecture. See Roberto Gabetti and Paolo Marconi, "L'insegnamento dell'architettura nel sistema didattico franco-italiano (1789–1922)," part 4, *Controspazio*, October–November 1971, p. 44.

21 Not one major Italian architect was involved in public housing. See M. Grandi and A. Pracchi, *Milano: Guida all'architettura moderna*, p. 105.

22 Gabetti and Marconi, "L'insegnamento dell'architettura," p. 44.

23 Nicoletti, "Art Nouveau in Italy," in *The Anti-Rationalists*, p. 33.

24 On Brera, see Eva Tea, *L'Accademia di Belle Arti a Brera-Milano*, Florence, 1941.

25 Significantly, Moses Ginzburg, later to become one of the USSR's most famous architects, enrolled in the same *corso comune,* on the very same day. Although Ginzburg's work in Milan was a far cry from his later rationalist projects, it is interesting to see how these two future exponents of modern architecture were already in touch in 1909.

26 On Mentessi, see Guido Marangoni, "L'insegnamento artistico in Italia: La scuola dell'Accademia di Brera," *Emporium* (Bergamo), February 1913, pp. 102–118. See also *Giuseppe Mentessi,* Ferrara, 1972.

27 Anselmo Bucci, "Scapigliatura 1906," *La Lettura* (Milan), 1941, p. 274.

28 Very little is known of Cattaneo. He designed the Hotel Corso (1904–1905), one of the most spectacular Liberty buildings in Milan, in collaboration with Giacomo Santamaria. See the unsigned obituary "La morte dell'architetto Angelo Cattaneo," *Arte Cristiana*, December 1936, p. 261. Cesare Fratino, "Angelo Cattaneo," *La Martinella*, vol. 14, 1960, p. 324; and also Paolo Mezzanotte, "L'edilizia milanese dalla caduta del Regno Italico alla prima guerra mondiale," *Storia di Milano*, vol. 15, Milan, 1962, pp. 442–443, 451.

29 See G. Fontana, "Sant'Elia maestro comacino," *La Provincia di Como,* August 19, 1957, p. 3. See also Jörn-Peter Schmidt-Thomsen, *Floreale und futuristische Architektur: Das Werk von Antonio Sant'Elia*, Berlin, 1967, p. 145.

30 Paolo Thea, "Nuove Tendenze a Milano," in *Nuove Tendenze—Milano e l'altro futurismo*, Milan, 1980, p. 10.

31 Quoted in Fontana, "Sant'Elia maestro comacino," p. 3. The "Maestri Comancini" were great master builders, renowned for their ecclesiastical architecture during the Romanesque period.

32 See Ambrogio Annoni, "Un maestro dell'architettura tra l'800 ed il '900: Gaetano Moretti," *Bolletino del Po-litecnico di Milano,* no. 3, 1952; M. Calzavara, "L'architetto Gaetano Moretti," *Casabella,* no. 218, 1958, pp. 69–83.

33 Sant'Elia's grades were, based on a scale of 10: Perspective, 5; Architecture, 9 1/2; and Ornament, 6.

34 Dates are necessarily conjectural: Sant'Elia did not always sign or date his works. Moreover, his entire output was compressed in the space of more or less six years, so that one cannot really trace the evolution that a longer career would allow.

35 Some of the early drawings were done on paper watermarked with the arms of Milan and the words "Comune di Milano," as the photographs themselves make clear. This has led Alberto Longatti and Luciano Caramel to date these drawings between 1906 and 1909, when Sant'Elia worked for the city administration (*Antonio Sant'Elia,* Milan, 1987, p. 127). Stylistically, however, this theory is doubtful, and Sant'Elia could have kept the stationery as scrap paper for years.

36 Carrà, *La mia vita,* Rome, 1943, rpt. in *Tutti gli scritti,* Milan, 1978, p. 638.

37 Ibid., p. 642. For Carrà's views on Moretti, see also the manifesto "Contro la critica," December 1913, rpt. in *Archivi del futurismo,* ed. Maria Drudi Gambillo and Teresa Fiori, Rome, 1958, vol. 1, p. 177 (hereafter cited as *Archivi*).

38 Marinetti, "Le Futurisme," *Le Figaro,* February 20, 1909, p. 1. For the best annotated modern edition of the manifesto, see Jean-Pierre Andreoli de Villiers, *Le premier manifeste du futurisme*, Ottawa, 1986.

CHAPTER 3: THE IMPACT OF VIENNA

1 Carlo Santi, "Milanino: La 'garden city' italiana," *Comunità*, February 1960, pp. 72–82.

2 *Le Case Popolari e le Città-Giardino,* year 1, nos. 10–11, 1911, pp. 226, 259. The projects were republished in the volume *Il villino moderno: Raccolta di progetti per il concorso omonimo, dicembre 1910–gennaio 1911*, Milan, n.d. (but 1911).

3 According to an interview granted to Schmidt-Thomsen by Luigi Pellini. Schmidt-Thomsen, *Floreale*, pp. 111–112.

4 For this event, see *Roma 1911*, ed. Gianna Piantoni, Rome, 1980.

5 See A. Manfredini, "Il IX Congresso Internazionale degli Architetti e l'Esposizione Internazionale di Architettura in Roma," *Il Monitore Tecnico*, October 10, 1911; Enrico Valeriani, "Il concorso nazionale d'ar-

chitettura," in *Roma 1911,* pp. 305–326; G. Accasto, V. Fraticelli, and R. Nicolini, "Il concorso per la casa moderna all'Esposizione dell'11 e l'aggiornamento dell'eccletismo," *L'architettura di Roma capitale, 1870–1970,* Rome, 1971, pp. 259–261.

6 "Of all the buildings of Italy in the last century," declared Carroll Meeks of the Palazzaccio, "this one has probably come in for more obloquy and objuration than any other, except possibly the 'Vittoriano.'" *Italian Architecture,* p. 353.

7 See Eduard Sekler, "Josef Hoffmann e il suo padiglione austriaco all'Esposizione internazionale di Belle Arti in Roma nel 1911," in *Artisti austriaci a Roma dal barocco alla Secessione,* Rome, 1972, n.p.; M. Marchetti, "Il padiglione austriaco," in *Roma 1911,* pp. 274–278.

8 See *Der Architekt,* no. 17, 1911, plate 42.

9 Specifically, from a project for a Trade Bank in Prague designed by Josef Hoffmann and Franz Krásny in 1897.

10 On Sommaruga, see Ugo Monneret de Villard, *L'architettura di Giuseppe Sommaruga,* Milan, n.d. (1908); F. Tentori, "Contributo alla storiografia di G. Sommaruga," *Casabella,* 1957, no. 217, pp. 70–87; E. Bairati and D. Riva, *Giuseppe Sommaruga: Un protagonista del Liberty italiano,* Milano, 1982.

11 The two female nudes on either side of the entrance caused such an uproar that they had to be removed, and Sommaruga was mercilessly lampooned in the local press over the issue.

12 On Mazzucotelli, see R. Bossaglia and A. Hammacher, *Mazzucotelli: L'artista italiano del ferro battuto Liberty,* Milan, 1971.

13 Daniela Poli claims that the recurrent figures in Sant'Elia's oeuvre prove that he thought of his works as drawings or paintings rather than as a means to an end. See "I disegni di Sant'Elia," *I Quaderni del Conoscitore di Stampe,* May–June 1974, p. 31.

14 As Robert Schmutzler remarks, "Illustrated and decorated books and magazines were the most effective transmitters of the new style, because in them the significant tendencies towards flat pattern and symbolism could express themselves in all purity." "The English Origins of Art Nouveau," *Architectural Review,* February 1955, p. 109.

15 Tschudi Madsen, *Sources of Art Nouveau,* p. 410.

16 In addition to the two gold medals received in Rome in 1908 and 1911, he scored a great personal triumph in the Venice Biennale of 1910. For his influence on Italian architects, see Bossaglia, *Il Liberty in Italia,* pp. 150–155.

17 According to Gerolamo Fontana, he and Sant'Elia had also visited Klimt's one-man show at the Venice Biennale that summer. See Caramel and Longatti, *Antonio Sant'Elia,* 1987, p. 11.

18 For the connection between Art Nouveau and eroticism, see Hilton Kramer, "The Erotic Style: Reflections on the Exhibition of 'Art Nouveau,'" *Arts,* September 1960, pp. 22–26; Albino Galvano, "L'erotismo del Liberty e la sublimazione astrattista," *Cratilo,* Turin, 1963, no. 3, pp. 39–60.

19 For an overall view of this issue see Bram Dijkstra, *Idols of Perversity: Fantasies of Feminine Evil in Fin-de-Siècle Culture,* New York, 1986.

20 Nietzsche's views on women were part of the cultural baggage of the Milanese, no less than the Austrian, artists of the time. See Tschudi Madsen, *Art Nouveau,* p. 37.

21 G. Fontana, "Sant'Elia e il 'Liberty,'" *Como,* 1963, no. 2, p. 55.

22 Carlo Cresti, *Appunti storici e critici nell'architettura italiana dal '900 ad oggi,* Florence, 1971, p. 113.

23 In particular, his misogynist, phrenological approach to female delinquents: see Cesare Lombroso and Guglielmo Ferrero, *La donna delinquente, la prostituta e la donna normale,* Turin, 1893. For Lombroso's influence on the art of the turn of the century, see Bram Dijkstra, *Idols of Perversity.*

24 On Romani, see Guido Ballo, *Preistoria del futurismo,* Milan, 1960, pp. 122–126; Giovanni Anzani, "Per una revisione critica dell'opera di Romolo Romani," *Storia dell'Arte,* no. 33, 1978, pp. 155–180; Renato Barilli, ed., *Romolo Romani,* Milan, 1982.

25 See Anzani, "Per una revisione critica dell'opera di Romolo Romani," p. 155. Given Sant'Elia's intellectual makeup, it is improbable that he knew anything about Freud, whose *Interpretation of Dreams* had been translated into Italian in 1900. At the time Freud was known only to a restricted circle of intellectuals in Milan, mainly through the work of Lombroso.

26 See Caramel and Longatti, *Antonio Sant'Elia,* Como, 1962, p. 18 (not to be confused with their recent publication of the same name, published in Milan in 1987). Anzani, "Per una revisione critica dell'opera di Romolo Romani," p. 177; Nicoletti, *L'architettura Liberty,* p. 370.

27 For Previati's influence on futurism, see Ballo, *Preistoria del futurismo,* pp. 137–150.

28 Caramel and Longatti, *Antonio Sant'Elia,* 1962, p. 39.

29 Ibid., p. 16.

30 It was based on a hasty interpretation of an article by Sant'Elia's old friend Gerolamo Fontana, in which the

latter compares Sant'Elia's Liberty drawings with those of Poe. Schmidt-Thomsen, *Floreale,* p. 139.

31 Many of Sant'Elia's projects have to do with funerary buildings: the Monza cemetery, the funeral monuments to the Caprotti family and to Luigi Sant'Elia, the cemetery of the Brigata Arezzo, and several Liberty tombs (fig. 22).

32 "L'arte nei cimiteri: Al monumentale di Milano," *Corriere della Sera,* November 1, 1910, p. 4. See also F. S. Borri, *Il cimitero monumentale di Milano,* Milan, 1966; Bossaglia, "Scultura cimiterale a Milano tra Scapigliatura e simbolismo," in *La scultura nel XIX secolo,* Bologna, 1984, pp. 209–214.

33 In addition, both St. Leopold and the Postal Savings Bank had been published in Italy in *L'Arte Decorativa Moderna,* year 3, 1908, pp. 124ff, and later in *Emporium,* August 1910, pp. 102–115.

34 The pact, signed by Germany, Austria, and Italy, was aimed chiefly at countering French and English power in Europe and required that if any of the three allies was attacked, the other two would come to its assistance.

35 The Viennese Secession was heavily represented both at the Venice Biennale and at Ca' Pesaro. See Ballo, *Preistoria del futurismo,* pp. 89–90.

36 See Maria Grazia Messina, "Historismus e *Nutzstil:* Il ruolo di Wagner e della Wagnerschule nell'architettura Liberty in Italia," *Wien und die Architektur des 20. Jahrhunderts,* Vienna, 1986, pp. 37–53.

37 On this issue, see Iain Boyd Whyte, "Antonio Sant'Elia: Un Wagnerschüler in absentia," *Antonio Sant'Elia: l'architettura disegnata,* Venice, 1991, pp. 73–87.

38 On the Wagnerschule, see Otto Antonia Graf, *Die vergessene Wagnerschule,* Vienna, 1969; Marco Pozzetto, *Die Schule Otto Wagners, 1894–1912,* Munich, 1980; Liliana Grueff, *Disegni della Wagnerschule,* Florence, 1989. Iain Boyd Whyte, *Three Architects from the Master Class of Otto Wagner: Emil Hoppe, Marcel Kammerer, Otto Schönthal,* Cambridge, Mass., 1989.

39 Arata, "La Prima Mostra d'Architettura promossa dall'Associazione degli Architetti Lombardi," *Vita d'Arte,* March 1914, p. 71. See also Prampolini, "Il gruppo 'Nuove Tendenze' plagiario del futurismo," *L'Artista Moderno,* June 1914, p. 217.

40 *Wagnerschule 1902,* Vienna, 1903.

41 See Ezio Godoli, *Il futurismo,* Bari, 1983, p. 12. G. Bernasconi, "Rilettura di Mario Chiattone," *Necropoli,* September–December 1970, p. 44.

42 Belief in the permanence of the Austro-Hungarian empire, with its ethnic and aristocratic stratification, died

hard. See Claudio Magris, *Il mito absburgico nella letteratura austriaca moderna,* Turin, 1963.

43 Graf, *Die vergessene Wagnerschule,* p. 27.

44 Marinetti, "Tripoli italiana," rpt. in *Sintesi del futurismo,* ed. Luigi Scrivo, Rome, 1968, p. 40.

45 Mussolini, quoted in C. Cresti, "Sulle origini del gap architettonico," *Necropoli,* February 1969, p. 15. Trento and Trieste were part of the "unredeemed" lands that Italy claimed as its own "natural" frontiers (and indeed Austria was forced to relinquish them after World War I). Tripolitania, a Libyan province, was coveted and eventually conquered on the grounds that it had once belonged to the Roman Empire.

46 See *La Provincia di Como,* April 21, 1911.

47 Gabetti and Marconi, "L'insegnamento dell'architettura," p. 44.

48 Wagner, *Modern Architecture,* trans. Harry F. Mallgrave, Santa Monica, 1988, p. 65.

49 Nicoletti, "Art Nouveau in Italy," in *The Anti-Rationalists,* p. 32.

50 *Concorsi di architettura in Italia,* Milano, n.d.

51 One of Bastl's many versions of this project, significantly, was for a church in the Central Cemetery in Vienna. See *Wagnerschule 1901,* Vienna, 1902.

52 Rossana Bossaglia and Mauro Cozzi, *I Coppedè,* Genoa, 1982, p. 168.

53 For the underlying ethnic and political assumptions implicit in this fascination with the East, see the trenchant and illuminating book by Edward Said, *Orientalism,* New York, 1979.

54 For the use of typologies from the Far East by the Milanese architects, see Nicoletti, *L'architettura Liberty,* p. 83. Godoli, *Il futurismo,* p. 14.

55 Nicoletti, *L'architettura Liberty,* p. 371.

56 Bossaglia, *Il Liberty in Italia,* p. 52.

57 Filippo Quaglia, "Per il nuovo cimitero di Monza," *La Lombardia,* October 18, 1912, n.p. Quaglia mentions the "extremely elegant and audacious decoration that recalls Klimt in certain coloristic orgies." See also Luigi Angelini, "Concorsi d'architettura in Italia," p. 48.

58 See Francesco Tentori, "Le origini Liberty di Antonio Sant'Elia," *L'Architettura,* July–August 1955, p. 206.

59 See *Silvio Gambini: Opere, 1903–1915,* Busto Arsizio, 1976. G. Pacciarotti, *Situazione degli studi sul Liberty,* Florence, n.d. (but 1977), pp. 208–210.

60 *Relazione della commissione giudicatrice del concorso per un progetto architettonico per il nuovo cimitero,* Monza, 1912, p. 7.

61 *Concorsi di architettura in Italia,* pp. 71–75.

62 For this interesting competition, see *La Stazione Centrale di Milano,* Milan, 1981; G. Lavini, "Ciò che dovrebbe insegnare un concorso," *Architettura Italiana,* September 1912, p. 133.

63 For illustrations, see P. Mezzanotte, "L'edilizia milanese dalla caduta del regno italico alla prima guerra mondiale," *Storia di Milano,* p. 452.

64 The importance of the competition is evidenced by the list of jury members, which included Camillo Boito and Gaetano Moretti. See Ferdinando Reggiori, *Milano, 1800–1943,* Milan, 1947, p. 474.

65 Nicoletti, *L'architettura Liberty,* p. 370. See also Caramel and Longatti, *Antonio Sant'Elia,* 1962, p. 24; Tentori, "Le origini Liberty di Antonio Sant'Elia," p. 208.

66 Wagner took these wreaths from his revered Gottfried Semper, for whom they constituted one of the embryos of architecture in the remote past. See Semper, *Der Stil in den technischen und tektonischen Künsten oder praktische Ästhetik: Ein Handbuch für Techniker, Künstler und Kunstfreunde,* 1860, rpt. Mittenwald, 1977, p. 14.

67 Godoli, *Il futurismo,* p. 15.

68 *Aus der Wagnerschule 1898,* Supplementheft, *Der Architekt,* Vienna, 1898, p. 13.

69 Nicoletti, "Memoria e linguaggio in Raimondo D'Aronco," *Atti del Congresso Internazionale,* p. 217.

70 Silvia Evangelisti, "Dal simbolismo alla non-figurazione e ritorno: Il percorso artistico di Romolo Romani," in *Romolo Romani,* p. 28.

71 For the influence of Mestrovič, see G. Fontana, "Sant'Elia e il 'Liberty,'" p. 55; Anzani, "Per una revisione critica dell'opera di Romolo Romani," p. 172.

72 Evangelisti, "Dal simbolismo alla non-figurazione," p. 28.

73 The main projects for the competition are illustrated in *Concorsi di architettura in Italia.*

74 Carroll L. Meeks, *The Railroad Station,* New Haven, 1956, pp. 141–142.

75 Caramel and Longatti, *Antonio Sant'Elia,* 1962, p. 21. Sartoris alone mentioned "un refuge alpin dans les environs de Brunate." *Encyclopédie de l'architecture nouvelle,* Milan, 1948, vol. 1, p. 143.

76 Sant'Elia's original plan has not come down to us. The plan illustrated here is taken from Caramel and Longatti, *Antonio Sant'Elia,* 1962, fig. 16.

77 Schmidt-Thomsen noted that a similar plan by the architect V. Borzani had appeared in the well-known magazine *L'Architettura Italiana,* May 1909; see Schmidt-Thomsen, *Floreale,* p. 134.

78 See Bernasconi, "Rilettura di Mario Chiattone," p. 48.

79 At the preliminary exams the candidate had to choose one of the following options: (1) the facade of a pavilion of fine arts; (2) the facade of a rich seignorial villa with two stories in addition to the ground floor; or (3) the facade of a hall of fame for a cemetery in a medium-sized city.

80 Bossaglia, "Antonio Sant'Elia," *Mostra del Liberty italiano,* p. 110.

81 Cresti, "Sulle origini del gap architettonico," p. 19.

82 The date of fig. 47, which is almost illegible, seems to read 21-11-1909. But it is so close in style, format, and subject matter to other dated drawings of 1912 that I am inclined to accept the latter date. This was also Longatti's earlier position on the subject. Cf. Caramel and Longatti, *Antonio Sant'Elia,* 1962, p. 74.

83 Paolo Portoghesi noted that these slanted planes function as reflecting surfaces, their intense luminosity contrasting sharply with the vertical pylons. Portoghesi, *L'angelo della storia,* Bari, 1982, p. 226.

84 G. Veronesi, *L'opera di Mario Chiattone architetto,* Pisa, 1965, p. 8.

85 Quoted in Hugh Ferriss, *Architectural Visions,* New York, 1980, p. 31.

86 Wolfgang Pehnt, *Expressionist Architecture,* New York, 1973, p. 19.

87 Nicoletti, *L'architettura Liberty,* p. 83.

88 Carlo Ragghianti, "Sant'Elia: Il Bibbiena del duemila," *Critica d'Arte,* no. 56, March–April 1963, p. 10. On the "impenetrability" of Sant'Elia's buildings, see Pehnt, *Expressionist Architecture,* p. 119.

89 Giulio Carlo Argan, "Il pensiero critico di Antonio Sant'Elia," *L'Arte,* September 1930, p. 494.

90 "Whenever Sant'Elia suggests a topographical setting, it is in the Expressionist tradition of plunging slopes or precipitous cliffs." Pehnt, *Expressionist Architecture,* p. 176.

91 Corrado Maltese, *Storia dell'arte italiana, 1785–1943,* Turin, 1960, 273.

92 Cresti, "Sulle origini del gap architettonico," p. 19.

93 Little is known of this fascinating architect, whose career, like Sant'Elia's, was cut short by World War I. Baroncini graduated from the Politecnico in 1909 but followed the core curriculum at Brera, where Sant'Elia may have met him. Cf. Raffaello Giolli, "Impressioni d'architettura indiana," in *Vita d'Arte,* April 1914, pp. 92–93; and Leonardo Borgese, "Milano 1870–1920: Architettura, edilizia, urbanistica," *La Famiglia Artistica milanese nel centenario,* Milan, 1972, p. 34.

94 Pier Giorgio Gerosa correctly points out that Otto Wag-

ner reserved the last of the three-year architectural course that he gave at Vienna for fantasy buildings beyond utility or contingency. *Mario Chiattone: Un itinerario architettonico fra Milano e Lugano,* Milan, 1985, p. 37.

95 See Ragghianti's unsigned article "Sant'Elia," in *seleArte,* November–December 1955, p. 47. See also A. Giusti Baculo, "Gli studi architettonici di Emil Hoppe," *L'Architettura,* December 1969, pp. 552–556; and Boyd Whyte, *Three Architects,* p. 32.

96 "Hoppe in particular was more concerned with mood than with topographical exactitude." Boyd Whyte, *Three Architects,* p. 31.

97 Baculo, "Gli studi architettonici di Emil Hoppe," p. 554.

98 Umbro Apollonio, *Antonio Sant'Elia,* Milan, 1958, p. 15.

99 Mendelsohn's drawings are slightly later than Sant'Elia's (i.e., 1914), but it is unlikely that he had a chance to see any of Sant'Elia's works until after World War I. See Pehnt, *Expressionist Architecture,* p. 215 n. 9.

100 Reyner Banham, *Theory and Design in the First Machine Age,* 2d ed. New York, 1967, p. 168.

101 A. Sartoris, *L'architetto Antonio Sant'Elia,* Milan, 1930, p. 20.

102 Karel Teige, "Il futurismo e l'arte italiana moderna," 1925, rpt. in *Il Verri,* October 1970, p. 38.

103 Ragghianti, "Sant'Elia," p. 46.

104 For Appia's influence on Heinrich Tessenow, see Adolphe Appia, *Oeuvres complètes,* ed. Marie L. Bablet-Hahn, vol. 3, Lausanne, 1983, p. 99.

105 In the case of Gordon Craig, there is at least a connection with the futurists, since he lived in Florence, where Carrà had met him. See Carrà, *Tutti gli scritti,* p. 676.

106 Banham, *Theory and Design,* pp. 130–131.

107 See his letter to Herwarth Walden, dated May 8, 1912, rpt. in Boccioni, *Gli scritti editi e inediti,* Milan, 1971, p. 354.

108 On the importance of electricity for the futurists, see Pär Bergman, *"Modernolatria" et "Simultaneità": Recherches sur deux tendances dans l'avant-garde littéraire en Italie et en France à la veille de la première guerre mondiale,* Uppsala, 1962, pp. 132–134.

109 Many of Milan's famous architects, including Gaetano Moretti, had designed power plants, but unlike Sant'Elia's, theirs were always historicist.

110 Caramel and Longatti, *Antonio Sant'Elia,* 1962, p. 30.

111 Baculo, "Gli studi architettonici di Emil Hoppe," p. 554.

112 Argan, "Il pensiero critico di Antonio Sant'Elia," p. 496.

113 Baculo, "Gli studi architettonici di Emil Hoppe," p. 554.

114 Renato De Fusco was the first to point this out in his admirable book on the aesthetic foundations of architectural theory in the twentieth century: *L'idea di architettura,* Milan, 1964.

115 "Looking more closely at the issue, Einfühlung also transformed itself into formalism inasmuch as it was a theory of sensory emotion leading to the representation of objects. Hence the *optisches Formgefühl,* the *Raumästhetik,* etc. *Sichtbarkeit,* on the other hand, rejected emotional content, and neither excluded nor neglected the emotions triggered by the forms . . . thus confirming the hedonist underpinnings of their aesthetic nature." Guido Morpurgo-Tagliabue, *L'esthétique contemporaine,* Milan, 1960, p. 46.

116 De Fusco, *L'idea di architettura,* p. 55.

117 Ibid., p. 47.

118 Lipps, quoted in De Fusco, *L'idea di architettura,* p. 45.

119 Wölfflin, *Prolegomena zu einer Psychologie der Architektur,* rpt. in *Kleine Schriften,* Basel, 1946. For a specifically architectural approach to Wölfflin's ideas on Einfühlung, see the illuminating pages in Francesco Dal Co, *Figures of Architecture and Thought: German Architecture Culture, 1880–1920,* New York, 1990, pp. 132ff. *Empathy, Form, and Space: Problems in German Aesthetics, 1873–1893,* edited by Harry Francis Mallgrave and Eleftherios Ikonomov, Santa Monica, 1994, came out while I was reading galleys.

120 Wilhelm Worringer, *Abstraction and Empathy,* New York, 1953.

121 De Fusco, *L'idea di architettura,* p. 8.

122 Argan, *Walter Gropius e la Bauhaus,* Turin, 1951; Morpurgo-Tagliabue, *L'esthétique contemporaine;* Carlo, Ragghianti, *Mondrian e l'arte del XX secolo,* Milan, 1962; De Fusco, *L'idea di architettura;* Adriana Giusti Baculo, *Otto Wagner,* Naples, 1970.

123 Van de Velde, "La linea è una forza," *Casabella,* March 1960, p. 37. Although published in Brussels in 1923, this essay was going back to van de Velde's book *Kunstgewerbliche Laienpredigten,* Leipzig, 1902.

124 Henry van de Velde, "La via sacra," *Casabella,* March 1960, p. 29. Again, this essay was published in 1933 but was a summation of his long-standing interest in the subject.

125 Traces of Lipps's Raumästhetik can be found even in F. L. Wright. See De Fusco, *L'idea di architettura,* p. 62. See also Morpurgo-Tagliabue, *L'esthétique contemporaine,* p. 357.

126 Mendelsohn, for example, had always acknowledged his debt to van de Velde, particularly to the latter's idea that "the line is a force." See his *Three Lectures on Architecture,* Berkeley, 1944, p. 7.

127 Baculo, *Otto Wagner,* pp. 58, 59 (emphasis in the original).

128 Wagner, *Modern Architecture,* p. 109.

129 "The loss of touch as a conceptual component of vision meant the unloosening of the eye from the network of referentiality incarnated in tactility and its subjective relation to perceived space." Jonathan Crary, *Techniques of the Observer,* Cambridge, Mass., 1991, p. 19.

130 For an excellent article addressing this issue, see Sanford Kwinter, "La Città Nuova: Modernity and Continuity," *Zone,* vols. 1/2, 1986, pp. 81–121.

131 Croce analyzed Lipps's aesthetics in his *Aesthetic,* London, 1909, pp. 347–348. For Sichtbarkeit, see Croce's "La teoria dell'arte come pura visibilità," 1913, rpt. in *Nuovi saggi di estetica,* Bari, 1920, pp. 247–254.

132 For the impact of Einfühlung on Boccioni, see Maurizio Calvesi and Ester Coen, *Boccioni,* Milan, 1983, pp. 72–79. See also Ragghianti, "Il significato dell'opera di Konrad Fiedler," in K. Fiedler, *L'attività artistica,* Venice, 1963, p. 19.

133 Both letters are now in Boccioni, *Gli scritti editi e inediti,* pp. 343–344, 346–347. Barbantini was one of Italy's most farsighted connoisseurs of modern art. Under his direction, Ca' Pesaro became the most advanced artistic institution in Italy.

134 *Les peintres futuristes italiens,* Paris, Galerie Bernheim Jeune, February 1912. Although the text appeared as a joint effort of all the futurist artists, it was chiefly the work of Boccioni. The English version is taken from the show's presentation in England: *Exhibition of the Works by the Italian Futurist Painters,* London, Sackville Gallery, March 1912, pp. 16–17.

135 Ibid., pp. 14–15.

136 Ibid., pp. 15–16.

137 Boccioni, *Pittura scultura futuriste (dinamismo plastico),* Florence, 1977, p. 137.

138 *Kunstgewerbliche Laienpredigten,* Leipzig, 1902. For van de Velde's influence on Boccioni, see Franco Camporesi, "L'idea di 'architettura' nella poetica di Umberto Boccioni," *Atti e memorie dell'Accademia Clementina di Bologna,* vol. 14, 1981, pp. 100–101.

139 Annie-Paul Quinsac, *La peinture divisionniste italienne,* Paris, 1972, p. 66.

140 Calvesi and Coen, *Boccioni,* p. 47. See also Giovanni Lista, "Boccioni et le futurisme," in Boccioni, *Dynamisme plastique (peinture et sculpture futuristes),* Lausanne, 1975, p. 13.

141 Caramel and Longatti, *Antonio Sant'Elia,* 1962, p. 85.

142 Schmidt-Thomsen, *Floreale,* pp. 130–131.

143 The project came to nought. Construction of the winning project was put off by the outbreak of the war, after which the Piazza delle Erbe was declared untouchable. G. L. Mellini and O. Tognetti, "1866–1961, Griglia per una storia della cultura architettonica a Verona: 1914, Concorso internazionale per la sede della Cassa di Risparmio di Verona," *Architetti Verona,* October 1961, pp. 4–6, 10–12.

144 Even favorable critics considered this impossible to build unless one made use of iron, i.e., a method abhorred by a Ruskinian like Boito because lacking in "sincerità."

145 Lorenzo Priuli-Bon, quoted in "L'esito del Concorso della Cassa di Risparmio per la sua sede in Piazza delle Erbe," *Verona Fedele,* April 17, 1914. The perspective of the "magnificent corner entrance" was by Dudreville.

146 *Concorso per la Cassa di Risparmio di Verona,* Milan, 1914, n.p.

147 Ibid., n.p. The same idea appears in Sant'Elia's almost contemporary "Messaggio," where he calls for "salutary demolitions."

148 Quoted in L. Priuli-Bon, "Il secondo concorso per i progetti della nuova Sede della Cassa di Risparmio," *Verona Fedele,* December 23, 1914.

149 Armando Lovato, "Ancora la questione di Piazza Erbe di Verona," *Il Messaggero* (Rome), December 27, 1914, p. 3.

150 See Ragghianti, "Sant'Elia: Il Bibbiena del duemila," p. 9. Exceptions to the rule are Eleonora Bairati and Daniele Riva, who point out the influence of these designs on Giovanni Muzio, in *Il Liberty in Italia,* Bari, 1985, p. 67.

151 "L'esito del concorso per la sistemazione della Piazza Erbe di Verona," *Pagine d'Arte,* January 15, 1915, p. 10. See also Arata's "La Piazza delle Erbe di Verona e la sua sistemazione," *Emporium,* March 1915, pp. 192–199.

152 Zevi, *Cronache di Architettura,* vol. 2, no. 82, Bari, 1970–1973, n.p.

153 Originally built in the cemetery of San Gregorio at Monza, the tomb was later transferred, with minor modifications, to the Cimitero Monumentale in the same city. The bronze mask was executed by Caprotti's son, who was both a sculptor and a painter.

154 Longatti, *Disegni di Sant'Elia,* Lecco, 1984, p. 59.

155 In particular, the tomb by Hans Bolek in *Der Architekt,* 1909, p. 23.

156 Luigi Russolo speaks of the prodigious amount of work Sant'Elia put into his projects and of the truly amazing speed with which he drew. See "Un ricordo di Luigi Russolo," *La Martinella di Milano,* October 1958, p. 536.

1 Tancredi Motta claims that Sant'Elia took part in this competition while working for Cantoni and under the aegis of the latter's studio. See Schmidt-Thomsen, *Floreale*, p. 191.

2 "Il concorso per la chiesa parocchiale," *Pagine d'Arte*, June 15, 1915, pp. 95–96. For Salsomaggiore, see also *Gli avvenimenti*, January 16–23, 1916, and "La nuova cattedrale di Salsomaggiore," in *Bianco Rosso e Verde*, December 15, 1915, n.p.

3 Longatti, *Disegni di Sant'Elia*, p. 14.

4 Poli, "I disegni di Sant'Elia," p. 30.

5 As his contemporaries had already noted: see Marco Ramperti, "L'architetto Sant'Elia," *La Stampa*, April 30, 1930.

6 Schmidt-Thomsen, *Floreale*, p. 132. See also "Concorso per villini al Lido," in *Pagine d'Arte*, January 15, 1914.

7 Banham, "Footnotes to Sant'Elia," *Architectural Review*, June 1956, p. 344.

8 Ragghianti, "Sant'Elia: Il Bibbiena del duemila," p. 3.

9 Vincent Scully, foreword to *Ausgeführte Bauten und Entwürfe von Frank Lloyd Wright*, Tübingen, 1986, p. 31.

10 *Ausgeführte Bauten und Entwürfe*, Berlin, 1910. Both Wright's Unitarian Temple and the Coonley house were published in Italy in Sant'Elia's day: see *Annuario di Architettura*, Milan, 1914.

11 For Wright's early influence in Europe, see H. Russell Hitchcock, "Wright's Influence Abroad," *Parnassus*, December 1940, pp. 11–15. See also N. Pevsner, "Frank Lloyd Wright's Peaceful Penetration in Europe," *Architects' Journal*, May 4, 1939, pp. 731–734.

12 Edoardo Baroncini and Marcello Piacentini also took part. For a full list of participants, see Arata, "La prima mostra di architettura," pp. 66–72.

13 Ibid., p. 67.

14 "Arata, i morti pela patria: Antonio Sant'Elia," *Pagine d'Arte*, November 15, 1916, p. 140.

15 This information is borrowed from Schmidt-Thomsen, who was the last to see a copy of this catalogue, which no longer exists. See "Sant'Elia architetto oder die Achillesferse des Futurismus," *Daidalos*, no. 2, 1981, pp. 37, 38.

16 Carrà, *Tutti gli scritti*, p. 656. See also Carrà's "L'esposizione futurista alla Galleria Pesaro," *L'Ambrosiano* (Milan), October 22, 1930, p. 3.

17 Marinetti, *La grande Milano tradizionale e futurista*, Milan, 1969, p. 98. U. Nebbia, "Trent'anni dopo," *L'Esame*, July–December 1942, p. 29.

18 On the Famiglia Artistica, see P. Chiesa, "La Famiglia Artistica e l'arte lombarda dell'ultimo cinquantennio," *Emporium*, January 1914, pp. 3–13; *La Famiglia Artistica milanese nel centenario*; Carrà, *Tutti gli scritti*, pp. 649–652.

19 Evangelisti, "Dal simbolismo alla non-figurazione," p. 24.

20 An earlier version of this manifesto, undated, was signed by Sant'Elia's friends Romolo Romani and Aroldo Bonzagni, but in the definitive version they were replaced by Balla and Severini.

21 As Guido Ballo remarks, "By 1915, the dynamism and the hue and cry of the previous years had already begun to die down. The group that was founded in Milan and that exhibits at the Nuove Tendenze show in 1914 is indicative of this trend." *Boccioni e il suo tempo*, Milan, 1973, p. 27.

22 The name was in all probability taken from Nouvelles Tendances, an art association founded by Auguste Rodin and Paul Adam in Paris a few years earlier, which had counted Pelizza da Volpedo among its members. Pelizza, of course, was already a legend in Milan, after his tragic suicide in 1907.

23 Enrico Crispolti, *Il mito della macchina e altri temi del futurismo*, Trapani, 1969, p. 77.

24 Thea, "Nuove Tendenze a Milano," *Nuove Tendenze*, p. 5.

25 Leonardo Dudreville, "Ai margini di una polemica: Antonio Sant'Elia," *Corriere della Provincia*, August 12, 1957, p. 3. See also Thea, "Nuove Tendenze a Milano," p. 8.

26 In his somewhat romanticized memoirs, written thirty years later, Dudreville says that he asked to meet Sant'Elia when putting the group together: see "Inizi," in *Nuove Tendenze: Milano e l'altro futurismo. Documenti*, Milan, 1980, pp. 130–138 (typescript distributed by the Padiglione d'Arte Contemporanea di Milano; hereafter cited as *Documenti*). Ugo Nebbia claimed it was founded during the winter of 1913–1914: "I futuristi e il manifesto di Sant'Elia," *L'Espresso* (Rome), December 9, 1956.

27 "Prima esposizione del gruppo 'Nuove Tendenze,'" in *Documenti*, pp. 3–4.

28 The other artists were represented as follows: Bisi-Fabbri (2 works), Chiattone (3), Dudreville (10), Erba (9), Fidora (4), Funi (9), Nizzoli (6), Possamai (4). It is noteworthy that two works in the exhibition were inspired by Sant'Elia: Dudreville's *Ritmi emanati da Antonio Sant'Elia* and Possamai's *Sant'Elia* (lost).

29 Nebbia, "We do not want to be incomprehensible in the extreme, nor do we wish to profane the aesthetic sense

of the majority out of sheer love of the new." *Prima esposizione d'arte del gruppo Nuove Tendenze alla Famiglia Artistica di Milano,* Milan, 1914, p. 5.

30 Margherita Sarfatti, "I pittori delle 'Nuove Tendenze' alla Famiglia Artistica di Milano," *L'Avanti!* June 17, 1914. Sarfatti was at the time a militant socialist, and *L'Avanti!* was the official organ of the Socialist Party. A mistress of Mussolini for many years, she was also the author of the most famous biography of the Duce, the brassy, best-selling *Dux,* Milan, 1926.

31 Giuseppe Carfagna, "Nuove Tendenze d'arte alla Famiglia Artistica milanese," *Luce del Pensiero,* June 30, 1914.

32 Prampolini, "Il gruppo 'Nuove Tendenze' plagiario del futurismo," p. 217.

33 Thea, "Nuove Tendenze a Milano," p. 7.

34 Ibid., p. 11. See also *Archivi,* pp. 102–103.

35 He was, in fact, supposed to have signed the *Manifesto of Futurist Painting* of February 11, 1910. See the letter written by Boccioni to Severini (August 1910), in *Archivi,* vol. 1, p. 231. See also Dudreville's version in his memoirs, in *Documenti,* pp. 126–129. Dudreville finally joined the futurist movement in 1919.

36 Raffaele Giolli, "La mostra delle Nuove Tendenze," *Pagine d'Arte,* May 15, 1914, p. 126. See also Marco Rosci, "Dudreville fra futurismo ed espressionismo," *Arte Illustrata,* January–February 1967, pp. 38–45; and *Dudreville: Opere su carta, 1905–1967,* Milan, 1987.

37 Nebbia, "La prima mostra delle 'Nuove Tendenze' a Milano," *Vita d'Arte,* May 1914, p. 118.

38 Rosci, "Dudreville fra futurismo ed espressionismo," p. 41.

39 On Erba, see *Carlo Erba: Una memoria nel futurismo, 1884–1917,* Rome, 1981.

40 Crispolti, "Futuristi di destra," *Bolaffiarte,* April–May 1979, p. 29.

41 See *Documenti,* pp. 246, 248, for Boccioni's letters to Bisi-Fabbri and her husband concerning this exhibition.

42 Germano Celant, *Marcello Nizzoli,* Milan, 1968, p. x.

43 Ironically, it was Possamai who made a name for himself in architecture. Encouraged by Sant'Elia, he studied architecture at Brera, after having finished his degree in fine arts. See Crispolti, "Futuristi di destra," p. 33.

44 Rosci, "Dudreville fra futurismo ed espressionismo," p. 40. Written in Paris in 1913, Severini's manifesto was not published until the late 1950s, but Dudreville had been in correspondence with him for several years.

45 Dudreville, in *Prima esposizione d'arte,* pp. 6–7.

46 Funi, in *Prima esposizione d'arte,* p. 23.

47 Prampolini, "Il gruppo 'Nuove Tendenze' plagiario del futurismo," p. 217.

48 See Crispolti, "Zang Tumb Tuum: I futuristi vanno alla guerra," *Bolaffiarte,* May 1978, pp. 9–15.

49 Guido Ballo, *Boccioni,* p. 374. See also Crispolti, *Il mito della macchina,* p. 109.

50 Crispolti, "Futuristi di destra," p. 29.

51 "The two extremes of its research are: on the one hand the symbolist and secessionist tradition of Central Europe in its latest developments; on the other hand, it partakes of the futurist dynamism of interpenetration." Crispolti, *Il mito della macchina,* p. 75.

52 For Chiattone, see Gerosa, *Mario Chiattone.*

53 See *Collezione familia Gabriele Chiattone,* Lugano, 1968.

54 *Mostra di pittura e scultura rifiutata alla esposizione nazionale di Brera,* Milan, 1912.

55 Veronesi, *L'opera di Mario Chiattone,* p. 10.

56 Many of their projects, kept by Chiattone, were destroyed during World War II, when his house was bombarded in August 1943.

57 Cresti, "Contributo per una revisione critica dell'opera di Mario Chiattone," *Necropoli,* September–December 1970, p. 52.

58 C. Lodovici, "Le mostre delle Nuove Tendenze a Milano," *Corriere del Ticino,* May 26, 1914; J. J. P. Oud, "Architectonische beschouwing bij bijlage III," *De Stijl,* no. 3, January 1920, pp. 25–27; Veronesi, "Disegni di Mario Chiattone, 1914–1917," *Comunità,* March–April 1962, p. 54.

59 Pehnt, *Expressionist Architecture,* p. 177.

60 Veronesi, "Tutto Sant'Elia a Como," *Comunità,* October 1962, p. 78.

61 Ibid., p. 12. Pehnt, *Expressionist Architecture,* p. 178.

62 "The prospect of a considerable increase . . . of the motive power destined to replace part of the consumption of fossilized coal was in fact received as the tidings of liberation from a situation of secular inferiority and consecrated for the first time, at the level of public opinion, the hopes in the industrial future of the nation." Valerio Castronovo, "La fase espansiva in età giolittiana," in *Storia d'Italia dall'Unità a oggi,* p. 153.

63 Marinetti, Boccioni, Carrà, Russolo, "Contro Venezia passatista," April 27, 1910, in *Archivi,* p. 20.

64 This plant was of the old historicist kind and was situated in Piazza Trento in Milan. See V. Fontana, *Il nuovo paesaggio,* p. 126.

65 Visits to these sites were in fact de rigueur in architectural congresses held in Milan.

66 See L. Caramel and L. Patetta, eds., *L'idea del lago: Un*

paesaggio ridefinito, 1861–1914, Como, 1984, p. 10; V. Fontana, *Il nuovo paesaggio,* pp. 137–142.

67 Poli, "I disegni di Sant'Elia," p. 32.

68 Donatella Poli, "Proposta per un catalogo critico dei disegni di Antonio Sant'Elia," Tesi di Laurea, University of Pavia, 1969–1970, p. 115. I wish to thank Professor Poli for having put her thesis at my disposal.

69 The plants should undoubtedly be read as structures of concrete, though Italy's first dam in prestressed concrete (in Tirso, Sardinia) was not completed until 1923. V. Fontana, *Il nuovo paesaggio,* p. 136.

70 Bairati and Riva, *Il Liberty in Italia,* p. 20.

71 As already noted by Joseph Masheck, "The Panama Canal and Some Other Works of Art," *Artforum,* May 1971, p. 39.

72 Nicoletti, *L'architettura Liberty,* p. 382.

73 Caramel and Longatti, *Antonio Sant'Elia,* 1962, p. 60.

74 Marinetti, *Le futurisme,* 1912, quoted in Banham, "Futurism and Modern Architecture," *Journal of the Royal Institute of British Architects,* February 1957, p. 133.

75 See, e.g., "Buildings like Mountains," by Hugh Ferriss, in *The Metropolis of Tomorrow,* New York, 1929, frontispiece.

76 Longatti, "Il caso Sant'Elia," *Nuove Tendenze,* p. 15.

77 Ibid., p. 33.

78 The term "casa a gradinata" appeared for the first time in the *Manifesto of Futurist Architecture.*

79 Nicoletti, *L'architettura Liberty,* p. 379. Schmidt-Thomsen points out that Sant'Elia may have seen the other well-known gallerie in Florence and Naples: *Floreale,* p. 143.

80 *Traité de l'association domestique-agricole,* Paris, 1822, quoted in E. Poisson, *Fourier,* Paris, 1932, pp. 141–142.

81 Nicoletti, *L'architettura Liberty,* p. 380.

82 Banham, *Theory and Design,* p. 133. Sant'Elia was fascinated by elevators: they are mentioned in each of the six captions to the drawings published in the manifesto.

83 Caramel and Patetta, *L'idea del lago,* p. 11.

84 Quoted in S. Fauchereau, "Aviation," in *Futurism and Futurisms,* ed. Pontus Hulten, Milan, 1986, p. 423.

85 For an excellent description of Milan's industrial architecture in Sant'Elia's day, see Antonello Negri, "Milano, 1881–1914: La città che sale," in *Boccioni a Milano,* pp. 77–86.

86 In Milan the most famous example was the Stigler tower built in 1894 by the elevator firm of the same name and later incorporated into the Pro Sempione show of 1906, which Sant'Elia undoubtedly saw.

87 Banham, *Theory and Design,* p. 133.

88 Cf. Boccioni's celebrated passage: "The yellow, red, and green advertisements, the large letters in black, white, and blue, the lurid and grotesque sign-boards of the shops, the bazaars, the 'SALES,' the resplendent English bathrooms, the black dances to the brutal rhythm of the gypsies amid lights and beautiful prostitutes, this is what inspires and fascinates us." *Pittura scultura futuriste (dinamismo plastico),* p. 15.

89 *Iron* is often wrongly rendered as *steel* in some translations of his *Manifesto of Futurist Architecture.* See, e.g., *Futurist Manifestos,* ed. Umbro Apollonio, London, 1973, pp. 160–172.

90 See Otto Wagner's enthusiastic remarks about iron in *Modern Architecture,* p. 98.

91 "Manifesto dei pittori futuristi," February 11, 1910; quoted in Pehnt, *Expressionist Architecture,* p. 173.

92 "Manifesto of Futurist Architecture," quoted in Pehnt, *Expressionist Architecture,* p. 176; rpt. in *Archivi,* p. 85.

93 See the strictures of Robert van't Hoff, "Aanteekeningen bij bijlage XX," *De Stijl,* August 1919, p. 115. See also Nicoletti, *L'architettura Liberty,* p. 379, and Schmidt-Thomsen, *Floreale,* p. 145.

94 Hanno Walter Kruft, *Geschichte der Architekturtheorie von der Antike bis zur Gegenwart,* Munich, 1985, p. 468.

95 Schmidt-Thomsen, *Floreale,* p. 160. For the relationship between Sauvage and Sant'Elia, see François Loyer and Hélène Guéné, *Henri Sauvage: Les immeubles à gradins,* Brussels, 1987. R. Jullian, "Sauvage et Sant'Elia: Le problème des maisons à gradins," *Bulletin de la Société de l'Histoire de l'Art Français,* Paris, 1978, pp. 291–298. Richard Etlin, *Modernism in Italian Architecture, 1890–1940,* Cambridge, Mass., 1991, pp. 82–86.

96 F. Honoré, "La maison à gradins," *L'Illustration,* March 21, 1914; *La Construction Moderne,* September 20–27, 1914, pp. 577–578.

97 *Henri Sauvage, 1873–1932,* Brussels, 1976, p. 59.

98 Schmidt-Thomsen, *Floreale,* p. 160.

99 Ibid., p. 161.

100 Etlin correctly points out that Dudreville confused the French periodical with the Milanese *L'Illustrazione Italiana.* See *Modernism in Italian Architecture,* p. 83.

101 Michele and Maria Costanzo, "Boccioni e Sant'Elia," in *Rassegna dell'istituto di architettura e urbanistica,* April–August 1978, p. 33.

102 Nicoletti, *L'architettura Liberty,* p. 380.

103 The stratification of urban soil into different planes of reference for pedestrians and vehicles was introduced at the beginning of the century. Gerosa, *Mario Chiattone,* p. 28.

104 Marinetti, *Archivi*, p. 17. On Sant'Elia's predilection for bridges, see Schmidt-Thomsen, *Floreale*, p. 171.

105 "Contro Venezia passatista," in *Archivi*, p. 20.

106 S. Giedion, *Space, Time and Architecture*, Cambridge, Mass., 1967, p. 243. See also Günther Feuerstein, "Traffic Storeys: Otto Wagner and Antonio Sant'Elia," *Daidalos*, December 1991, pp. 62–75.

107 Boyd Whyte, *Three Architects*, p. 15.

108 Longatti is quite right in linking them to the Ponte del Risorgimento inaugurated in Rome in 1911 (*Disegni di Sant'Elia*, p. 14). Designed by the Porcheddu firm, with the collaboration of the Hennebique studio, it was a thin waferlike strip of exposed concrete thrown across the Tiber. Its startling appearance elicited such distrust that it had to be sheathed in stone.

109 For Wagner's treatment of bridges in the modern city, see his *Modern Architecture*, pp. 111–113.

110 Ivo Tagliaventi, "Sant'Elia e l'architettura futurista," *Ingegneri-Architetti-Costruttori*, November 1954, p. 259. It was Sommaruga's design rather than the hotel as actually built that shows great affinity with Sant'Elia's project.

111 Nicoletti, *L'architettura Liberty*, p. 368. See also Caramel and Longatti, *Antonio Sant'Elia*, 1962, p. 29.

112 Recent scholarship has called attention to the profound ambiguity of the futurists with regard to technology. See Roberto Tessari, *Il mito della macchina: Letteratura e industria nel primo Novecento italiano*, Milan, 1973, pp. 210–212; G. Celli, "In margine al futurismo: Storia di una ambivalenza," *Il Verri*, nos. 33–34, 1970, pp. 118–124; G. Lista, *Giacomo Balla*, Lausanne, 1984, p. 23.

113 See M. Calvesi, *Le due avanguardie*, Bari, 1971, p. 72.

114 For a similar tendency in Boccioni, see the excellent article by Noëmi Blumenkranz-Onimus, "La ville des futuristes," *Revue d'Esthétique*, nos. 3–4, 1977, pp. 96–97.

115 In a manifesto written in the trenches shortly before Sant'Elia's death, Mario Carli gives vent to the futurists' disdain of the snail-like pace of the pedestrian: "Whoever wrote 'pedestrian crossing' for the first time in one of these metropolitan boulevards perpetrated the first great crime of the century since this encouraged that spirit of cautious and bourgeois sheepishness that teaches young people to look carefully around themselves before crossing a street." "Vulcanizziamo le grandi città," *L'Italia Futurista*, August 25, 1916, p. 2.

116 Godoli, *Il futurismo*, p. 126.

117 In the Città Nuova, streets and buildings have lost their separate identities. They have become what Sergio Los calls urban communications centers: "In the past the road was only a link between distinct urban blocks, in the present the town is only an interchange at the points in which the road network has its nodes." *La città macchina*, Vicenza, 1974, p. 70.

118 Sant'Elia, *Prima esposizione d'arte*, p. 16.

119 Ragghianti, "Sant'Elia: Il Bibbiena del duemila," p. 17.

120 S. Kwinter, "La Città Nuova," p. 100.

121 Marinetti, "Noi rineghiamo i nostri maestri simbolisti ultimi amanti della luna," 1915, rpt. in *Teoria e invenzione futurista*, ed. Luciano De Maria, Milan, 1968, p. 260.

122 Giedion, *Space, Time and Architecture*, p. 321.

123 Russolo, *L'arte dei rumori*, March 11, 1913, rpt. in L. De Maria, ed., *Per conoscere Marinetti e il futurismo*, Milan, 1973, p. 94. See also Carrà's manifesto, "La pittura dei suoni, rumori e odori," August 11, 1913, *Archivi*, pp. 73–76. Blumenkranz-Onimus, "La ville des futuristes," pp. 78, 82.

124 Tentori, "Le origini Liberty di Antonio Sant'Elia," p. 208. For a good analysis of Sant'Elia's syntax, see Portoghesi, *L'angelo della storia*, pp. 221–230; and Kwinter, "La Città Nuova."

125 Cresti, *Appunti storici e critici*, p. 118.

126 Portoghesi, *L'angelo della storia*, p. 229.

127 See Germano Celant, "Speed," p. 578, and Gerald Silk, "Automobile," p. 421, both in *Futurism and Futurisms*.

128 Sant'Elia writes "areoplani" rather than "aeroplani."

129 In a text that has only recently come to light, Boccioni complains that "aeroplanes . . . are too logical with their dragon-fly wings! Oh for hippogriphs—those dear horses that spring upward with the force of their legs." "Il plastico magico," *Corriere della Sera*, January 14, 1973, p. 12.

130 On the role of airplanes and aviation in futurism, see Serge Fauchereau, "Aviation," in *Futurism and Futurisms*, p. 423.

131 Marinetti, "Fondazione e manifesto del futurismo," February 11, 1909, in *Archivi*, p. 18.

132 Boccioni, *Pittura scultura futuriste*, p. 11.

133 Ibid., p. 13, ellipsis in original.

134 Marinetti, "La declamazione dinamica e sinottica," in *Teoria e invenzione futurista*, pp. 106–107. This text was published in March 11, 1916, but its effects can be seen long before.

135 Marinetti, "La guerra elettrica" (1915), in *Teoria e invenzione futurista*, p. 274.

136 Sartoris, *Encyclopédie*, p. 37.

137 For Leonardo's architectural drawings, see Luigi Firpo, *Leonardo: Architetto e urbanista*, Turin, 1963, pp. 68–78.

See also the exhibition catalogue *Leonardo da Vinci, Engineer and Architect,* Montreal, 1987, pp. 298–299.

138 Luca Beltrami, distinguished architect and professor at Brera, was publishing studies on Leonardo's architecture during those very years.

139 George R. Collins, introduction to *Visionary Drawings of Architecture and Planning, Twentieth Century through the 1960s,* Cambridge, Mass., 1979, n.p.

140 Ibid. This idea was given lasting expression after Sant'Elia's death by Lamb's friend Harvey Wiley Corbett, who entrusted the architectural rendering to Hugh Ferriss.

141 Vincent Scully, *American Architecture and Urbanism,* New York, 1969, p. 148.

142 "La più grande stazione del mondo inaugurata a New York," *L'Illustrazione Italiana* (Milan), February 23, 1913. See Ulrich Conrads and Hans Sperlich, *The Architecture of Fantasy,* New York, 1962, p. 159.

143 "La circolazione futura e i grattanuvole a New York," *L'Illustrazione Italiana,* August 31, 1913. This drawing was first published by Schmidt-Thomsen, *Floreale,* p. 168. Both Grand Central Station and the idealized view of New York had originally been published in *Scientific American* on December 7, 1912, and July 26, 1913, respectively.

144 There is no doubt that Sant'Elia knew the two drawings. In conversation with Schmidt-Thomsen, Pellini remembered a visionary illustration of the city of New York, which he claimed Sant'Elia had seen, adding that the reproduction occupied almost an entire page. Schmidt-Thomsen, *Floreale,* p. 233 n. 206.

145 Cf. Banham: "The intellectual ins and outs of provincial coteries are always biographically fascinating, but the specifically Milanese motivations of futurism, and their political entanglements are as irrelevant to the main story of modern art as the rent-collector farces of Bateau-Lavoir cubism." "Futurism for Keeps," *Arts,* December 1960, p. 33.

146 See E. Belloni, "Il Corso d'Italia a Milano," *Le Case Popolari e le Città-Giardino,* 1909–1910, pp. 110–118. On the Corso d'Italia, see also Grandi and Pracchi, *Milano: Guida all'architettura moderna,* p. 97.

147 On Soria y Mata, see George R. Collins and Carlos Flores, eds., *Arturo Soria y Mata y la ciudad lineal,* Madrid, 1976.

148 Belloni, "Il Corso d'Italia," p. 115.

149 Bossaglia and Cozzi, *I Coppedè,* p. 24.

150 Stroppa (1880–1964) had made his name more as an architectural illustrator than as an architect. He had studied at Brera somewhat irregularly, not unlike Sant'Elia, who had had ample occasion to meet him personally. Both men had taken part in the competition for the Central Station of Milan in 1912. For an illustration of his work, see *Boccioni a Milano,* p. 181; see also *Mostra del Liberty italiano,* pp. 260–261.

151 See P. Nurra, "Un nuovo grande quartiere a Milano nella zona compresa tra Milano e Sesto San Giovanni," *Le Case Popolari e le Città-Giardino,* 1909–1910, p. 163. See also L. V. Bertarelli, "Città che nasce," *Touring Club Italiano,* August 1908, pp. 345–352.

152 Selvafolta, "La città dei servizi," *Boccioni a Milano,* p. 84.

153 Grandi and Pracchi, *Milano: Guida all'architettura moderna,* p. 100.

154 See Selvafolta, *Boccioni a Milano,* p. 85.

155 Quoted in Paul Goldberger, *The Skyscraper,* New York, 1982, pp. 58–59.

156 The futurist architect Virgilio Marchi saw this very well: "The American skyscraper has been Europeanized by our Baroque trappings: those of Sant'Elia . . . function exclusively as planes, scaffoldings, silhouettes, as light and shade." *Noi,* no. 2, May 1923, p. 3 (emphasis in the original).

157 Crispolti, *Ricostruzione futurista dell'universo,* Turin, 1980, p. 67.

158 Quoted in E. Coen, "City," in *Futurism and Futurisms,* p. 452.

159 On Sant'Elia's "Americanismo," see Sarfatti, "Sant'Elia e le sue opere," *Gli Avvenimenti,* October 29–November 15, 1916, p. 14.

160 Crispolti, *Ricostruzione,* p. 65.

161 "Il primo 'skyscraper' di Milano," *Corriere della Sera* (Milan), October 28, 1910, p. 5.

162 L. Broggi, "In difesa dei 'grattanuvole,'" *Corriere della Sera* (Milan), November 6, 1910, p. 6.

163 Luca Beltrami, "La questione dei 'grattacielo,'" *Corriere della Sera,* November 7, 1910, p. 5.

164 The Commissione Edilizia, of which Manfredini had formerly been a member, was responsible for the decision.

165 Armando Foresta, "Il tentativo di un 'Americanata' a Milano," *La Casa,* November 16, 1910, p. 427.

166 Derogatory comments about American architecture and urbanism were common in Europe at the time. See George Collins and Christiane Collins, *Camillo Sitte: The Birth of Modern City Planning,* New York, 1986, p. 345.

167 Crispolti, *Attraverso l'architettura futurista,* Modena, 1984, p. 33.

168 De Finetti, *Milano*, p. 210.

169 "There are architects," wrote Adolf Loos in "The Principle of Cladding" (1898), "who work in a different way. Their imagination doesn't form spaces, but mass. Whatever the mass of wall leaves over, are the spaces." Quoted in Max Risselada, introduction to *Raumplan versus Plan Libre*, New York, 1988, p. 7.

170 Nicoletti, *L'architettura Liberty*, p. 372.

171 Godoli, *Il futurismo*, p. 124.

172 Kwinter, "La Città Nuova," p. 112.

173 F. T. Marinetti and Christopher Nevinson, "Manifesto futurista (contro l'arte inglese)," June 11, 1914, in *Teoria e invenzione futurista*, p. 95.

174 Godoli, *Il futurismo*, pp. 121–122.

175 De Fusco, "Un'avanguardia verosimile," *Controspazio*, April–May 1971, p. 62.

176 Cresti, *Appunti storici e critici*, pp. 116–117.

177 Sartoris, *Encyclopédie*, p. 116.

178 Ragghianti, "Sant'Elia: Il Bibbiena del duemila," p. 7.

179 For Morasso, see Virgilio Vercelloni, *Macchinolatria e modernolatria di Mario Morasso*, San Lazzaro di Savena, 1972; Roberto Tessari, *Il mito della macchina: Letteratura e industria nel primo Novecento italiano*, Milan, 1973. Ugo Piscopo, "Mario Morasso: Anticipazioni e divergenze," in *Questioni e aspetti del futurismo*, Naples, 1976, pp. 33–71; Carlo Gentile, "A proposito di F. T. Marinetti e Mario Morasso," *Atti e memorie dell'Accademia Clementina di Bologna*, Bologna, 1974, pp. 117–132. Etlin, *Modernism in Italian Architecture*, pp. 69–81.

180 Schmidt-Thomsen, *Floreale*, p. 233, n. 206.

181 Ragghianti, "Sant'Elia: Il Bibbiena del duemila," p. 14.

182 For the negative connotations attaching to the metropolis, see Massimo Cacciari, "Note sulla dialettica del negativo nell'epoca della metropoli," *Angelus Novus*, 21, 1971, pp. 1–54.

183 See Blumenkranz-Onimus, "La ville des futuristes."

184 Marinetti, "Fondazione e Manifesto del Futurismo," February 11, 1909, rpt. in *Archivi*, p. 17.

185 Unanimism was a turn-of-the century movement of artists and writers who celebrated the city, modern life, and the collective personality of the crowd. It found its clearest formulation in Jules Romains's *La vie unanime* (Paris, 1908), which had enormous impact on the Italian avant-garde. In Milan the most important exponent of unanimist art was the sculptor Medardo Rosso, to whom Boccioni was much indebted.

186 See Maria Costanzo and Michele Costanzo, "Boccioni e Sant'Elia," pp. 7–36; Crispolti, *Ricostruzione*, p. 75.

187 *Technical Manifesto of Futurist Sculpture*, 1912, rpt. in *Archivi*, p. 70 (emphasis in the original).

188 Ibid.

189 Marianne Martin, *Futurist Art and Theory, 1909–1915*, Oxford, 1968, p. 127.

190 Boccioni, "Architettura futurista: Manifesto," in *Altri inediti e apparati critici*, ed. Zeno Birolli, Milan, 1972, p. 40.

191 Zevi, *Storia dell'architettura moderna*, Turin, 1955, p. 226.

192 Ibid. See also Anton Giulio Bragaglia's differentiation of *movimentismo* and the futurist *dinamismo* in *Fotodinamismo futurista*, Rome, 1912.

193 Pier Giorgio Badaloni, "Il futurismo, Antonio Sant'Elia e la nuova dimensione umana," *Moebius*, 1970, p. 60.

CHAPTER 5: THE MANIFESTO OF FUTURIST ARCHITECTURE

1 Giovanni Bernasconi, who first republished the "Messagio" in 1956, designated it as such in order to distinguish it from the *Manifesto of Futurist Architecture*. "Il messaggio di Antonio Sant'Elia del 20 maggio 1914," *Revista Tecnica della Svizzera Italiana*, July 1956, pp. 145–152.

2 Banham, "Futurism and Modern Architecture," p. 130.

3 To date there is no faithful transcription of the original "Messaggio" in print. All quotations, therefore, refer to the translated version given in appendix 1.

4 Boccioni, "Fondamento plastico della scultura e pittura futuriste," *Lacerba*, March 15, 1913, rpt. in *Archivi*, p. 142.

5 Boccioni, *Altri inediti*, p. 37.

6 Wagner, *Modern Architecture*, p. 78.

7 *Archivi*, p. 17. Longatti had already noted this parallel in Caramel and Longatti, *Antonio Sant'Elia*, 1962, p. 53.

8 Calvesi, "Il futurista Sant'Elia," *La Casa*, no. 6, 1959, p. 124; and "Antonio Sant'Elia," *Edilizia Popolare*, November 1954, p. 83.

9 Significantly, Boccioni's famous painting *The City Rise*s was entitled *Labor* when first exhibited in 1911.

10 Marinetti, *Le futurisme*, Paris, 1911, p. 116; quoted in Blumenkranz-Onimus, "La ville des futuristes," p. 94.

11 Boccioni, see "Prefazione al catalogo della prima esposizione di scultura," La Boétie, Paris, June 1913, p. 3, rpt. in *Archivi*, p. 118: "I thought, therefore, that by taking apart this material ensemble into various materials . . . one might obtain a dynamic element."

12 Boccioni, *Archivi*, p. 72.

13 Boccioni, *Altri inediti*, p. 39. It is interesting that Boccioni comes closer to Wagner than Sant'Elia, with his

insistence on the need for time-saving materials. See Wagner, *Modern Architecture,* p. 97.

14 Papini, *Lacerba,* December 15, 1913, rpt. in *Archivi,* p. 183. Schmidt-Thomsen noted this parallel in *Floreale,* p. 174.

15 "It is well known that these manifestos, though signed by Carrà, Russolo, Balla, Severini, were conceived and drafted primarily by Boccioni (who signed his own name first)." Calvesi, *Le due avanguardie,* p. 55.

16 Boccioni, *Pittura scultura futuriste,* pp. 6–7.

17 Carrà, "La pittura dei suoni rumori e odori," originally published in *Lacerba,* September 1, 1913, rpt. in *Archivi,* p. 73. Calvesi had already noted this relationship in "Il futurista Sant'Elia," p. 126.

18 Carrà, *Archivi,* p. 74.

19 Calvesi, "Il futurista Sant'Elia," p. 132. For Carrà's criticism of the cubists' "static" conception of art, see his "Piani plastici come espansione sferica nello spazio," *Lacerba,* March 15, 1913, rpt. in *Archivi,* pp. 145–147.

20 Boccioni, "Prefazione al catalogo della prima esposizione di scultura," rpt. in *Archivi,* p. 118. For Boccioni's evolving concept of architecture, see Franco Camporesi, "L'idea di 'architettura' nella poetica di Umberto Boccioni," pp. 81–109.

21 Boccioni, "Prefazione," *Archivi,* p. 119. Once more, it was Calvesi who first published this parallel in "Il futurista Sant'Elia," p. 126.

22 Boccioni, *Altri inediti,* p. 39.

23 Boccioni, *Archivi,* p. 71. Calvesi, "Il futurista Sant'Elia," p. 125.

24 Valerie Jaudon and Joyce Kozloff, "Art Hysterical Notions of Progress and Culture," *Heresies,* Winter 1977–1978, p. 222.

25 Marinetti, "Distruzione della sintassi—Immaginazione senza fili—Parole in libertà," May 11, 1913, rpt. in *Teoria e invenzione futurista,* p. 66.

26 Marinetti, *Technical Manifesto of Futurist Literature,* May 11, 1912, rpt. in *Teoria e invenzione futurista,* p. 41 (emphasis in the original).

27 Boccioni, Carrà, Russolo, Balla, Severini, *Archivi,* p. 63. See Banham, "Futurism and Modern Architecture," p. 130.

28 Ugo Piscopo, "Significato e funzione del gruppo nel futurismo," in *Questioni e aspetti del futurismo,* p. 226.

29 Marinetti et al., *Teoria e invenzione futurista,* p. 44 (emphasis in the original).

30 Calvesi, "Il futurista Sant'Elia," p. 126.

31 Boccioni, Carrà, Russolo, Balla, Severini, *Archivi,* p. 65.

32 See the unsigned article by Persico in *La Casa Bella,* June 1930, rpt. in *Tutte le opere (1923–1935),* ed. G. Veronesi, vol. 2, Milan, 1964, p. 27. "The 'machine à habiter' of Le Corbusier, who creates the master plans of the new cities, is presented by Sant'Elia as the 'futurist house like a gigantic machine,' within the panorama of modern Europe."

33 Quoted in O. A. Graf, "Wagner and the Vienna School," in *The Anti-Rationalists,* p. 95.

34 Banham, "Futurism and Modern Architecture," p. 130.

35 Once more Otto Wagner comes to mind: "The starting point for all artistic production must be the needs, the skills, the means and the characteristics of 'our' age." From the "Inaugural Lectural at the Academy of Fine Arts," quoted in Pozzetto, *Die Schule Otto Wagners,* p. 144.

36 Argan, "Il pensiero critico di Antonio Sant'Elia," p. 498.

37 Ibid. Argan was quoting from Sant'Elia's manifesto because at the time of writing, the "Messaggio" had not yet come to light. In the manifesto this passage differs from the "Messaggio" only by the substitution of the word "futurist" for "real" (*vera*).

38 Tafuri, *Theories and History of Architecture,* New York, 1980, p. 33.

39 See Robert van't Hoff, "Aanteekeningen bij bijlage XX," and also Sartoris, *L'architetto Antonio Sant'Elia,* p. 24.

40 "Altogether it is remarkable," wrote Nikolaus Pevsner, "how often functionalist theory in the nineteenth century contradicts freely ornamental performance." *Pioneers of Modern Design,* p. 228.

41 Calvesi, "Il futurista Sant'Elia," p. 133.

42 Ibid., p. 132.

43 Tentori, "Le origini Liberty di Antonio Sant'Elia," p. 206.

44 Calvesi was the first to point out Sant'Elia's immense debt to Boccioni in "Antonio Sant'Elia" and "Il futurista Sant'Elia." See also Banham, "Futurism and Modern Architecture."

45 Godoli, *Il futurismo,* p. 11.

46 Calvesi, "Il futurista Sant'Elia," p. 132.

47 Tafuri, *Theories and History of Architecture,* p. 33.

48 Ibid., p. 32 (emphasis in the original). "On the opposite side," Tafuri continues, "are Gropius, Le Corbusier and Mies van der Rohe. . . . They do not accept the industrial *new nature* as an external factor and claim to enter into it as producers and not as interpreters."

49 Ibid.

50 Sant'Elia, "Manifesto of Futurist Architecture," *Lacerba,* August 1, 1914, pp. 228–231.

51 Bernasconi, "Il messaggio di Antonio Sant'Elia del 20

maggio 1914." Chiattone first alluded to the existence of the "Messaggio" in his article "L'espressionismo nei disegni di Mario Chiattone," *Rivista Tecnica della Svizzera Italiana,* September 1955, p. 219.

52 Ivo Tagliaventi, "Contributo alla storiografia santeliana," *Ingegneri-Architetti-Costruttori,* January 1957, p. 10 (emphasis in the original). The adverb "diabolically" applied to Marinetti is characteristic of the ebbing reputation of futurism in the postwar decade because of its connection to fascism.

53 Carrà, *Tutti gli scritti,* p. 677.

54 Significantly, in Marinetti's personal copy of the Nuove Tendenze catalogue, now in the Beinecke Library at Yale, Sant'Elia's essay is missing. To judge from the yellowed edges, the pages were cut out many years ago.

55 Cf. Marinetti: "Sant'Elia's having been the precursor of the new architecture . . . is all the more indisputable since *the first and only manifesto of architecture* by him in 1914 still constitutes the definitive authority on the matter" (emphasis added). *Enciclopedia italiana,* Milan, 1936, vol. 30, p. 779.

56 "The futurist, and for that very reason prefascist Sant'Elia . . . ," wrote Ragghianti in "Sant'Elia: Il Bibbiena del duemila," p. 5.

57 Nicoletti, *L'architettura Liberty,* p. 364.

58 Zevi, "I disegni smentiscono il manifesto futurista," *L'Espresso* (Rome), October 28, 1956, p. 13.

59 All quotations from the manifesto are from *Archivi,* pp. 81–85. Zevi, "Sant'Elia non era futurista," *L'Espresso* (Rome), September 2, 1956, p. 15.

60 Claude Leroy, "La fabrique du lecteur dans les manifestes," *Littérature,* Paris, 1980, p. 125.

61 "The *Messaggio* is wanting in the structural and programmatic clarity of the futurist manifestos. It lacks— and this is crucial—the premise of a 'technical' nature." Costanzo and Costanzo, "Boccioni e Sant'Elia," p. 14.

62 Boccioni, Carrà, Russolo, Balla, Severini, *Archivi,* p. 63. Cf. Calvesi, "Antonio Sant'Elia," p. 83.

63 E.g., Marinetti's "Discorso futurista di Marinetti ai Veneziani" and Boccioni's "Fondamento plastico della scultura e pittura futurista," and *Pittura scultura futuriste.*

64 Calvesi, "Il futurista Sant'Elia," p. 128.

65 Chiattone, quoted in Giulia Veronesi, "L'architetto Sant'Elia non era futurista," *La Nazione Italiana* (Florence), February 5, 1957, p. 3.

66 Boccioni, *Archivi,* p. 67. See Calvesi, "Il futurista Antonio Sant'Elia," p. 129. Apropos of Boccioni's recantation, see Carrà's sarcastic comment to Severini in a let-

ter of March 3, 1914: "Four years ago, [Boccioni] loved Klimt more than Renoir in art—loved the pre-Raphaelites, and could not, in fact, understand the great impressionists, not even the 'post' Matisse and Picasso." *Archivi,* p. 319.

67 Ivo Tagliaventi, "Contributo alla storiografia santeliana," p. 12.

68 Schmidt-Thomsen, *Floreale,* p. 180.

69 See his letter to Balilla Pratella of August 12, 1914: "I am returning from Florence where I went to transform *Lacerba* into a political journal with the sole aim of preparing the Italian atmosphere for war against Austria." *Archivi,* p. 344.

70 Schmidt-Thomsen, *Floreale,* p. 180.

71 Ibid.

72 Carrà, *Archivi,* p. 74. Calvesi first noted this parallel in "Il futurista Sant'Elia," p. 126.

73 Longatti, *Antonio Sant'Elia,* 1962, p. 46.

74 Godoli, *Il futurismo,* p. 7.

75 Carrà, *Archivi,* p. 74.

76 Boccioni, "Architettura futurista: Manifesto," in *Altri inediti,* p. 38.

77 Marinetti and C. R. W. Nevinson, *Manifesto futurista (contro l'arte inglese),* June 11, 1914, rpt. in *Teoria e invenzione,* p. 96.

78 Marinetti, *Ricostruire l'Italia con l'architettura futurista Sant'Elia,* rpt. in *Teatro F. T. Marinetti,* ed. Giovanni Calendoli, Rome, 1960, vol. 3, pp. 507–602.

79 "I did not give up, however, but insisted, showing him the advantageous aspect: I made him realize how his name would leave the obscurity that surrounded it, despite his great merit, and how his adhesion would show abroad that Italy too could boast of a truly modern architect." Carrà, *Tutti gli scritti,* p. 677.

80 Ibid., p. 678.

81 Giovanni Lista shrewdly remarks that it is hardly conceivable that Marinetti—who was known to criss-cross Europe in search of proselytes—should have sat by passively while Carrà tried to persuade Sant'Elia to join futurism. *Giacomo Balla,* p. 61.

82 Carpi De' Resmini, "Sant'Elia non era futurista," *L'Architettura,* December 1956, p. 549.

83 Borgese, "Il Manifesto di Sant'Elia," *L'Espresso* (Rome), November 11, 1956, n.p.

84 Nebbia, "I futuristi e il manifesto di Sant'Elia."

85 On Nebbia, see Piero Gazzola, "Il pensiero critico di Ugo Nebbia," *Arte Lombarda,* vol. 12, 1st semester, 1967, pp. 91–102.

86 He was undoubtedly up-to-date with futurist experi-

ments in art and even reviewed them in print. See his "Sul movimento pittorico contemporaneo," *Emporium*, December 1913, pp. 421–438.

87 Caramel and Longatti, *Antonio Sant'Elia*, 1962, p. 59.

88 Buggelli's letter was not published in full. For the unabridged text, see *La Provincia di Como*, November 28, 1956, p. 3.

89 Buggelli, then in his eighties, actually challenged Zevi to a duel. See his letter to the editor (Zevi), "Il manifesto di Sant'Elia," *L'Espresso* (Rome), November 11, 1956.

90 See the following articles by Marinetti: "L'architettura alla Triennale," in *Sant'Elia*, October 22, 1933; "I nuovi poeti futuristi," rpt. in *Teoria e invenzione futurista*, p. 165; "Sant'Elia," in *Enciclopedia italiana*, p. 779; *L'architettura e le arti decorative negli stili dei vari tempi*, Rome, 1937, pp. 5–6.

91 The manuscript is a holograph copy by Boccioni, but the title ("Architettura futurista: Manifesto") is in Marinetti's handwriting. See *Altri inediti*, pp. 36–40.

92 Prampolini, "Anche l'architettura futurista . . . E che è?" *Il Piccolo Giornale d'Italia*, January 29–30, 1914, p. 3. The first part was not published until four years later, in Prampolini's magazine *NOI*, February 2–4, 1918. For the annotated text of the manifesto, see Crispolti, *Ricostruzione*, pp. 82–87.

93 Crispolti, *Ricostruzione*, p. 57. Crispolti also attempts to correlate the two manifestos by Boccioni and Prampolini, but his arguments on this score have not met with critical acclaim. See his *Attraverso l'architettura futurista*, Modena, 1984, pp. 20–27.

94 In this manifesto, Boccioni refers to his book *Pittura scultura futuriste (dinamismo plastico)*, which came out in March 1914, thus permitting Birolli to establish a *terminus post quem* for his manifesto. See *Altri inediti*, p. 87.

95 Birolli, *Altri inediti*, p. 86. The similarities between the two texts are mentioned in the notes to the first part of this chapter.

96 Zevi, "La profezia di Umberto Boccioni," *L'Architettura*, April 1974, pp. 704–705; Godoli, *Il futurismo*, p. 10.

97 Tagliaventi, "Contributo alla storiografia santeliana," p. 14.

98 Longatti, "Il caso Sant'Elia," *Nuove Tendenze*, p. 18.

99 See Schmidt-Thomsen, *Floreale*, p. 178.

100 "Dearest Severini, Walden [Herwarth Walden, editor of *Der Sturm*] wrote me yesterday to say that he had sent Marinetti the dues corresponding to July. When our friend M. [Marinetti] returns, we shall send you your allotted share." Letter from Carrà to Severini, July 11, 1914, *Archivi*, p. 341.

101 Schmidt-Thomsen, *Floreale*, p. 177.

102 Dudreville, "Ai margini di una polemica," p. 3. See also Chiattone, in Veronesi, "L'architetto Sant'Elia non era futurista," p. 3.

103 Accetti, "Omaggio a Sant'Elia, architetto futurista," *L'Arte*, July–December 1957, p. 181.

104 Calvesi, "Il futurista Sant'Elia," p. 130.

105 See Chiattone, in Veronesi, "L'architetto Sant'Elia non era futurista," p. 3; Carpi De' Resmini, "Sant'Elia non era futurista," p. 549; Accetti, "Omaggio a Sant'Elia," p. 177.

106 Dudreville, *Documenti*, pp. 130–138. Dudreville wrote under a pseudonym and consequently referred to himself in the third person.

107 Schmidt-Thomsen, *Floreale*, p. 180.

108 Dudreville, "Ai margini di una polemica," p. 3.

109 It is noteworthy that the title is the same as the one Marinetti added in his own hand to Boccioni's text: "Architettura futurista: Manifesto."

110 See Zevi, "Sant'Elia non era futurista"; Veronesi, "L'architetto Sant'Elia non era futurista"; Bernasconi, "Il Messaggio di Antonio Sant'Elia"; C. Accetti, "Sant'Elia fu o no futurista?" in *La Provincia di Como*, October 19, 1956, p. 3; Borgese, "Milano 1870–1920: Architettura, ediliza, urbanistica," *La Famiglia Artistica milanese*, p. 38.

111 Chiattone, in Veronesi, "L'architetto Sant'Elia non era futurista," p. 3. Nebbia says essentially the same thing: "These are ideas that the futurist loudspeaker, without my knowledge and, I believe, without that of Sant'Elia's, wanted to broadcast as loudly as possible, by means of their own rewriting of the original text." See his "I futuristi e il manifesto di Sant'Elia."

112 Quoted in Tagliaventi, "Contributo alla storiografia santeliana," p. 11.

113 Ibid.

114 Dudreville, "Ai margini di una polemica," p. 3.

115 Accetti, "Omaggio a Sant'Elia," p. 177.

116 Birolli, *Altri inediti*, p. 87.

117 Ibid.

118 "We often lamented this lacuna [architecture] amongst ourselves, but we could not see any architect willing to step forth." Carrà, *Tutti gli scritti*, p. 676.

119 See Camporesi, "L'idea di 'architettura,'" and *L'architettura e il dinamismo: Studio della poetica di Umberto Boccioni*, Bologna, 1982. See also C. De Seta, *Architetti italiani del novecento*, Bari, 1982, pp. 3–14. A. Sartoris, "Boccioni e l'architettura futurista," in *Boccioni cento anni*, Rome, 1982, pp. 137–142.

120 Boccioni, "Architettura futurista: Manifesto," *Altri inediti,* p. 39. In the "Messaggio" Sant'Elia spoke of "the house of cement, glass, iron, stripped of painting and sculpture, enriched solely with the innate beauty of its lines and its relief, extraordinarily ugly in its mechanical simplicity."

121 Boccioni, *Altri inediti,* p. 38.

122 Godoli, *Il futurismo,* p. 9.

123 Boccioni, *Altri inediti,* pp. 39–40.

124 Zevi, "La profezia di Umberto Boccioni," p. 705.

125 Godoli, *Il futurismo,* p. 10.

126 Zevi believes that Marinetti suppressed it because it was too revolutionary. "La profezia di Umberto Boccioni," p. 705.

127 See Yvonne Casagrande, Mémoire de licence, University of Geneva, 1979, p. 37.

128 Schmidt-Thomsen, "Sant'Elia architetto oder die Achillesferse des Futurismus," p. 37.

129 See Marinetti's two letters to Ardengo Soffici, editor-in-chief of *Lacerba,* July 21, 23, 1914, rpt. in *Archivi,* pp. 341–342.

130 Bernasconi, "Vent'anni di polemica su Sant'Elia," *Rivista Tecnica della Svizzera Italiana,* October 1976, p. 32.

131 Boccioni, *Gli scritti editi e inediti,* p. 427.

132 Marinetti, *Archivi,* p. 342.

133 Bernasconi, "Vent'anni di polemica su Sant'Elia," p. 32.

134 Marinetti, *Archivi,* p. 342.

135 Carrà, *Archivi,* p. 341.

136 Bernasconi, "Vent'anni di polemica su Sant'Elia," p. 32. One should note, however, that Bernasconi's excellent detective work is geared toward proving that Marinetti appropriated the "Messaggio" without Sant'Elia's consent.

137 On the two versions of Balla's manifesto, see Lista, "Marinetti et le futurisme politique," in *Marinetti et le futurisme: Etudes, documents, iconographie,* Lausanne, 1977, p. 11: "A comparison of the original manuscript and the definitive version of this manifesto illustrates beyond any possible doubt the way Marinetti manipulated the collective ideas of his group in order to instill them with his political ideology and his bellicosity."

138 Quoted in Thea, "Nuove Tendenze a Milano," p. 8.

139 Dudreville, "Ai margini di una polemica," p. 3.

140 Arata, *Costruzioni e progetti—Con alcune note sull'architettura contemporanea,* Milan, 1942, p. xviii.

141 Chiattone, in Veronesi, "L'architetto Sant'Elia non era futurista," p. 3; Carpi De' Resmini, "Sant'Elia non era futurista," p. 549.

142 Carrà, *Tutti gli scritti,* p. 677.

143 Claudia Salaris points out that joining futurism was the goal of many young artists who wanted to make themselves known through Marinetti's numerous contacts and the generous funds at his disposal. *Storia del futurismo,* Rome, 1985, p. 35.

144 G. Arata, "L'architettura futurista," *Pagine d'Arte,* August 30, 1914, pp. 193–195.

145 Ibid., p. 193. The opening line is a reference to an article by Giovanni Papini in which he attacked Boccioni ("Il cerchio si chiude," *Lacerba,* February 15, 1914). See Schmidt-Thomsen, "Sant'Elia architetto oder die Achillesferse des Futurismus," p. 37.

146 Arata, "La prima mostra di architettura promossa dall'associazione degli Architetti Lombardi."

147 Decio Buffoni and Gustave Macchi, art critics both, did not contribute to the catalogue either, but in Macchi's case, at least, this can hardly be interpreted as hostility, because he gave a conference on Nuove Tendenze at the Famiglia Artistica, where the show was being held.

148 Arata, "L'architettura futurista," p. 195.

149 For the political persuasion of the members of Nuove Tendenze, see Crispolti, "Futuristi di destra." See also Thea, "Nuove Tendenze a Milano."

150 Crispolti, *Il mito della macchina,* p. 110.

151 See, e.g., Zevi, "Sant'Elia non era futurista," p. 15; Veronesi, "L'architetto Sant'Elia non era futurista," p. 3; Borgese, "Milano 1870–1920," p. 38.

152 Banham, "Poetica di Sant'Elia e ideologia futurista," *L'Architettura,* January 1957, p. 626.

153 How little critical and philological attention the "Messaggio" actually received can be gathered from the fact that all available versions are faulty. E.g., Bernasconi, "Il Messaggio di Antonio Sant'Elia del 20 maggio 1914"; Zevi, "Poetica di Sant'Elia e ideologia futurista," *L'Architettura,* November 1956, pp. 516–517; *Archivi,* pp. 81–85; Caramel and Longatti, *Antonio Sant'Elia,* 1962, pp. 121–124.

154 Apollonio, *Antonio Sant'Elia,* p. 11.

155 Banham, *Theory and Design,* p. 134.

156 Longatti, "Il caso Sant'Elia," p. 18.

CHAPTER 6: THE LATE WORK

1 The artist Rinaldo Belluschi executed the actual painting, according to the information given me by his son, Riccardo Belluschi.

2 Des Esseintes, the main character of the novel *A rebours* (Paris, 1884), by Joris-Karl Huysmans, was considered the very prototype of the languid voluptuary whom

decadents and symbolists tried to emulate and whom the futurists execrated.

3 Folgore (1888–1966)—or Lightning—was the pseudonym of a Roman poet whose given name, it has been said, was unpardonable for a futurist: Omero Vecchi.

4 *Ponti sull'oceano* (Bridges over the Ocean) was published in Milan by Poesia, Marinetti's editing house, in 1914.

5 Folgore and Marinetti, *Carteggio futurista*, Rome, 1987, p. 67.

6 For futurist experiments in typography, see E. Godoli and G. Fanelli, *Il futurismo e la grafica*, Florence, 1988; G. Lista, *Le livre futuriste de la libération du mot au poème tactile*, Modena, 1984.

7 "Distruzione della sintassi—Immaginazione senza fili —Parole in liberta," rpt. in *Teoria e invenzione futurista*, p. 66.

8 Lista, "Marinetti et le futurisme politique," p. 20.

9 He was elected by 2,434 votes. See *La Provincia di Como*, July 7, 1914, p. 1.

10 It is not known when Sant'Elia joined the party. Most of the archives of the PSI (Partito Socialista Italiano) were destroyed after Mussolini's rise to power, often by the socialists themselves, in order to prevent their falling into the hands of the fascists. According to a socialist newspaper in Como, he had only recently joined the party. See *Il Lavoratore Comasco*, October 21, 1916.

11 "Lettera aperta al futurista Mac Delmarle," *Lacerba*, August 15, 1913, rpt. in *Archivi*, p. 25. Marinetti's contempt for the socialists was echoed by Carrà, who numbered four categories of pacifists in his taxonomy of antipatriots: "professors, whores, priests, and socialists." *Guerra pittura: Futurismo politico, dinamismo plastico, disegni guerreschi, parole in libertà*, 1915, rpt. Florence, 1978, p. 21.

12 But see the strictures of Ugo Piscopo, "I futuristi e Sorel," in *Georges Sorel: Studi e ricerche*, Florence, 1974, pp. 159–167. For Marinetti's political background, see Gian Battista Nazzaro, *Introduzione al futurismo*, Naples, 1984, and his *Futurismo e politica*, Naples, 1987. E. Gentile, "La politica di Marinetti," *Storia contemporanea*, September 1976, pp. 415–438. See also Giovanni Lista, ed., *Marinetti et le futurisme*, pp. 11–28, 79–107, and 122–129; N. Zapponi, "La politica come espediente e come utopia: Marinetti e il partito politico futurista," *F. T. Marinetti futurista*, Naples, 1977, pp. 221–239. G. Lista, *Arte e politica: Il futurismo di sinistra in Italia*, Milan, 1980. Ugo Carpi, *L'estrema avanguardia del Novecento*, Rome, 1985.

13 See Gramsci's famous letter to Trotsky concerning the great appeal that futurism held for the Italian working class: "Before the war the futurists were very popular among the workers. The magazine *Lacerba* had a distribution of 20,000 copies, four-fifths of which was disseminated among the workers. During the various demonstrations of futurist art in the theaters of the large Italian cities it so happened that the workers defended the futurists against more or less semiaristocratic or bourgeois youth who fought against the futurists." "Marinetti rivoluzionario?" quoted in Nazzaro, *Introduzione al futurisme*, p. 14.

14 Carrà, *Tutti gli scritti*, p. 631.

15 Severini, *La vita di un pittore*, Milan, 1965, p. 18.

16 According to Libero Altomare, Boccioni said that "he admired the leader of the futurist movement and sympathized with his agenda in matters of art, even though he held to his own marxist convictions when it came to politics." *Incontri con Marinetti e il futurismo*, Rome, 1954, p. 22. Libero Altomare was the nom de plume of the futurist poet Remo Mannoni.

17 See M. Isnenghi, *Il mito della grande guerra*, Bari, 1970, pp. 7–70; R. Luperini, *La crisi degli intellettuali nel periodo giolittiano*, Messina, 1978.

18 Party members were in fact expressly forbidden to belong to interventionist groups.

19 For Marinetti's account, see his *La grande Milano tradizionale e futurista*, Verona, 1969, pp. 110–112.

20 See Gentile, "La politica di Marinetti," pp. 415–438.

21 See *L'Avanti!* April 12, 1915.

22 Letter from Mussolini to Paolo Buzzi, November 21, 1914, published by Carlo Belloli in *Il Nuovo Milanese*, October 15–21, 1976, p. 27.

23 Quoted in Calvesi and Coen, *Boccioni*, p. 27.

24 On *trasformismo*, see De Fusco, *Il floreale a Napoli*, p. 19: "Though progressive, these [Basile, Sommaruga, D'Aronco] underwent a 'trasformismo' very similar to that of the parliamentarians of the historical Left."

25 See Graf, *Die vergessene Wagnerschule*, p. 27.

26 "We have in fact lost the sense of the monumental, the massive, the static. . . . We feel we are no longer the men of cathedrals and meeting halls."

27 On Boccioni's "crisi di linguaggio," see Ballo, "Boccioni a Milano," in *Boccioni a Milano*, pp. 70–72.

28 See Carrà's "Parlata su Giotto," *La Voce*, March 31, 1916, and "Paolo Uccello costruttore," ibid., September 30, 1916.

29 See Lista's introduction to Russolo, *L'art des bruits*, Lausanne, 1975, p. 21.

30 "The poetic and logical construction of the architect Sant'Elia," wrote Nicoletti, "was hardly influenced by his entry into Marinetti's movement. The event, however, had a radical influence on his destiny as a man, and on the success of his ideas." *L'architettura Liberty,* p. 361.

31 They were actually the minority. The vast majority of the nation, including Parliament and the Vatican, opposed war.

32 Quoted in Thea, "Nuove Tendenze a Milano," p. 9.

33 Bernasconi, "Vent'anni di polemica su Sant'Elia," p. 31. Bernasconi's testimony should be treated with caution. A Swiss citizen by birth, Chiattone became a fervid interventionist and was even imprisoned with the other futurists for demonstrating against Austria.

34 Ramperti, "Rispettare i morti," *L'Avanti!* November 13, 1920, p. 3.

35 Philip Cannistraro and Brian Sullivan, *Il Duce's Other Woman,* New York, 1993, p. 145.

36 Marinetti, "Il futurista Sant'Elia," in *Testa di Ferro,* Milan, November 21, 1920.

37 Quoted in Longatti, *Disegni,* p. 49.

38 Caramel and Longatti claim that Sant'Elia chose the Lombard Battalion only to be with his friends, since he was called to arms anyway. But Sant'Elia's letter makes it quite clear that he was called up on June 1, whereas he had enrolled in the Lombard Battalion in May. *Antonio Sant'Elia,* 1987, p. 59.

39 For the role of the futurists in the Lombard regiment, see Crispolti, "Zang Tumb Tuum: I futuristi vanno alla guerra."

40 For a description of the futurist decorations and Sant'Elia's participation, see Russolo, "Un ricordo di Luigi Russolo," pp. 537–538. See also "La serata d'addio dai Volontari Ciclisti al 'Condominio,'" *Cronaca Prealpina,* July 17, 1915.

41 See Balilla Pratella's recollections in his *Autobiografia,* Milan, 1971, p. 139. See also Marinetti's description of the euphoric atmosphere that reigned in the Lombard Battalion in *Mostra delle opere dell'architetto futurista comasco Sant'Elia,* Como, 1930, pp. 9ff.

42 Bucci, "Scapigliatura 1906," p. 279.

43 Marinetti, "Quinte e scene della campagna del Battaglione Lombardo Volontari Ciclisti sul Lago di Garda e sull'Altissimo," *La Gazzetta dello Sport,* January 13, February 7, 1916, rpt. in *Bolaffiarte,* May 1978, pp. 12–15. See also Boccioni's enthusiastic letters from the front, in *Gli scritti editi e inediti,* pp. 379–387.

44 Thea, "Nuove Tendenze a Milano," p. 10.

45 Mario Massai, "La Bandiera del Battaglione Lombardo," *Corriere della Sera,* October 18, 1930, p. 5.

46 Marinetti, Boccioni, Russolo, Sironi, Piatti, and Sant'Elia, *L'orgoglio italiano,* January 15, 1916, rpt. in *Archivi,* pp. 32–34. All further quotations are from this source. It appeared as a flyer that also contained Balilla Pratella's manifesto "Il futurismo e la guerra."

47 Quoted in Sarfatti, *Dux,* p. 170 (emphasis in the original).

48 See Edoardo Sanguinetti, "La guerra futurista," *Quindici,* December 1968, p. 28.

49 For Marinetti's manipulations of futurist manifestos, see Russolo, *L'art des bruits,* pp. 158–159, and Lista, "Marinetti et le futurisme politique," p. 11.

50 The same instability of mood can be found in Boccioni's last letters. Euphoric during the heroic period of the Lombard Battalion, a profound disillusionment comes over him shortly before his death. See Salaris, *Storia del futurismo,* p. 82.

51 This postcard is now in the collection of Paride Accetti in Milan.

52 On the difficulties of the Italian front, see C. Seton-Watson, *Italy from Liberalism to Fascism, 1870–1925,* London, 1967, pp. 450–504.

53 Apparently, the painter Mario Bazzi was also responsible for the project. But the photograph of the cemetery that has come down to us shows a work by Sant'Elia alone. See Cinzio Vaccari, "Dalla caserma del Gentilino alle trincee del Carso: L'architetto Sant'Elia tempra d'eroe," *La Provincia di Como,* October 7, 1928.

54 C. Vaccari, "Antonio Sant'Elia," *Il Gagliardetto* (Como), October 23, 1921, pp. 1–2.

55 The highly romanticized account is related by Jeri in two slightly different versions: *I razzi e le stelle,* Milan, 1928, p. 93, and "Come Sant'Elia morì combattendo," *La Provincia di Como,* April 1, 1932, p. 3.

56 Vaccari, "Antonio Sant'Elia," pp. 1–2.

57 "Fra i nostri morti valorosi: Antonio Sant'Elia," *La Sera* (Milan), October 19, 1916. See also "L'architetto Sant'Elia e sepolto nel cimitero da lui ideato," *La Provincia di Como,* October 27, 1916.

58 On Sant'Elia's cemetery, see Sandro Scarrocchia, "Antonio Sant'Elia's Last Project," *Journal of Architectural Education,* forthcoming.

CHAPTER 7: EPILOGUE

1 "The fascists did well not to break his head," wrote a local reporter, "because next to them lay the great De-

ceased." GIM. [sic], "I funerali dell'eroico concittadino Sant'Elia," *Il Gagliardetto* (Como), October 30, 1921.

2 Como had a street, a district, a kindergarten (built by Terragni), a theater group, and a fascist militia named after him.

3 Giuseppe Bottai (1895–1959), ex-futurist, former editor of the magazine *Roma Futurista*, governor of Rome, and later minister of education, was an active supporter of modern art and one of the main representatives of so-called left-wing fascism (*sozialfascismo*). On Bottai, see Alexander J. De Grand, *Bottai e la cultura fascista*, Rome, 1978.

4 Published in *Il Popolo d'Italia*, October 6, 1926, rpt. in *Opera omnia di Benito Mussolini*, Florence, 1957, vol. 22, p. 230.

5 "I believe," wrote Ernesto Rogers years later, "that our mistake lay in a philosophical confusion. We based ourselves on a syllogism which, *grosso modo*, went like this: fascism is a revolution, modern architecture is revolutionary. Hence it should be the architecture of fascism. As you see, the first proposition was wrong, and the corollary could not but be disastrous: fascism was not a revolution." Cesare De Seta, *La cultura architettonica in Italia tra le due guerre*, Bari, 1983, pp. 220–221.

6 E.g., the exhibition of the Decennials of the regime (1932) and the competitions for the train station in Florence and for the town of Sabaudia, both of 1933, were all entrusted exclusively to the young modernists.

7 Marinetti, in "Al di là del Comunismo," *Testa di Ferro*, August 15, 1920, p. 2.

8 Prezzolini, "Fascismo e futurismo," *Il Secolo*, July 3, 1923, rpt. in L. De Maria, ed., *Per conoscere Marinetti e il futurismo*, p. 289 (emphasis in the original).

9 Soffici, "Opinioni sull'arte fascista," *Critica Fascista*, October 15, 1926, p. 384. Soffici (1879–1964), a former futurist turned archconservative, was one of the main intellectuals behind the regressive, anti-urban movement Strapaese (super-village), which was violently opposed to the idea of the metropolis.

10 Piacentini, "Difesa dell'architettura italiana," *Il Giornale d'Italia*, May 2, 1931, quoted in Dennis Doordan, "The Political Content in Italian Architecture during the Fascist Era," *Art Journal*, Summer 1983, p. 130.

11 Pensabene, "L'internazionale dell'architettura," *Quadrivio*, November 27, 1933, p. 2; Pensabene, "Libro giallo dell'architettura italiana," a series of eight installments published in *Il Tevere* from December 16, 1932, to January 6, 1933. For Pensabene's enthusiastic appraisal of Sant'Elia, see "Sant'Elia, Le Corbusier e la nuova architettura," in *Futurismo*, April 30, 1933, p. 4.

12 "Europeanism is the first artistic attempt sufficiently widespread that was carried out by the Jews after millennia: . . . rationalism, surrealism, the so-called metaphysical art and magic realism, are Jewish creations." Giuseppe Pensabene, "L'europeismo e i giovani," *Quadrivio*, February 23, 1936.

13 See Marinetti, "THAT WHICH THE VENERABLE TRADITIONALISTS CALL THE NORTHERN-BOLSHEVIK STYLE in their desperate defense of *passéisme* is THE FUTURIST, ITALIAN BOCCIONI-SANT'ELIA STYLE," untitled entry published in the futurist magazine *Sant'Elia*, June 1, 1934, p. 6 (emphasis in the original).

14 For the best account of the feud, see Crispolti, *Il mito della macchina*, pp. 601–648; L. Patetta, "Neofuturismo, novecento e razionalismo: Termini di una polemica nel periodo fascista," *Controspazio*, April–May 1971, pp. 87–98; Silvia Evangelisti, ed., *Fillia e l'avanguardia futurista negli anni del fascismo*, Milan, 1986.

15 See Prampolini, "L'architettura dell'Italia fascista," *Stile Futurista*, July 1934, p. 7; Fillia, "Architettura di stato," *L'Ambrosiano* (Milan), February 25, 1931.

16 Bardi, "Architettura di stato e confusioni futuriste," *L'Ambrosiano* (Milan), February 19, 1931; Terragni, "Tre lettere sull'architettura," *L'Ambrosiano*, February 25, 1931.

17 On Bardi, see Riccardo Mariani, *Razionalismo e architettura moderna*, Milan, 1989. See also Francesco Tentori, *P. M. Bardi*, Milan, 1990. I wish to thank Ellen Shapiro for having brought this book to my attention.

18 Bardi, "Architettura, arte di stato," *L'Ambrosiano* (Milan), January 30, 1931, p. 1. See also his article "Petizione a Mussolini per l'architettura," *L'Ambrosiano*, February 13, 1931, p. 1. For Terragni's answer to Bardi, see "Architettura di stato?" *L'Ambrosiano*, February 10, 1933, p. 1. Sartoris, *Introduzione all'architettura moderna*, Milan, 1943, p. 331.

19 Quoted in Bruno La Padula, "Notiziario di architettura," *Futurismo*, January 8, 1933, p. 6.

20 Bardi, *Rapporto sull'architettura (per Mussolini)*, Rome, 1931, p. 101.

21 Ibid.

22 Somenzi, "La funzione politica dell'arte," *Futurismo*, July 15–30, 1932, p. 1.

23 Somenzi, "L'arte fascista," *Futurismo*, June 15–30, 1932, p. 2.

24 Marinetti, "Stile futurista," *Futurismo*, November 6, 1932, p. 1.

25 Bartoli, "E necessaria la violenza?" *Futurismo*, April 23,

1933, p. 2 (emphasis in the original).

26 Ghezzi, "L'organizzazione degli artisti in regime fascista," *Nuovo Futurismo,* May 30, 1934, p. 1.

27 Mario Rispoli, "Caratteri dell'architettura fascista," *Sant'Elia,* December 17, 1933, p. 5.

28 Argan, "Il pensiero critico di Antonio Sant'Elia," *L'Arte,* September 1930, pp. 491–498; rpt. in *Dopo Sant'Elia,* Milan, 1935, a book of essays written in defense of rationalism, but using Sant'Elia as a figurehead.

29 Ibid., p. 497.

30 Persico, "L'architettura mondiale," *L'Italia Letteraria,* July 2, 1933, rpt. in *Tutte le opere,* vol. 2, p. 143.

31 All their important exhibitions acknowledged Sant'Elia as the fountainhead of the new architecture: the Monza Triennale (1927); the first and the second exhibitions of rationalist architecture (1928 and 1931); Gruppo Sette; and the Programma di Architettura (1933).

32 Sartoris, "L'architettura Sant'Elia, influenza e sviluppi," *Meridiano di Roma,* December 17, 1939, p. v.

33 The engineer Guido Fiorini declared that in the case of the Città Nuova these were actually redundant; "such was the exemplary transparency of the exterior of the building." "L'influenza mondiale di Antonio Sant'Elia," p. 18. *Stile Futurista,* October 1934, p. 18.

34 See Marinetti, "La vittoria di Sant'Elia," *Futurismo,* February 26, 1933, p. 1.

35 "Il genio di Sant'Elia glorificato dall'accademico F. T. Marinetti al Broletto," *La Provincia di Como,* September 16, 1930. This falsehood was republished numerous times. See *Mostra delle opere dell'architetto futurista comasco Sant'Elia,* p. 9; C. M. Boesmi, "Commemorazione veloce di Sant'Elia," *Il Regime Fascista,* September 21, 1930, p. 5.

36 Godoli, *Il futurismo,* p. 70.

37 Highly romanticized accounts of Sant'Elia's death were legion in the late 1920s and after: Alfredo Jeri, *I razzi e le stelle,* Milan, 1928; "Per un architetto morto in guerra: Antonio Sant'Elia," *Corriere della Sera,* July 5, 1930, p. 3; "Come è morto Sant'Elia," *L'Ambrosiano* (Milan), September 17, 1930, p. 3; Marinetti, "L'Italia onora in Sant'-Elia l'architetto del futuro," *Oggi e Domani,* September 29, 1930, p. 6; Emilio Zanzi, "L'architettura dell'avvenire è nata a Como," *Nord-Milano,* October 1930, pp. 230–233; L. Vanni, "Ricordo di Sant'Elia," *Corriere della Sera,* June 24, 1933, p. 3; A. Jeri, "Come è caduto Sant'-Elia," *La Stampa,* October 10, 1944, p. 2.

38 E.g., Marinetti's "Sant'Elia e la nuova architettura," *Oggi e Domani,* September 29, 1930, p. 13; Marinetti and M. Del Bello, *Antonio Sant'Elia,* Rome, 1933, p. 15. *Mostra delle opere dell'architetto futurista comasco Sant'Elia,* p. 9.

39 "Trieste, la nostra bella polveriera," Milan, 1917, rpt. in *Teoria e invenzione futurista,* p. 247. See also "Battaglie di Trieste: Discorso ai Triestini," ibid., pp. 210–216. The futurists liked to stress the contrast between Venice, decadent and passéist, and nearby Trieste, industrialized and warriorlike.

40 See the relatively sober account given by Sant'Elia's commanding officer, Lieutenant Colonel A. Miravalle: "L'architetto Antonio Sant'Elia è caduto da eroe," *La Provincia di Como,* October 19, 1916. According to Lieutenant Nino Dabbusi, who was responsible for Sant'Elia's cemetery at Montfalcone, Sant'Elia's last words were "We shall meet again on high" ("arrivederci lassù"). See "L'architetto Sant'Elia è sepolto nel cimitero da lui ideato," *La Provincia di Como,* October 27, 1916.

41 Republished in *L'Italia Futurista,* November 1, 1916, p. 1.

42 Marinetti and Del Bello, *Antonio Sant'Elia,* Rome, 1933.

43 Ellen Shapiro has suggested to me that the Concordat of 1929, signed jointly by Mussolini and the Vatican, is what brought about this change of attitude.

44 Marinetti and Del Bello, *Antonio Sant'Elia,* p. 25. These words reappear verbatim in Marinetti's introduction to the futurist show at the Galleria Pesaro in Milan: *Mostra futurista architetto Sant'Elia e 22 pittori futuristi,* Milan, 1930, p. 11.

45 M. Del Bello, "Antonio Sant'Elia: L'uomo, l'artista, l'eroe," *Sant'Elia,* October 10, 1933, p. 6.

46 The year 1933 marked the beginning of what was known as the Starace era, during which political conformism reached its peak. Achille Starace (1889–1945), secretary of the PNF (Fascist National Party) from 1931 to 1939, is most widely known for his attempt to endow fascism with a set of rules and rituals called *costume e mistica fascista.* The booklet by Marinetti and Del Bello is characteristic of this period.

47 Untitled article, *Futurismo,* January 29, 1933, p. 1; originally published in *La Penna dei Ragazzi,* a magazine for fascist youth, the phrase was often used in futurist publications.

48 Van Doesburg, "Rinnovamento dell'arte e dell'architettura in Italia," *Het Bouwbedrijf,* April 29, 1929, rpt. in *Casabella,* August–September 1973, pp. 80–81.

49 Over sixty magazines affiliated with futurism have been documented. For a full record, see V. Vercelloni, "Neofuturismo nella cultura italiana degli anni '30," *Controspazio,* April–May 1971, p. 98.

50 "Furthermore, we use the label FUTURIST STYLE as we have, for some time, used the designation SANT'ELIA ARCHITECTURE to shut up the 'foreignophiles,' always prone to attribute to foreigners our own creations." Untitled article, *Stile Futurista,* July 1934, p. 5 (emphasis in the original).

51 Untitled article, *Futurismo,* July 15–30, 1932, p. 1.

52 Vercelloni astutely remarks that the tiresome custom of labeling as futurist all the great names of modern architecture has its origin in a cultural inferiority complex. "Neofuturismo nella cultura italiana degli anni '30," p. 99.

53 This is not to disparage the importance of these magazines. *La Città Futurista* of April 1929, e.g., was the first to publish Le Corbusier in Italy.

54 Untitled article, *Sant'Elia,* October 10, 1933, p. 1.

55 Ibid.

56 Lista, "Marinetti et le futurisme politique," p. 26.

57 The list of "materiali Sant'Elia" is far from exhaustive, as even a cursory perusal of the magazine will show. See also Vercelloni, ''Neofuturismo nella cultura italiana degli anni '30."

58 See the pathetic letter written in July 1934 by Sant'Elia's younger brother, Guido, to the magazine *Nuovo Futurismo,* in which he bitterly complains about the unlawful usurpation of his brother's name for industrial products.

59 *Onoranze all'architetto futurista Antonio Sant'Elia,* Milan, 1930 (flyer).

60 "Il genio di Antonio Sant'Elia glorificato."

61 Actually, Como had announced a competition for the Monumento ai Caduti in 1926, but none of the entries, including those of Giuseppe Terragni and Pietro Lingeri, met with the approval of the jury. Four years later, Terragni, Lingeri, and Gianni Mantero were asked to submit new projects, and once more the authorities demurred. Terragni thus prepared two projects for the monument. For the best account of the War Memorial, see the following works: Longatti, "Marinetti, Terragni e il Monumento ai Caduti," *La Provincia di Como,* October 2, 1980, pp. 8–9; Longatti, "Futurismo e razionalismo a Como: Terragni e il Monumento ai Caduti," *Como,* Autumn 1983; Caramel and Patetta, *L'idea del lago,* pp. 193–199. See also Thomas Schumacher, *Surface and Symbol: Giuseppe Terragni and the Architecture of Italian Rationalism,* New York, 1991, pp. 115–117.

62 The rationalists protested immediately. "In effect," wrote Persico, "it is inconceivable that a sketch of Sant'Elia for a power plant, a skyscraper, an airport, a hangar and so forth be used indifferently as a memento to the dead." Persico, "Echi riflessi chiose," *La Casa Bella,* October 1930, p. 58.

63 As he once wrote, "Como will have rendered a poor service to its great Sant'Elia, by dedicating to the memory of its dead a none too orthodox reconstruction of a sketch for a power plant, left us by the bold pioneer of the New Architecture." Quoted in "Omaggio a Terragni," *L'Architettura,* July 1968, p. 178.

64 See Terragni's own version in "Precisazioni," *La Provincia di Como,* August 2, 1936, p. 4.

65 I wish to thank the Terragni family for kindly allowing me to look at Terragni's drawings and for having assisted my research in every possible way.

66 "Como, nel XV annuale della Vittoria, inaugura il Monumento ai suoi Caduti," *La Provincia di Como–Il Gagliardetto,* November 5, 1933, p. 3.

67 On this competition, see the excellent work of Giorgio Ciucci, *Gli architetti e il fascismo: Architettura e città, 1922–1944,* Turin, 1989, pp. 139–151.

68 Fillia [Luigi Colombo] and E. Prampolini, "Futurismo!" *Futurismo,* November 20, 1932, p. 6. See also Prampolini's "I futuristi e la via dell'Impero," *Futurismo,* December 4, 1932, p. 6. Bruno La Padula, "Notiziario di architettura," *Futurismo,* January 1, 1933, p. 6. Lino Cappuccio, "Palazzo Littorio," *Nuovo Futurismo,* October 15, 1934, p. 2.

69 Pound's original words in Italian were: "Una Casa Littoria a Rapallo potrebbe benissimo contenere almeno una biblioteca accessibile ai forestieri dilettanti o di passaggio, aiutandoli a subito comprendere la Nuova Italia. Questa costruzione, se ispirata ad un progetto di Sant'-Elia, aprirebbe l'occhio e probabilmente la mente alla contemporaneità della Nazione." "Rapallo centro di cultura," *Il Mare,* May 2, 1936, p. 1.

70 The letter was published in *Il Giornale di Genova,* March 23–May 2, 1936. There is also a short note from Pound to Marinetti on the subject, undated but written soon after this first letter.

71 Pound's two letters to Marinetti, as well as Marinetti's letter to Pound, are now in the Beinecke Library at Yale.

72 This was immediately noted by the futurists themselves. V. Marchi, "Antonio Sant'Elia architetto futurista," *L'Impero,* 1922, p. 4. Gerardo Dottori, "La mostra di Sant'Elia al Circolo Artistico di Roma," *Oggi e Domani,* December 11, 1930, p. 5.

73 *La Carta del Carnaro nei testi di Alceste De Ambris e Gabriele D'Annunzio,* ed. Renzo De Felice, Bologna, 1973, p. 73. It was probably De Ambris who brought

Sant'Elia's manifesto to D'Annunzio's attention: the futurists were fervid supporters of the conquest of Fiume, and he occasionally published in their magazines.

74 Alberto Longatti recently found a copy of Sant'Elia's manifesto in D'Annunzio's lodgings at the Vittoriale. Caramel and Longatti, *Antonio Sant'Elia,* 1987, p. 63.

75 See, e.g., also Vincenzo Costantini, "Sant'Elia," *Italia Letteraria,* October 12, 1930, p. 4 .

76 For many years it was believed that Hitler pressured Mussolini into accepting an official policy of anti-Semitism. But according to recent scholarship Mussolini's institutionalization of anti-Semitism stemmed from a firm conviction that such measures were necessary to consolidate the alliance between the two regimes. See Renzo De Felice, *Storia degli ebrei italiani sotto il fascismo,* Turin, 1961. Meir Michaelis, *Mussolini and the Jews: German-Italian Relations and the Jewish Question,* New York, 1978.

77 "'Modern,' naturally, took on the specific meaning of Jewish: only that which is Jewish is 'modern.'" G. Pensabene, "La cultura e la razza," *Quadrivio,* August 7, 1938, p. 6.

78 Quoted in Crispolti, *Il mito della macchina,* pp. 815–816.

79 *Origini,* March 2, 1939. I was unable to locate a copy of this magazine in Italy. This list is quoted from Enrico Mantero, *Giuseppe Terragni e la città del Razionalismo italiano* (n.p.), 1969, p. 175.

80 "Panorama sintetico di tutti gli inventori dell'arte moderna," *Artecrazia,* January 11, 1939. Yet a third variant, unsigned, appeared a few years later in the short-lived *Mediterraneo Futurista,* December 1943.

81 Interlandi, "L'arte e la razza," *Quadrivio,* December 11, 1938, pp. 1–2; December 18, 1938, pp. 1–2; December 25, 1938, pp. 1–2; January 1, 1939, pp. 1–2; January 29, 1939, pp. 1–2. See also Alberto Schiavo, *Futurismo e fascismo,* Rome, 1981, p. 56.

82 See Claudia Salaris, *Artecrazia: L'avanguardia futurista negli anni del fascismo,* Florence, 1992, pp. 205–210.

83 See their manifesto in *L'Ambrosiano,* October 14, 1940.

84 Interlandi, *Il Tevere,* November 24–25, 1938.

85 Nicoletti, *L'architettura Liberty,* p. 361.

86 Banham, "Sant'Elia," *Architectural Review,* May 1955, p. 301.

87 Banham, "Futurism for Keeps," *Arts,* December 1960, p. 39.

88 Banham, "Futurism and Modern Architecture," p. 137. However, he also adds that "the surviving plans . . . are competent but dull."

89 Banham, *Theory and Design,* pp. 130–131.

90 Ragghianti, "Sant'Elia: Il Bibbiena del duemila," p. 9. For an equally severe opinion, see Cresti, "Sulle origini del gap architettonico," p. 18: "To hang on to the figurative models of the Secession as late as 1911, that is, when Gropius was tackling concretely the problems of improving work conditions in the Fagus plant by developing an activity of effective social policy, was tantamount to putting oneself *voluntarily* at least ten years behind European reality" (emphasis mine).

91 See chapter 5, note 58.

92 Mariani, "Disegni inediti di Sant'Elia," *L'Architettura,* July–August 1955, pp. 210–215; "Altri disegni inediti di Antonio Sant'Elia," ibid., January–February 1956, pp. 704–707; and "Antonio Sant'Elia urbanista," ibid., January 1959, p. 631.

93 There is as yet no catalogue raisonné of Sant'Elia's work. The recent publication by Caramel and Longatti (*Antonio Sant'Elia,* 1987) includes several drawings that are not by Sant'Elia.

94 But see Donatella Poli's careful analysis of these forgeries in her "Proposta per un catalogo critico," p. 212.

95 E.g., Bruno Zevi: Sant'Elia "questions and restructures the city, taking the components apart and then reassembling them at a large scale. Sant'Elia deserves a chapter in the history of modern urbanism, [a chapter] whose critical content still awaits an adequate interpretation." *Cronache di Architettura,* vol. 2, no. 82, Bari, 1970–1973, n.p.

96 "Taciturn" is the word that recurs most often in his friends' descriptions of his personality. See G. Fontana, "Sant'Elia," *Como,* Summer 1955, n.p.

97 Bucci, "Scapigliatura 1906," p. 280.

98 Longatti, "Antonio Sant'Elia," in *Nuove Tendenze,* p. 108.

99 In this sense, statistics are telling. Of the three hundred or so drawings currently attributed to Sant'Elia, only about ten show plans, and only three show interiors.

100 Ragghianti, "Sant'Elia: Il Bibbiena del duemila," p. 22.

101 Henri Bresler, "Dessiner l'architecture," in *Images et imaginaires d'architecture,* Paris, 1984, pp. 33–37.

102 See Giulia Veronesi's penetrating comments apropos of similar traits in Chiattone. "Disegni di Mario Chiattone," p. 54.

103 C. Cresti, "Il tema della città nella cultura architettonica del Liberty," *Situazione degli studi sul Liberty,* p. 57.

104 Crispolti, *Ricostruzione,* p. 65.

105 John Jacobus, review of Stephan Tschudi Madsen's "Sources of Art Nouveau," *Art Bulletin,* December 1958, p. 371.

106 Lista, "Marinetti et le futurisme politique," p. 17.

107 Cresti, "Sulle origini del gap architettonico," p. 24.

108 Argan, "Il pensiero critico di Antonio Sant'Elia," p. 497. Bossaglia, "L'architettura," *Mostra del Liberty italiano,* p. 40.

109 M. Nicoletti, "Flash Gordon and the Twentieth Century Utopia," *Architectural Review,* August 1966, p. 89.

110 Zevi, *Storia,* p. 225.

111 Portoghesi rightly observes that Sant'Elia's drawings were dominated by the primacy of the image ("primato dell'immagine") over that of the concept. *L'angelo della storia,* p. 230.

Select Bibliography

Accetti, Carlo, "Omaggio a Sant'Elia, architetto futurista," *L'Arte,* July–December 1957, 177–182.

Angelini, Luigi, "Concorsi d'architettura in Italia," *Emporium,* January 1916.

———, "La piazza delle Erbe di Verona e la sua sistemazione," *Emporium,* March 1914, 192–198.

Antonio Sant'Elia: L'architettura disegnata, Venice, 1991.

Anzani, Giovanni, "Per una revisione critica dell'opera di Romolo Romani," *Storia dell'Arte,* no. 33, 1978, 155–180.

Apollonio, Umbro, *Antonio Sant'Elia,* Milan, 1958.

Arata, Giulio Ulisse, "La prima mostra di architettura promossa dall'associazione degli Architetti Lombardi," *Vita d'Arte,* March 1914, 66–72.

———, "L'architettura futurista," *Pagine d'Arte,* August 30, 1914, 193–195.

———, "I morti per la patria," *Pagine d'Arte,* November 15, 1916, 139–140.

Argan, Giulio Carlo, "Il pensiero critico di Antonio Sant'Elia, *L'Arte,* September 1930, 491–498.

Ashton, Dore, and Guido Ballo, *Antonio Sant'Elia,* New York, 1986.

Atti del congresso internazionale di studi su "Raimondo D'Aronco e il suo tempo," Udine, 1982.

Baculo, Adriana Giusti, *Otto Wagner,* Naples, 1970.

———, "Gli studi architettonici di Emil Hoppe," *L'Architettura. Cronache e Storia,* December 1969, 552–556.

Bairati, Eleonaora, and Daniele Riva, *Il Liberty in Italia,* Bari, 1985.

Ballo, Guido, *Preistoria del futurismo,* Milan, 1960.

Ballo, Guido, ed., *Boccioni a Milano,* Milan, 1982.

Banham, Reyner, "Footnotes to Sant'Elia," *Architectural Review,* June 1956, 343–344.

———, "Futurism and Modern Architecture," *Journal of the Royal Institute of British Architects,* February 1957, 129–139.

———, "Futurism for Keeps," *Arts,* December 1960, 33–39.

———, "Sant'Elia," *Architectural Review,* May 1955, 95–301.

———, *Theory and Design in the First Machine Age,* New York, 1960.

Bernasconi, Giovanni, "L'espressionismo nei disegni di Mario Chiattone," *Rivista Tecnica della Svizzera Italiana,* Lugano, September 1955, 218–226.

———, "Il messaggio di Antonio Sant'Elia del 20 maggio 1914," *Rivista Tecnica della Svizzera Italiana,* July 1956, 145–152.

———, Rilettura di Mario Chiattone," *Necropoli,* September–December 1970, 42–48.

———, "Vent'anni di polemica su Sant'Elia," *Rivista Tecnica della Svizzera Italiana,* October 1976, 27–36.

Blumenkranz-Onimus, Noëmi, "La ville des futuristes," *Revue d'Esthétique,* nos. 3–4, 1977, 96–97.

Boccioni, Umberto, *Altri inediti e apparati critica,* ed. Zeno Birolli, Milan, 1972.

———, *Pittura scultura futuriste (dinamismo plastico),* Florence, 1977.

———, *Gli scritti editi e inediti,* Milan, 1971.

Boito, Camillo, *Architettura del medio evo in Italia,* Milan, 1880.

Borsi, Franco, *L'architettura dell'Unità d'Italia,* Florence, 1966.

Bossaglia, Rossana, *Il Liberty in Italia,* Milan, 1968.

Bossaglia, Rossana, and Mauro Cozzi, *I Coppedè,* Genoa, 1982.

Boyd Whyte, Iain, *Three Architects from the Master Class of Wagner: Emil Hoppe, Marcel Kammerer, Otto Schönthal,* Cambridge, Mass., 1989.

Bucci, Anselmo, "Scapigliatura 1906," *La Lettura,* Milan, March 1941, 273–280.

Calvesi, Maurizio, "Antonio Sant'Elia," *Edilizia Popolare,* November 1954, 83–84.

———, *Le due avanguardie,* Bari, 1971.

———, "Il futurista Sant'Elia," *La Casa,* no. 6, 1959, 120–134.

Calvesi, Maurizio, and Ester Coen, *Boccioni,* Milan, 1983.

Camporesi, Franco, "L'idea di 'architettura' nella poetica di Umberto Boccioni," *Atti e memorie dell'Accademia Clementina di Bologna,* vol. 14, 1981, 81–109.

Caramel, Luciano, and Alberto Longatti, *Antonio Sant'Elia,* Como, 1962.

———, *Antonio Sant'Elia,* Milan, 1987.

Caramel, Luciano, and Luciano Patetta, eds., *L'idea del lago: Un paesaggio ridefinito, 1861–1914,* Como, 1984.

Carpi De' Resmini, Aldo, "Sant'Elia non era futurista," *L'Architettura. Cronache e Storia,* December 1956, 549.

Carrà, Carlo, *La mia vita,* Milan, 1943; reprint, *Tutti gli scritti,* Milan, 1978.

Le Case Popolari e le Città-Giardino, Milan, 1911, nos. 10–11, 55–56.

Ciucci, Giorgio, *Gli architetti e il fascismo: Architettura e città, 1922–1944,* Turin, 1989.

Collins, George R., *Visionary Drawings of Architecture and Planning, Twentieth Century through the 1960s,* Cambridge, Mass., 1979.

Concorsi di architettura in Italia, Milan, n.d.

Costanzo, Maria, and Michele Costanzo, "Boccioni e Sant'-Elia," *Rassegna dell'Istituto di Architettura e Urbanistica,* April–August 1978, 7–36.

Cresti, Carlo, *Appunti storici e critici nell'architettura italiana dal '900 ad oggi,* Florence, 1971.

———, "Contributo per una revisione critica dell'opera di Mario Chiattone," *Necropoli,* September–December 1970, 49–53.

———, "Intorno a due disegni quasi sconosciuti di Antonio Sant'Elia," *Necropoli,* December 1972, 45–50.

———, "Sulle origini del gap architettonico," *Necropoli,* February 1969, 13–26.

Crispolti, Enrico, *Attraverso l'architettura futurista,* Modena, 1984.

———, "Futuristi di destra," *Bolaffiarte,* April–May 1979, 28–33.

———, *Il mito della macchina e altri temi futurismo,* Trapani, 1969.

———, *Ricostruzione futurista dell'universo,* Turin, 1980.

———, "Zang Tumb Tuum: I futuristi vanno alla guerra," *Bolaffiarte,* May 1978, 9–15.

De Finetti, Giuseppe, *Milano: Costruzione di una città,* Milan, 1969.

De Fusco, Renato, "Un'avanguardia verosimile," *Controspazio,* April–May 1971, 60–63.

———, *Il floreale a Napoli,* Naples, 1959.

———, *L'idea di architettura,* Milan, 1964.

De Seta, Cesare, *Architetti italiani del Novecento,* Bari, 1982.

———, *La cultura architettonica in Italia tra le due guerre,* Bari, 1983.

Dijkstra, Bram, *Idols of Perversity: Fantasies of Feminine Evil in Fin-de-Siècle Culture,* New York, 1986.

Doordan, Dennis, *Building Modern Italy: Italian Architecture, 1914–1936,* Princeton, 1988.

———, "The Political Content in Italian Architecture during the Fascist Era," *Art Journal,* Summer 1983, 121–131.

Drudi Gambillo, Maria, and Teresa Fiori, eds., *Archivi del futurismo,* Rome, 1958.

Etlin, Richard, *Modernism in Italian Architecture, 1890–1940,* Cambridge, Mass., 1991.

Evangelisti, Silvia, "Dal simbolismo alla non-figurazione e ritorno: Il percorso artistico di Romolo Romani," in *Romolo Romani,* ed. Renato Barilli, Milan, 1982.

La Famiglia Artistica milanese nel centenario, Milan, 1972.

Feuerstein, Günther, "Traffic Storeys: Otto Wagner and Antonio Sant'Elia," *Daidalos,* December 1991, 62–75.

Fontana, Gerolamo, "Sant'Elia," *Como,* Summer 1955, n.p.

———, "Sant'Elia e il 'Liberty,'" *Como,* no. 2, 1963, 54–55.

Fontana, Vincenzo, *Il nuovo paesaggio dell'Italia giolittiana,* Bari, 1981.

Gabetti, Roberto, and Paolo Marconi, "L'insegnamento dell'architettura nel sistema didattico franco-italiano (1789–1922)," pt. 4, *Controspazio,* October–November 1971, 41–44.

Gerosa, Pier Giorgio, *Mario Chiattone: Un itinerario architettonico fra Milano e Lugano,* Milan, 1985.

Giedion, Siegfried, *Space, Time and Architecture,* Cambridge, Mass., 1967.

Godoli, Ezio, *Il futurismo,* Bari, 1983.

Graf, Otto Antonia, *Die vergessene Wagnerschule,* Vienna, 1969.

Grandi, Maurizio, and Attilio Pracchi, *Milano: Guida all'architettura moderna,* Bologna, 1980.

Hanson, Anne, ed., *The Futurist Imagination: Word and Image in Italian Futurist Painting, Drawing, Collage and Free-Word Poetry,* New Haven, 1983.

Hulten, Pontus, ed., *Futurism and Futurisms,* Milan, 1986.

L'Italia Liberty, Milan, 1973.

Jullian, René, "Marinetti et Sant'Elia," in *Présence de F. T. Marinetti: Actes du colloque international tenu à l'UNESCO,* ed. Jean-Claude Macadé, Lausanne, 1982, 86–91.

———, "Sauvage et Sant'Elia: Le problème des maisons à gradins," *Bulletin de la Société de l'Histoire de l'Art Français,* 1978, 291–298.

Kwinter, Sanford, "La Città Nuova: Modernity and Continuity," *Zone,* vols. 1/2, 1986, 81–121.

Lista, Giovanni, *Giacomo Balla,* Lausanne, 1984.

———, "La représentation futuriste de l'architecture," *Images et imaginaires d'architecture,* Paris, 1984, 42–45.

Lista, Giovanni, ed., *Marinetti et le futurisme: Etudes, documents, iconographie,* Lausanne, 1977.

Longatti, Alberto, *Disegni di Sant'Elia,* Lecco, 1984.

Los, Sergio, *La città macchina,* Vicenza, 1974.

Mallgrave, Harry Francis, and Eleftherios Ikonomov, eds., *Empathy, Form, and Space: Problems in German Aesthetics, 1873–1893,* Santa Monica, 1994.

Marinetti, F. T., *La grande Milano tradizionale* e *futurista,* Milan, 1969.

———, "Sant'Elia," *Enciclopedia italiana,* vol. 30, Milan, 1936, 779.

———, *Teoria e invenzione futurista*, ed. Luciano De Maria, Milan, 1968.

Meeks, Carroll L., *Italian Architecture, 1750–1914*, New Haven, 1966.

Monneret de Villard, Ugo, *Opere di architettura moderna*, Milan, 1909.

Mostra del Liberty italiano, Milan, 1972.

Mostra delle opere dell'architetto futurista comasco Sant'Elia, Como, 1930.

Nebbia, Ugo, "La prima mostra delle 'Nuove Tendenze' a Milano," *Vita d'Arte*, May 1914, 116–120.

Nicoletti, Manfredi, *L'architettura Liberty in Italia*, Bari, 1978.

Nuove Tendenze: Milano e l'altro futurismo, Milan, 1980.

Nuove Tendenze: Milano e l'altro futurismo: Documenti, Milan, 1980, typescript distributed by the Padiglione d'Arte Contemporanea di Milano.

Oud, J. J. P., "Architectonische beschouwing bij bijlage III," *De Stijl*, no. 3, January 1920, 25–27.

Pehnt, Wolfgang, *Expressionist Architecture*, New York, 1973.

Perloff, Marjorie, *The Futurist Movement: Avant-Guard, Avant-Guerre, and the Language of Rupture*, Chicago, 1986.

Persico, Edoardo, *Tutte le opere, 1923–1935*, ed. G. Veronesi, vol. 2, Milan, 1964.

Pevsner, Nikolaus, *Pioneers of Modern Design*, Harmondsworth, 1987.

Piantoni, Gianna, ed., *Roma 1911*, Rome, 1980.

Piscopo, Ugo, *Questioni e aspetti del futurismo*, Naples, 1976.

Poli, Donatella, "I disegni di Sant'Elia," *I quaderni del conoscitore di stampe*, May–June 1974, 28–35.

———, "Proposta per un catalogo critico dei disegni di Antonio Sant'Elia," Tesi di Laurea, University of Pavia, 1969–1970.

Il Politecnico di Milano, 1863–1914, Milan, 1981.

Portoghesi, Paolo, *L'eclettismo a Roma, 1870–1922*, Rome, n.d. (1968?).

———, *L'angelo della storia*, Bari, 1982.

Pozzetto, Marco, *Die Schule Otto Wagners, 1894–1912*, Munich, 1980.

Prampolini, Enrico, "Il gruppo 'Nuove Tendenze' plagiario del futurismo," *L'Artista Moderno*, June 1914, 217–218.

Prima esposizione d'arte del gruppo Nuove Tendenze alla Famiglia Artistica di Milano, Milan, 1914.

[Ragghianti, Carlo Ludovico], "Sant'Elia," *seleArte*, November–December 1955, 46–47.

———, "Sant'Elia: Il Bibbiena del duemila," *Critica d'Arte*, no. 56, March–April 1963, 1–23.

Richards, J. M., and N. Pevsner, eds., *The Anti-Rationalists*, London, 1973, 32–62.

Rosci, Marco, "Dudreville fra futurismo ed espressionismo," *Arte Illustrata*, Milan, January–February 1967, 38–45.

Russolo, Luigi, "Un ricordo de Luigi Russolo," *La Martinella di Milano*, October 1958, 536–539.

Salaris, Claudia, *Storia del futurismo*, Rome, 1985.

Sant'Elia, Antonio, "L'architettura futurista: Manifesto," *Lacerba*, August 1, 1914, 228–231.

Sant'Elia, Guido, "Scrive G. Sant'Elia," *Il Nuovo Futurismo*, July 1934, 1.

Sarfatti, Margherita, "I pittori delle 'Nuove Tendenze' alla Famiglia Artistica di Milano," *L'Avanti!* June 17, 1914.

———, "Sant'Elia e le sue opere," *Gli Avvenimenti*, October 29–November 15, 1916, 14.

Sartoris, Alberto, *L'architetto Antonio Sant'Elia*, Milan, 1930.

———, *Encyclopédie de l'Architecture nouvelle*, 3 vols., Milan, 1948.

———, *Sant'Elia e l'architettura futurista*, Rome, 1943.

Schmidt-Thomsen, Jörn-Peter, *Floreale und Futuristische Architektur: Das Werk von Antonio Sant'Elia*, Berlin, 1967.

———, "Sant'Elia architetto oder die Achillesferse des Futurismus," *Daidalos*, no. 2, 1981, 37–44.

Scully, Vincent, Foreword to *Ausgeführte Bauten und Entwürfe von Frank Lloyd Wright*, Tübingen, 1986.

Situazione degli studi sul Liberty, Firenze, n.d. (1977).

"Studio per villa: Disegni inviatici dal signor Antonio Sant'Elia—Milano," *La Casa*, January 1909, 10–11.

Tafuri, Manfredo, *Theories and History of Architecture*, New York, 1980.

Tagliaventi, Ivo, "Contributo alla storiografia santeliana," in *Ingegneri-Architetti-Costruttori*, January 1957, 9–14.

———, "Sant'Elia e l'architettura futurista," *Ingegneri-Architetti-Costruttori*, October 1954, 233–237; November 1954, 256–261; December 1954, 284–287.

Tentori, Francesco, "Le origini Liberty di Antonio Sant'Elia," *L'Architettura. Cronache et Storia*, July–August 1955, 206–209.

Terragni, Giuseppe, "L'architettura Sant'Elia invano rosicchiata da Ugo Ojetti," *Origini*, April 5, 1942, 1–2.

Tschudi Madsen, Stephan, *Art Nouveau*, New York, 1967.

———, *Sources of Art Nouveau*, Oslo, 1956.

Van Doesburg, Theo, "Rinnovamento dell'arte e dell'architettura in Italia," *Het Bouwbedrijf*, April 29, 1929; reprint, *Casabella*, August–September 1973, 80–81.

van't Hoff, Robert, "Aanteekeningen bij Bijlage XX," *De Stijl*, August 1919, 114–116.

Veronesi, Giulia, "Disegni di Mario Chiattone, 1914–1917," *Comunità*, March–April 1962, 47–66.

———, *Joseph Maria Olbrich*, Milan, 1948.

———, *L'opera di Mario Chiattone architetto*, Pisa, 1965.

————, "Tutto Sant'Elia a Como," *Comunità*, October 1962, 78–81.

Wagner, Otto, *Modern Architecture*, trans. Harry F. Mallgrave, Santa Monica, 1988.

Zevi, Bruno, *Cronache di architettura*, vol. 2, no. 82, Bari, 1970–1973.

————, "Poetica di Sant'Elia e ideologia futurista," *L'Architettura*, November 1956, 516–517.

————, "La profezia di Umberto Boccioni," *L'Architettura*, April 1974, 704–705.

————, *Storia dell'architettura moderna*, Turin, 1955.

Index

Pirovano, Ernesto, 41, 44, 63

Plečnik, Josef, 39, 180

Poe, Edgar Allan, 35

Poelzig, Hans, 60, 93

Pogány, Maurice, 24, 63

Poli, Daniela, 219n13, 226n68, 239n94

Politecnico of Milan, 19, 20

Portoghesi, Paolo, 124, 240n111

Possamai, Giovanni, 54, 94, 96, 98, 167, 182, 183

Pound, Ezra, 202, 238n69

power plants, 108–110

Prampolini, Enrico, 97, 98, 155, 157, 164, 194, 200, 204

Pratella, Balilla, 175

Previati, Gaetano, 21, 34–35, 79

Preziosi, Giovanni, 203

Prezzolini, Giuseppe, 192–193

Prutscher, Otto, 81

Quaglia, Filippo, 166

Quartiere Industriale Nord Milano, 131–132

Ragghianti, Carlo, 68, 121, 206, 208

Ramperti, Marco, 182–183

rationalism, 193; versus futurism, 194–195

Reed, Stem, Warren, and Wetmore, 129

Repossi, Luigi, 15

Riegl, Alois, 75, 77

Risorgimento, 1, 209–210

Rogers, Ernesto, 236n5

Romains, Jules, 229n185

Romani, Romolo, 34, 53

Rosci, Marco, 216n36

Rummel, Richard, 146

Ruskin, John, 5, 8, 216n41

Russolo, Luigi, 34, 78, 94, 95, 97, 123, 125, 138, 155, 156, 174, 176, 191, 223n156; in World War I, 183, 184, 185

Sacconi, Giuseppe, 5, 29, 63

Salaris, Claudia, 233n143

Salsomaggiore church, 89–90, 181

Sant'Elia, 198

Sant'Elia, Antonio: at the Accademia di Belle Arti di Brera, 19–25, 56–57; American skyscraper as influence on, 133–134; approach to architecture, 208–209; birth of, 1, 13; Boccioni as influence on, 79; Chiattone as influence on, 99–101; church designs of, 89–90, 176–181; Como architecture as influence on, 90; use of concrete, 115; death of, 188–189, 196–197; dinamismi, 66–75; education of, 14; and fascism, 191–192, 197–198; first project of, 16–19; futurism as influence on, 71–74, 138; association with futurists, 94–96; influences on, 31–37, 208–210; kinesis in work of, 140; last sketches of, 176–182; *Manifesto of Futurist Architecture,* 89, 117, 123, 149–155, 156–162; "Messaggio," 141–149, 151–153, 158–162, 168, 211–212, 233n120; in Milan, 14–19; Milan architecture influence on, 129–131; and Milan train station designs, 51–54, 93; monumental buildings, 56–66; and Monza competition, 40–51; mythologizing of, 196–199; "Onoranze," 199; oriental influences on, 41–44, 63; use of perspective, 59; as pioneer, 194–196; politics of, 173–176; posthumous buildings, 199–203; power plants, 108–110; reburial of, 191, 196; in Rome, 27–29; Secession as influence on, 18, 31, 33, 35–36, 47, 83, 86, 177; Sommaruga as influence on, 31–32, 41; symbolist literature as influence on, 35; urban vision of, 136–140; and Verona Savings Bank, 79–85, 170; Viennese influence on, 30–40; Villa Elisi, 54–56, 114, 207; *villino moderno,* 27; Wagner as influence on, 30, 35, 37–40, 47, 52, 88, 118, 119, 177–180; images of woman in work of, 34, 35; during World War I, 182–189. *See also* Città Nuova

Sant'Elia, Guido, 13

Sant'Elia, Luigi, 13; funeral monument to, 86

Sarazin, Charles, 115, 116

Sarfatti, Margherita, 96–97, 182–183, 225n30

Sartoris, Alberto, 128, 191, 194, 203, 204

Sauvage, Henri, 115, 116, 121

Scheerbart, Paul, 147

Schmarsow, August, 77

Schmidt-Thomsen, Jörn-Peter, 35, 115, 154, 159, 218n3, 228n144

Schmutzler, Robert, 219n14

Schönthal, Otto, 30, 39

Schopenhauer, Arthur, 167

science fiction, 137–138

Scully, Vincent, 91, 224n9

Selvatico Estense, Pietro, 3, 68

Semenza, Guido, 124

Semper, Gottfried, 5, 37, 118–119, 221n66

Severini, Gino, 95, 97, 98, 174

Shapiro, Ellen, 234n43, 236n17

Sichtbarkeit, 75

Sironi, Mario, 98, 183, 184, 185

Sitte, Camillo, 77, 121, 136

skyscrapers, 133–136

socialism: and the Liberty, 8, 10–11; under Mussolini, 175–176

Soffici, Ardengo, 165, 193

Somenzi, Mino, 195, 204

Sommaruga, Giuseppe, 31–32, 41, 43, 44, 63, 92, 115, 119, 120, 219n11

Sorel, Georges, 174

Soria y Mata, Arturo, 129, 130, 131

Stacchini, Ulisse, 49, 54, 57, 92

Starace, Achille, 237n46

Stazione Centrale, Milan, 51–54

Stefini, Evaristo, 131, 132

Stirner, Max, 174

Strauss, Richard, 34